Re-Writing the Script: Gender and Community in Elin Wägner

Helena Forsås-Scott

Norvik Press
2014

© 2009, 2014 Helena Forsås-Scott
The moral right of the author has been asserted.
Norvik Press Series A: Scandinavian Literary History and Criticism, No. 32.

A catalogue record for this book is available from the British Library.

ISBN 9781909408142
First published in 2009, second revised edition 2014.

Norvik Press
Department of Scandinavian Studies
University College London
Gower Street
London WC1E 6BT
United Kingdom
Website: www.norvikpress.com
E-mail address: norvik.press@ucl.ac.uk

Managing editors: Sarah Death, Helena Forsås-Scott, Janet Garton, C. Claire Thomson.

Cover illustration: detail from a photograph entitled *Tolv kvinnor* (Twelve Women), reproduced courtesy of *KvinnSam, Göteborgs universitetsbibliotek* (KvinnSam, Göteborg University Library). The occasion is *Kvinnornas vapenlösa uppror mot kriget* (The Women's Unarmed Revolt against War) in August 1935, and the likely location is the Stockholm flat belonging to Ada Nilsson. Jane Hermelin is seated on the far left, and Honorine Hermelin, her stepdaughter, is sitting opposite. The identity of the woman on the right, facing the camera, is unknown.
www.ub.gu.se/kvinn

Till Bill
och
till Allan och May

Contents

Preface to the second edition..7

Preface to the first edition..9

Chapter 1: A New Approach..13
1. Text..13
2. Gender..25
3. Community..30
4. Re-Writing...39

Part I. Suffrage and Beyond, 1907-21

Chapter 2: Contexts..47
1. Economic...47
2. Political..50
3. Social...54
4. Cultural..57

Chapter 3: Discourses: The Family...67
1. Dominant Discourses..67
2. Alternative Discourses..79

Chapter 4: Texts..99
1. Reportage...100
2. Essays...121
3. Light-Hearted Columns..132
4. Prose Fiction: *Norrtullsligan*, *Pennskaftet*, *Åsa-Hanna*,
   Den befriade kärleken, *Kvarteret Oron*,
   Den förödda vingården..144

Chapter 5: Gender, Community and the First World War......193

Part II. New Communities: A New Society? 1922-47

Chapter 6: Contexts 199
1. Economic 199
2. Political 202
3. Social 204
4. Cultural 206

Chapter 7: Discourses: Citizenship 211
1. Dominant Discourses 213
2. An Alternative Discourse 223

Chapter 8: Texts 1922-36 237
1. Opinion Pieces 237
2. *Från Seine, Rhen och Ruhr* 252
3. Radio Drama 260
4. Prose Fiction: *Den namnlösa, De fem pärlorna,*
   Dialogen fortsätter, Mannen vid min sida 271

Chapter 9: Texts 1937-47 297
1. *Väckarklocka* 297
2. *Tusen år i Småland* 317
3. *Selma Lagerlöf* 327
4. Prose Fiction: *Genomskådad, Hemlighetsfull,*
   Vinden vände bladen 340

Chapter 10: Gender and Community 1922-47:
Pacifism into Ecocentrism 357

Chapter 11: Connecting, Circulating, Moving On 361

Chronology 370

Select Bibliography 377

Select Bibliography: Second Edition, updates 409

Index 411

Preface to the second edition

I am grateful to my fellow Directors at Norvik Press, Sarah Death, Janet Garton and Claire Thomson, for suggesting a new edition of this book. The role of the work of Elin Wägner in the context of modern Swedish society has attracted a considerable amount of attention recently, with Sofi Qvarnström (2009) reading some of her texts, in conjunction with work by Anna Lenah Elgström and Marika Stiernstedt, in relation to the First World War, and Anna Bohlin (2008) choosing texts by Wägner, Selma Lagerlöf and Klara Johanson for her investigation into the feminine political voice in Sweden in the 1920s, just after the introduction of female suffrage. Like the present study, both Qvarnström and Bohlin illustrate the importance of working across the conventional genre boundaries. Using a more traditional starting-point, Peter Forsgren (2009) has shed new light on a handful of Wägner's novels. Wägner's work also figures prominently in Bibi Jonsson's (2008) study of Swedish women writers and antimodernism in the 1930s. The lavish anthology edited by Marianne Enge Swartz (2009) presents a range of perspectives on Wägner and her work. A short summary in Swedish of the present book is available in my article from 2011.

In this edition occasional errors with regard to spelling and typography have been corrected, and the odd translation into English has been amended. I have also added a short update to the original bibliography.

At Norvik Press I particularly want to thank Dr Elettra Carbone, Editorial Assistant, and Marita Fraser, Production Assistant, for their practical help with this new edition. Marita's expert work on design and typography has done much to enhance the appearance of the book.

As I write, a statue of Elin Wägner is about to be put up in a public space in Stockholm. It is an enlarged version of a statue made in 1945 by Siri Derkert (1888-1973), and shows Elin Wägner in the midst of making a speech, so eager to get her message across that she seems about to take off from the surface she is standing on. There could be no better reminder of her continuing relevance in the twenty-first century. I hope this new edition will help make new audiences aware of her work.

Helena Forsås-Scott
Edinburgh, March 2014

Preface to the first edition

This study has benefited from the support and encouragement of many people, and from conversations and discussions often extending over long periods of time – and, I hope, continuing far beyond the completion of this project.

Sarah Death and I started discussing a joint Elin Wägner project several years ago. I was delighted when Sarah agreed to translate one of Wägner's novels, and when Norvik Press offered us contracts for Sarah's translation of *Pennskaftet* (*Penwoman*) and the present volume. The collaboration with Sarah and with Neil Smith of Norvik Press has been a joy, and I want to thank them both for some of the best samarbete I know.

The expanding range of research on Wägner and her work has also been an important source of inspiration, the vitality of the field illustrated by the fact that Peter Forsgren's study *I vanskligbetens land. Genus, genre och modernitet i Elin Wägners smålandsromaner* (In the Perilous Land: Gender, Genre and Modernity in Elin Wägner's Småland Novels) is due out just ahead of the present volume (and so does not figure in the analyses presented here). The formation of *Elin Wägner-sällskapet* (The Elin Wägner Society) in Berg, Småland, in 1990 was a key event, focusing the wide-ranging interest in Wägner and also providing scholars, myself included, with unique opportunities to present and discuss our work. But I have drawn just as much inspiration from developments on this side of the North Sea, especially from the establishment of the Masters and Diploma programmes in Gender Studies (Gender, Society and Representation) at University College London and the network of colleagues that has emerged as a result, and from the transformation of the Department of Scandinavian Studies since 2006.

Some of the material that has fed into this study has been presented as invited lectures and conference papers. A special thank you to the organisers of the annual meetings in the United States of the Society for the Advancement of Scandinavian Study for several opportunities to air aspects of my research on Wägner in a conference environment that is one of the most positive and exciting I know. At Göteborg University Library I have enjoyed exceptional support and assistance. *Kvinnohistoriska samlingarna* (The Women's History Collections) has provided an unrivalled working environment for this project too, and I want to thank Inger Eriksson, Berith Backlund, Helena Brännström, Elisabeth Hammarberg, and Anna Sjödahl Hayman. Kristina Göransson has not only offered professional help but generous hospitality. Thank you, Kristina!

Sarah Death, Janet Garton of Norvik Press, and Birgitta Ney have read parts or all of the manuscript of this book, and I am most grateful to them for constructive comments and helpful suggestions. Sarah and Janet have also helped improve my translations into English. Needless to say, I am responsible for the remaining errors and shortcomings with regard to both content and translations.

I also want to thank Irene Andersson, Margareta Benner, Johan Bernander, Elettra Carbone, Eli Cook, Barbro Ek, Marianne Enge Swartz, Jane Fenoulhet, Curt Gustafsson, Theo Hermans, Mary Hilson, Birgitta Holm, Katarina Leppänen, Elvy Löwall, Anna-Lisa Murrell, Anna Nordenstam, Karin Petherick, Michael Robinson, Bess Ryder, Linda Schenck, Märta Schlecker, Kristina Sjögren, Birgitta Svanberg, Claire Thomson, and Ebba Witt-Brattström. With Solveig Hammarbäck, who has facilitated my work in various ways, I have also enjoyed inspirational spells in Småland and on Öland; and although Stephen Walton is no longer my colleague, our conversations go on. My mother, Britta Forsås, has shown remarkable understanding and patience, and I am grateful to my sister and my niece, Anna Forsås and Sofia Forsås, for their unstinting support. Sadly, my thanks can no longer reach Karl-Fredrik Bernander, Alvar Carlsson, Flory Gate, and Börje Schlecker. Several bodies have helped fund this project. The generous grant from *Svenska Akademien*, which supported both the final phase of my own project and Sarah Death's translation of *Pennskaftet*, was most welcome. My work has also benefited from several grants from The Dean's Travel Fund at University College London. Magn. Bergvalls

Preface to the first edition

stiftelse, Stockholm, supported the earliest phase of my Wägner research, including my first trip to *S:t Sigfrids folkhögskola*, Växjö, which houses Wägner's library. In addition, I want to thank Norstedts förlag for publishing a selection of journalism and essays by Wägner (1999), *Svenska Akademien* for the opportunity to edit *Pennskaftet* in the Swedish Academy's Classics Series (2003), and Albert Bonniers Förlag for involving me in the work on new editions of Ulla Isaksson and Erik Hjalmar Linder's biography of Wägner (2003) and Wägner's *Väckarklocka* (Alarm Clock) (2007). In various ways, all these projects have helped inspire the present study.

The chronology of Wägner's life towards the end of this volume is based on the one I drew up for the new edition of Isaksson and Linder's biography, and I am grateful to Albert Bonniers Förlag and Hans Isaksson for permission to use the Swedish version as a template for the version published here.

The texts analysed in the present volume are quoted in Swedish, from the original newspapers or magazines or from the first editions of Wägner's works published in book form (in the case of the dramas for radio from the scripts available in the archives of *Sveriges Radio*, the Swedish Broadcasting Corporation, in Stockholm), with translations into English given in brackets. I have used Sarah Death's published translations of *Pennskaftet* and extracts from *Tusen år i Småland* (A Thousand Years in Småland) and *Väckarklocka*; otherwise, the English versions are my own. In those cases where there are published translations of Swedish/Scandinavian texts that I have used as secondary material, I have quoted these, except for one translation that has sometimes been too free for my purposes. In these cases and in all other ones, I have provided my own translations of the material quoted. Full references have been given throughout.

This book is dedicated to Bill, whose encouragement continues to mean most, and to the next generation, Allan and his wife May.

Helena Forsås-Scott
London, 30 December 2008

Chapter 1:
A New Approach

> Det är mycket vi har att ändra i manus. Också småsaker. Också spår i snön. Oupphörligt oupphörligt skriva om. Generation efter generation. Tills vi finner uttrycksformerna för samspelet på lika villkor kvinna och man, människa och natur.
>
> Elisabet Hermodsson, *Ord i kvinnotid* (1979, p.119)

(There's a lot we need to change in the script. Details too. Tracks in the snow too. Continuously continuously re-write. Generation after generation. Until we find the forms of expression for the collaboration on equal terms of woman and man, human being and nature.)

1. Text

Preamble

This is a study of texts by Elin Wägner (1882-1949). In other words, this is not a biography of the Swedish journalist, suffragist, novelist, and environmentalist who was elected to the Swedish Academy in 1944, as only the second woman ever to become a member. Lisbeth Larsson has traced the impact of the anti-biographical trend in a number of feminist monographs on Swedish women writers published in the 1970s and 1980s (Larsson 2001, 363-78). But Wägner's texts did not become the subject of a monograph at this time; instead the definitive biography, by Ulla Isaksson and Erik Hjalmar Linder, was published in two volumes in 1977 and 1980, with a new one-volume edition appearing in 2003. It was Isaksson and Linder's biography that first aroused my interest in Wägner's work three decades ago; yet at the same time this biography inevitably continued to sanction the biographical readings of the texts that had been established by the standard literary histories. But however much the present study distances itself from biographical readings, texts are of course written by authors in specific circumstances. Consequently the analyses here are related to the economic, political, social, and cultural contexts of the periods in which they were produced (and readers wanting information about Elin Wägner's life will also find a chronology at the end of this volume). However, one of the main aims of this study is to call into question the seemingly automatic linkage of the author's life, the author's political position, and the author's ideas on the one hand with the author's texts on the other. While the appearance in recent years of a number of book-length studies of aspects of Wägner's work has been greatly encouraging, these studies all use the notions of authorial ideas and authorial control as starting-points and so read the texts as instances of the unproblematic transposition of thought into words. This is true of Bibi Jonsson's study of the utopian vision in Wägner's novels from the 1930s (2001); of Katarina Leppänen's exploration of ecofeminist ideas in Wägner's pamphlet *Väckarklocka* (1941; Alarm Clock) (2005); and of Birgitta Wistrand's investigation into Wägner's contacts, thought, and writing in the 1920s (2006).

I am also keen to move away from the over-emphasis on the prose fiction in Wägner's output, so conspicuous in the literary histories and also prominent in the studies by Jonsson and Wistrand. In addition to twenty novels and six volumes of short stories, Wägner published a vast quantity of journalism, including well over 600 signed articles just in the radical weekly *Tidevarvet* (1923-36; The Epoch); a considerable number of essays; a volume of 'anecdotes' from contemporary Europe, *Från Seine, Rhen och Ruhr* (1923; From the Seine, the Rhine and the Ruhr); a travelogue that is also a local history with an ecological slant, *Tusen år i Småland* (1939; A Thousand Years in Småland); the pamphlet *Väckarklocka* (1941); and a two-volume biography (1942-43) of the author Selma Lagerlöf (1858-1940). A total of seven of Wägner's dramas for radio were also broadcast, one of these co-written with Ragnar Hyltén-Cavallius. While large sections of Wägner's output were neglected up to around 1990, the texts that did receive attention continued to be read in accordance with the grid established by Erik

Hjalmar Linder, the first literary historian to cover virtually all her prose fiction along with a handful of other texts: after some early works in which the modern professional woman and the campaign for women's suffrage are prominent, there is a shift in the late 1910s towards a preoccupation with ethics and religion which continues to predominate throughout the 1920s (with some modifications, this perspective still determines Wistrand's recent study of the journalism and prose fiction of the 1920s), before a renewed interest in feminism in the early 1930s is gradually transformed into a preoccupation with feminine difference and more specifically the notion of a matriarchal past, which predominate in the output from the late 1930s onwards (Linder 1949). In an important study of the treatment of women writers in twentieth-century histories of Swedish literature, Anna Williams has demonstrated the extent to which Linder's sometimes disparaging comments on Wägner's output tended to be characteristic of his treatment of women writers generally, and also how his perspectives on her work have been reiterated by subsequent authors of literary histories (Williams 1997, 103-109).

In stating that the present study covers a very wide range of genres, I am using the concept of genre as a convenient shorthand. As Alastair Fowler has reminded us, 'the character of genres is that they change', with genre 'best thought of, perhaps, as a collective or group creative process' (Fowler 1997, 18, 277). With regard to the texts by Wägner, the 'collective or group creative process' is most obvious in those cases where the texts did not fit into existing genre categories when they were published and where the process of categorisation is in effect still going on: *Från Seine, Rhen och Ruhr*, *Tusen år i Småland*, and *Väckarklocka* are examples here. In addition, the series of light-hearted columns often have much in common with prose fiction, some of the opinion pieces have affinities with essays, and the Lagerlöf biography arguably shares many features with the genre of the novel. Genre categorisations have been necessary for the structuring of this study, but as I am applying them, I am acutely aware of their tentativeness and fluidity, and in some of the analyses these aspects become prominent.

This study assesses the innovative potential of a range of texts by Wägner by investigating, throughout her output, the construction of gender and the construction of community. As Judith Butler has pointed out, construction is 'the necessary scene of agency, the very terms in which agency is articulated and becomes culturally intelligible' (Butler 2006, 201). My decision to focus on the constructions of gender and community, along with the periodisation of the material, are the results of my reading of a vast quantity of texts by Wägner rather than of preconceived notions of Wägner's ideas or political position. The remainder of this introduction contains sections on feminist poststructuralism and narratology, with a special emphasis on dialogue; gender; community; and existing research, along with an outline of the structure of this book. The two chronological sections that constitute the main sections of this study, 1907-1921 and 1922-1947 respectively, each begin with surveys of contextual material – economic, political, social, and cultural – followed by chapters that attempt to pinpoint dominant and alternative discourses on gender and on community by exploring family and citizenship respectively. Texts representing a range of genres are then analysed within the framework of these contexts. By freeing Wägner's texts from the biographical bond and instead exploring them in the wider contexts of economic, political, social, and cultural conditions, and with an emphasis on constructions of gender and community, I hope to highlight both the range of narratives – also taking into account the radio drama – published around the same time and the potential of these texts for innovation and change. And this potential is no small thing: as has been pointed out by Elizabeth Frazer and Nicola Lacey, '[i]n a real sense, to change discursive practice is to change the world' (Frazer and Lacey 1993, 210).

Feminist Poststructuralism and Narratology

The narrator in Virginia Woolf's *A Room of One's Own* (1929) refers to the fact that the middle-class woman, towards the end of the eighteenth century, began to write, as 'a change [...] which, if I were rewriting history, I should describe more fully and think of greater importance than the Crusades or the Wars of the Roses' (Woolf 1977, 62-63).

Arguably, her claim has become all the more persuasive in the light of the flood of rediscoveries, reprintings, and scholarly studies of texts by women writers that began in the 1970s and that has transformed our perception and understanding of writing by women. Today, the study of gender and text is likely to range more widely across aspects of sex, sexuality, and gender but with the text, if anything, more pre-eminent, not just as the site for the exploration of marginalisation and oppression, but as the site of new possibilities, of change.

Chris Weedon has defined feminist poststructuralism as 'a mode of knowledge production which uses poststructuralist theories of language, subjectivity, social processes and institutions to understand existing power relations and to identify areas and strategies for change' (Weedon 1997, 40). In a poststructuralist perspective, language is not the transparent, reliable medium of liberal humanism: following on from Ferdinand de Saussure who highlighted, early in the twentieth century, the arbitrariness of signifier and signified but then described their combination as 'a positive fact' (quoted in op. cit., 24), poststructuralists view the relationship between signifier and signified as one of non-fixity, with meaning constantly deferred. While the specific discursive context provides a temporary fixing of meaning, the result is that meaning is also 'always open to challenge and redefinition with shifts in its [the signifier's] discursive context' (op. cit., 25).

The work of Michel Foucault provides a range of familiar examples of the role and impact of discourses, in the penal system, in psychiatry, with regard to sexuality. In Chris Weedon's summary,

> [d]iscourses are more than ways of thinking and producing meaning. They constitute the 'nature' of the body, unconscious and conscious mind and emotional life of the subjects which they seek to govern. Neither the body nor thoughts and feelings have meaning outside of their discursive articulation, but the ways in which discourses constitute the minds and bodies of individuals is always part of a wider network of power relations, often with institutional bases. (Weedon 1997, 105)

A well-known example from Foucault's analysis of the 'mechanisms of knowledge and power centering on sex' that he has traced from the eighteenth century onwards is the 'hysterization of women's bodies', i.e. the construction of the female body in terms of its reproductive function (Foucault 1990, 103-104). The power of discourse, however, is by no means absolute: as Foucault has pointed out, discourse 'transmits and produces power; it reinforces it, but also undermines and exposes it, renders it fragile and makes it possible to thwart it' (op. cit., 101). One effect is 'reverse discourse', exemplified by homosexuality which, in the nineteenth century, was not only defined as a 'perversity' and subjected to social controls, but which also 'began to speak in [sic] its own behalf' (ibid.). Referring to the turn of the century 1900 and foregrounding the figure of the New Woman – who is highly relevant for the early phase of Wägner's output – Ebba Witt-Brattström has read 'women' as 'balancing on the edge' of reverse discourse (Witt-Brattström 2004, 9-10).

To speak, Chris Weedon has pointed out, is 'to assume a subject position within discourse and to become *subjected* to the power and regulation of the discourse' (Weedon 1997, 116; italics original). In the context of the present study, this observation might at first sight appear to be most relevant to the author Elin Wägner, whose texts that can be seen as representing different genres such as reportage, prose fiction, pamphlet, and biography could be read as expressions of the author's range of voices, subjected to the frameworks of different discourses. But while I am in no way denying the significance of the author, I have chosen in this study to make a clear distinction between author and texts, one of my aims being the one defined by Mieke Bal as the emancipation of 'both author and reader from the stronghold of a misconceived interpretive authority' (Bal 1999, 17). In other words, it is the subject positions constructed in the texts, along with their relations to and implications for constructions of gender and community, that are at the forefront of this study. The concept of 'the nomadic subject', coined by Rosi Braidotti and defined as 'a situated, postmodern, culturally differentiated understanding of the subject in general and of the feminist subject in particular', has been an important source of inspiration; 'nomadism' in this context refers to 'the kind of critical consciousness that resists settling into socially coded modes of thought and behavior' (Braidotti 1994, 4, 5). While Braidotti's understanding of nomadism as a process, a 'becoming', is directly relevant to the prominence in the present study of narrative, her foregrounding of nomadic becoming as 'emphatic proximity, intensive interconnectedness' points, in *Nomadic Subjects*, to the interrelationship between subjectivity and community (op. cit., 5, 200-201). Braidotti's development, in a subsequent work such as *Transpositions* (2006), of the concepts of subjectivity and community in the contexts of post-humanism and environmentalism, is also relevant to the present study, and especially to my explorations of some of Wägner's late texts.

The methodological basis of this study is narratology, defined by Bal as 'the theory of narratives, narrative texts, images, spectacles, events; cultural artifacts that "tell a story"' (Bal 1999, 3). This is quite different from the narratology that emerged after the New Criticism and which, in the words of Mark Currie, was characterised by 'rigorous formalism' and 'the arid scientificity of linguistics' (Currie 1998, 24). Indispensable though it is, the work of Gérard Genette, most importantly *Narrative Discourse* (in French in 1972, English translation 1980) and *Narrative Discourse Revisited* (in French in 1983, English translation 1988), probably constitutes the most important example of the type of analysis to which Currie is referring. Bal, however, has increasingly distanced herself from any notion of narratological analysis for its own sake, instead highlighting narrative as '*a cultural attitude, [and] hence, narratology [as] a perspective on culture*' (Bal 1999, 222; italics original). The clearest signal of her growing preoccupation with narratology as a 'heuristic tool, not an objective grid providing certainty' (op. cit., xiii), is the reversal of the structure of her highly influential *Narratology: Introduction to the Theory of Narrative* between the first English edition in 1985 (a revised version of the second, revised edition [1980] of the Dutch original) and the second English edition in 1997. The earlier order of (1) fabula, 'a series of logically and chronologically related events that are caused or experienced by actors'; (2) story, 'a fabula that is presented in a certain manner'; and (3) narrative text, defined as 'a text in which an agent relates a narrative' (Bal 1997, 5) has thus been turned on its head. Not only has the definition of 'narrative text' been expanded to encompass 'a text in which an agent relates ("tells") a story in a particular medium, such as language, imagery, sound, buildings, or a combination thereof' (Bal 1999, 5), but most importantly, the reversal of the original order highlights the significance of the text encountered by the reader and thus the role of narratology as 'a readerly device [...] that provides focus to the expectations with which readers process narrative' (op. cit., xv).

The methodological basis provided by Bal is also helpful in the context of this study because it is relevant to narratives representing a range of genres and not just to prose fiction. While for the analyses of texts such as pamphlets and reportages I draw on some of Norman Fairclough's models in *Discourse and Social Change* (1992), which represent an approach grounded in theoretical premises very similar to those used by Weedon but slanted more emphatically towards the social context, I rely on Bal for the distinction between author and narrator which, in the present study, has been applied to texts of all genres. This means that even in texts in which the identification of the narrating 'I' with the author might seem obvious, for example in the travelogue-cum-local-history *Tusen år i Småland*, the pamphlet *Väckarklocka*, or the biography *Selma Lagerlöf*, I insist on distinguishing the historical person called Elin Wägner from '"that agent which utters the linguistic signs which constitute the text" or the equivalent of that agent in other media', which is Bal's definition of the narrator (Bal 1999, 18). In line with Bal, but unlike a theorist such as Shlomith Rimmon-Kenan whose *Narrative Fiction: Contemporary Poetics* (1983) continues to be influential, I do not use the concept of 'implied author' (Rimmon-Kenan 1988, 86-89) since this, as Bal has pointed out, 'is the result of the investigation of the meaning of a text, and not the source of that meaning' (Bal 1999, 18). Consequently the 'implied reader' is not relevant in the present study either. But the 'narratee' certainly is, in other words the 'abstract function' that constitutes 'the receiver of the narrated text' (op. cit., 63). As I shall demonstrate, the narratees often become prominent in Wägner's texts, with the frequent occurrences of an indefinite pronoun such as *man* (one/you/they/people) or a personal pronoun such as *vi* (we) constructing narratees as part of groups, of textual communities, and the appearance of questions and, in non-fiction, sentences and paragraphs in italics, contributing to the construction of informed and engaged readers.

Some of the features I have just referred to can be labelled dialogic, and as we shall see, dialogism is a prominent dimension of a number of the texts analysed in this study. The obvious instances are the radio dramas broadcast in 1930-34, which will be considered here on the basis of the original manuscripts available in *Sveriges Radios arkiv* (the archives of the Swedish Broadcasting Corporation); there are few recordings from these early years (public broadcasting had begun in Sweden in 1925), and I have made no attempt to work from the copies used by the directors. In other words, my analyses of the radio dramas are based almost entirely on the dialogue between the characters which, just as in stage drama, establishes character, space, and action (Aston and Savona 1991, 52). But dialogue is also prominent in other texts and especially in the prose fiction (and not just in the novel entitled *Dialogen fortsätter* (1932; The Dialogue is Continuing): novels such as *Den namnlösa* (1922; The Anonymous Woman) and *Mannen vid min sida* (1933; The Man at My Side) contain sections of dialogue that are in fact presented in the format of a drama. However, the interdependence of dialogism clearly does not require a drama format; as I shall show, it is also highly relevant in texts such as *Från Seine, Rhen och Ruhr* and *Väckarklocka*. As Lynne Pearce has emphasised in *Reading Dialogics* (1994), in which the theory of Mikhail Bakhtin is related to a gendered perspective, there is a direct link between dialogism and subjectivation in the sense that 'the Bakhtinian subject', which is 'incontrovertibly *social*', is formed 'through an ongoing process of dialogic exchange with his or her various interlocutors' (Pearce 1994, 4; italics original). In terms of the dialogic contract, 'all of us are engaged in our effort to speak, to "mean", to "be"' (op. cit., 5). Bakhtin's 'profoundly interdependent view of human communication' (ibid.) has played an important role for the analyses that follow.

My analyses of texts by Wägner, then, focus on constructions of gender and of community. Bal sometimes highlights gender dimensions, for example in her comparison of Alice Walker's novel *The Color Purple* and Steven Spielberg's film of the same title (Bal 1999, 165-67); and in her *Narratology* it is not difficult to distinguish parts of the 'ensemble of signs' that make up a text, or aspects of a story or elements of a fabula, to reinforce Bal's terminology (op. cit., 5, 7-8), that would be central to an analysis from a perspective of gender, for example narrator, narratee, dialogue, free indirect speech, character, space, focalisation, and, within an analytical framework drawing on Greimas, subject and object, power and receiver, helper and opponent. Here I have also drawn inspiration from Susan S. Lanser, the theorist who has done most to develop narratology in a context of gender, and whose *Fictions of Authority: Women Writers and Narrative Voice* (1992) remains a seminal text. Lanser's chapter on 'Sexing Narratology: Toward a Gendered Poetics of Narrative Voice' (1999) is an argument for the need to integrate 'questions of sex, gender, and sexuality into a descriptive poetics of narrative' (Lanser 2004, 123), and this work by Lanser has also been of significance for the present study. In so far as they have not been defined already, narratological terms will be defined when they become relevant for my analyses.

Drawing on a phrase from Raymond Williams, Lanser has defined 'narrative voice' as 'situated at the juncture of "social position and literary practice"' and embodying 'the social, economic, and literary conditions under which it has been produced' (Lanser 1992, 5). Here 'communal voice' turns out to be one of Lanser's categories, and it is defined as 'a spectrum of practices that articulate either a collective voice or a collective of voices that share narrative authority', with narrative authority 'invested in a definable community and textually inscribed either through multiple, mutually authorizing voices or through the voice of a single individual who is manifestly authorized by a community' (op. cit., 21). While I cannot agree with Lanser's use of the term 'individual' which, in contrast to Bal's strict schemas, seems to sanction the notion of the narrator as a living human being rather than a textual construct, Lanser's definition of 'communal voice' highlights some of the aspects of the fabula and the story relevant to a narratological analysis with a focus on the construction of community. In addition to narrator, dialogue, and character, we might mention here both the space of the story and the place of the fabula, along with focalisation and memory, the latter defined by Bal as 'a special case of focalization' (Bal 1999, 147). Perhaps one of the most striking props in the narrative construction of community is the use of the feature that Lanser, following Genette, labels 'maxims' – Bal calls them 'argumentative textual passages' (op. cit., 32-33) – and defines as 'reflections, judgments, generalizations about the world "beyond" the fiction' (Lanser 1992, 16-17). While Lanser's analysis of 'maxims' belongs in the context of narrative authority, as demonstrated in her chapter on the role of 'maxims' in George Eliot (op. cit., 81-101), 'maxims' clearly also contribute to the constructions of the narratee and the larger community of readers.

Given the increasing prominence of past times in some of Wägner's late texts in particular, I have found the linkage of memory with community in a study such as Peter Middleton and Tim Woods's *Literatures of Memory: History, Time and Space in Postwar Writing* (2000) both illuminating and helpful. In the reading of Middleton and Woods a text is 'a form of memory' while 'memories are themselves textual', with the new historical literature of the recent decades being part of 'the historical turn in literary studies and the turn to memory in historical studies' (Middleton and Woods 2000, 6, 9). In common with the work of Weedon and Braidotti that of Middleton and Woods, in other words, is grounded in poststructuralism. As I hope to show in due course, poststructuralism can open up new perspectives on Wägner's texts and help focus new possibilities. The notion of the past as 'a rewritable text' is a useful one as we approach a number of the texts, as is the idea of texts '[engaging] with the resistances and desires of an audience actively in search of pasts' and so offering 'ample room for their audiences to become historians' (op. cit., 10, 34).

The Present Study

Elizabeth Grosz has outlined the potential of the feminist text in the following terms: such a text, she has written, 'must [...] help, in whatever way, to facilitate the production of new and perhaps unknown, unthought discursive spaces – new styles, modes of analysis and argument, new genres and forms – that contest the limits and constraints currently at work in the regulation of textual production and reception' (Grosz 1995, 23). In the analyses that follow, I make no attempt to determine whether texts by Wägner are feminist or not, and as should be clear from my discussion so far, I am certainly not going to argue that the fact that Wägner was a feminist – and I think it is safe to say that this represents the consensual view – somehow automatically makes all her texts feminist. But I do believe that the contextualisation of a text in terms of gendered relations of power can help to highlight the role of textual space as a potential for change. My conviction that such spaces are significant underpins the present study.

My study takes its starting-point in a series of questions. What happens in texts by Wägner once we begin to free them from the fetters of those biographical readings which, in this case, so often have seemed merely to confirm Christiane Rochefort's dictum, 'A man's book is a book. A woman's book is a woman's book' (Rochefort 1981, 183)? How do the constructions of gender and community in the differing textual spaces constituted by different genres (the term used with the caveats about genre categorisation expressed above) relate to the dominant discourses on gender and community, and how do they compare and contrast with each other, especially given the fact that texts that can be labelled as belonging to different genres were often produced and published simultaneously? How innovative are the various textual spaces with regard to constructions of gender and community, in what ways are they innovative, and what are the implications with regard to subjectivation and agency? To what extent does the picture of Wägner's output change when we take into consideration genres that have not previously been read side by side with the prose fiction, such as reportage, pamphlets, essays, and radio drama? How accurate are the literary histories that have effectively defined her output as becoming increasingly conservative, with issues of gender becoming more and more marginal? How does the environmentalism of the late texts emerge in the context of constructions of gender and community? Might the texts of Wägner be more innovative and more radical than has been realised? And, irrespective of how we answer the previous question, what may be the implications of the present study for histories of literature? Might there also be an argument emerging here for much more broadly based histories of texts?

2. Gender

A recent text by Yvonne Hirdman, whose work has dominated the Swedish debate about gender theory since the late 1980s, provides both an up-to-date outline of the predominant understanding of Wägner's feminism and an introduction to the theorisation of gender. According to Hirdman's analysis in a chapter published in 2006, 'Feminismens dilemma. Variationer på ett (oändligt) tema...' (The Dilemma of Feminism. Variations on a (Never-ending) Theme...), the feminist has two options: (1) to accept 'the world of the male norm', or (2) not to accept it (Hirdman 2006, 121). Simone de Beauvoir and Alva Myrdal are examples of feminists who chose the first option, while Hirdman's example of the second option is Wägner, 'the main representative of Swedish difference feminism' (op. cit., 122, 121). In Hirdman's reading, Wägner combined the rejection of 'the world of the male norm' with a belief in the gender stereotypes produced by this very same world and so found herself in an impossible position, advocating 'the society of the female norm' when notions of femaleness and femininity were necessarily the products of subordination and oppression (op. cit., 125, 127-28).

Hirdman's analysis of Wägner's feminism is a classic example of the predominant categorisation of Wägner in ideological and political terms, a categorisation which, in a circular argument, is derived from Wägner's texts and is then taken to underpin and determine these texts. It is this automatic linkage of the ideological and political position on the one hand and the texts on the other that the present study is calling into question by foregrounding the texts and their potential for change. But Hirdman's discussion of 'the dilemma of feminism' also provides useful insights into the Swedish debate about feminism and gender towards the end of the twentieth century.

As long ago as 1983, Harriet Clayhills pointed out that Ellen Key (1849-1926) was continuing to overshadow the debate in twentieth-century Sweden 'about what women have been, what they are and what they can become' (Clayhills 1983, 11). The significance of Key, an author and lecturer who enjoyed considerable international fame around the turn of the century 1900, will be considered in Part I,

Chapter 3 below; what matters in this context is the fact that her texts distinguish femininity from masculinity on biological grounds and advocate separate and specific social roles for women, with *samhällsmoderlighet* (social motherliness) a central concept. Key's texts, in other words, epitomise the notion of femaleness and femininity as different; and I broadly agree with Clayhill's analysis of the impact of these texts on the Swedish feminist debate, which has been very much preoccupied with discussions about maleness and masculinity, femaleness and femininity in terms of difference and equality. Indeed, Hirdman's insistence on analysing gender in binary terms, reduced to the three formulas A – Not-A, A – a, A – B, in which A stands for man/male/masculine, elaborated in her book *Genus – om det stabilas föränderliga former* (2001; Gender: Changeable Forms and Stable Content) and reiterated in the chapter discussed above along with the claim that in 'the gender order', 'stable patterns' are to be discerned (Hirdman 2006, 127), also points to the continuing impact of Key.

While Clayhills has provided some useful clarification of the distinctions between the positions of Key and Wägner, emphasising that a work such as Wägner's *Väckarklocka* by no means amounts to a call for 'a return to the past', she has insisted on continuing to read Wägner in terms of difference, albeit of the pioneering variety (Clayhills 1983, 20-22). As I have made clear above, the present study is one of texts and not of ideological positions or political ideas; indeed, as a study of texts it has some of its roots in my analyses of a handful of texts by Wägner in the introduction to an edition of selected texts published in 1999, *Vad tänker du, mänsklighet?* (Humankind, What Are You Thinking?), which focused on the destabilisation of the polar opposites of masculinity and femininity (Forsås-Scott 1999, 26-56). However, the present study is clearly also political. As Joan Wallach Scott has pointed out, feminists 'cannot give up "difference"; it has been our most creative analytic tool', nor can we give up equality, 'at least as long as we want to speak to the principles and values of our political system' (Scott 1994, 260-61). Scott's solution amounts to a combination of the two: 'the unmasking of the power relationship constructed by posing equality as the antithesis of difference and the refusal of its consequent dichotomous construction of political choices' (op. cit., 261). Rosi Braidotti has elaborated on 'poststructuralist feminist reaffirmations of difference' in terms of 'a radical redefinition of the text and of the textual away from the dualistic mode' of equality and difference in terms that are directly relevant to the present study (Braidotti 1994, 154). The text, according to Braidotti,

> is now approached as both a semiotic and a material structure, that is to say not an isolated item locked in a dualistic opposition to a social context and to an activity of interpretation. The text must rather be understood as a term in a process, that is to say a chain reaction encompassing a web of power relations. What is at stake in the textual practice, therefore, is less the activity of interpretation than that of decoding the network of connections and effects that link the text to an entire sociosymbolic system. In other words, we are faced here with a new materialist theory of the text and of textual practice. (ibid.)

In the present study, the impact of the theory of the text and of textual practice outlined by Braidotti is noticeable not just in the analyses of individual texts, but also in the foregrounding of economic, political, social, and cultural contexts, and of dominant and alternative discourses on gender and community. In the sections on contexts, politics is largely defined in institutional terms; but elsewhere, and especially in the chapters on discourses, the definition of politics is the much broader one spelled out by Joan Wallach Scott: 'politics is the process by which plays of power and knowledge constitute identity and experience' (Scott 1988a, 5).

To expand my analyses of texts, I will draw on material on gender theory in addition to the discourse theory, feminist poststructuralism, and feminist narratology outlined above. Most importantly, this material consists of some of the work of Judith Butler and, as I have indicated already, some of that of Rosi Braidotti.

First published in 1990, Judith Butler's *Gender Trouble* comprehensively demolished the element of certainty underpinning the familiar distinction between 'sex' and 'gender', according to which 'sex' refers to biological difference and 'gender' denotes social and cultural construction. 'There is no gender identity behind the expressions of gender', Butler argued; 'that identity is performatively constituted by the very "expressions" that are said to be its results'

(Butler 2006, 34). She explained the concept of performativity in terms of 'acts, gestures, and desire' that produce

> the effect of an internal core or substance, but produce this *on the surface* of the body, through the play of signifying absences that suggest, but never reveal, the organizing principle of identity as a cause. Such acts, gestures, enactments, generally construed, are *performative* in the sense that the essence or identity that they otherwise purport to express are *fabrications* manufactured and sustained through corporeal signs and other discursive means. (op. cit., 185; italics original)

While I find Butler's concept of performativity particularly relevant in the context of textual analysis, the main aim of the argument in *Gender Trouble* is political, with Butler pointing out that 'acts and gestures, articulated and enacted desires create the illusion of an interior and organizing gender core, an illusion discursively maintained for the purposes of the regulation of sexuality within the obligatory frame of reproductive heterosexuality' (op. cit., 185-86). By definition, performativity involves repetition, and the possibilities of gender transformation are thus to be found 'in the arbitrary relation' between these repeated acts as well as 'in the possibility of a failure to repeat, a de-formity, or a parodic repetition that exposes the phantasmatic effect of abiding identity as a politically tenuous construction' (op. cit., 192). Consequently concepts such as masquerade, drag, and cross-dressing are prominent in the discussion in *Gender Trouble*, with Butler highlighting the complexity of the relation between the 'imitation' and the 'original':

> If the anatomy of the performer is already distinct from the gender of the performer, and both of those are distinct from the gender of the performance, then the performance suggests a dissonance not only between sex and performance, but sex and gender, and gender and performance. As much as drag creates a unified picture of 'woman' (what its critics often oppose), it also reveals the distinctness of those aspects of gendered experience which are falsely naturalized as a unity through the regulatory fiction of heterosexual coherence. *In imitating gender, drag implicitly reveals the imitative structure of gender itself – as well as its contingency.* (op. cit., 187; italics original)

I have found the notion of performativity a useful one in the analyses of the texts that follow, and as we shall see, there are also examples of masquerade and cross-dressing. My analyses of Wägner's texts in these terms will thus help to highlight what Butler has called the 'critical task for feminism' and defined as follows: 'to locate strategies of subversive repetition enabled by those constructions [of identity], to affirm the local possibilities of intervention through participating in precisely those practices of repetition that constitute identity and, therefore, present the immanent possibility of contesting them' (op. cit., 201).

The 'nomadic subject', the notion of Rosi Braidotti introduced above, has marked similarities with Butler's concept of performativity. The nomadic subject, according to Braidotti, is 'a performative image'; and Braidotti's reading of the significance of parody highlights both the connections with the thought of Butler and the political implications of the concept of the nomadic subject:

> what is politically effective in the politics of parody, or the political practice of 'as if,' is not the mimetic impersonation or capacity for repetition of dominant poses, but rather the extent to which these practices open up in-between spaces where new forms of political subjectivity can be explored. In other words, it is not the parody that will kill the phallocentric posture, but rather the power vacuum that parodic politics may be able to engender. (Braidotti 1994, 7)

The nomadic subject, by definition, is a challenge and alternative to phallocentrism ('a system that privileges the phallus as the symbol or source of power' [Moi 1985, 179]): Braidotti describes it as 'a suitable theoretical figuration for contemporary subjectivity', glossing 'figuration' as 'a style of thought that evokes or expresses ways out of the phallocentric vision of the subject' (Braidotti 1994, 1). The nomad, in Braidotti's reading, is 'a figuration for the kind of subject who has relinquished all idea, desire, or nostalgia for fixity', in other words 'a postmetaphysical, intensive, multiple entity, functioning in a net of interconnections' (op. cit., 22, 36). *Nomadic Subjects* presents a 'new vision of subjectivity as process' (op. cit., 99), and in this vision Donna Haraway's notion of the cyborg plays a prominent role. As a 'hybrid of machine and organism' and a 'creature in a post-gender world' (Haraway 1991, 149, 150), the cyborg may seem far removed from the texts of Elin Wägner, especially for readers familiar with some of the traditional approaches to Wägner's texts outlined above. As Haraway has clarified, however, the cyborg is 'resolutely committed to partiality, irony, intimacy, and perversity' as well as being a concept in which nature and culture are reworked: 'the one can no longer be the resource for appropriation or incorporation by the other' (op. cit., 151); in Braidotti's shorthand it is 'a connection-making entity, [...] a figure of interrelationality, receptivity, and global communication that deliberately blurs categorical distinctions' (Braidotti 1994, 105). I have found the perspective towards the cyborg a useful one when analysing Wägner's texts.

Outlining 'nomadic aesthetics' on the basis of her own experience as a 'nomadic polyglot', Braidotti describes writing in terms I believe can also usefully contribute to a model for the reading of texts, with Braidotti referring to writing as 'a process of undoing the illusory stability of fixed identities, [...] disengaging the sedentary nature of words, destabilizing commonsensical meanings, deconstructing established forms of consciousness' (Braidotti 1994, 15). Defining the function of the nomadic subject in terms of 'a relay team: s/he connects, circulates, moves on', Braidotti highlights the significance in her writing of the voices of others and their contribution to the 'dethroning of the "transcendental narcissism" of the philosophizing "I"', as well as the role, in *Nomadic Subjects*, of the variations between texts of different types (op. cit., 35, 37-38). To me these are also useful markers as we prepare to approach the texts of Wägner.

3. Community

Conny Svensson, author of the chapter on Elin Wägner in what has for the past two decades been the standard handbook of Swedish literature, has chosen to begin with *Väckarklocka* (1941), and more specifically with the pamphlet's linkage of the Second World War with masculinity. 'Life', he writes, 'was certainly better in the matriarchies from the dawn of history that Elin Wägner had come across in popular science texts' (Svensson 1999, 453-54). Here Svensson is effectively reinforcing the notion that the attention given to matriarchy makes *Väckarklocka* so divorced from reality that the text verges on irrelevance. However, more important in the present context is the underlying concept of community which has biologism, and in this case the relationship between the mother and child, as its bedrock. In other words, gender and community fuse in a construction that underlines the significance of binarism. But as Jennifer Burwell has pointed out, an

> examination of feminist 'utopias of reversal' reveals that, while attempts to construct a utopia based on difference effectively turn our gaze to that other space against which the dominant order has defined itself, these attempts end up sustaining a complementary relation between the two terms of the opposition without significantly challenging the structure of that opposition. (Burwell 1997, 204)

Let us take a look at the construction of a community beyond gender binarism. The study by Lena Eskilsson of *Kvinnliga medborgarskolan* (The Women Citizens' College) at Fogelstad (1925-54) – which Elin Wägner helped found and at which she taught for many years – has the title *Drömmen om kamratsamhället* (1991), which translates as 'The Dream of a Society of Comrades'. (It should be noted that in the case of the Swedish *kamrat*, the connotation 'fellow socialist or communist' is less prominent than in the case of the English *comrade*.) Eskilsson's investigation into the ideas underpinning the Women Citizens' College during its first ten years highlights the significance of personal relations and the informal group, of the foregrounding of the circle of comrades, equal yet different, rather than the family circle (Eskilsson 1991, 209), and of the emphasis on 'the role of the individual human being, the responsibility that went with citizenship, and the necessity to abolish the dualism between public and private, male and female characteristic of a society based on masculine principles' (op. cit., 202). Eskilsson has referred to the ideas cultivated at Fogelstad as a type of 'feminine humanistic cultural critique' (op. cit., 205); but it is significant that the concept of community developed at Fogelstad was *not* synonymous with a feminine utopia. Indeed the concept, by definition, was incomplete, dependent as it was on the inspiration and creativity of work in progress and not on any specification of the meaning of 'community'. As Eskilsson has pointed out, the leading women at Fogelstad argued not just that the new women citizens had a special contribution to make to society but that they also had the capacity to change the world (ibid.); however, it is important to emphasise that this vision did not exclude men.

According to a recent study of *gemenskap* (community) in Sweden, Anders P. Lundberg's investigation into community in the Evangelical Free Church and the Swedish Social Democratic Party respectively, 'the understanding of community and national integration' in twentieth-century Sweden has primarily been determined by the concept of the *folkhem* (the home of the people), i.e. the Swedish welfare state as developed by the social democrats from the early 1930s onwards (Lundberg 2005, 64). Lundberg goes on to endorse the point made by Johan Asplund in terms of Ferdinand Tönnies's *Gemeinschaft und Gesellschaft* (1887; *Community and Society*, 1957), namely that the concept of 'the home of the people' introduced, in 'a single catchword, [...] the ideology that a *Gemeinschaft* can be realised within the framework of a *Gesellschaft*' (Asplund 1991, 13; see also Lundberg 2005, 66). In Asplund's study, 'the home of the people' thus effectively becomes an illustration of his central thesis, which is that the concepts of *Gemeinschaft* and *Gesellschaft* are interrelated as in a puzzle picture: 'When one has initially discerned a *Gemeinschaft*, the image has to be reorganised for a *Gesellschaft* to emerge, and vice versa' (Asplund 1991, 43).

While the concept of 'the home of the people' clearly has to be a focal point in any consideration of community in twentieth-century Sweden, some definitions and categorisations have to be introduced before we can proceed. In Raymond Williams's *Keywords*, the greater part of the article on 'community' is taken up by clarifications of the contrast between 'community' and 'society', with Williams emphasising both the impact of industrialisation which resulted, in the nineteenth century, in the strong development of a contrasting 'sense of immediacy or locality', and the pivotal role of Tönnies's work

A New Approach

(Williams 1988, 75-76). In Williams's summary, the complexity of the term 'community' relates to 'the difficult interaction between the tendencies originally distinguished in the historical development: on the one hand the sense of direct common concern; on the other hand the materialization of various forms of common organization'; but he also finds that in contrast to all other terms of social organisation, that of 'community' seems 'never to be used unfavourably' (op. cit., 76).

Tönnies's categorisations remain prominent in a recent textbook such as Gerard Delanty's *Community*, first published in 2003. As Delanty underlines, the term 'community' can refer both to an idea and to a particular social phenomenon, and on this basis he distinguishes four approaches: (1) 'community' is associated with disadvantaged urban localities requiring government support for community regeneration etc.; (2) 'community' is seen as 'the search for belonging', with the emphasis on 'cultural issues of identity'; (3) in the context of postmodern politics and radical democracy, 'community' is approached 'in terms of political consciousness and collective action'; and (4) 'community' is 'cosmopolitanized' in the context of global communications, including the internet (Delanty 2008, 3-4). Delanty points up the theme of loss in the concept of community of Tönnies, the role of community as a moral force in the work of Durkheim, and the understanding of community in opposition to structure in the work of Victor Turner; he notes that the common denominator is that of community concerning belonging (op. cit., 15, 32-34, 36-39, 44-46, 4). With the search for belonging being the focal point of the second of Delanty's approaches, he develops the positions involved in a chapter on communitarianism and citizenship, summing up the 'communitarian turn' in the phrase 'from contract to community', and underlining that communitarians argue that 'citizenship is based on a social concept of the individual as a member of a community', with 'community' in this sense meaning 'the civic community of the polity as opposed to a small-scale traditional community' (op. cit., 73-74). Here Delanty discerns four versions of communitarianism: liberal communitarianism, radical pluralism, civic republicanism, and governmental communitarianism (op. cit., 74). Disappointingly, however, the version of greatest relevance to the present study, radical pluralism, is given the shortest treatment.

As Elizabeth Frazer and Nicola Lacey have pointed out in *The Politics of Community: A Feminist Critique of the Liberal-Communitarian Debate* (1993), gender 'remains a conceptual irrelevance for communitarian political theory: it is either ignored, or gestured at in a way which assumes that gender issues can be incorporated without conceptual modification' (Frazer and Lacey 1993, 158). Highlighting the absence of a theory of power in liberal communitarian arguments, Frazer and Lacey have emphasised that the inclusion of such a theory, covering 'power with' as well as 'power over', has the effect of rendering inappropriate 'the liberal conception of public and private spheres, and suggests that every area of social life must be opened up to political critique' (op. cit., 195, 196). This project involves the deconstruction of the dichotomy individual - society as a means of showing 'how power is exercised through social practices', along with the inclusion of the notion of a social group 'as a tool of political theoretical analysis' and a means of recognising

> that our social positions, our identities, the operations of power on us, are largely determined not just by our actions as 'individuals', but by our social relations and locations, which will, of course, be multiple and shifting. Only by placing the relevance of different kinds of social groups and group membership, including questions of power and access to that membership, at the core of political theory can we properly acknowledge the importance of group membership in the constitution of human identity, and recognise and attend to the question of social justice raised by group-based patterns of disadvantage. (op. cit., 197)

Frazer and Lacey advocate the ideal of 'dialogic communitarianism', describing this as dialogic in the sense that it 'assumes democratic institutions providing real access to political processes for all citizens'; as dialogic and communitarian in the sense that it proceeds 'from the relational theory of the self, recognising the importance of both dialogue and identification with various "communities" in the constitution of subjectivity and human identity'; and communitarian in the sense that it places 'questions of both public goods and the institutions needed to support them, and the ideal of collective life based on mutual acceptance and recognition, at the heart of politics' (op. cit., 203). The openness of language is central to Frazer and Lacey's argument about the role of dialogic communitarianism in suggesting 'ways in which we can begin to see what possibilities for political change exist' (op. cit., 207), and an example of the dialogic process in concrete political practice is the feminist consciousness-raising group:

> As multiple experiences are exchanged, new interpretations emerge and find strength and validity from the collective practice. These interpretations generate new concepts, new languages, new frameworks through which we interpret the world, and hence in turn change our perceptions and with them, in a significant sense, social reality. (op. cit., 208)

But the consciousness-raising group is just one example among many: 'A chance scene in a film or a passage in a novel; reflection on a dream; recollection of one's past feelings and behaviour in certain situations; an argument at work; all these are capable of generating reinterpretations and reconceptualisations of the world' (op. cit., 209).

In *Transpositions*, Rosi Braidotti has gone on to develop the concept of nomadism in terms that problematise and significantly expand the notion of community. In terms of citizenship (in Part II below, constructions of gender and community will be considered with a focus on dominant and alternative discourses on citizenship), nomadism leads on to flexible forms of citizenship, with Braidotti arguing for 'complex allegiances and multiple forms of cultural belongings' that would involve the dismantling of the us/them binary and the replacement of

> a fixed notion of European citizenship with a functionally differentiated network of affiliations and loyalties. For the citizens of the member states of the European Union this leads to the disconnection of the three elements of citizenship, nationality and national identity. These effects boil down to one central idea: the end of pure and steady identities, or in other words, creolization and hybridization producing a multicultural minoritarian Europe, within which 'new' Europeans can take their place alongside others. (Braidotti 2006, 79)

But the most powerful part of Braidotti's argument concerns the need to 'move beyond anthropocentrism', the need to develop a very different perspective underpinned by the notion of *zoe*, the 'affirmative power of life' (op. cit., 107, 109). Braidotti's critique of 'the classical humanistic *hubris* which declares "Man" as the measure of *all* things, oblivious to the sexism and the ethnocentrism of such a position' (op. cit., 130; italics original), is also relevant to the present study. The remainder of Braidotti's paragraph may seem too radical and perhaps too obviously postmodern to be relevant to texts by Wägner, the last of them published as long ago as 1947, but I am quoting it as a means of flagging up the possibilities of present-day theorisation and new directions for the reading of Wägner's texts. Having emphasised her bond of empathy and responsibility 'towards non-human others' and the 'real hindrance' of the notion of 'Man' as the measure of all things, Braidotti continues:

> This is why I want to reclaim my *zoe*-philic location and enlist it in support of the project of undoing anthropocentrism and its spin-off, androcentrism. I want to unfasten their joint reliance on the phallic signifier, i.e. the political economy of Sameness and of its specular, binary and constitutive 'Others'. I want to run with the she-wolves against the gravitational pull of the humanization and hence the commodification of all that lives. And I want to celebrate instead not so much the mystery of nature – a sentimental notion dear to deep ecology which sounds unconvincing to my agnostic ears – but rather the immense generative power, the intelligence and artistry of the non-human, of *zoe* as generative force. (op. cit., 130-31; italics original)

As I shall show in due course, Braidotti's notion of *zoe* can be helpful in pointing up directions and possibilities with regard to some of Wägner's late texts in particular.

A number of the distinctions and definitions from this brief survey will provide useful markers in the chapters that follow, and while some of them will be relatively prominent in the chapters on contexts and discourses, others will underpin the textual analyses. But although Sweden in the first half of the twentieth century might seem the ideal focal point for a study of community (the late transition from an agricultural to an industrial economy, the strength of the popular movements, the organisation of labour, democratisation, the campaign for women's suffrage), the present study is of course not a sociological one but primarily a study of texts. The exploration of communities of women, of feminine utopias, was a prominent project in feminist literary criticism in the 1970s and 1980s, with Nina Auerbach's *Communities of Women: An Idea in Fiction* (1978) as one of the landmarks, and Birgitta Svanberg persuasively applying the concept to the seventh and final volume in Agnes von Krusenstjerna's (1894-1940) series *Fröknarna von Pahlen* (1930-35; The Misses von Pahlen) (Svanberg 1989, 351-410). Eva Heggestad's *En bättre och lyckligare värld* (2003; A Better and Happier World), which investigates utopian visions by Swedish women writers 1850-1950 and to which I shall refer in my analysis of Wägner's *Norrtullsligan*, represents a recent example. But the main emphasis in the present study, with regard to constructions of community as well as constructions of gender, is on narrative, and a number of the features defined by a narratologist such as Mieke Bal will help us pinpoint the constructions of community in texts by Wägner. These may include the role of the narrator, and more particularly the issue of narratorial control, especially with regard to other characters or actors in the story. The representation of speech may well also be relevant in this context, with the difference between – in the terminology of Shlomith Rimmon-Kenan – a diegetic summary by the narrator on the one hand and instances of direct discourse on the other (Rimmon-Kenan 1988, 109-16), possibly with many voices in the form of direct discourse, potentially having a significant impact on constructions of community. Focalisation, the 'relation between the vision and that which is "seen", perceived' (Bal 1999, 142), may vary considerably within a single text and may of course also be important to the construction of community. So may a text's frames of reference, in Bal's definition 'information that may with some confidence be called communal' (op. cit., 119). As mentioned above, Susan S. Lanser uses the term 'maxim' to define the type of comments and truths that constitute '"extrarepresentational" acts' referring to 'the world "beyond" the fiction' (Lanser 1992, 16-17); and given Lanser's feminist perspective, her comment on the potential significance of maxims also points in the direction of alternative communities as she underlines that '[i]deologically oppositional writers might wish [...] to "maxim-ize" their narratives in order either to posit alternative textual ideologies or to establish the writer, through her authorial narrator-equivalent, as a significant participant in contemporary debates' (op. cit., 17). Also relevant here is the potential community of narratees, with the narratee, in the basic definition of Gerald Prince, being another textual construct, the 'someone whom the narrator addresses' (Prince 1996, 214). As Prince has pointed out, the construction of the narratee may involve direct addresses by the narrator, but personal pronouns in the second person – you – and in the first person plural – we – may also contribute to the construction of the narratee (op. cit., 220-21). Beyond the narratees, readers buy, borrow, read, and discuss texts, and so form communities of readers.

The past, history, and memory are of particular relevance with regard to the constructions of community in a number of the texts to be analysed below. As Middleton and Woods remind us, '[n]ot only is the text a form of memory, [but] memories are themselves textual'. Reading, moreover, 'itself is a practice of memory, because texts are forms of prosthetic social memory by which readers increase and correct their own limited cognitive strengths and participate in a public memorial space' (Middleton and Woods 2000, 5-6). In addition, textual memory also looks forward: 'It not only empowers societies to manage territories and plan for the future, it also contains a promise that this can be a democratic process' (ibid.). As we shall see, textual memory functions in a range of different ways in texts by Wägner, but in some of the late texts in particular references to what is presented as documentation – notes, letters, manuscripts and much else which may be historical or fictitious – adds to the prominence of what Middleton and Woods have highlighted as the 'room for [...] audiences to become historians' (op. cit., 34). Probably the most familiar version of this room is intertextuality, in Bal's definition 'the quotation, in a text, of another text' which does not need to be marked as such (Bal 1999, 64). While Middleton and Woods consider intertextuality chiefly in relation to Roland Barthes's 'From Work to Text' (Middleton and Woods 2000, 83-84), Bal highlights the impact of the work of Mikhail Bakhtin and emphasises its 'strong liberating potential' in terms that are highly relevant to the present study:

The very notion that language is not unified provides access to bits and pieces of culturally different environments within a single text. It makes readers aware of the limited importance of the individual author and the impossibility of completely repressing ideological and social others. To realize that any text is a patchwork of different strata, bearing traces of different communities and of the contestations between them, is an essential insight. (Bal 1999, 65-66)

In summary, then, the present study takes its theoretical starting-point in feminist poststructuralism and draws on material chiefly from Chris Weedon, Susan S. Lanser, Judith Butler, and Rosi Braidotti to explore constructions of gender and community in texts by Wägner which can be categorised as representing a range of different genres, albeit with the caveat that the notion of genre is a fluid and variable one. The texts are approached within the frameworks of contexts (economic, political, social, and cultural) and discourses focusing on gender and community; and the emphasis on construction contributes to foregrounding agency.

4. Re-Writing

Only a handful of scholarly studies of Wägner appeared prior to the publication of Isaksson and Linder's biography in 1977-80. The first substantial article, 'Elin Wägner. En översikt' (1936; Elin Wägner. A Survey) by the author Karin Boye (1900-1941), was boldly feminist and offered detailed and innovative readings, but this was the exception. Most of the early studies tended to place considerable emphasis on aspects of Wägner's biography, her ideas, and the sources of inspiration for various works of prose fiction. Several articles were published in 1949, the year Wägner died, and John Landquist's 'Några drag av Elin Wägners berättarkonst' (Some Aspects of Elin Wägner's Narrative Art), Örjan Lindberger's 'Hjärtat och nycklarna' (The Heart and the Keys), and Bengt Tomson's '*Släkten Jerneploogs framgång* och *De fem pärlorna*' (The Rise of the House of Jerneploog and The Five Pearls) all belong to this category. The prefaces by Holger Ahlenius to the 15 volumes of Wägner's *Valda skrifter* (1950-54; Selected Works) similarly focused on the biographical background and especially on the sources of narratives and models of characters; in addition, Ahlenius outlined the reception of the chosen texts. Barbro Alving (1909-1987), a journalist who became a close friend of Wägner and began writing her biography – the task subsequently carried out by Isaksson and Linder – published several articles; for obvious reasons, these also related Wägner's work to her biography. There was a new wave of interest from 1980 onwards, much of it undoubtedly inspired by the publication of the biography. Karl Lindqvist's *Individ grupp gemenskap. Studier i de unga tiotalisternas litteratur* (1980; Individual Group Community: Studies in the Literature of the Young Writers of the 1910s) approaches work by Ludvig Nordström and early texts by Wägner such as the series of lighthearted columns entitled *Klubben* (1907; The Club) and *Norrtullsligan* from a sociological perspective. Bertil Björkenlid's *Kvinnokrav i manssamhälle. Rösträttskvinnorna och deras metoder som opinionsbildare och påtryckargrupp i Sverige 1902-21* (1982; Women's Demands in Men's Society: The Women Suffragists and their Methods as Opinion-Makers and as a Pressure Group in Sweden 1902-21) covers much material in addition to texts by Wägner, but the treatment of her work is comparatively detailed, and the meticulous contextualisation provided by Björkenlid is very useful. Sarah Death's doctoral thesis *The Female Perspective in the Novels of Fredrika Bremer and Elin Wägner* (University of London, 1985; unpublished) investigates the treatment in Bremer and Wägner of themes such as upbringing and education, marriage, and feminine creativity. Sarah Death has also published articles about two of Wägner's novels, *Släkten Jerneploogs framgång* and *Silverforsen* (The Silver Rapids).

It is possible to speak of a new phase in Wägner research from 1990 onwards. Previously the emphasis had chiefly been on Wägner as an author of prose fiction, but since 1990 Wägner has attracted at least one sociologist, two intellectual historians, and one historian in addition to literature specialists. Margareta Lindholm compared and contrasted the thought of Alva Myrdal (1902-1986) and Elin Wägner during the 1930s in a sociological study entitled *Talet om det kvinnliga. Studier i feministiskt tänkande i Sverige under 1930-talet* (1990; Discourses on'Women': Studies in Feminist Thinking during the 1930s in Sweden). Lindholm's study, boldly couched in terms of a dialogue between

Myrdal and Wägner, plays a prominent role in Chapter 7 below, 'Discourses: Citizenship'. The intellectual historian Lena Eskilsson completed her doctoral thesis – referred to above – in 1991, *Drömmen om kamratsamhället. Kvinnliga medborgarskolan på Fogelstad 1925-35* (Female Citizenship: The Women Citizens' School at Fogelstad 1925-35), and among other things her study contextualises Wägner's contributions in relation to *Frisinnade Kvinnors Riksförbund* (The National Association of Liberal Women), the weekly *Tidevarvet*, and the Women Citizens' College. In 2001 Bibi Jonsson published the first doctoral thesis wholly devoted to texts by Wägner, *I den värld vi drömmer om. Utopin i Elin Wägners trettiotalsromaner* (In the World We Dream of: The Utopian Scheme in Elin Wägner's Novels of the Thirties); focusing on encounters and meetings, Jonsson analysed relations between male and female characters, feminine creativity, and motherliness and utopia. The historian Irene Andersson also published her doctoral thesis in 2001: in *Kvinnor mot krig. Aktioner och nätverk för fred 1914-1940* (Women Against War: Actions and Networks for Peace, 1914-1940), the focus is on three pacifist actions by women in Sweden, with Wägner playing a prominent role in two of these. Andersson's mapping of the field and contextualisation of a number of texts by Wägner have been important to the present study. Inger Larsson's study of three Swedish literary biographies (2003) includes one written by Wägner, and I will refer to *Text och tolkning i svenska författarbiografier. Elin Wägners Selma Lagerlöf, Elisabeth Tykessons Atterbom och Fredrik Bööks Verner von Heidenstam* (Text and Interpretation in Swedish Literary Biographies: Elin Wägner's *Selma Lagerlöf*, Elisabeth Tykesson's *Atterbom* and Fredrik Böök's *Verner von Heidenstam*) in my section on the Lagerlöf biography below. In 2005, the intellectual historian Katarina Leppänen published the first Swedish doctoral thesis on Wägner in English: her *Rethinking Civilisation in a European Feminist Context: History, Nature, Women in Elin Wägner's Väckarklocka* draws on ecofeminist theory and archival material in the United States, Germany, and Sweden to relate Wägner's pamphlet to European ideological contexts in the interwar period. Birgitta Wistrand's doctoral thesis from 2006, *Elin Wägner i 1920-talet. Rörelseintellektuell och internationalist* (Elin Wägner in the 1920s: Movement Intellectual and Internationalist) explores Wägner's ideas and texts during the period 1922-30, defining Wägner's significance as a 'movement intellectual' in both sociological and psychological terms, and pinpointing as central her preoccupations with women, love, and war. Wägner's journalism remained a neglected field up to the late 1990s, but since then media scholars such as Birgitta Ney, Kristina Lundgren, and Margareta Stål have published chapters and articles on various aspects of the journalism, and Margareta Stål is currently researching Wägner's contributions to *Idun* in the early decades of the twentieth century. Gunilla Domellöf has also explored aspects of the journalism with an emphasis on *Tidevarvet*; in addition, she has published articles about the reception and canonisation of Wägner's work. My own work, starting with articles published in the 1980s, has been inspired by second-wave feminism and then increasingly by feminist poststructuralism and narratology. My editions of Wägner's texts include a collection of opinion pieces and essays, *Vad tänker du, mänsklighet? Texter om feminism, fred och miljö* (1999; Humankind, What are You Thinking? Texts on Feminism, Peace and the Environment).

The research survey above is not exhaustive, and I will refer to additional and mostly short studies as part of my analyses. Boel Hackman's biography (2005), written as part of a series, is also indicative of the current interest in Wägner and her work, as is the new one-volume edition of Isaksson and Linder's biography (2003).

Following the introductory material in this chapter about feminist poststructuralism and theories of gender and community, the bulk of the present study is divided into two chronological sections, 1907-21 and 1922-47. The dividing line has been dictated by the introduction in Sweden of suffrage for women in 1921; the start and end years, on the other hand, derive from the dates of publication of the earliest and latest texts by Wägner analysed in this study. Each of the two sections is structured in the same way. There is a short chapter outlining the economic, political, social, and cultural contexts, and this is followed by a chapter setting out dominant and alternative discourses on gender and community. For each of the two chronological periods, I have chosen to explore the conjunction of the discourses on gender and community in terms of a key concept, the family for the period 1907-21, and

A New Approach

citizenship for the period 1922-47. Within the framework of contexts and dominant and alternative discourses, I then move on to analysing the constructions of gender and community in a range of texts. The texts representing the period 1907-21 consist of a selection of journalistic reportages, a handful of essays, two series of light-hearted columns, and six novels. The range of texts from the period 1922-47 is considerably greater, and on the basis of a shift in the texts from the final decade with regard to constructions of community in particular, I have divided my analyses of the texts from 1922-47 into two chapters. The first of these, covering the period 1922-36, begins with a range of opinion pieces and then turns to the volume entitled *Från Seine, Rhen och Ruhr* before moving on to the radio drama dating from 1930-34 and the prose fiction as represented by four novels. The subsequent chapter covers the period 1937-47 and begins with an analysis of the pamphlet *Väckarklocka*. This is followed by a section on the travelogue-cum-local-history *Tusen år i Småland*, and one on the biography of Selma Lagerlöf. The concluding section, on prose fiction, covers Wägner's last three novels. There is a chapter providing a short summary at the end of each of the two major chronological sections, 1907-21 and 1922-47, and there is of course also a general conclusion.

In the text by Elisabet Hermodsson from which I have taken the epigraph of this chapter, a heavy fall of snow inspires a new text as the narrator 'pulsar genom det oskrivna' (Hermodsson 1979, 118) (plods through the unwritten), the re-modelling of the landscape by a thick layer of snow tangibly opening up possibilities of change. This sense of adventure, of the excitement of exploring new landscapes, has been important in inspiring the present study, and I hope I have been able to convey some of this excitement in my analyses. But before we begin to explore a range of textual spaces and their potential, I shall sketch the contexts of the period 1907-21 and explore constructions of gender and community in terms of discourses on the family. Both the contexts and the discourses are indispensable frameworks for the analyses of Wägner's texts that follow.

Part I.
Suffrage and Beyond
1907-21

Chapter 2: Contexts

1. Economic

At the turn of the century 1900 the Swedish economy was in a period of strong growth which, in the analysis of Lennart Schön, was to last until the middle of the century, with the two world wars and the international recession of the late 1920s and early 1930s causing mere dips in the upward curve. Sweden's economic success was based on timber, increasingly turned into pulp and paper and widely exported; a flourishing engineering industry; a well-established textile industry; the development of a modern banking system; the increasing use of electrical power; and the building of railways (Schön 2000, 223-32).

By 1900, Sweden had a population of 5.1 million. Of those in work, around 55 per cent were to be found in agriculture, with around 20 per cent in industry (Schön 2000, 233). Swedish agriculture had become more efficient in the second half of the nineteenth century, but at the point when the volume of production of Swedish industry overtook that of agriculture, around 1900, well over half the working population was still earning their living from agriculture (ibid.). In Nils Edling's analysis, Sweden in 1900 was at once an agricultural nation and a young industrial one (Edling 1996, 31). With small-scale family farms continuing to predominate, well over one third of Swedes in employment were still to be found in agriculture as late as 1930 (Schön 2000, 233).

Gendered analyses of employment have added to this picture and also raised some pertinent questions. Exploring the relationships between the traditional household economy and the market economy, Anita Göransson has emphasised the extent to which the contribution of the Swedish household economy, long prevalent within agriculture and traditionally shouldered by women, has been underestimated. The reasons are twofold: production that did not take place within the market economy and thus was not priced has tended to be grossly underestimated; and the statisticians' perspectives on the household have long obscured many of those working there, with the economic contribution of farmers' wives not appearing in Swedish statistics until 1960 (Göransson 1996, 59). Thus Schön's figure of around 55 per cent working in agriculture by 1900 necessarily excludes, as he indeed points out, all those doing unpaid work in agricultural households (Schön 2000, 233). As Göransson has underlined, the tendency to underestimate women's work and household-based production generally has had major implications for the understanding of economic growth overall and the roles of specific sections of the economy. Thus the inclusion of women's work may add still further to the role of agriculture in relation to industry, including, of course, during the period that concerns us here. On the other hand, the interpretation of the industrialisation of Sweden may well have to be modified if we are prepared to accept the extensive production of goods and services in Swedish households as home or proto industrial (Göransson 1996, 59-60).

While the proportion of women in employment, outwith agriculture, almost doubled in the period 1890-1920, this increase primarily involved unmarried women in urban areas (Silenstam 1970, 38, 40). By 1900, according to the official census, women made up 24 per cent of those in full-time employment outwith agriculture (quoted in Widerberg 1980, 58). What types of work did these women do? The biggest proportion (17.7 per cent) was to be found in domestic service, with smaller proportions in industry (9.6 per cent), commerce (4.8 per cent) and public services (3.9 per cent). By 1930, the closest point of comparison available to me, the biggest proportion was instead to be found in industry (20.8 per cent), followed by commerce (16.9 per cent), domestic service (16.1 per cent) and the public services (9.7 per cent) (Kyle and Qvist 1974, 71-72). The growth in the employment of women in public service posts (state and local authority) requiring an academic qualification was very slow, with only 15 physicians and not a single woman lawyer or dentist in this type of post by 1900, and 155 physicians, 32 lawyers, and 250 dentists by 1930. In lower-ranking public service posts the pattern was, at least in part, somewhat different, with twice as many women as men teaching in the compulsory school system (including primary school), and women constituting 80 per cent of those working in telecommunications and 100 per cent in nursing in 1900. By 1930, these gender divisions had become more pronounced, with women constituting nearly three quarters of the teachers in the compulsory school system, 90 per cent of those working in telecommunications, and – still – 100 per cent of nurses (op. cit., 73).

Women, as Anita Göransson has pointed out, have always been working; the key problem has been the lack of access to status positions (Göransson 1996, 63). Although women had gained access to the Swedish universities in 1873 (with the exception of the faculties of theology and law), they remained barred from the state upper-secondary schools until 1927. Elin Wägner, whose father was a head master with a doctorate in philosophy and whose younger brother received a university education as a matter of course, was refused the private tuition in philosophy that she had asked for and that would presumably have paved the way for her university entrance (Isaksson and Linder 2003, 73, 76). Women, moreover, were barred from most public service posts requiring an academic qualification until new legislation was introduced in 1923.

Highlighting the fact that the abolition of legal obstacles to gendered equality in Sweden in the first half of the twentieth century coincided with the introduction of new obstacles to equality at work, Ulla Wikander, following Olwen Hufton, has concluded that 'industrial "development"' brought about a 're-ordering of the subordination of women' (Wikander 1993, 87). In Wikander's pan-European perspective, the gendered division of work up to around 1900 was comparatively malleable, complete with openings offering new possibilities for women (Wikander 1999, 83). Her research into gender and work at the Gustavsberg porcelain factory in Stockholm has shown that in the period 1880-1910, women more frequently did the same types of work as men than was the case after this period (Wikander 1988). Margareta Berger in her history of Swedish women journalists has highlighted the significance of the emergence of the *pennskaft* (women journalists, literally 'pen holders'), named after Elin Wägner's novel about a woman journalist, *Pennskaftet* (1910; *Penwoman*). Although Berger has calculated that by 1913, 11 per cent of the Stockholm journalists were women (the figure for the provinces was very much lower), she has also found that the number of women journalists at some Stockholm papers declined throughout this decade (Berger 1977, 135-36). Elin Wägner became a journalist in 1903, working at the provincial daily *Helsingborgs-Posten*, and was assistant editor at the Stockholm-based women's weekly *Idun* from 1907 to1916. Thus it would seem that the latter part of this phase of her journalistic career coincided with a trend towards a more traditionally gendered division of journalistic work.

While Sweden remained neutral throughout the First World War, the war had a huge impact on the country's foreign trade. The rationing of some foodstuffs was introduced in 1916, and during the winter of 1917-18 there were severe shortages of both food and fuel (Carlsson 1968c, 309-11). Applying a pan-European perspective and referring to both World Wars, Ulla Wikander has distanced herself from the notion that the World Wars amounted to turning points as regards women's participation in paid employment. In her analysis, they instead contributed to widening the gulf between 'masculine'and 'feminine', with all the implications this continuing division would have (Wikander 1999, 147).

2. Political

Some key events in the first couple of decades of the twentieth century help pinpoint the democratisation of Swedish politics. Following a lengthy political conflict, the union with Norway was dissolved by negotiation in 1905, the more democratic and radical politics of Norway having long exerted pressure on the more conservative politics of Sweden. The General Strike of 1909 involved as many as 300,000 Swedish workers, making it the biggest trades union mobilisation in the world prior to the events in France in May 1968 (Therborn 1988, 45). General suffrage for men was introduced in 1909, along with proportional representation in both parliamentary and local elections. In

1914 a speech by the king sparked a constitutional crisis, with parliamentary democracy finally introduced in 1917. In 1919 the Swedish *riksdag* (parliament) voted in favour of suffrage for women; and the first women members of parliament took their seats in 1921, one in the First Chamber and four in the Second Chamber.

Sweden was neutral throughout the First World War, although many conservative Swedes took a pro-German stance. The impact of the revolutions in Russia in 1917 and in Germany in 1918 was considerable. As Kjell Östberg has demonstrated, Swedish women played a leading role in the food riots that occurred in a great number of Swedish towns in the spring of 1917. However, both the Social Democratic Party and the Communist Party preferred to avoid making use of the expertise of women who had headed the proletarian mass movements in the spring of 1917, just as they sidelined the women who had headed political women's organisations and the unionisation of women workers (Östberg 2000, 19-36, 97).

Soon after the turn of the century 1900, Sweden had modern political parties of the kind that have subsequently dominated the country's political life. While the Social Democratic Party had been founded in 1889, a liberal party (*Frisinnade landsföreningen*) was founded in 1902 and a conservative party (*Allmänna valmansförbundet*) in 1904. The emergence of the Swedish Social Democratic Party and the organisation of labour have been seen as closely related to other contemporary popular movements such as the temperance movement and the free church (Therborn 1988, 42-43). In 1896 Hjalmar Branting, leader of the Social Democratic Party, was elected to the Second Chamber. In 1920, he was to head the country's first Social Democratic government – the first in the world to come to power by peaceful and democratic means and not as the result of a revolution (Carlsson 1968d, 18). Following the introduction of general suffrage for men, the Social Democrats had rapidly gained ground in the *riksdag*, achieving 28.5 per cent of the votes in 1911 and 36.4 per cent in September 1914 (Hadenius, Molin, Wieslander 1971, 286). In the meantime, Social Democratic women had lost ground in the sense that *Kvinnornas fackförbund* (The Women's Trades Union Association) which had contributed to promoting women's representation in the

Swedish Trades Union Confederation, had been dissolved in 1909 (Carlsson 1986, 193-99), leaving Social Democratic women to channel most of their activities through the Social Democratic women's clubs. When *Sveriges Socialdemokratiska Kvinnoförbund* (The Swedish Social Democratic Women's Association) was established in 1920, its aims were to promote education and 'women's issues'; moreover, as Östberg has shown, relations between the Social Democratic Party and the Women's Association remained difficult at least until the mid-1930s (Östberg 2000, 59-61). *Sverges socialdemokratiska vänsterparti* (The Swedish Social Democratic Party of the Left) was founded in 1917, and *Sveriges kommunistiska parti* (The Swedish Communist Party) in 1921.

Throughout much of the first two decades of the twentieth century, Sweden was governed by either the conservatives or the liberals. The conservatives were markedly hostile to women's suffrage, but *Sveriges Moderata Kvinnoförbund* (The Swedish Conservative Women's Association), formed in 1915, became a significant pressure group (Nicklasson 1992, 80), and the Conservative Women's Suffrage Association was established in 1917. While general suffrage was one of the central planks of the Liberal Party programme and the emphasis on equality had the effect, at least for a time, of suggesting that a separate women's association would be superfluous (Nilsson 1940, 10), the constitutional crisis of 1914 and the subsequent policy shift to the right, along with the growing international tension, precipitated the formation in March 1914 of *Föreningen Frisinnade Kvinnor* (The Swedish Women's Liberal Association), the core items on the agenda being (1) peace and (2) full citizenship for women in the context of democracy (op. cit., 27). A number of leading figures in *Landsföreningen för kvinnans politiska rösträtt* (The National Association for Women's Suffrage) also became members of the Women's Liberal Association, among them Elin Wägner, who was also on the committee from 1914 to 1917. While the first few years of the Association were characterised by the efforts to safeguard the humanitarian and cultural ideals threatened by the First World War, the subsequent years, up to the introduction of suffrage for women, were focused on political work in preparation for universal suffrage (op. cit., 22).

Frisinnade Kvinnors Riksförbund (The National Association of Liberal Women) was established in 1921, and in 1923, following the splitting of the Liberal Party, the National Association of Liberal Women asserted its independence in relation to the two liberal parties. Both the Association of Liberal Women and the National Association of Liberal Women, along with the weekly *Tidevarvet* (The Epoch) and *Kvinnliga medborgarskolan* (The Women Citizens' College) at Fogelstad, established by some of the leading figures in the National Association in 1923 and 1925 respectively, are key examples of feminist counter-publics in Sweden, and I shall return to them in the analyses that follow.

The organised campaign for women's suffrage had begun with the formation of the Stockholm Association for Women's Suffrage in 1902 and the establishment of the National Association for Women's Suffrage in 1903. The National Association was dominated by non-socialist women, and by liberal women in particular. According to Josefin Rönnbäck, Sweden in effect had two women's suffrage organisations, one bourgeois and the other social democratic (Rönnbäck 2004, 193). The Swedish suffrage campaign was markedly peaceful, involving a single public demonstration (in Göteborg in 1918), focusing instead on petitioning, lecturing, and leafleting. Courses for women, covering for example social issues and local politics, were introduced as early as 1907 and considerably expanded from 1912 (op. cit., 153-60); and in 1912 the National Association also launched a fortnightly newspaper, *Rösträtt för kvinnor* (Votes for Women). While the total membership of the National Association for Women's Suffrage peaked in 1913 (17,057) and the highest number of local associations was achieved in 1917 (237), the most successful year for *Rösträtt för kvinnor* was 1916, with the 24 issues printed in a total of 148,000 copies (Björkenlid 1982, 263). Although the work of both the Associations – local as well as national – and the educational initiatives, including the publication of pamphlets and journalism, would have contributed significantly to the new understanding of suffrage and politics which Rönnbäck has defined as a key outcome of the process of democratisation in Sweden (Rönnbäck 2004, 269), the impact at the level of national politics after 1921 was to remain very limited indeed for several decades. There were just 5 women in the *riksdag* in 1922 (out of a total of 380 members), the figure rising to 6 in 1933 and 10 in 1937 (Östberg 2000, 70). Swedish cabinets did not include women prior to 1947, when Professor Karin Kock was appointed Minister without portfolio, becoming Minister of National Economy the following year.

3. Social

The population of Sweden rose from 5.1 million in 1900 to 5.9 million in 1920 (Carlsson 1968a, 30). There was a considerable surplus of women, e.g. 1,022 women to 1,000 men in the age group 15-39 in 1900, and 1,149 in the age group 40-64, figures which had changed only marginally by 1920 (Kyle and Qvist 1974, 69). The main reason for the imbalance was emigration: during the period 1840-1930 more than one million Swedes emigrated to the United States (Carlsson 1968b, 40), with very much smaller numbers emigrating to other countries. Men emigrated to a greater extent than did women. But women left rural Sweden for the towns and urban areas to a greater extent than did men, which resulted in a shortage of women in the age group 15-39 in the rural areas and a considerable surplus in the urban areas in all age groups from the age of 15 upwards (Kyle and Qvist 1974, 69). In 1900, the percentage of women in Sweden aged 20-64 who were married was 56.7, while 35.8 per cent were unmarried. Over the next two decades, the number of married women declined, reaching 55.5 per cent in 1920, while the number of unmarried women rose, reaching 37.4 per cent in the same year (op. cit., 67). Over this period nativity, although still high, was declining: while the figure had been 27.1 per mil in 1891-1900, it was 22.1 per mil in 1911-20 (Carlsson 1968a, 30).

The first few decades of the twentieth century marked a breakthrough for social policy in Sweden, with the establishment of structures and systems that were to provide the first steps towards the modern welfare state. While Lennart Schön has linked these developments to the industrial breakthrough (Schön 2000, 267-69), Nils Edling has interpreted them in the context of the wider pattern I have referred to above, of a Sweden that in 1900 was both an agricultural nation and a young industrial one. Although the concept of *den sociala frågan* (the social issue) was primarily taken to refer to the situation of industrial workers, covering aspects such as industrial conflicts, unemployment, inadequate housing, alcohol abuse, illness, and poverty, the social issue, as Edling has emphasised, was also relevant in rural Sweden. Here the efforts to expand owner-occupied housing (*egnahemsfrågan*) constituted a central plank of the struggle to tackle social problems, and as Edling has argued, these efforts should be included in any consideration of the social issue (Edling 1996, 19-22). I shall survey social policy in the first couple of decades of the twentieth century firstly in terms of the rural areas, with an emphasis on the efforts to expand owner-occupied housing and also small-holdings, and secondly in terms of the more urbanised and industrialised areas, with an emphasis on the broader range of efforts to achieve social reform.

Against the background of the combined impact of industrialisation, the accelerating acquisition of small Norrland farms by timber companies, and large-scale emigration, there were major moves towards the end of the nineteenth century to increase the numbers of owner-occupiers and small-holders. In 1904, the *riksdag* decided to introduce loans for these categories, thus laying the foundation for the expansionist agricultural policy that would characterise the decades up to the Second World War (Edling 1996, 12). In the same year, the government-appointed Norrland Committtee delivered its six-volume report, the gist of which was that the land in Norrland should be preserved for the local people (Sörlin 1988, 187-88). In both cases, the underlying ambitions were partly political, with ownership of land, however limited, perceived as guaranteeing social stability (Sörlin 1988, 191; Edling 1996, 21), and including a strong nationalist element that was reinforced after the dissolution of the union with Norway in 1905. Country cottages, as Edling has pointed out, should be both salubrious and Swedish, with the notion of the typical Swedish cottage, made of wood and painted red with white corners, emerging just after the turn of the century 1900 (Edling 1996, 298). But there was also a moral dimension to the promotion of owner occupancy, with the rural cottage or small-holding seen as central to the reinforcement of the role of the home and family life. The images by the artist Carl Larsson (1853-1919) have become well-known, in the form of books, calendars, and postcards, to audiences world wide as celebrations of Swedish rural home and family life of this period. While Edling has argued for the policy promoting owner occupancy as the missing link between the nineteenth-century (bourgeois) celebration of the home and the social democratic construction of *folkhemmet* (the home of the people) from the early1930s onwards, he has also highlighted the extent to which the promotion of owner occupancy was based on a traditional construction of gender, with men and women perceived as having distinct and 'natural' spheres of work (op. cit., 324).

Other and probably more familiar aspects of Swedish social policy developed in the early decades of the twentieth-century would at first sight seem both to draw on and to promote a gendered framework constructed in quite different terms. Some of the landmarks were: the legislation in 1900 that placed further restrictions on the employment of children and prevented women from working for four weeks after the birth of a child; the establishment in 1912 of *Socialstyrelsen* (The National Social Welfare Board); the introduction in 1913 of legislation regarding old-age pensions as well as legislation to curb the consumption of alcohol and promote abstention; the establishment in 1919 of *Socialdepartementet* (The Ministry for Social Affairs) as well as the introduction of legislation on poor relief; the introduction in 1920 of new legislation regarding marriage and the family; and the introduction in 1924 of legislation pertaining to child welfare (Ohrlander 1996, 44). Many of those working for social reform in Sweden at the time were simultaneously active in the women's movement, and in the reading of Kajsa Ohrlander the result was the feminisation of relations in the field of social work. Relations that had previously been hierarchical, distant, and impersonal became interactive, empathic, and personal, with women able to highlight their special competence in this field (op. cit., 34, 35).

Following the establishment of *Centralförbundet för socialt arbete* (The National Association of Social Work) in 1903, which brought together 16 existing organisations, and the creation in 1906 of *Svenska fattigvårdsförbundet* (The Swedish Organisation for Poor Relief), there followed an intense period of meetings, conferences, courses, and reports (Ohrlander 1996, 42-43). By the late 1920s, virtually all the areas of social policy that had been mapped out by 1906 had seen the introduction of reforms (op. cit., 33-34). But although women were prominently involved in this work, their participation, as Ohrlander has emphasised, was conditional: women were welcome as long as they focused on the welfare of others and refrained from promoting interests of their own (op. cit., 35). By the late 1920s Swedish social policy was largely institutionalised, and as a result women ceased to play the kinds of prominent role they had enjoyed during the previous couple of decades (op. cit., 34). Although in a wider perspective it would seem clear that social policy in Sweden provides women with a stronger position than does social policy in for example Germany or France (op. cit., 65), the relevance for the early reforms of the ideal of the family and the role of the mother points up the connection with the traditional construction of gender underlying the efforts to increase the numbers of owner occupiers and small-holders in the rural areas.

4. Cultural

How, then, did the far-reaching changes I have traced above – economic, political, social – relate to cultural life in Sweden in the period from around 1900 to 1921? For the purposes of this study, I am defining 'cultural life' in rather narrow terms, as referring chiefly to the production and consumption of books, newspapers, journals, plays, and films. To what extent did the improved financial and social conditions, including better education, help create new audiences? What was the effect of the increases in the production of books and newspapers, and their availability, during this period? What was the relevance of the theatre and the cinema, the latter emerging in Sweden at the very beginning of our period? And what, in the context of all these developments, was the significance of gender? Johan Svedjedal has defined the period 1887-1943 in Sweden as 'the society of the book', concluding that despite the economic growth and democratisation characterising the half-century under scrutiny, the society of the book remained both a class society and, to a large extent, a patriarchal society (Svedjedal 1993, 778, 781). Yet there were a number of significant developments with regard to gender, and these will be central to the survey that follows.

Education

The development of elementary education in Sweden meant that by 1880 close to 90 per cent of children were acquiring the skills of reading and writing (Nilsson and Pettersson 1996, 174), although the schooling of many children remained patchy up to the First World War (Sjöstrand 1968, 236). Åke Åberg, who has provided an overview of reading habits of the working class during the period 1890-1940, has given some indication of the effect on reading habits of both class and gender. While the lack of space and privacy in combination with inadequate heating and lighting would have affected all the members of a household, it is clear from Åberg's material that women's opportunities for reading tended to be particularly restricted. For women the working-hours were often so long as to make reading impossible, but there was also a notion, linked by Åberg to the dominance of Lutheranism, that practical, physical work was more appropriate for the working class in general and for women in particular (Åberg 1983, 394-98).

In the decades with which we are concerned here, only a minority of the cohorts of school-children was able to continue their education beyond the compulsory school. In 1910 a total of 1,502 students passed the newly-introduced middle-school examination, *realexamen*, 21.7 per cent of whom were female; while a total of 1,544 students passed the equivalent of A-levels, *studentexamen*, 12.1 per cent of whom were female. Although the figures for both qualifications had risen by 1920 (a total of 2,197 for the *realexamen*, 34.8 per cent of whom were female, and 2,048 for *studentexamen*, 18.4 per cent of whom were female) (Kyle and Qvist 1974, 75), these, clearly, were not educational options available to the majority of the population. Of particular importance to the working class were the folk high-schools, the first of which had been founded in the 1860s, drawing on a model imported from Denmark. The folk high-school has been described as a 'citizen's school' for the working class, opening up a route to political, social, and cultural influence parallel to the one it had initially provided to the sons of farmers (Thorsell 1957, 70). These were routes, however, that were predominantly used by men, who continued to constitute the majority of students at the folk high-schools until well into the 1940s. The Women Citizens' College at Fogelstad, founded in 1925 by a group of women belonging to the National Association of Liberal Women, Elin Wägner among them, was modelled on the folk high-school.

Books

Surveying the half-century from 1870 to 1920 (and stressing the unreliability of the statistics from the period), Johan Svedjedal has shown that the production of books in Sweden grew steadily up to around 1900 and then accelerated up to around 1920, with much of the increase in the early decades of the twentieth century due to the introduction of cheap editions (Svedjedal 1993, 182). With the introduction of regulations curbing the use of works in translation and, more specifically, the introduction of the Berne Convention of 1904 which banned the free use of translations for ten years following the original publication, Swedish prose fiction for adults enjoyed a considerable boost, the output doubling from the period 1901-1905 to 1906-1910 (op. cit., 186-89). Some of these texts were quickly republished in cheap editions, the precursors of modern paperbacks, which flourished in Sweden from 1904 to around 1920. Wägner's *Norrtullsligan* (1908), which had originally been serialised in the liberal daily *Dagens Nyheter* in 1907-08, was published by Bonnier in a cheap edition, price 25 öre, in 1912, the cost roughly the equivalent of .02 per cent of the average worker's annual income (SEK 1,076 by 1913), and just under 1.5 per cent of the sum spent on 'intellectual pursuits' in the same year by the average worker and low-income salaried employee (op. cit., 347, 351). Novels were also serialised in supplements appended to magazines. Wägner's *Vansklighetens land* (The Perilous Land), the original version of the novel subsequently retitled *Åsa-Hanna*, appeared in *Iduns romanbibliotek* (*Idun*'s Novel Library) in 1917; and *Den befriade kärleken* (Love Liberated) was serialised in *Vecko-Journalen* in 1918-19 and also published in book form by Åhlén & Åkerlunds Förlag, the publisher of this magazine, in 1918, the year before the publication of the novel by Bonnier.

Who, then, were the authors of the new literature published in the period 1900-1921? There was a gradual shift in the social composition of the cohorts of authors producing their first book, with a decline in the numbers coming from aristocratic, academic, and bourgeois backgrounds and an increase in the numbers coming from backgrounds such as farming, the lower middle class, and the working class (Thorsell 1957, 120-27; Svedjedal 1993, 216-19). While there was an increase in the number of female writers during the period 1900-1920, the proportion of women remained around 25 per cent (Thorsell 1957, 122; Svedjedal 1994, 82-83). Pia Lamberth, who has studied female Swedish authors in the period 1900-1949, has concluded that the chief obstacles to women's literary activities were the demands of family and household duties (Lamberth 1991, 40), but a study by Svedjedal of women and the Swedish book market points to more complex patterns. Women authors made some of their major contributions in genres linked with education and edification, producing 77 per cent of prose fiction for children and young people by 1900, and more than half of the prose fiction published by religious publishers in the period 1916-1940 (Svedjedal 1994, 83). Women also found it easier to get published in journals than to publish books (ibid.). Overall, they were more successful in low-status genres, while their male colleagues continued to dominate the high-status ones.

As Svedjedal has demonstrated, the distribution of state financial support and other grants to authors also played a key role in reinforcing the dominance of male writers (Svedjedal 1993, 222-26). And publishing in Sweden was totally male-dominated, with no women publishers nor, indeed, women in top positions, in the 20 or 30 publishing-houses that played a leading role in literature between the

1880s and the 1940s (Svedjedal 1994, 91). The first Swedish publishing-house to specialise in texts by women, Trevi, was founded in 1971.

The Press

The transformation of the Swedish press in the first two decades of the twentieth century added significantly to the role of the press by fostering new communities of readers (the workers' movement had begun to establish its own newspapers towards the end of the nineteenth century); by providing an expanding market for writers; and by opening up new opportunities for employment, some of which also began to attract women.

While the total production of Swedish daily papers, per day, had been around 1 million in 1895, this figure had doubled by 1920 (Svedjedal 1993, 367), over a period when the population of the country had grown from 5,1 million (1900) to 5,9 million (1920) (Carlsson 1968a, 30). The average Swedish daily around 1900 consisted of between four and six pages (Nilsson 1975, 65). The headlines rarely reached beyond a single column, the texts were mostly short and not arranged in top-specific sections, and there were very few illustrations (op. cit., 60). By the 1920s, Swedish dailies had acquired the appearance of modern newspapers with more pages, bigger headlines, longer and more varied texts, including feature material such as exclusive reportages and interviews, a more structured arrangement of the material, and a more generous use of illustrations (Nilsson 1975, 64-65; Stål 2002, 64-77). This was the impact of 'the new journalism' which, towards the end of the nineteenth century, had transformed the press in the United States (see Stål 2002, 64-65). The changes required a considerable expansion of a paper's editorial staff, and also far greater specialisation among its members (Nilsson 1975, 65).

The weekly press also developed rapidly in the early decades of the twentieth century. *Idun*, where Wägner was employed as assistant editor from 1907 to 1916, had been founded in 1887 as *Praktisk Veckotidning för Qvinnan och Hemmet* (Practical Weekly for Woman and the Home). According to Birgit Petersson, there were dual – and contradictory – reasons why women were beginning to be perceived as an important audience around this time, to do with the early women's movement and the emergence of women in the labour market on the one hand, and with the dominance of the bourgeois discourse on women as wives and mothers on the other (Petersson 2001, 326). As Margareta Frostegren's study of *Idun* in 1906 has shown, as much as 25 per cent of the material by then consisted of news and reportage, with the same proportion devoted to literature and 15 per cent to reviews and articles on art and artists (Frostegren 1979, 19). By 1909, *Idun* had achieved a circulation of 50,000, a remarkably high figure (op. cit., 13). In 1910, the publisher Åhlén & Åkerlund launched *Illustrerad Vecko-Journal* (The Illustrated Weekly Journal), later renamed *Vecko-Journalen* (The Weekly Journal), and early the following year this highly successful journal, which placed a special emphasis on prose fiction, achieved an average circulation of 120,000 (Svedjedal 1993, 319). In 1913, the Swedish cooperative movement launched *Konsumentbladet* (The Consumer Magazine), from 1937 renamed *Vi* (We); its emphasis on literature was to be particularly important to Swedish authors beginning to publish in the 1930s (op. cit., 730-31). One of Wägner's novels, *Vändkorset* (1935; The Turnstile), was commissioned by *Konsumentbladet* which serialised it in 1935, prior to its publication in book form by Bonnier.

According to Margareta Berger, the total number of journalists employed on the Stockholm dailies in 1913 was around 220, with 11 per cent of these being women (Berger 1977, 136; Stål 2002, 59). In her book on the journalist Ester Blenda Nordström (1891-1948), Margareta Stål has included a survey of the women journalists in Stockholm who, from 1909-10 onwards, formed the group *Ligan* (The League). Elin Wägner was one of the founding members; and in a survey of the first ten members, Stål has found a number of recurring patterns, with these women journalists being employed on just three Stockholm dailies, the majority coming from bourgeois backgrounds, and the majority having academic degrees (Stål 2002, 87-88). The exceptions were Ester Blenda Nordström and Elin Wägner, neither of whom had academic qualifications. Wägner, however, added to her

Contexts

symbolic capital by her marriage in 1910 to the philosopher and author John Landquist (1881-1974), whose sister Ellen Landquist was also a founder member of *Ligan* (op. cit., 88). Wägner's novel *Pennskaftet* (1910) is the iconic work of prose fiction about this generation of women journalists.

With women playing an increasingly important role as readers and consumers, newspapers in Sweden, in common with newspapers in many other countries, began to devote sections to material deemed to be of special interest to women (Stål 2002, 96). In the Swedish press this represented a clear shift in comparison with the situation twenty years previously; and as Margareta Stål has pointed out, several of the journalists who were members of *Ligan* complained about having to produce material for the women's sections of their papers (op. cit., 96-97). While these women journalists were eager to work on the same conditions as their male colleagues and with the same types of material, they tended to be caught up in a process of gender segregation which, in Stål's reading, was a product of their professionalisation (op. cit., 95). This segregation, however, would have been part of the increasingly marked gender segregation that had begun to characterise the Swedish labour market as a whole from around the turn of the century 1900. And as Stål has emphasised, the low-status 'women's sections' could also offer the women journalists a considerable amount of freedom (op. cit., 97).

Drama and Film

Around 1900 there were more theatres in Stockholm than in many other European cities (Ericsson 1994, 185), but the quality of the productions varied greatly. A number of women playwrights had emerged in the 1880s and 1890s. One of these was Frida Stéenhoff (1865-1945) whose texts, including the drama *Lejonets unge* (1896; The Lion Cub) will be considered in the section on discourses on the family below. Elin Wägner wrote a couple of works for the stage but was reasonably successful only with her dramas for radio, which I shall discuss in due course.

During the period with which we are concerned here, the cinema emerged as a source of entertainment appealing to wide sections of society. The first Swedish film, less than a minute long, had been shot and shown in 1897 (Werner 1970, 11), and in 1919, Sweden had a total of 703 cinemas (Furhammar 2003, 45). In 1911 the number of cinema visits was around 12 million, a figure which had risen to more than 40 million by 1919-20 (ibid.). A remarkably big proportion of cinema goers were working class, and women were also frequent visitors to the cinema (Sjöholm 2003, 48).

Up to 1912, film making in Sweden was characterised by individual initiatives. In 1911 Elin Wägner had written a film script entitled *Hon fick platsen* (She Got the Job), which was shot early that year with herself and a number of journalist colleagues in the cast and which became a considerable success, the proceeds going to a fund for women journalists (Åhlander 1986, 136-37). Later in the same year, a short story by Wägner became the script of the film *Systrarna* (The Sisters), which was directed by Sweden's first female film director, Anna Hofman-Uddgren (1868-1947), who was only the second female director in the world, the pioneer being Alice Guy-Blaché (Koskinen 1983, 3). The film based on Wägner's script, about two sisters whose different paths in life nevertheless confront them both with the untrustworthiness of men, placed considerable emphasis on the Stockholm setting, and would appear to have been a success (ibid.; Åhlander 1986, 149-51).

In 1911-12 *Svenska Biografteatern* (The Swedish Cinema Theatre), commonly known as Svenska Bio, moved from Kristianstad to Stockholm, where it was to play a key role in the development of silent film in Sweden. Hofman-Uddgren made a few more films, including film versions of August Strindberg's *Fröken Julie* (*Miss Julie*) and *Fadren* (*The Father*), both in 1912, but the great era of silent film was dominated by male actors and directors, notably Mauritz Stiller (1883- 1928) and Victor Sjöström (1879-1960). In the period 1917-23 Sjöström and Stiller were to produce a number of epoch-making films, including Sjöström's *Berg-Ejvind och hans hustru* (1917; *The Outlaw and His Wife*) and *Körkarlen* (1920; *The Phantom Carriage*), the latter based on a text by Selma Lagerlöf (1858-1940) and renowned for the revolutionary photography by Julius Jaenzon (1885-1961). While *Erotikon* (1920) is usually regarded as Stiller's most original film, he too produced work based on texts by Lagerlöf, including *Herr Arnes pengar* (1919; *Sir Arne's Treasure*) and *Gösta Berlings saga* (1923; *The Story of Gösta Berling*), the latter with Greta Garbo (1905-1990) in the leading female role.

Wägner maintained her interest in film. Several films based on her novels were produced from 1923 onwards, and she also turned her novel *De fem pärlorna* (1927; The Five Pearls) into a film script, although no film was ever made.

*

To sum up, it was in the contexts outlined above that Wägner's texts published up to and including 1921 were produced and initially consumed. We have seen how extensive economic changes opened up employment opportunities for women, but also how a creeping gender conservatism became apparent during this period. Organisations of women in employment resulted in new communities of women, but the most prominent organisation during this period was the National Association for Women's Suffrage. The Swedish campaign for female suffrage met much resistance over a long period of time, and in institutional politics women remained in a minority throughout the entire period covered by this study. Conflicts in terms of gender were also apparent in the field of social politics, with traditional constructions of gender contrasting with the prominent contributions by women to the organisation and institutionalisation of social work that was to form a corner stone of the Swedish welfare state. The extensive cultural changes during this period including the expansion of education, the greater availability of books, the transformation of the press, and the emergence of film constitute a key part of this changing society.

In the chapter that follows I shall move on to focus on discourses on gender and community in Sweden in the period from around 1900 up to 1921.

Chapter 3:
Discourses: The Family

What were the dominant discourses on gender and on community in Sweden during the period with which we are concerned here? What were the alternative ones? To what extent did these discourses inflect each other, especially given the context of rapid and extensive changes with regard to economics, politics, and social conditions in Sweden at the time?

I shall outline some answers to these questions by exploring discourses on the family. Discourses on the family do not just provide a series of intersections of discourses on gender and discourses on community: given that we are dealing with a period of extensive changes, economically, politically, socially and culturally, 'the family' is likely to be at the cross-roads of many of these transformations, thus shedding light on continuity and conservatism on the one hand and radicalism and innovation on the other. The survey that follows, of (1) dominant discourses on the family and (2) alternative discourses on the family, will provide a set of prisms for the analyses of texts in the subsequent chapters.

1. Dominant Discourses

The encyclopedia *Nordisk Familjebok*, the relevant volume of which was published in 1907, defined *familj* in the social sense as 'the form of personal life between human beings the natural foundation and prerequisite of which is the sexed contrast between the man and the woman', and specified the chief relationships involved as those 'between the man and the woman (the spouses), and between these (the parents) and the children'. Think Carl Larsson, whose images of his family reached wide audiences in Scandinavia and Germany in his life-time and, since the 1970s, have found new audiences all over the world (Lengefeld 1997, 196). Whether the Larsson family is enjoying breakfast in the open on a summer's morning, celebrating Christmas Eve, catching crayfish or gathering around the lamp in the evening, there is never any doubt as to the gender roles that are pivotal to these idylls. As if further confirmation was needed, Larsson the narrator in his immensely popular volume *Ett hem* (1899; *Our Home*, 1976), which appeared in six editions between 1899 and 1917, proudly indicates to the visitor/reader the lines he has painted above the entrance to Lilla Hyttnäs:

*Var välkommen, kära du,
Till Carl Larsson och hans fru!* (Larsson 1969, 6; italics original)

(*Welcome, dear guest
to Carl Larsson and his wife!*)

As the host guides the visitor/reader around his home he highlights the examples of his own work, side-stepping the fact that 'hans fru' (his wife), the artist Karin Larsson (1859-1928), had played a key role in designing the interiors at Lilla Hyttnäs (see Rydin 1997). We are left with examples of 'homo economicus' and 'femina domestica' (Cominos 1973) and their offspring that have acquired an iconic status. As is clear from *Nordisk Familjebok*, the distinctive gender roles of husband and wife were perceived as fundamental to the stability of the family unit. The basic community, constituted by the nuclear family, was essential to the stability of society.

When Norway terminated the union with Sweden in June 1905, a procession consisting of 'Sweden's women, side by side with Sweden's men' made its way to the royal summer palace at Djurgården in Stockholm to express their loyalty to the king; according to Dagny, the journal of the Fredrika Bremer Association, the event was 'a significant historical act, symbolic of the unity and assembled strength that have always animated the people of Sweden in times of real danger' (Anon. 1905, 238). The account in Dagny highlighted the significance of the nation as an 'imagined community' which, in Benedict Anderson's definition, 'is always conceived as a deep, horizontal comradeship'; Anderson, indeed, uses the word 'fraternity' (Anderson 2003, 7). As the Norwegian historian Ida Blom has pointed out, the women taking part in the procession in June 1905 did not have the right to vote and so were not full citizens: it was in their roles as wives and mothers they constituted part of 'the people of Sweden' (Blom 1996, 8). In the agricultural economy, the rationale of the family unit on the farm had been production, the work distinctly gendered *and* indispensable (Löfgren 1996, 92). But the bourgeois family that had emerged in Sweden in the nineteenth century increasingly became a unit of consumption, i.e. a different type of community, and this change was underpinned by a reconstruction of gender. The differences between husband and wife remained clearly marked, but there was a new emphasis on the role of emotional affinities, most importantly on the love between husband and wife (op. cit., 93-94). Emotional affinities were similarly pivotal to the relationships between parents and children (ibid.). Family love is the predominant emotion constructed in Carl Larsson's paintings in *Ett hem*, and arguably it was family love that inspired the wives and mothers to demonstrate 'unity and assembled strength' side by side with their husbands on 7 June 1905. But beneath the surface there were frequently major asymmetries – all the more important, in the analysis of Orvar Löfgren, in that these also had a profound impact on the patterns of marriage and on gender relations in twentieth-century Sweden (Löfgren 1999a, 83).

Firstly, there was often a considerable difference in age between husband and wife as the middle-class husband tended to be considerably older (Löfgren 1996, 101-02). Secondly, the difference in age made for differences with regard to knowledge and experience (op. cit., 102). Thirdly, there was an asymmetry with regard to the emotional background, expectations, and commitment of the spouses (op. cit., 102-103). Well before the marriage the ground had been prepared for the distinction between the active husband and the passive wife. The distinction was reinforced by developments in the field of medicine where, towards the end of the nineteenth century, Social Darwinism had contributed to defining the female body as not just different but of lower standing (see Johannisson 1994). Fourthly, there was a difference with regard to moral standards (Löfgren 1996, 102-105). As in Britain, there was an intense debate about the double moral standards during the last few decades of the nineteenth century (Jackson 1994, 23-31), not just in Sweden but throughout Scandinavia, but what made the Scandinavian debate special was the prominent role played by works of literature, including dramas such as Ibsen's *Gengangere* (1881; *Ghosts*) and Bjørnson's *En hanske* (1883; *A Gauntlet*). In Sweden prostitution had been regulated in 1847, and *Federationen* (The Federation), founded in 1878 as the Swedish branch of Josephine Butler's Ladies' National Association for the Repeal of the Contagious Diseases Act and attracting primarily Christians and activists for the women's cause, had developed into the country's leading women's organisation as early as 1880 (Lundquist 1982, 322). The state regulation of prostitution was abolished in 1918, but throughout the first two decades of the twentieth century, 'the double view of women' (Löfgren 1996, 103) remained a threat to the bourgeois construction of the family.

The asymmetries distinguished by Löfgren helped reinforce the gender polarisation in the family. While the husband was focused on developing his career, he expected his wife to devote herself to catering for his every need in the haven of the home (Löfgren 1996, 105). Inspired by Michelle Zimbalist Rosaldo, Löfgren has also traced, in Sweden in the second half of the nineteenth century and into the twentieth, the emergence of what might be termed a feminine counter-culture, based on the notion of women as purer and morally superior to men (op. cit., 106). While this counter-culture would have added a new dimension to the polarisation of gender, by far the most significant reinforcement of the gender polarisation at this time came from the work of Ellen Key (1849-1926). Writing about Key's influence in England in an essay in honour of her seventieth birthday, Havelock Ellis highlighted the emphasis in her texts on 'the right of woman to be different from man' (Ellis 1919, 126).

Key's *Missbrukad kvinnokraft* (1914a; The Abuse of Woman's Power), first published in 1896, argued that the women's movement was misguided in demanding equality between women and men and thus marginalising the role of motherliness; and *Kvinnorörelsen*

Discourses: The Family

(1909; *The Woman Movement*, 1912) defined motherhood as a vocation (Key 1912, 43). Indeed, 'Samhällsmoderlighet' (Social Motherliness), an essay published in 1903, had painted motherhood as the vocation of vocations: the mother should

> in her tasks in the home [...] develop the qualities of a statesman, a spiritual guide, a military leader, a law-maker, a national economist, an artist in order to maintain the calm and strong authority by which all the members of the household are governed while believing themselves to be following their own will; in order to bring out the best in everybody; in order to educate children and servants, make the work enjoyable, and innovate day-to-day life by creating an atmosphere of festivity. (Key 1976c, 183)

Claudia Lindén in her doctoral dissertation *Om kärlek. Litteratur, sexualitet och politik hos Ellen Key* (2002; On Love: Literature, Sexuality and Politics in Ellen Key), has highlighted the significance in Key's texts of the distinction between biological motherhood and the cultural phenomenon of motherliness, arguing that the concept of motherliness in Key's work was tantamount to the rewriting of the Nietzschean *Übermensch* as a woman (Lindén 2002, 153-88). Interesting though Lindén's reading is, the influential notion of 'natural areas of work for women' was based on the prominence of biological motherhood: the young woman, according to *Naturenliga arbetsområden för kvinnan* (1896; Natural Areas of Work for Woman), should preferably find for herself 'an activity [...] in agreement with her nature' that did not make her 'less suited, either physically or spiritually, to her calling as a mother' (Key 1914b, 73). The majority of Key's contemporaries would have taken literally the clarification of 'natural areas of work' as those in which women without children would be able to develop their motherly instincts, e.g. education, health care, and branches of farming such as dairy work and gardening (Key 1914b). They would also have been familiar with the dictum in 'Samhällsmoderlighet' that women with ambitions to influence politics and matters of war and peace could only hope to do so indirectly, via the education of their sons (Key 1976c, 162).

Not surprisingly, the home is celebrated in texts by Key. 'Skönhet i hemmen' (1899; Beautiful Homes) referred to Carl Larsson's Lilla Hyttnäs as a model and also quoted from his *Ett hem* (Key 1976b, 90-91). Criticising the dark décor and cluttered appearance of the typical bourgeois home of this period, Key's text advocated a judicious use of colour and a tasteful simplicity, with the necessary objects combining usefulness with beauty as in the traditional Swedish peasant culture. And there was no doubt as to the identity of the central source of inspiration, the creator of beauty in the home:

> by striving for beauty while at the same time satisfying usefulness, woman will satisfy not only a demand *characteristic of her nature*: she will also exercise a deep influence on the members of the home whose soul she is. The minds of the children will be educated and refined thanks to the experience of beauty; the adults will enjoy a sense of peace and happiness which will always make them kinder and often nobler; and woman herself will be happier as a result of the creative pleasure which the practice of art will always entail. (op. cit., 83-84; my italics)

'[W]oman' in this quotation is clearly synonymous with 'the mother'. The close connection between the community represented by the nuclear family with its well-defined gender roles and the state was illustrated when the weekly *Idun*, during the International Woman Suffrage Alliance's sixth congress in Stockholm in June 1911, produced a special issue which included accounts not just by women who had become suffragists but also by men married to suffragists. The five accounts on the page headed 'Rösträttskvinnan i hemmet' (The Suffragist in the Home) were an attempt to counter the concern that 'the woman who is working for suffrage and who is granted suffrage will no longer find herself suited to the duties of the home and the household', described as 'one of the most personal and weighty reasons for the male and even the female resistance to the demands of the women' (Anon., 1911). What is interesting about these accounts is not just the fact that the management of the home and the household was perceived as the key duty of the wife, but also the absence of any hint that the enlightened husbands might have been prepared to share these responsibilities. (The fact that they all belonged to the professional class and presumably employed maids would no doubt have made any such suggestion risible.) In other words, when the majority of these husbands compared the home to the state and argued that the good housewife ought to be sufficiently aware of wider issues to take an interest in developments in the bigger home that was the state, they would necessarily have perceived the tasks involved as sharply gendered. These husbands would have taken their cue not just from Ellen Key's 'Samhällsmoderlighet' which had argued, on the basis of the family as 'the first "state"', for the replacement of the current 'state celibacy' with a 'state marriage' (Key 1976c, 162-63), but also from the author Selma Lagerlöf, who had delivered a seminal speech on 'Hem och stat' (Home and State) to the IWSA congress (Lagerlöf 1915). As Yvonne Hirdman has emphasised, the connection between this linkage of the home and the state and the origins of the Swedish welfare state, 'the home of the people', is unmistakable (Hirdman 1993, 81-91). In December 1927 Per Albin Hansson, leader of the Swedish Social Democratic Party, was to outline in *Morgonbris*, the journal of the Social Democratic Women's Association, the vision of 'the home of the people' in the following terms:

> *We have advanced far enough to begin to furnish the big home of the people. It will be a matter of creating in it a cheerful atmosphere, of making it pleasant and warm, bright and happy and free. For a woman, there should be no more attractive task. Perhaps all we need to do to alert her to it is to make her see that it is here, and then she'll come along with all her eagerness and enthusiasm.* (quoted in Hirdman 1983, 37; italics original)

We have traced, then, the discourses on gender and community as focused in the prism of the family with an emphasis on the first two decades of the twentieth century. Using as our lens the middle-class family, we have found traditional discourses on gender rooted in the construction of biological differences between husband and wife. Moreover, throughout what was an economically and politically turbulent period in Sweden the family, with gender discourses of this type at its core, was frequently perceived as fundamental to the (ideal) state. The dominant discourses on gender and community fused in the the middle-class nuclear family. And as we have seen, there are clear connections between this notion of the family and the social democratic welfare state, 'the home of the people', that began to take shape in Sweden just after the period with which we are concerned here.

But of course the family model popularised by Carl Larsson was not the only one. Here are a couple of different ones.

Emma is a poor seamstress and single mother whose pride and joy is her four-year-old daughter, smiling towards her from a photograph framed in red velvet. Yet Emma does not hesitate to give her last scrap of food to her friend Ida: she has five children, but her husband is unemployed and Ida, who is expecting her sixth, is pitifully thin. Emma also answers the question that Ida cannot bring herself to complete: 'Would it be a crime, Emma? Would I become a murderess if...?' (Sandel 1908, 144). But between the question and the answer, the omniscient narrator elaborates on Emma's plight, the powerful metaphors engaging the narratee in discourses on community and society quite different from those we have traced above. The narrator refers to

> the social cruelty that made her its victim again and again, whether it left her, with total indifference, to fight as best she could in the eddies of the social maelstrom, or mercilessly chopped one finger after the other off her hands as she, her strength multiplied by her motherly love, was hanging on to the gunwales of the ship of society. (op. cit., 145)

Emma's firm 'No' in response to Ida's question marks the end of the text.

In these families, then, the fathers are either absent or reduced to economic impotence, and the mothers are left to provide for their children despite the fact that their means for doing so are limited or non-existent. 'Femina economica' has replaced 'homo economicus', and 'femina domestica' has become irrelevant. There is no way the two families in this text, effectively headed by single mothers, could epitomise the state. On the contrary, the state that emerges here is one that does not hesitate to exploit the concept of motherly love – even to the point where it becomes synonymous with the mother's plan to abort the baby for which she will have no means of providing. To the extent that there is a community here, it consists of Emma and Ida.

Maria Sandel (1870-1927), the author of 'Bland malströmmens hvirflar' (In the Eddies of the Maelstrom) from which I have quoted above, belonged to the first generation of working-class writers in Sweden and published this short story in her first volume, *Vid svältgränsen* (1908; Close to Starving). Supporting herself as a machine-knitter, she went on to publish two more volumes of short stories and three novels. In comparison with the work of Carl Larsson, that of Sandel has remained relatively obscure, yet as the only writer of her generation to focus on the daily life of working-class women, she has made a unique contribution to Swedish literature (Witt-Brattström 1977, 268). Both the struggling mother figures of Maria Sandel's text and Carl Larsson's idylls of the nuclear family are indicative of the changes that were transforming Sweden at the time and that impacted so comprehensively on the discourses on both gender and community. While, in the agricultural economy, the rationale of the family unit on the farm was production, the struggle for survival in the rural proletariat, from which the workers for the country's industries were largely recruited, often forced the family members to work and live apart, with their home, in Orvar Löfgren's analysis, reduced to a 'base from which the members of the family were sent out to earn money' (Löfgren 1996, 144). According to Löfgren, a similar pattern was common in the urban Swedish working class around the turn of the century 1900 (ibid.). Yet housework would of course have to be done, and a study by Yvonne Hirdman has highlighted, at least implicitly, the gender bias inherent in Löfgren's analysis. Focusing specifically on the significance of housework, Hirdman has investigated the attempts by the Social Democratic Women's movement in Sweden in the period 1890-1939 to relate the situation of working-class women to the ideology and policies of the Social Democratic Labour Party. Hirdman's study sheds light on the discourses on gender and community as crystallised in the notion of the family in working-class contexts in Sweden during the period with which we are concerned here, and in what follows I shall focus on some of its key findings.

Sveriges Socialdemokratiska Arbetarparti (The Swedish Social Democratic Labour Party), founded in 1889, had originally advocated change by revolution, but during the period with which we are concerned here there was a shift to reformism as general suffrage for men was introduced in 1909, the elections in the autumn of 1914 made the Social Democratic Party the biggest in the Second Chamber of the *riksdag*, and the spell in government of the Social Democrats in coalition with the Liberals in 1917-20 saw the introduction of parliamentarism and suffrage for women (Lindqvist 1968, 162-64). But Hirdman's analysis of the ideology underpinning the Swedish Social Democratic women's movement begins with Clara Zetkin (1857-1933), the German Marxist. In common with the work of Marx, Engels, and Bebel, that of Zetkin defined women's contribution to production as the key to their emancipation (Dahlerup 1973, 358). However, while the texts of Marx, Engels and Bebel continued to envisage a gendered division of work, those of Zetkin argued that society should take responsibility for the children and housework (Hirdman 1983, 17). Texts by Zetkin were prominent in the early issues of *Morgonbris*, the journal that the Swedish Social Democratic women's movement had founded in 1904, and which thus made a significant contribution to the construction of alternative discourses on gender and community. Viewing socialism in an international perspective, Hirdman has contrasted this early willingness in Sweden to tackle, at least in theoretical terms, the situation of working-class women characterised by the conflicts between paid work, children, and housework, with the subsequent tendency simply to marginalise the latter two (op. cit., 18-19). According to Christina Carlsson the focus, in practical terms, continued to be on the impact of women in the labour market, where their male colleagues perceived them as competitors (Carlsson 1986, 187). In Hirdman's reading, the result was an ideological vacuum which the women in the Social Democratic women's movement were left to fill themselves (Hirdman 1983, 19). Here Hirdman traces, in Sweden around the turn of the century 1900, two main sources of influence: the 'housewife movement' – effectively a new type of community reinforcing traditional gender roles – and, perhaps surprisingly in the light of my survey so far, the texts of Ellen Key.

Discourses: The Family

In its origins the 'housewife movement' was conservative, its emphasis on the home as a platform for reforms and on the role of the housewife as a profession in its own right an attempt to stem the impact of the bourgeois women's movement (Hirdman 1983, 19). But its emphasis on the 'new' home, drawing on recent research in chemistry, medicine, and technology to ensure cleanliness, nutritious food, and a rational approach to cookery and housework, appealed to social democratic women too (op. cit., 19-20). Around the turn of the century 1900, there was a proliferation of courses in cookery and home economics. Intended primarily for the daughters of the middle classes, such courses helped ensure that the notion of the 'new' home spread to the working classes (op. cit., 20). These were already becoming influenced by middle-class concepts of the home, as the most common types of employment for young working-class women were those of maid or servant in middle-class homes (Löfgren 1996, 149; see above p.48). With the outbreak of the First World War, rising prices and food shortages turned the rationalisation of the household into a matter of political importance (Hirdman 1983, 27). State and local authority support was introduced to teach women good household practices, and the home adviser emerged as a new category of expert (ibid.). Indeed, as Charlotte Tornbjer has demonstrated, the home at this time acquired a national significance: with husbands and fathers called up to safeguard Sweden's neutrality, it was the duty of the wives and mothers to make their contribution by safeguarding the home and so provide a basis for the wellbeing of the nation (Tornbjer 2002, 201). In Hirdman's analysis, the home increasingly came to be regarded as the only significant sphere of working-class women, and Hirdman has highlighted the symbolism inherent in the formation in June 1919, in the immediate wake of the abolition of the state measures designed to alleviate the war-time food shortages, of *Sveriges husmodersföreningars riksförbund* (The National Alliance of the Swedish Housewives' Associations) (Hirdman 1983, 30).

If Hirdman's first strand, the 'housewife' movement, had the effect of pushing working-class women away from the liberation which, according to the texts of Zetkin, had been beckoning as the result of paid work and channelling them back into the more traditional role of home-makers, what was the effect of the texts of Ellen Key? And how could Key, who appealed so strongly to the middle classes, appeal to working-class audiences too? The answer, I think, is partly to be found in the pull of the ideological vacuum identified by Hirdman. While some of Zetkin's texts were highlighted in the early issues of *Morgonbris*, the very first issue in 1904 was a celebration of central ideas in the texts of Key (Hirdman 1983, 23). The appeal of the emphasis on motherhood as a vocation, developed in the context of the modern, rationally run home, clearly transcended the class barriers, and the same was true of the vision in Key of a new order, originating in the nuclear family and based on the following corner stones:

> *Children* born of parents whose souls and bodies are qualified and prepared for a worthy parenthood and who can thus create for their children sound and beautiful conditions of life.
> *Mothers* won back to the husbands, the children, the homes, but under such circumstances that *as free human personalities they perform the most important work of society*: the bearing and rearing of children.
> *Fathers* with time and leisure to share with the mothers the task of education and to share with them and the children the joys of the home life, as well as of the remainder of existence. (Key 1912, 43; italics original)

As is clear from Key's 'Samhällsmoderlighet', the health of the individual human organism was directly linked to the health of the organism of the 'samhälle', a term that here combines the meanings of 'community' and 'society':

> When it is accepted that the purpose of the society is to give every member the opportunity to use and develop her/his powers to the greatest potential for the highest possible goals, then the criteria for the health of a society will no longer be sought in abstract constructions of state justice, but in the laws of human life. (Key 1976c, 161)

The affinity between the organisms of society and the human being foregrounds the significance and, indeed, the interdependence of the 'masculine' brain and the 'feminine' heart, with the predominance of the former explaining many of the inadequacies of the existing society (op. cit., 164-70). The emphasis in this text on the need to develop solidarity, and on the linkage between solidarity and that which is specifically feminine (ibid.), helps profile the characteristics of the ideals of community and society.

With the growing gender segregation in the labour market that was not just a Swedish but a European phenomenon, Key's texts became increasingly influential, and many of her works were also made available in English and German translations. In Sweden, the Social Democratic women's movement was left trying to combine socialism with Key. By 1914 *Morgonbris*, seemingly without difficulty, could highlight the home of the nuclear family as one of the main elements of the socialism of the future: 'the home will become what it ought to be, a nest of love in which the wife and mother can stay at home with her nearest and dearest, providing her children with the education and care that they now often have to do without as mother is having to work in the factory or elsewhere' (quoted in Hirdman 1983, 27). An increasingly segregated labour market in combination with the impact of the First World War helped to emphasise, in working-class as well as middle-class contexts, not just the significance of the mother and the home but the community of the nuclear family. The Swedish 'home of the people' had strong roots both in the middle classes and in the working class.

2. Alternative Discourses

Despite the dominance of the bourgeois discourse on the family in Sweden in the first two decades of the twentieth century, it is not difficult to find examples of alternative discourses. The overview that follows covers just a handful of examples, but the attention given to alternative thinking on the family, and thus to gender and community, is indicative of the radicalism of the debates taking place in sections of Swedish society at the time. Works by Rosa Mayreder, Olive Schreiner, Charlotte Perkins Gilman, and Frida Stéenhoff were part of these debates, which thrived on the process of democratisation and the expanding campaign for women's suffrage.

Rosa Mayreder

Rosa Mayreder (1858-1938), singled out by Harriet Anderson in *Utopian Feminism: Women's Movements in fin-de-siècle Vienna* as one of only three Austrian women to create a 'coherent visionary feminist theory' at this time (Anderson 1992, 145), was given an enthusiastic introduction in *Dagny*, the journal of the Fredrika Bremer Association, in 1910. A front-page article on 14 April 1910 announced the Swedish translation of Mayreder's *Zur Kritik der Weiblichkeit* (1905), entitled *Kvinnlighet, manlighet och mänsklighet* (Femininity, Masculinity and Humanity), describing the book as an 'intellectual feat, an ethical achievement and a work of art besides' (Anon., 1910, 169). The review of the volume by the editor of *Dagny*, Ellen Kleman, hailed *Zur Kritik der Weiblichkeit* as a 'master-piece'. Kleman drew attention to the significance in Mayreder's analysis of the constructedness of gender, quoting the lines that had also appeared in a list of quotations from the book published in an earlier issue of *Dagny* (Mayreder 1910, 175), 'We will know what women are only when we no longer dictate to them what they should be' (Kleman 1910, 294). Underlining the fact that to the majority of human beings, the concepts of masculinity and femininity were still clearly defined and delimited, Kleman highlighted the innovative significance of Mayreder's concept of the 'synthetic' human being and her vision of a future underpinned by this new unity between women and men.

The primary synthesis proposed by Mayreder's texts was one between *Geschlecht*, 'sex', and *Geist*, 'intellect' (Anderson 1992, 165). While the former concept was characterised by 'those psychological qualities needed for reproduction, the teleological function of humanity', the latter was characterised by 'that which is individual to each person' (ibid.). In *Zur Kritik der Weiblichkeit*, translated into English as *A Survey of the Woman Problem* (1913), these concepts belonged in an evolutionary hierarchy. With *Geschlecht* at the bottom, the English translation described as the most common type of human being 'the partially developed being of unmitigated sexuality whose whole personality is determined by teleological sex characteristics' (Mayreder 1913, 262). It was among human beings of this type that we found '[a]ll the hackneyed declarations as to what the "wholly male" and the "truly female" should be'; and carried to its extremes, this 'tendency [produced] licentious domineering masculinity and weak, insignificant and passive, or else crafty, false and ludicrous femininity, forms of sex-differentiation which [were] the complements of each other and equal in nature and in origin' (ibid.). This concept of masculinity still ruled in modern society, 'like an ancient idol which [was] still publicly worshipped and served with prescribed sacrifices, although it [had] long ceased to work miracles'(op. cit., 91); indeed, if we considered

> the conception of masculinity as it [was] depicted in general outlines in everyday life, or in those writings which [had] need of a normal basis, in pedagogic, popular medical, didactic-moral works, we [found] the primitive, teleological sexual type handed on from generation to generation, without having been put to the test of the actual conditions of life. (op. cit., 92)

While Mayreder's text emphasised that war was 'the state in which primitive man [was] essentially in his element', the retardation with regard to the construction of masculinity was in fact becoming all the more marked as '[c]ivilisation and culture' were bringing man closer to woman (op. cit., 99, 93). At the intermediate level in the evolutionary hierarchy, human beings were struggling to rise above the teleological characteristics of *Geschlecht*, which in the case of woman included weakness of will, patience, and passivity as these best equipped her 'for her generative tasks of conceiving, bearing and bringing up children' (Anderson 1992, 165). With *Geist* being individual and not sex specific, 'it stands on a higher evolutionary level than *Geschlecht* and is a distinguishing feature of the present level of evolution' (op. cit., 166). In *A Survey of the Woman Problem*, motherhood was unproblematically combined with intellectual labour (Mayreder 1913, 55), and as the text underlined, there were modern women – sometimes referred to as *Mannweib*, 'man-woman' (op. cit., 167-68) – who had risen above 'the teleological sex-character of femininity' (op. cit., 167). At the top of the evolutionary hierarchy was the 'hermaphrodite' personality, the human being who had reached far beyond the characteristics of *Geschlecht* to confirm the significance of the 'synthetic' human being. A personality became hermaphrodite 'not only as a result of overpowering love causing a mingling of two beings and an "exchange of souls," but also through that great preponderance of intellect which [was] produced by living in the domain of the higher culture' (op. cit., 254). In other words, the mind of the creative genius was androgynous (Anderson 1992, 168).

Anderson has summed up Mayreder's project as the 'forward-looking ideal of the world's essential equilibrium and the harmony of polarities' (Anderson 1992, 171); and this project was further developed in *Geschlecht und Kultur* (Sex and Culture), which was published in 1923 and appeared in Swedish translation in the same year entitled *Sexualitet och kultur*. (There was no translation into English.) But as early as 1915 *Hertha*, the re-named journal of the Fredrika Bremer Association, had published two texts, 'Rosa Mayreder om kön och kultur', I-II (Rosa Mayreder on Sex and Culture). According to Klara Johanson's introduction these summarised – in Johanson's translation – a recently published essay or dissertation by Mayreder also entitled 'Geschlecht und Kultur' (Johanson 1915, 212-13). (There is no trace of this published essay or dissertation in the bibliography in Anderson's book.) Some of the main arguments in *Geschlecht und Kultur* about gender, culture, and civilisation would thus have been familiar in Sweden 1915, at least to readers of *Hertha*; and the survey that follows is based on the two articles.

Mayreder's texts make a fundamental distinction between 'culture' and 'civilisation'. While 'civilisation' is associated with technical developments and the machine age, 'culture' is associated with terms such as *organisk* ('organic'), *samfundserfarenhet* ('community experience') and *gemensamhet i kulturskapande* ('a sense of community in the creation of culture') (Mayreder 1915a, 216). Pointing up the parallel position of the sociologist Ferdinand Tönnies, Anderson, referring to *Geschlecht und Kultur*, has highlighted the 'progressive reaction' according to which what was 'formerly culture has [...] been converted into a state-ridden civilisation in which culture is at risk of total suffocation' (Anderson 1992, 170). Mayreder's second article in *Hertha* set out the gendering of this development in an historical perspective, highlighting the pivotal role of the emergence of the concepts of private property and fatherhood (*Geschlecht und Kultur* was to refer explicitly to Engels, i.e. his *The Origin of the Family, Private Property and the State* [first published in German in 1884], and to Lewis Henry Morgan, i.e. *Ancient Society*, 1877, as well as Bachofen's *Das Mutterrecht*, 1861 [Mayreder 1923b, 94]). Modern warfare marks the nadir of masculine civilisation. Women, however, have the potential to restore the balance between culture and civilisation: 'Motherhood, literally as well as metaphorically, can function as a kind of regulator, but on condition that women learn to elevate their lack of sexual freedom into a cultural power capable of countering the sexual freedom of men' (Mayreder 1915b, 234). While the historical perspective culminating in modern warfare thus reduces the constructedness of gender and returns us to the kind of essentialism that is based on reproduction, it is worth noting that *Geschlecht und Kultur* also highlights the brand-new work by Vaerting (here with double first names, Mathias and Mathilde, rather than just Mathilde which is the correct version [Mayreder 1923b, 92; see also Leppänen 2005, 61]), *Neubegründung der Psychologie von Mann und Weib* (1921-23; *The Dominant Sex*, 1923 [transl. of vol. 1]). In the reading of R. W. Connell, Vaerting created 'what might be seen as the first extended theory of gender' (Connell 2005, 122). According to Vaerting, constructions of gender were the products of relations of power. The potential inherent in the constructedness of gender underpins the celebration of love in which *Geschlecht und Kultur* culminates, with the concluding chapter about the significance of love – the longest in the volume – highlighting the role of love in transcending the boundary between subject and object and founding a new *livsgemenskap* ('community of life') (Mayreder 1923b, 246) – with Mayreder's original phrase, 'die Gemeinschaft des Lebens' (Mayreder 1923a, 262), echoing a phrase also found in Tönnies (quoted in Lundberg 2005, 61).

Olive Schreiner

The South African writer Olive Schreiner (1855-1920) was a feminist, socialist, and pacifist. As Liz Stanley has pointed out, Schreiner regarded all her writings as political (Stanley 1983, 237). Her texts quickly appeared in Swedish translation: her novel *The Story of an African Farm*, 1883, was published in 1890 (*Under Afrikas himmel: historien om en farm i Kaplandet)*, and another two works of prose fiction, *Dreams* (1890) and *Trooper Peter Halket of Mashonaland* (1897), appeared in 1897 and 1901 respectively (Drömmar and Soldaten Peter Halket: en berättelse från Sydafrika). While Schreiner's biographers, Ruth First and Ann Scott, have made a point of listing translations, they have not included the translations into Swedish. *Dagny*, the journal of the Fredrika Bremer Association, published in 1900 a text by Schreiner entitled 'Kvinnorörelsens mål' (The Aims of the Women's Movement), which would appear to be a draft version of Chapter I in *Woman and Labour*, 'Parasitism'. (The source of the article is given as *The Cosmopolitan* [Schreiner 1900, 233]). When Schreiner's pamphlet *Woman and Labour* appeared in 1911, a Swedish translation, *Kvinnan och arbetet*, was published in the same year.

Around the turn of the century 1900, then, Swedish readers would have been reasonably familiar with the work of Schreiner. An article in the journal *Ord & Bild* in 1897 had likened her ability to represent 'the finest, deepest life of the soul' to that of Selma Lagerlöf (Kleen 1897, 521), and had provided an assessment of *The Story of an African Farm* that was at once lyrical and committed, parallelling the striving for liberation for women represented by Lyndall with the striving for religious liberation represented by Waldo (op. cit., 522-23). In *A Literature of Their Own*, Elaine Showalter has read Lyndall as the 'first wholly serious feminist heroine in the English novel' (Showalter 1978, 199). It is Lyndall who points out to her childhood friend Waldo, after having spent four years away from the small South African farm, that her biggest asset is the dimple in her chin: 'though I had a knowledge of all things under the sun, and the wisdom to use it, and the deep an angel, it would not stead me through life like this little chin' (Schreiner 1979, 188). The analysis of sex and gender in Schreiner, it has been emphasised, 'anticipated later twentieth-century directions of feminist thinking' (Berkman 1989, 91); and Lyndall, as is clear from a key speech to Waldo, certainly reads masculinity and femininity as cultural constructs:

> We all enter the world little plastic beings, with so much natural force, perhaps, but for the rest – blank; and the world tells us what we are to be, and shapes us by the ends it sets before us. To you it says – *Work!* and to us it says – *Seem!* (Schreiner 1979, 188; italics original)

Unable to accept wedlock, Lyndall never marries, but her pregnancy and the birth of a baby who lives for just a few hours result in a terminal illness. For all her struggle, Lyndall thus becomes an illustration of the point she has once made to Waldo: 'We [women] fit our sphere as a Chinese woman's foot fits her shoe, exactly' (op. cit., 189). All she can do is outline a future 'when love is no more bought or sold, when it is not a means of making bread, when each woman's life is filled with earnest, independent labour' (op. cit., 195). These points were to be elaborated in *Woman and Labour*, the text which, to Vera Brittain and 'many of the early twentieth-century feminists', was to become the 'Bible of the Woman's Movement' (First and Scott 1980, 265).

In the reading of First and Scott, *Woman and Labour* was rooted in the evolutionism of the 1880s and heavily influenced by the intellectual radicalism that Schreiner encountered while in London 1881-89 (First and Scott 1980, 285). Here she got to know the sexual psychologist and social reformer Havelock Ellis (1859-1939), Eleanor Marx (1855-1898), and perhaps most importantly Karl Pearson (1857-1936), a mathematician and statistician at University College London who founded, in 1885, the Men and Women's Club. In the words of Elaine Showalter, this club brought together twenty middle-class feminist and socialist intellectuals 'to discuss everything from Buddhist nuns to contemporary marriage' (Showalter 1992, 47). According to Showalter, Schreiner was the most distinguished member of 'the women's group' in the club (op. cit., 47-48).

As First and Scott have pointed out, the institution of the family was neither endorsed nor questioned in *Woman and Labour* (First and Scott 1980, 277). Gender roles, however, certainly were. The central argument of the text was that the contemporary women's movement had developed in response to the drastic shrinkage of the 'field of woman's ancient and traditional labours' (Schreiner 1978, 66-67). The text spells out what this 'field' had involved in the post-nomadic phase:

> While man went forth to hunt, or to battle with the foe who would have dispossessed us of all, we laboured on the land. We hoed the earth, we reaped the grain, we shaped the dwellings, we wove the clothing, we modelled the earthen vessels and drew the lines upon them, which were humanity's first attempt at domestic art; we studied the properties and uses of plants, and our old women were the first physicians of the race, as, often, its first priests and prophets. (op. cit., 34)

The often lyrical prose of *Woman and Labour* does not include references, but underlying the account of the development of human societies it is not difficult to discern, as in the texts of Mayreder, an authority such as Engels. But the emphasis on the role of labour makes for some significant shifts in comparison with Mayreder with regard to the construction of gender. For the human male the choice, according to *Woman and Labour*, in the present as in the past, has been *'Find labour or die'* (op. cit., 75; italics original), but for the modern female the choice is 'one far more serious in its ultimate reaction on humanity as a whole – [...] the choice between finding new forms of labour or sinking slowly into a condition of more or less complete and passive *sex-parasitism*' (op. cit., 77; italics original). The 'peculiar conditions of our modern civilisation' mean that sex-parasitism has now become a danger 'to the mass of civilised women, perhaps ultimately to all' (op. cit., 79).

There is no doubt that the text generalised on the basis of the situation of white middle-class women. But the insistence on the significance of work was crucial, and all the more so given the insistence on the absence of any kind of gender categorisation of work: *'We take all labour for our province!'* (Schreiner 1978, 167; italics original). The emphasis was on the usefulness of work to society as a whole: '[t]hat even one individual in a society should be debarred from undertaking that form of social toil for which it is most fitted, makes an unnecessary deficit in the general social assets' (op. cit., 165). In *Woman and Labour*, moreover, there clearly is no difficulty in combining demands arising from similarity with demands arising from difference as the basis for the women's movement:

> That demand, which to-day in all democratic self-governing countries is being made by women, to be accorded their share in the electoral, and ultimately in the legislative and executive duties of government, is based on two grounds: the wider, and more important, that they find nothing in the nature of their sex-function which exonerates them, as human beings, from their obligation to take part in the labours of guidance and government in their state: the narrower, but yet important ground, that, in as far as in one direction, i.e., in the special form of [sic] their sex function takes, they do differ from the male, they, in so far, form a class and are bound to represent the interests of, and to give the state the benefit of, the insight of their class, in certain directions. (op. cit., 192-93)

In Schreiner's text, it is the contribution of women as human beings in general and as women in particular that will eventually bring war to an end. *Woman and Labour* contains a chapter on 'Woman and War', and as First and Scott have pointed out the book, appearing just three years before the outbreak of the First World War, went on to become 'a powerful reference-point in the argument for a specifically female pacifism' (First and Scott 1980, 282). A number of the succinct claims in this chapter have been quoted by subsequent feminists, perhaps most importantly the one about women's contribution to battle:

> There is no battlefield on earth, nor ever has been, howsoever covered with slain, which it has not cost the women of the race more in actual bloodshed and anguish to supply, than it has cost the men who lie there. *We pay the first cost on all human life*. (Schreiner 1978, 169; italics original)

According to *Woman and Labour*, there is no doubt that wars will end once 'the woman takes her place beside the man in the governance and arrangement of external affairs of her race' (op. cit., 170-71).

In *Woman and Labour*, the women's movement emerges as part of a 'general modification' that modern life is undergoing, and in a reading that comes close to that developed in Mayreder's texts, the women's movement is defined as *'essentially a movement of the woman towards the man, of the sexes towards closer union'* (Schreiner 1978, 252; italics original). Here the New Woman is complemented by the New Man (op. cit., 253-55), with the prospect of not just marriage as 'increasingly a fellowship of comrades' (op. cit., 256), but of work as the seedbed of new communities:

> It is more especially because the sharing by woman of the labours of man will tend to promote camaraderie and the existence of common, impersonal interests and like habits of thought and life, that the entrance of women into the very fields shared by men, and not into others peculiarly reserved for her, is so desirable. (op. cit., 279)

Charlotte Perkins Gilman

Charlotte Perkins Gilman (1860-1935) has been called 'the leading intellectual in the women's movement in the United States during the first two decades of the twentieth century' (Degler 1966, xiii). Her best-known book, *Women and Economics*, was not translated into Swedish, but two of her subsequent books soon appeared in Swedish: *The Home: Its Work and Influence* (1903) was published in 1907 in a translation by Frigga Carlberg, the chairperson of the women's suffrage association in Göteborg, as *Hemmet: dess verksamhet och inflytande*; and *The Man-Made World or, Our Androcentric Culture* (1911) appeared in 1912 in a translation by Alma Faustman as *Den av mannen skapade världen eller Vår maskulina kultur*.

Gilman was a socialist in the American tradition. As represented around the turn of the century 1900 by Edward Bellamy, Lester F. Ward, Thorstein Veblen, and Gilman, this socialism was not indebted to Marx but inspired by the utopian socialist tradition, underpinned by the work of for example Robert Owen and Charles Fourier (Zauderer 1999, 152). As has been pointed out this socialism, pre-Marx, provides 'a stronger basis for socialist feminism than traditional Marxism does because it recognizes that social transformation need not begin with a change in the mode of production; the family can be acted on independently and simultaneously' (ibid.). In Gilman's scheme – her subsequent books effectively represent developments of ideas first formulated in *Women and Economics* (see e.g. Degler 1966, xiii) – the family is significant chiefly in a historical perspective. In the context of Gilman's reform Darwinism (Määttä 1997, 99-133), 'the horde' was the hunting unit and the family, and later the tribe, the pastoral unit, with the contemporary family no more than 'a decreasing survival of the earliest grouping known to man' (Gilman 1966, 215). The sharp distinction between the family and marriage is pivotal to the argument in *Women and Economics*. While the family is a 'purely social phenomenon', marriage is a 'form of sex-union', complicated by the fact that it has also been made into 'an economic relation' (op. cit., 213). In the text's succinct wording, 'She gets her living by getting a husband. He gets his wife by getting a living' (op. cit., 110). Developing the 'sex-parasitism' of *Woman and Labour*, *Women and Economics* underlines that 'we have painfully and laboriously evolved and carefully maintain among us an enormous class of non-productive consumers, – a class which is half the world, and mother of the other half' (op. cit., 118).

While the tendency to generalise on the basis of the position of white middle-class women is clearly problematic, the forceful argument in *Women and Economics* is undoubtedly innovative. Emphasising that '[m]aternal energy is the force through which have come into the world both love and industry' (Gilman 1966, 126), the text defines the contemporary situation in which a woman has to rely on 'sex-distinction' not just to attract a mate but, 'as is the case with no other creature under heaven', to get her livelihood (op. cit., 38), as a transient phenomenon. The emergence of both the women's movement and the labour movement prove as much (op. cit., 138). *Women and Economics* makes a powerful plea for economic independence for women; and while the text underlines the significance of both motherhood and the home, the argument is for far-reaching reforms in both areas: 'It is a melancholy fact that the vast majority of our children are reared and trained by domestic servants, – generally their mothers, to be sure, but domestic servants by trade' (op. cit., 211). Given that '[n]o mother knows more than her mother knew' (op. cit., 293), uneducated mothers by definition make bad educators of children. And although modern, professional women with families want homes, 'they do not want the clumsy tangle of rudimentary industries that are supposed to accompany the home' (op. cit., 243). In a move that is more radical than anything suggested in Schreiner's *Woman and Labour*, the solution as set out in *Women and Economics* is to leave both education and housework in the hands of experts, thus allowing the majority of women to develop their economic freedom. In the analysis of *Women and Economics*, the practice of making women dependent on marriage for their living is in fact holding humankind back, but

> as women become free, economic, social factors, so becomes possible the full social combination of individuals in collective industry. With such freedom, such independence, such wider union, becomes possible also a union between man and woman such as the world has long dreamed of in vain. (op. cit., 145)

Gilman's utopian novel *Herland*, which she wrote for her journal *The Forerunner* and published in instalments in 1915 (*Herland* only appeared in book form in 1979), provides a glimpse of this kind of ideal union in the form of the relationship between Ellador and Vandyck Jennings. But she belongs to Herland, the country in which women have been free to develop peace, harmony, and beauty over 2,000 years, and he is a sociologist able to cope with the fact that the women of Herland treat men 'just as they do one another': 'It's as if our being men was a minor incident' (Gilman 1979, 30). As the three male characters – including Jennings, who is also the narrator – spend a year in Herland, the narrative's indirect and often humourous commentary on the gendering of western society emerges as one of the strengths of the novel. With Terry arguing that in a society without men there is 'not only no fun [...] – no real sport – no competition; but these women aren't *womanly*' (op. cit., 58; italics original), the incomprehension that meets a question about feathers in hats has the effect of ridiculing the use of hats for anything but practical purposes (op. cit., 49-50), just as the puzzled reaction to the statement that western women are 'loved – idolized – honored – kept in the home to care for the children' calls into question one of the corner-stones of the dominant discourse on the family: '"What is 'the home'?" asked

Somel' (op. cit., 61). In Herland children are 'the *raison d'être*' (op. cit., 51), and their education is a key task of the community, but significantly the 'heavenly babies' observed by Jennings

> never knew they were being educated. They did not dream that in this association of hilarious experiment and achievement they were laying the foundation for that close beautiful group feeling into which they grew so firmly with the years. This was education for citizenship. (op. cit., 108)

In this country where there have been no wars because the women '[have grown] together – not by competition, but by united action' (op. cit., 60), the sense of community and of communal responsibility is not just limited to the present but also reaches far into the future, with the inhabitants of Herland perceiving their country as

> a unit – it was theirs. They themselves were a unit, a conscious group; they thought in terms of the community. As such, their time-sense was not limited to the hopes and ambitions of an individual life. Therefore, they habitually considered and carried out plans for improvement which might cover centuries. (op. cit., 79)

Jennings has to conclude that in contrast to western societies, 'women [are] "the world"' (op. cit., 137). Transforming the 'private world of mother – child, isolated in the individual home, into a community of mothers and children in a socialized world' (Lane 1979, xxiii), Gilman's utopian novel challenges not just the dominant discourse on the family but the relations of gender and power shaping the western world at the time.

Frida Stéenhoff

In Wägner's novel *Pennskaftet* (1910; *Penwoman*, 2009), the central character sells a brochure at a suffrage meeting with the title 'Hvarför skola kvinnorna vänta?' (Wägner 1910, 226-27) (Why Should Women Wait? [Wägner 2009, 150]). The title was that of an existing brochure, the date of publication was 1905, and the name of the author was Frida Stéenhoff (1865-1945).

During the period we are concerned with here, Stéenhoff was a leading Swedish radical. But as Christina Carlsson Wetterberg has pointed out, Stéenhoff's ideas tended to be approached piecemeal, the result being that issues relating to the liberation of women were marginalised 'in favour of the family, the whole, the nation', and that these 'attempts to speak in a different voice' were thus silenced (Carlsson Wetterberg 2002, 207). Carlsson Wetterberg has also suggested that the limited interest in Stéenhoff's work subsequently shown by Swedish scholars has been due to the fact that the ideas formulated in her texts do not fit neatly into existing categories, be they party political or feminist (Carlsson Wetterberg 1994, 83). There is no doubt, however, that Stéenhoff 'perceived the liberation of women as closely connected with a radical transformation of social institutions and ways of thinking' (op. cit., 82).

With her drama *Lejonets unge* (The Lion Cub), performed and published in 1896, Stéenhoff tore apart the dominant discourse on the family. Here a young woman sculptor, Saga Leire, challenges the standards of a provincial Swedish town. Not only does she refute the conservative headmaster who doubts that a woman can be a genius – '"Feminine genius"? Is genius gendered?' (Stéenhoff 1896, 54) – but she also insists that the sanctity of marriage stems from the husband and wife and not from God (op. cit., 133). As a relationship develops between her and Adil, a young journalist introduced as the nephew of the wife of the bishop in whose house they are both staying, it is Saga who takes the initiative and invites Adil to her room. Their relationship encourages the bishop's wife to reveal that Adil is her son, born as the result of a pre-marital relationship; and it is with the blessing of the bishop that Saga and Adil set out for Paris: 'For those who are happy, everything is pure' (op. cit., 213).

Stéenhoff worked in a range of genres, including prose fiction, her texts concise, stringently argued, and frequently provocative. Originating as a lecture, the pamphlet 'Feminismens moral' (1903; The Moral Standards of Feminism) – which introduced the concept of *feminism* into the Swedish debate about society (Carlsson Wetterberg 1994, 80) – argued that marriage could be tantamount to the 'chaining' of innocent human beings to 'criminals of all kinds', pointed out that 'in our legislation' the married woman was in many respects placed 'on a par with children, delinquents and idiots', and denounced marriage as 'legalised slavery' (Stéenhoff 1903, 27, 21, 27). In Stéenhoff's texts – as in those of Rosa Mayreder – marriage and the family emerge as the corner-stones of a society based on private property (Carlsson Wetterberg 1994, 86); and 'Feminismens moral' lists some of the key privileges that have accrued to men thanks to their role as family breadwinners. Men have become the sole legislators; the work of women has been deemed to be worth less than that of men even when exactly the same; and women have been kept away from all well-paid official positions (Stéenhoff 1903, 23). The dominant moral standards, according to this pamphlet, have amounted to the worship of power and of those in power, with 'the trinity' of 'weapons, ceremonies and banknotes' idolised both at home and in the churches (op. cit., 14). By siding with the powerful against the weak, the dominant moral standards have emboldened men to oppress women (op. cit., 15). The impact on the construction of gender has been fundamental: the dominant moral standards have tried to allocate all sensibility to the woman and all reason to the man and thus, 'as a means of maintaining a relationship of subservience between them, distorted their mental personalities' (ibid.). This is in direct contrast to the influential construction of gender advocated around the same time by Ellen Key. Stéenhoff disagreed with Key's argument that motherliness would somehow improve the world: 'Women had had the opportunity, for a long time, to be mothers, yet the world had remained masculine, in a negative sense' (quoted in Zade 1935, 210). Like Vaerting, Stéenhoff instead took her starting-point in the unequal distribution of power, which in turn had impacted on the construction of gender. Her texts argue that the dominant moral standards have then reduced women to instruments for the transfer of property from one generation to the next, circumscribing their right to give birth, and nurturing double moral standards (Carlsson Wetterberg 1994, 87).

Stéenhoff clearly drew some of her inspiration from Engels (Carlsson Wetterberg 1994, 86-87), and 'Feminismens moral' points up the parallels between feminism and socialism: they were both against clericalism and for free thought; against militarism and for peace; and against the oppression caused by class and capital and for social reorganisation (Stéenhoff 1903, 9). Feminism, according to Stéenhoff's text, was a cry 'for truth and justice' (op. cit., 9-10); and signalling an evolutionist perspective, her text argued that the moral standards of feminism were 'more pure and more beautiful' than the dominant moral standards because the former had 'attempted to reach the height of the mental development achieved by humankind so far' (op. cit., 10). More specifically, the moral standards of feminism were human and social; they aimed at the perfection of each human being for her/his own sake and not for anyone else's; they aimed at an improved social environment for happier human beings; and the underlying principles were those of justice, truth, and goodness (op. cit., 14-17).

'Feminismens moral' devoted a considerable amount of space to the significance of women's work. Like Schreiner, Frida Stéenhoff highlighted the difference between self-sustenance and parasitism, but her text went on to make an important distinction: the parasitism of women was limited to the upper classes, while '[t]he majority of women were toiling like slaves from the cradle to the grave' (Stéenhoff 1903, 19). In other words, the class perspective in this text amounted to a correction of Schreiner. 'Feminismens moral' was of course published seven years before Schreiner's *Woman and Labour*, but in view of the fact that the text by Schreiner published in *Dagny* in 1900 reads like a draft of the first of the three big chapters on 'Parasitism' in *Woman and Labour* (see above, p.84), it is possible to read this section of 'Feminismens moral' as a response to Schreiner's text in *Dagny*. Stéenhoff's text went on to emphasise that women were making a very considerable contribution to Sweden's gross national product – and '[s]he who is productive is not a parasite' (op. cit., 20) – but that their position was complicated by their reproductive role. As Carlsson Wetterberg has underlined, a socialist theorist such as Engels viewed children chiefly as a problem, as an obstacle to the full equality of women; in Stéenhoff's works, on the other hand, the children were at the centre of the vision of a new society (Carlsson Wetterberg 1994, 86).

In *Lejonets unge* Stéenhoff had coined the phrase 'barnets århundrade' (Stéenhoff 1896, 211) (the century of the child), soon afterwards popularised by Ellen Key as the title of a book (1900). The phrase recurs in Stéenhoff's pamphlet of 1908, 'Penningen och kärleken' (Money and Love), introducing the argument that each child should be regarded as 'an independent economic unit' (Stéenhoff 1908, 42). The newborn baby represents the value of the work he (the text refers to the baby/child in the masculine throughout) will produce, and thus society ought to provide him with a good education as an advance. Each child should also be carefully looked after, and should be subject only to the existing laws and not 'the victim of personal arbitrariness' (op. cit., 43). The higher valuing of the child would result in the higher valuing of the mother.

In the pamphlet 'Kärleken som kulturproblem' (Love as a Cultural Problem), 1912, love was highlighted as a positive and ennobling element which, in contrast to enforced marriage, enforced celibacy or prostitution, increased 'the sum total of happiness in society' (Stéenhoff 1912, 6). Launching a stinging attack on 'ägendomsäktenskapet' (op. cit., 13) (marriage for the sake of property), the text pilloried the social anomaly of punishing the mothers for children born out of wedlock, while in the case of the fathers 'one pretended that *outwith* marriage there *was* no *fatherhood*' (op. cit., 14; italics original).

The repeated deconstruction in Stéenhoff's texts of the dominant discourse on the family, along with the suggestions as to how to improve the economic and social positions of women and children, have marked similarities with the texts of Charlotte Perkins Gilman. But while the innovative community that emerges in Gilman's *Herland* is conspicuously gendered, a text such as Stéenhoff's 'Kärleken som kulturproblem' highlights a concept of community that effectively has no boundaries and that is also continuing to evolve: 'We have reason to hope that the sense of community will grow as people's social awareness grows' (Stéenhoff 1912, 27). Defining 'solidarity' as 'the communal sense of responsibility', Stéenhoff's text singles out 'solidarity between the sexes in their work for the new generations' (op. cit., 31) as the pointer towards a better future:

all women have to develop a sense of solidarity for the sake of motherhood. [...] Men and women have to develop a sense of solidarity – for the sake of the child. In other words – for the sake of the future of humankind. (ibid.)

Stéenhoff was also a pacifist, and although she was not part of the Swedish delegation at the Women's International Congress at The Hague in 1915, she participated in the Ford Peace Expedition that was one of the results of the Congress, and she also became one of five Swedish delegates at the standing conference for continuous mediation set up by the Ford expedition (Wiltsher 1985, 157-63; Zade 1935, 184-85). Together with Elin Wägner and Anna Lenah Elgström she edited, in 1917, a volume in honour of Rosika Schwimmer, who had played a leading role at the Congress at The Hague and been instrumental in organising the Ford Peace Expedition. Stéenhoff's biographer concluded her volume with a series of 'aphorisms' by the author, none of them previously published. The last of these strikingly brings together gender, power, war, and justice in a positive perspective on the future:

> The masculine domination of the earth is maintained by means of violence and fear. This is why humankind is unable to achieve harmony and balance in their political relations. When the men finally realise that the governance of peoples has to take place in accordance with principles of justice, they will establish a law of mutuality between themselves and the women. At that point the moral standards of feminism will have achieved their goal: a judicial system with the same obligations for all. (quoted in Zade 1935, 216-17)

*

To sum up, the dominant discourse on the family during this period is epitomised by the nuclear family, with the asymmetries between wife and husband adding to the polarised constructions of femininity and masculinity. The texts of Ellen Key reinforced the significance of the concepts of motherliness and the home, and although the Social Democratic Women's movement early in the twentieth century debated issues such as childcare and housework in radical terms inspired by Clara Zetkin, this kind of radicalism was subsequently overshadowed by the professionalisation of housework epitomised by the 'housewife movement' and by the impact of the texts of Key. There is a clear connection between the dominant discourse on the family and the fundamental tenets of the Swedish welfare state, 'the home of the people', and this discourse had by then expanded its influence well beyond the middle class.

Alternative discourses on gender and community have been exemplified here by the work of Rosa Mayreder, Olive Schreiner, Charlotte Perkins Gilman, and Frida Stéenhoff. While in the dominant discourse on the family constructions of gender and community confirm each other in the form of husband-and-wife and the nuclear family respectively, the texts of Mayreder, Schreiner, Gilman, and Stéenhoff tend to separate gender and community and subject gender to a detailed analysis, often in an historical context inspired by socialism, and with attention to the role of power in general and economic power in particular. In the texts of these four writers, new constructions of gender that are more equal in terms of power highlight women's agency and form the basis of new communities. The community of women with its 2,000 years of peace and harmony in Gilman's *Herland* is an extreme example, but peace is a fundamental element in the new communities that emerge in these texts.

As we now move on to analyses of a selection of texts from the period 1907-21, the outlines of dominant and alternative discourses above will help point up and problematise the wide range of constructions of gender and community.

Chapter 4:
Texts

In this chapter, texts representing reportage, essay, light-hearted columns, and prose fiction will be analysed. As I have emphasised in the introductory chapter, the gender categorisations are to be perceived as tools; and in the analyses of the texts below, the fluidity of the categorisations is apparent throughout. The framework for the production of these texts, and an important dimension of my analyses of them, consists of the economic, political, social, and cultural conditions outlined in the chapter on contexts above; and following on from the chapter on gender and community in the dominant and alternative discourses on the family in Sweden in the first two decades of the twentieth century, the focus of my analyses will be on the constructions of gender and community in these texts. How are gender and community constructed in the examples of reportage, essay, light-hearted columns, and prose fiction examined below? To what extent do constructions of gender and community differ depending on genre, and if they do, how do they differ? Are there differences between for instance the clusters of reportages considered here, or between, say, novels with character-bound narration as opposed to those with external narration? And how does the dominant discourse on the family emerge in texts produced during a period that was dominated, in the national context, by extensive economic and political changes, including the struggle for women's suffrage and, in the international context from 1914, by the First World War and its aftermath?

1. Reportage

Elin Wägner began her career as a journalist. Her first contributions to the conservative provincial paper *Helsingborgs-Posten* appeared in 1901, and she was on the staff of the paper from 1903 to 1904. Kristina Lundgren and Birgitta Ney have categorised her contributions as book reviews and reportages from the streets of Helsingborg, plus lighthearted columns published under the heading 'I Helsingborg' (In Helsingborg), along with, most probably, translations from the foreign press (Lundgren and Ney 2000, 103-05). In addition, Wägner published short stories in *Helsingborgs-Posten*. In 1907 Wägner joined the women's weekly *Idun* as Assistant Editor and was employed in this capacity until 1916, when she left the magazine; she continued, however, to contribute to *Idun* in subsequent years. In the period 1907-21, she published a very wide range of material in *Idun*. Margret Halvardson and Susanne Töringe have listed a total of 278 items (Halvardson and Töringe 1979), but as I have found this list is not complete, and the number of items by Wägner is even greater. They represent a wide range of genres: apart from reportages, Wägner contributed opinion pieces, book reviews, obituaries, light hearted columns in the form of a series (which I shall consider in the section on light-hearted columns below), sketches, and short stories. A number of the early sketches and short stories from *Idun* were to form the core of Wägner's first book, *Från det jordiska museet* (From the Human Museum), which appeared in 1907. In the same year, she also began to contribute to the liberal daily *Dagens Nyheter*, and Ivar Ljungquist in his history of the paper has counted a total of 227 contributions by Wägner in the period 1909-21 (Ljungquist 1953, 412-13). This figure does not include the instalments of the novel *Norrtullsligan*, which were published in *Dagens Nyheter* in 1907-08; it appeared as a book in 1908 and is discussed in the section on prose fiction below. Wägner wrote numerous reportages for *Dagens Nyheter* on social and political issues, with the campaign for suffrage for women a prominent topic, but she also contributed book reviews and short stories.

I have chosen to refer to the category 'reportage' in preference to 'news story', which is certainly more common (see e.g. Randall 2000) but also more amorphous. 'Reportage' comes with more stringent definitions: according to John Carey's introduction to *The Faber Book of Reportage* (1987), a reportage must be written by an eye-witness (Carey 1989, ixxx). In journalistic terms, this has been translated into a substantial news report which is the work of a journalist who has usually been on the spot, and whose narrative is thus likely to be relatively prominent (Lundgren, Ney and Thurén 1999, 33). For a woman journalist in Sweden in the early decades of the twentieth century, being on the spot was tantamount to enjoying a freedom to move in public places that was by no means enjoyed by women generally. Birgitta Ney in her investigation of the work of Lotten Ekman, a woman journalist active in Stockholm in the period 1898-1910, has discerned examples of what she has called 'the text of a *flaneur*' in Ekman's work (Ney 1999, 95), and in Ney's analysis there is a direct link with the 'active journalism' introduced, by women journalists in particular, in the Stockholm press around this time (op. cit., 139).

The three clusters of reportages by Wägner that I have selected for analysis here take the significance of the freedom enjoyed by the women journalists in the first couple of decades of the twentieth century several steps further. While the first cluster, the series of eight reportages published in *Idun* in 1908-09 under the heading 'Kvinnan som arbetar' (The Working Woman), maps out conditions for women in employment in Stockholm and in Sweden more generally, the second cluster, the reportages published in spring 1915 when Wägner covered for *Idun* the Women's International Congress at The Hague, 27 April – 1 May, establishes the woman reporter in an international political context. The aim of the Congress was to initiate a ccasefire and thus help bring the First World War to an end; and from this point on, international pacifism in general and pacifist initiatives by national and international organisations, including women's organisations, and by individual women in particular, emerge as an important topic in Wägner's reportages, in *Idun* but more so in *Dagens Nyheter*. This topic acquires a new dimension in the reportages from Vienna that Wägner contributed to *Dagens Nyheter* in 1920, and which constitute my third cluster. Wägner had gone to Vienna in a dual capacity, as a reporter with a key interest in the first international project run by the recently established *Rädda barnen* (Save the Children), founded following the formation of the Save the Children Fund in Britain earlier in 1919. In addition to the series of reportages, she also turned the post-war plight of the population of Vienna into a work of fiction, and her novel *Den förödda vingården* (1920; The Ravaged Vineyard) is analysed in the section on prose fiction below.

'Kvinnan som arbetar' (The Working Woman), Idun, 1908-09

The series about women in employment under the heading 'Kvinnan som arbetar' (The Working Woman) consists of seven reportages published in 1908, about domestic servants, post office managers, factory workers (two articles), chicken farmers, and canteen managers (two articles), and one published in 1909, about stenographers. As I have pointed out in my outline of the economic context, there was a big increase in the number of women employed in sectors outwith agriculture in the decades leading up to 1920; and according to the preamble to the series, the aim of the reportages was to add to the knowledge of what was 'i stort sedt en ny företeelse inom samhället' (Wägner 1908g, 56) (on the whole a new phenomenon in society). The newness of the phenomenon along with the construction of women as 'en väsentlig faktor i det offentliga arbetslifvet' (ibid.) (a significant factor in the public life of work) and the equals of men was reinforced by military metaphors such as 'den arbetande kvinnoarmén' (ibid.) (the army of working women) and the reference to different professions as 'olika truppslag i den stora armén' (ibid.) (different branches of the great army). The two reportages on women factory workers in particular also highlight the need for improved social services (Wägner 1908i, Wägner 1908j). The women in employment inevitably call into question the dominant discourse on the family. There are parallels in these reportages with the constructions of gender in texts by writers such as Charlotte Perkins Gilman and Frida Stéenhoff; and in Wägner's texts these alternative constructions of gender also involve the constructions of new communities. But given their radicalism, how do these early texts tackle the central conflict between production and reproduction?

Texts

As these reportages foreground the subjectivation and professionalisation of women in employment, the alternative communities forged by several of these professions become prominent. The domestic servants have *Tjänarinneföreningen* (The Association of Women Servants) (Wägner 1908g), the female post office managers have united in their struggle with the Royal Swedish Mail for better conditions, and the women factory workers constitute *kåren* (the profession) (Wägner 1908j, 363). The reportage about women chicken farmers sets out the foundations of one such new profession by detailing information about finance and courses, and even if the glaringly inappropriate register in parts of this text – 'hönssaken har kräft sina martyrer' (Wägner 1908k, 473) (the poultry cause has claimed its martyrs) – suggests a critique of Ellen Key's argument about chicken farming as a 'natural area of work' for women (see e.g. Wägner 1908f, 73), there is no doubt as to the significance of the profession. And with a decisive shift from narrative to non-narrative comment, in other words to the type of comment in which, as Mieke Bal has pointed out, ideological statements are frequently made (Bal 1999, 31), the opening of the first reportage about women working in canteens turns into a manifesto for the employment of women with an emphasis on both subjectivation and community:

> jag förutsätter optimistiskt, att alla arbetsdugliga och arbetslediga kvinnor i vårt land icke ha någon högre önskan än att gripa fatt på arbetet. Förutsätter det, emedan det förefaller mig otänkbart, att man kan lefva i en tid full af arbetsdyrkan och arbetslidelse utan att ryckas med och tändas upp och gripas af hunger efter att få ta för sig. *Hur illa till mods, hur bortkommen bör icke den känna sig, som icke kommit med i ringen, ur hvars händer dagarna glida vissna och tomma till marken, som i stället för glädjen och tryggheten att vara med i ledet bär på den tryckande och pinsamma känslan af att stå utanför.* (Wägner 1908l, 584; my italics)

(I presume, optimistically, that all women in our country who are capable of being in employment and free to be so, have no higher wish than to set about working. I presume, because I find it unthinkable that anyone can be alive at a time full of the worship of work and passion for work without becoming involved and inspired and hungry to help herself. *How uncomfortable, how lost should she not feel who has not become part of the circle, she out of whose hands the days are slipping shrivelled and empty to the ground, she who instead of the happiness and safety of being part of the group is suffering under the oppressive and embarrassing feeling of being outside.)*

Indeed, this manifesto opens up perspectives towards a 'systemförändring' (op. cit., 585) (systemic change), with the work of the women canteen managers eventually resulting in 'ett godt missionsarbete bland folket, [...] höjande af folkhälsan, folktrefnaden och folkekonomien' (ibid.) (a successful missionary undertaking among the people, [...] the improvement of the health of the people, the comfort of the people, and the economy of the people). Beyond the alternative communities of women in employment, a new society can be glimpsed.

In the last reportage in the series, 'Kontorister och stenografer' (Office Workers and Stenographers), the conflict between production and reproduction is finally tackled as femininity, in contrast to masculinity, is constructed in terms of 'två oförenliga och hvarandra motsägande lifsmål' (Wägner 1909) (two incompatible and contradictory goals in life). The incongruity is enhanced by the outline of a programme for women in employment involving better education, better organisation, better pay, and better status, and the reappearance of military metaphors, introduced in the preamble, to indicate how such a programme could unite a work force: 'Vägen skulle vara svår men rak och den rätta, marschen långsam och med pauser, men utan plötsliga svängningar, och soldaterna skulle gå på utan att distraheras af den tanken, att det vore lyckligast och bäst att få gå ur ledet och ställa sig utom täflan' (ibid.) (The road would be difficult but straight and the right one, the march would be slow and with pauses yet without sudden deviations, and the soldiers would march on without being distracted by the thought that they would be happier and better off leaving the column and abstaining from the venture). While the resolution of the conflict between production and reproduction is left, somewhat disappointingly, to 'framtidens mera rådsnara och modiga kvinna' (ibid.) (the more capable and brave woman of the future), the construction of femininity in this series chiefly in terms of employment and, in principle, employment of all types, is conspicuous, with the military metaphors reinforcing a momentum that suggests that the solution to the problem of combining production and reproduction will in due course underpin the new and more gender-equal society that is taking shape.

The reportages about 'Kvinnan som arbetar' place the reader in the midst of some of the key changes transforming Swedish society in the early years of the twentieth century. Most immediately, these concern constructions of gender in the context of economics. While there is little or nothing in these texts about new constructions of masculinity, the reportages about 'Kvinnan som arbetar' amount to a multitude of new constructions of femininity, be the actors (I am using Mieke Bal's definition of 'structural [positions]' [Bal 1999, 115]) married women in employment, or single women like I. and D. Svensson, the two sisters who have launched *Stenografbyrån*, an institute training stenographers, as soon as they have come of age (Wägner 1909). The significance of the new communities constituted by women in employment is pointed up by the appropriation of military metaphors. The female reporter is clearly also part of these changes – economic, political, social, and cultural; and in the cluster of reportages about the Women's International Congress at The Hague in spring 1915 to be analysed below, this reporter steps straight into international politics. Constructions of gender could not be more prominent just as the stakes could not be higher: this Congress was an attempt by women, the majority still without franchise and citizenship, to bring the First World War to an end.

The Women's International Congress at The Hague 1915, Idun, 1915-16

The Women's International Congress, arranged at The Hague 27 April – 1 May 1915, brought together 1,136 delegates from Austria, Belgium, Canada, Denmark, Germany, Great Britain, Hungary, Italy, the Netherlands, Norway, Sweden, and the United States (Wiltsher 1985, 96), who had braved war-time travel restrictions to reach The Hague. Wägner was a member of the Swedish delegation (Andersson 2001, 94) as well as covering the Congress for *Idun*. Just a fortnight after the end of the Congress, on 16 May 1915, *Idun* devoted a six-page spread to the events at The Hague, the material consisting of three reportages by Wägner, one of them illustrated, along with a full page of photographs. The next issue of *Idun*, 23 May, contained two more reportages by Wägner, and another two appeared, in separate issues, later in the year, with Wägner's final reportage relating to the Congress and its aftermath published early in 1916.

The gathering of a congress of women in response to the biggest military conflict in the world so far made for constructions of gender and community that were far more radical and urgent than anything in the series on women in employment. What is remarkable is the relative unobtrusiveness with which the conceptual leaps are made as the focus on the professionalisation of women in the earlier series is replaced by a focus on women as agents in international politics in the midst of a world war. Three factors underpin the innovative constructions of gender and community and, by implication, society, in the reportages relating to the Congress. Firstly, women are constructed as agents in world politics. Secondly, these texts foreground the role of the female reporter who combines professionalism with knowledge and ideological commitment. Thirdly, several of these texts also foreground female readers and create new modes of subjectivity which, in the definition of Chris Weedon, offer 'both a perspective and a choice, and [open] up the possibility of political change' (Weedon 1997, 9). The analysis that follows is structured in terms of these three factors.

'Kongressen öppnas' (The Opening of the Congress) marked the uniqueness of the alternative community of the Congress by highlighting not just the difficulties of some of the delegations in reaching The Hague, but the fact that the delegations represented both nations at war and neutral nations. The second reportage illustrated the determination and efficiency of these delegations, with two pages of dense text detailing the proposals for resolutions, the discussions, and the decisions. The structure was chronological and in part the narrator had to rely on notes, but in comparison with the adopted resolutions as set out in Jane Addams, Emily G. Balch and Alice Hamilton, *Women at The Hague* (1915, reprinted 2003), the account offered to the readers of *Idun* was remarkably comprehensive, with any major gaps only in section IV, International Cooperation (Addams, Balch and Hamilton 2003, pp. 72-77). In this reportage, then, the professional, knowledgeable, and ideologically committed female reporter was constructed as crucial to the representation of women as agents in world politics.

The first five resolutions set out not just the parameters of the alternative community constituted by the Congress but also the outline of a new society: a protest against the madness and horrors of war; a protest against the specific forms of violence to which women were being subjected; an admonition to the women of all nations to work for political suffrage 'på det att ett förenadt inflytande af kvinnorna i alla länder måtte i framiden [sic] bli ett medel att förebygga krig' (Wägner 1915b, 312) (so that the joint influence of the women of all countries would, in future, be a means of preventing war); a promise by the delegates to work for greater understanding between the nations; an agreement about the need to make the ideal of peace central to children's education. Having summarised the majority of the resolutions, the narrative provides a maxim: 'Man begär det man anser som sin rätt, inte det man har hopp om att kunna drifva igenom, ty hur långt skulle man komma då?' (op. cit., 313) (You demand that which you regard as your right, not that which you hope to be able to drive through, for how far would you get then?). Maxims, as Susan S. Lanser has pointed out, is one of the 'conventional forms for authorial wisdom' (Lanser 1992, 82). This maxim is unique in this reportage and a measure of the extent of the renegotiation of gender and power taking place here. The construction of gender in binary terms is subdued, with the argument for women's agency rooted in the demands for justice and rights which emerge as part of an ongoing process of democratisation.

Avoiding any foregrounding of gender polarisation, the reportages analysed so far instead emphasise democratisation as a project involving both women and men. The third of the reportages published on 16 May 1915, 'Trots allt' (Against the Odds), expands the alternative community to include all those women who have not participated in the Congress. The media scholar Claes-Göran Holmberg has argued for the significance in journalism of archetypal narratives (Holmberg 1995);

and if the long list of obstacles helps to strengthen the expectation of eventual success, this final reportage is not just highlighting 'positions for interpreting subjects' (Fairclough 2006, 84) but emphatically constructing the female reader, any female reader, as a key agent. The concluding sentences cannot leave her in any doubt as to the work that is required and the transformation that could be achieved:

> Endast för den händelse att omkring de tusen på kongressen sluta nya och åter nya tusental i ständigt ökade ringar, kan man vänta det ögonblick, då vägvisaren vid sidan af vägen får myndighet i stämman och icke behöfver nöja sig med att blott bönfalla.
> Kongressens öde och eftermäle beror på, om de stora massorna stödja eller svika. (Wägner 1915c, 314)

> (Only if it were to happen that around the one thousand at the Congress new thousands form steadily increasing circles, can one expect the moment when the guide by the side of the road can begin to speak with authority and no longer has to be satisfied with mere pleading.
> The fate and the reputation of this Congress will depend on whether the great masses will give their support or fail to do so.)

The development of positions for interpreting subjects is a prominent aspect of the remaining reportages relating to the Congress. 'Färden genom Tyskland' (*Idun*, 23 May 1915; Travelling through Germany) consists of a series of snapshots of Germany at war, the material gathered during the three days the Swedish delegates have spent in Germany on their way to and from The Hague. The narrative provides close-ups of the impact of war as seen on the home front, with the German enthusiasm for the war so familiar from the press forming the backdrop to the harsh conditions represented here. This text is the first of Wägner's reportages from The Hague in *Idun* to gesture towards the polarisation of masculinity and femininity, but any hint of a binary conflict is quickly undermined by the highlighting of the suffering of the soldiers, and most importantly the effects of their psychological scars. The representations of psychologically injured men combine with a sketch of Hamburg's deserted harbour and an indication of the suffering of the civilians to suggest a community for which war is the very opposite of national triumphalism: 'Man undrar, när man ser denna stad, hvars hjärta stannat: hvad lefva människorna af, hur går tiden?' (Wägner 1915d, 328) (You wonder when you see this city whose heart has stopped, how are people surviving, how are they making the time pass?). The questions add to the urgency of the contribution by the interpreting subject in the face of the problematic that is pivotal to this reportage: given the profound effects of the war on the soldiers as well as on the civilians, is there likely to be a future at all for this community, this society, this nation whose citizens are being asked to make such enormous sacrifices?

Against this representation of war-stricken Germany, the subsequent reportage sets the alternative community of the Congress. In 'Croquiser från Haag' (*Idun*, 23 May 1915; Sketches from The Hague), a text with several features reminiscent of prose fiction, the focus is on some of the leading participants, most importantly Rosika Schwimmer (1877-1948) from Hungary and Emmeline Pethick-Lawrence (1867-1954) from Britain. The representation of Schwimmer in particular makes her not merely an actor, 'a structural position', but a character, 'a complex semantic unit' (Bal 1999, 115). Schwimmer emerges as 'revolten mot kriget förkroppsligad' (Wägner 1915e) (the embodiment of the revolt against war) with the focus on the words – in the form of indirect and direct discourse – with which she has tried to persuade the delegates to take action against the war:

> För att få dem till att vilja, tvang hon dem att se skyttegrafvarna, höra samtalen där, se de dödssårade krypa på marken med inälfvorna släpande efter sig, se de brända hemmen, de våldförda kvinnorna, tänka på det nya internationella släkte, som dessa kvinnor skulle föda till världen, på de veneriska sjukdomar, som skola för århundraden förgifta släktets blod. Upp därför att rädda, hvad som ännu finns att rädda, snart är det för sent! (ibid.)

> (To make them want [to take action], she forced them to see the trenches, listen to the conversations in them, watch the fatally wounded crawling on the ground dragging their intestines behind, watch the torched homes, the women who had been raped, reflect on the new international race that these women would bring into the world, on the venereal diseases that would poison the blood of the race for centuries to come. Up, then, to save what can still be saved, before it's too late!)

The most striking feature of this text is the application of military metaphors to the speeches of pacifist women. When speaking about the suffering of dying soldiers and women subjected to rape, Schwimmer 'öfveröste sina åhörare med shrapnels, hon sårade med afsikt att låta dem blöda' (ibid.) (was showering her listeners with shrapnel, she was injuring them, intent on making them bleed); and with a leading role in the Women's Social and Political Union, Pethick-Lawrence had 'drifvit fram hundratals af väluppfostrade engelskor mot polisen till fängelse och hungersträjk' (driven hundreds of well-mannered English women against the police and towards prison and hunger strike) and was now attempting 'med samma medel att drifva fram kvinnorna mot kriget, dock icke bokstafligen' (ibid.) (with the same means, to drive the women against the war, albeit not literally). Metaphors 'structure the way we think and the way we act, and our systems of knowledge and belief, in a pervasive and fundamental way' (Fairclough 2006, 194). We have previously encountered military metaphors in some of the reportages about women in employment where, I argued, they helped to underline that the progress of women in the labour market was as significant as that of men, but also eventually pointed up the difference of women as child-bearers. But in the reportage relating to the Congress at The Hague, the military metaphors do not just underline the urgency of the project: the use of such metaphors for the purposes of the women's peace movement becomes a means of undermining their conventional military significance, of prizing them apart, of appropriating them to new ends. Moreover, the phrase used with reference to Rosika Schwimmer, 'hon sårade med afsikt att låta dem blöda' (she was injuring them, intent on making them bleed), echoes a well-known phrase in the Swedish author Viktor Rydberg's (1828-1895) preface to his novel *Den siste atenaren* (1859; The Last Athenian): 'i krigarens lovliga uppsåt att såra och döda' (Rydberg 1945, 12) (with the legitimate intent of the warrior to wound and to kill). The intertext from Rydberg makes the appropriation of military metaphors to new ends more emphatic and more provocative, and points up the sophistication with which this short text sets out to alter existing systems of knowledge and belief.

Yet the construction of women as agents in world politics clearly remained problematic. The visit to Stockholm in June 1915 by one of the two delegations sent from The Hague to bring the resolutions of the Congress to most of the governments of Europe, 'an historic exercise in unofficial international diplomacy' (Wiltsher 1985, 103), resulted in a sixth reportage, charting the itineraries of the delegations, giving the names of some of the statesmen with whom they met, and also indicating some of the positive responses they had. But this reportage also pointed out that the attitude of the world press had hardened; and this would seem to be the likely explanation for the polarisation of the construction of gender in this text, in terms that were new in the context of Wägner's reportages relating to the Congress at The Hague: 'Dessa män [statsmännen] ha därmed erkänt kvinnornas rätt *som släktets mödrar* att säga sin mening och att bli respektfullt lyssnade till, när de uttala sin önskan om fredsslut och sin tanke om vägen till en bestående fred' (Wägner 1915f, 373; my italics) (With this, these men [the statesmen] have acknowledged the right of the women, *as the mothers of the species*, to express their opinion and to be listened to with respect when they voice their desire for peace and their ideas of a route to a lasting peace). Judging from a study of the language of the women at the Congress at The Hague by Harriet Hyman Alonso, Wägner's earlier reportages had been running counter to the types of gender constructions that predominated at The Hague. Alonso's quotations include not just Aletta Jacobs's words about the Congress having been called because 'the mother-heart of woman' had too long 'suffered in silence', but also Jane Addams's phrases from her concluding presidential address, raising the possibility that 'the appeals for the organization of the world upon peaceful lines' had been made 'too exclusively to the man's reason', and that it was time to look to women whose 'urgings to foster life and to protect the helpless' had prepared them for this important work (quoted in Alonso 2003, xxii, xxiii).

The sixth reportage has an epigraph: '"Haagkongressens värf är icke afslutadt, det är blott begynt."' (Wägner 1915f, 373) ("The Task of the Congress at The Hague Has not Been Completed, it Has Just Begun."). This type of '[comment] on the *text*' (Genette 2001, 157;

italics original) points up the prominence of positions for the readers as interpreting subjects in the second half of the reportage, the reference to the familiarity of 'våra läsare' (Wägner 1915f, 373) (our readers) with the resolutions adopted at the Congress underpinning an engagement which turns out to have strongly moral implications as the narrator appeals to the responsibility and duty of the readers to support the work of the women at The Hague.

Wägner's final reportage relating to the Congress at The Hague in *Idun* in 1915, 'Ett vägrödjningsarbete' (Clearing the Road), assesses the situation following the return of both delegations to the Netherlands. One of the sources is a statement from the International Committee of Women for Permanent Peace, established during the Congress and reconfigured in 1919 as the Women's International League for Peace and Freedom, WILPF (Bussey and Tims 1965, 32). The text highlights the three factors I have been teasing out in my analyses above, albeit in slightly different configurations. Positions for interpreting subjects are established from the beginning; the well-informed female reporter becomes prominent in the two paragraphs about the work of the French committee, partly designed to 'borttaga de falska föreställningar, som en dåligt underrättad press lyckats utbreda' (Wägner 1915g, 535) (remove the false notions that a badly informed press has managed to spread); and the agency of women in Sweden is manifested by the successful 'fredssöndag' (Peace Sunday) arranged on 27 June 1915 (Andersson 2001, 96-101), at this point in time about to be copied elsewhere (Wägner 1915g, 535).

In the reportages from the Congress at The Hague, then, the specifically Swedish contexts – economic, political, social, and cultural – become relatively less prominent as the construction of women as agents in world politics takes precedence. The well-informed and ideologically committed female reporter is part of this new community of women on the world stage; and an important aspect of her texts is the creation of new modes of subjectivity and thus the possibility, for her readers, of initiating change. Wägner's reportages from The Hague are made up of the details of debates and resolutions as well as the representations of leading characters, but the texts largely avoid the binary construction of gender that appears to have been prominent in the speeches at the Congress. Despite their preoccupation with a return to peace, these reportages leave the dominant discourse on the family far behind. As I have pointed out, the Congress also resulted in the formation of an international political community of women, the International Committee of Women for Permanent Peace, which in 1919 became the Women's International League for Peace and Freedom. Another new community, *Rädda barnen* (Save the Children), formed in Sweden in 1919, was pivotal to Wägner's spell in Vienna early in 1920 and thus to the series of reportages with an emphasis on the suffering in Vienna that she published in the liberal daily *Dagens Nyheter* in January-May 1920.

Vienna 1920, Dagens Nyheter 1920

In January 1920, Elin Wägner travelled to Vienna to report for *Dagens Nyheter* on the situation of the civilian population in the wake of the break-up of the Austro-Hungarian empire and the economic restrictions imposed by the peace agreement in Saint-Germain (10 September 1919). The first project run by *Rädda barnen*, the organisation founded in Sweden in 1919 on the model of the British Save the Children Fund, was under way in Vienna; and as one of the founders of *Rädda barnen* in autumn 1919 (Isaksson and Linder 2003, 286), Wägner also had a direct interest in this project.

A total of fourteen reportages by Wägner from Germany, Austria, and Hungary were published in *Dagens Nyheter* between January and May 1920. My analysis focuses on a selection dealing wholly or predominantly with conditions in Vienna. Wägner also wrote a novel based on the situation in Vienna, *Den förödda vingården*, and this text, published in October 1920, is analysed in the section on prose fiction below.

The fourteen reportages were all published under Wägner's full name, her name also appearing in five of the headings. By 1920, Wägner was well established both as a journalist and as one of Sweden's leading novelists. Highlighting the significance of the female reporter as an agent in an international context, her reportages from Germany, Austria, and Hungary reinforce the trend from her reportages from the Congress at The Hague in 1915. The narrator emerges as a reporter on the spot, presenting facts and figures gathered from a network of named contacts, a number of whom are also quoted in direct speech. This is also a reporter who meets with leading political figures, including Friedrich Ebert, the President of the Weimar Republic (Wägner 1920a), and Miklós Horthy, the regent of Hungary (Wägner 1920g). There is also an aside revealing that she has met Freud (Wägner 1920h). But while these reportages profile a professional female journalist, issues of gender are comparatively subdued, and there is no hint of the gender polarisation we have traced in some of the reportages from the Congress at The Hague.

How, then, do the reportages from Vienna construct gender and community? Most importantly, these texts construct community negatively, in terms of how it is no longer functioning, and issues of gender are largely superseded by the humanitarian crisis. The war and the suffering in its aftermath have effectively deconstructed the nuclear family. It is against this background that these reportages highlight the significance of the work of the Swedish Save the Children among the suffering children of Vienna – and thus also echo the emphasis on children in texts by Ellen Key, Charlotte Perkins Gilman, and Frida Stéenhoff. With many of the citizens profoundly damaged, psychologically as well as physically, these reportages, like some of the reportages from the Congress at The Hague, insistently pose the question about what kinds of communities and societies the new generations will be able to build. How, the reportages from Vienna are asking, can new generations suffering to such an extent possibly build societies better than those that resulted in the First World War?

I have chosen three reportages relating to/about Vienna which have struck me as particularly interesting with regard to the constructions of gender and community. Prominent in all three texts are non-narrative comments in which ideological statements tend to be made (Bal 1999, 31).

The reportage published in *Dagens Nyheter* on 20 January 1920 had the title 'Människor med eldsjäl i kamp för barnens väl: intryck från

Texts

Genève' (People with Fiery Spirits Fighting for the Well-Being of the Children: Impressions from Geneva), but offers a wealth of material from Austria and Vienna. The narrative begins *in medias res*: 'Medan jag sätter pennan till papperet dunkar hotellmusiken i våningen inunder: "Wien, du Stadt meiner Träume"' (Wägner 1920c) (As I am putting pen to paper, the music from the hotel is thumping on the floor below: 'Vienna, you city of my dreams'). The narratee is constructed as sharing the notion of Vienna as an attractive and sophisticated city only to have this torn apart, for – with a non-narrative comment – 'Wien erbjuder ju [...] det mest skärande exempel på den europeiska situationens orimlighet' (ibid.) (Vienna of course provides [...] the most glaring example of the absurdity of the European situation) as this great city, following the First World War, has become dependent on charity handouts from other nations. Vienna becomes a trope for a Europe that has become dysfunctional as a result of the war and its aftermath. The text piles on the evidence of the suffering of the citizens of Europe, from the Ukraine where epidemics are raging and Czechoslovakia where there are no doctors to Austria where the exchange rate is effectively imprisoning the citizens and cutting off all cultural contacts with other nations. The narratee is interpellated and provoked by the language in which Austria's exclusion from the international community is represented, the narrator referring to 'denna nedpressning av de ruinerade landens kurs som *ett djävulskt påfund*, i sin art fullkomligt ofelbart då det gäller *att mörda ett folk*. Det är *värre än krig*' (ibid.; my italics) (this reduction of the exchange rates of the ruined countries as *a devilish invention,* quite infallible when it comes to *murdering a people.* It is *worse than war*).

There is no doubt here as to the role of what Norman Fairclough has called the 'force', in other words the text's 'actional component, a part of its interpersonal meaning, what it is being used to do socially' (Fairclough 2006, 82), as this reportage prods the reader into awareness about the suffering in much of Europe just after the First World War. And the 'force' of this text crucially hinges on the construction of the narratee. The Congress of Save the Children, meeting in Geneva, has decided to tackle the disastrous effect of the exchange rate:

Man ville mobilisera världssamvetet mot den! Ingen smålog. *Man* gör sådant då *man* sitter tillsammans över det stora nödproblemet och känner strömmarna av klagan rinna från alla håll, känner också att hjälplösa människor hoppas något av *en*. (Wägner 1920c; my italics)

(*They/We* wanted to mobilise against it the conscience of the world. No one smiled. It is the kind of thing *you* do when *you* are sitting together trying to deal with the great problem of suffering, sensing the floods of lamentations from all directions, sensing too that helpless people are putting their hope in *you*.)

Here the English translation cannot do justice to the use of the pronoun *man* (one/you/they/people), traditionally categorised as an indefinite pronoun, although nowadays re-labelled a quantitative pronoun belonging to the sub-category generalising pronouns (Thorell 1973, 96; Hultman 2003, 117, 121-22). In a context such as the one in the quotation, *man* can either include or exclude the speaker/narrator (Hultman 2003, 121), and while the first instance, as I have indicated, is ambiguous in this respect, the second and third, in a sentence that also includes the accusative *en* (one), definitely include the speaker/narrator. And the inclusiveness of *man* does not end here. As Gerald Prince has pointed out, a personal pronoun such as 'we' or an indefinite pronoun can include the narratee (Prince 1996, 221); and in the quotation from Wägner's reportage the element of ambiguity combines with the urgency of the topic to make such a reading highly persuasive. With the opening up of this subject position, the narratee effectively becomes part of 'the conscience of the world', and this bridging of differences and creation of a new sense of unity is reinforced as the text goes on to present some of the key participants of the Congress, participants who come from different backgrounds, nationally, politically, and socially, but whose work has 'gjort dem alla [...] till kamrater' (Wägner 1920c) (made them all [...] comrades). Here issues of gender are largely sidelined as women and men work together to alleviate the suffering, with the reportage also implicating the reader as a contributor to the new community that is emerging from the ruins of the old one. With a quotation from the text in the heading, '"Alla onda drömmars land"' ('The Land of all Evil Dreams'), the reportage published on 3 February 1920 can be seen to allude directly to the text I have just analysed. In the reportage of 3 February, Vienna is explicitly the city where nothing is normal any longer, where 'man går omkring och förgäves väntar att man skall vakna upp till det verkliga livet' (Wägner 1920e) (you go around and wait in vain to wake up to real life). Note again the use of the pronoun *man*. To reinforce the inclusion of the narratee, the text adds a pedagogical example about what would happen if the axis of the earth were to shift, placing the whole of Sweden north of the Arctic Circle: in Austria, the upheaval has been far worse, and in the small republic that is all that remains of the dual empire 'är allt ställt på huvudet' (ibid.) (everything has been turned on its head). As we shall see, the trope of the-world-upside-down is also prominent in some of the prose fiction from 1919-20.

In the reportage of 3 February, the evidence reinforcing the validity of the trope of the-world-upside-down is drawn from the situation of the children. According to the Mayor of Vienna, the city has 300,000 children too many: in other words, conditions are such that there should be no children in Vienna at all. According to the narrator, 99 Viennese homes out of 100 lack the means to look after a child, with the 100th coping only thanks to foreign aid, and the rates of disease and mortality are extremely high. In what remains of the ravaged Wienerwald children gather firewood, including one stunted seventeen-year-old, 'en liten korsbärare' (Wägner 1920e) (a small bearer of his cross) with his burden. In the youth court, starving children who have stolen to eat are on trial, and so too is a boy who has killed his younger sibling because his parents have been unable to feed and clothe another child. The story of this murder is narrated casually, in a single sentence, and so reinforces the trope of the-world-upside-down, but the more prominent device in this text consists of a series of allusions to the Last Judgement and the Apocalypse. One of the four headings of the reportage equates the situation in Vienna with the biblical destruction of Jerusalem, the parallel highlighted in the text being the plight of pregnant women, breast-feeding mothers, and their babies: 've dem som i de dagarna äro havande eller giva di' (ibid.) (This is a free quotation from Matthew 24:19, Mark 13:17 or Luke 21:23; English version, Matthew 24:19: 'And woe unto them that are with child, and to them that give suck in those days!'). The construction of Vienna in early 1920 as the Apocalypse is reinforced by the youth court, with the narrator wishing for a defender at the Last Judgement similar to the one allocated to each of the children. The Bible, according to Northrop Frye – who is focusing on western culture – is 'a major element in our own imaginative tradition', a text '[sitting] [...] in the middle of our cultural heritage' (Frye 1981, xvi-xvii); to use a term from Peter Middleton and Tim Woods, it represents a 'public memorial space' (Middleton and Woods 2000, 5). In Wägner's reportage, the biblical intertexts construct the narratee as a participant in a cultural context familiar throughout the western world. But this reportage which appeared on the front page of Sweden's leading liberal daily on 3 February 1920, also appropriates the biblical parallels for new purposes. The context established by the reportage is markedly secular. The conditions in Vienna and elsewhere in Europe result from the First World War and its aftermath, and as the focus in the text on the children and their suffering is highlighting, the present and the future remain wholly dependent on human agency. As this text is signalling new, more peaceful, and inclusive types of community and society are needed to safeguard the future of the new generations. The biblical intertexts help reinforce the urgency of this joint project as Wägner's text advocates major 'social and cultural change' (Fairclough 2006, 102).

The third and final reportage to be analysed here, 'Mellan tiggaren och miljonpälsen' (Between the Beggar and the Fur Coat Worth a Million), published in *Dagens Nyheter* on 13 March 1920, foregrounds non-narrative comment making an ideological statement (Bal 1999, 31) by opening with a discussion about representation. There are different ways, the narrator explains, of conveying the suffering in Vienna, the most obvious of which is probably the juxtaposition of extreme contrasts. The implication of this narrative approach, however, is that 'den stora kristna tanken: allas lika värde som odödliga själar, är så övergiven och föraktad som aldrig förr' (Wägner 1920h) (the great Christian concept, the equal worth of everyone as an immortal soul, has become abandoned and disdained as never before). In line with the bridge-building foregrounded in some of the previous reportages from Vienna, this text focuses on the suffering of the social categories between the extremes; but as the problematisation of representation in the opening section suggests, the narratee needs to remain alert to the implications of the narrative that follows.

The non-narrative comments making an ideological statement are more emphatic and more explicit in this reportage than in any of the previous ones in the series. Again the pronoun *man* (one/you/they/people) plays a key role, as in the following passage:

> När *man* minns allt *man* tänkt och talat och predikat över krigets förbannelse sen augusti 1914, så var det ju ändå bara stoft och vind, papper och bläck tills *man* nu kom de människor nära som lida under denna förbannelse, vilkas liv blivit stympat, förvandlat och förött för alltid av kriget. (Wägner 1920h; my italics)
>
> (When *you* remember all *you* have thought and spoken and preached about the curse of war since August 1914, this has been mere dust and wind, paper and ink, until now that *you* have got close to the human beings who are suffering under this curse, whose lives have been maimed, reduced and devastated for ever by the war.)

The use of *man* throughout opens up the passage, engages the narratee, and connects the sentence directly to the subsequent one: '*Man* talar så mycket om fredens förbannelse här' (ibid.; my italics) (*One* talks so much here about the curse of peace). While the subject of the second sentence would seem to be the citizens of Vienna, the use of the indefinite pronoun again has the effect of breaking down the boundaries and, in this case, confronting the narratee with the seemingly paradoxical notion of peace as a curse. The bridge-building in this text, which is thus taking place in terms of vocabulary as well as in terms of narrative motifs, can be seen as a means of ensuring the participation of the narratee in the run-up to a new instance of non-narrative comments, a series of maxims. Maxims have not appeared previously in these reportages, nor do they appear in the remaining ones, but here it becomes apparent that the detailed accounts of the endless suffering of the civilian population in Wägner's earlier texts have been preparing the ground for statements such as: 'Det är kriget som gjort Österrikes elände, som är orsaken till att folket inte kan klara den nuvarande situationen' (ibid.) (It is the war that has created Austria's misery, that is the reason why people are unable to cope with the present situation); and 'kriget [har] förstört människorna, tagit deras mod, deras moral, satt upp dem mot varandra, gjort anarkien till en umgängesform, upplöst solidariteten och försvagat deras förnuft' (ibid.) (the war [has] ruined the human beings, deprived them of their courage, their moral standards, pitched them against each other, turned anarchy into a form of social intercourse, dissolved their solidarity, and weakened their common sense). The 'force' of these maxims, then, hinges on the construction of a narratee who engages with the narrative, and on the contribution of a narrator who has 'gått igenom dödsskuggans dal' (ibid.) (gone through the valley of the shadow of death [the reference is to Psalms 23:4]) to put her narrative together. One of the late reportages in the series quotes one of the 'andliga söner' (Wägner 1920l) (spiritual sons) of Bertha von Suttner (1843-1914), the Austrian author of the renowned pacifist novel *Die Waffen nieder!* (1889; *Lay Down Your Arms*, 1892), as saying 'Pacifismus, [...] so, was giebt's nicht mehr' (ibid.) (Pacifism, that doesn't exist any more). As a totality, Wägner's reportages from the Continent in general and from Vienna in particular during the first few months of 1920 comprehensively refute this claim.

*

In conclusion, the reportages relating to/about Vienna in early 1920 are clearly more distant both from the Swedish contexts, economic, political, social, and cultural, and from the dominant discourse on the family than either of the previous clusters about the working woman and the Congress at The Hague. While my selection of reportages is obviously a key factor here, the three clusters I have analysed give a fair indication of the range of reportages available from this early period and point up the decisive impact of the First World War. The pacifism, and the feminist pacifism in particular, foregrounded in the reportages relating to the Congress at The Hague in 1915 and in those relating to Vienna in 1920, can be linked to texts by Olive Schreiner and Charlotte Perkins Gilman considered in the section on alternative discourses on the family above; crucially, Wägner's texts also prominently reconstruct both gender and community. Leading the way, Sweden's new categories of working women marginalise the dominant discourse on the family with its traditional gender roles and community of family members; but as my comparisons between the three clusters of texts have demonstrated, the war gives the new textual constructions of gender and community a special prominence. Yet there is a distinct difference between the construction of female actors and characters as agents in world politics, and thus as members of new communities, in the reportages relating to the Congress at The Hague on the one hand, and the relative sidelining of constructions of gender along with the urgent problematisation of community in the chaos of Vienna on the other. The chaos of Vienna reinforces the structure and precision of the texts relating to the city, with the prominent biblical metaphors in particular adding up to a 'public memorial space' (Middleton and Woods 2000, 5) for a new community of readers. More emphatically than any of the other clusters of reportages, those relating to Vienna foreground the innovative potential of the text.

2. Essays

In a seminal text first published in 1958, Theodor W. Adorno argued that the essay does 'not permit its domain to be prescribed', that 'the effort of the essay reflects a childlike freedom' in its handling of existing material, and that the genre does 'justice to the consciousness of non-identity, without needing to say so, radically un-radical in refraining from any reduction to a principle, in accentuating the fragmentary, the partial rather than the total' (Adorno 1984, 152, 157). There are parallels here with, for example, Ruth-Ellen Boetcher Joeres and Elizabeth Mittman's definitions of the essay in a feminist context: they refer not only to the 'slippery nature of the form', but also to the tendency of the essay to 'enjoy the possibility of digression, of playfulness', and to 'partake of the elliptical, the elusive, the indirect'

(Joeres and Mittman 1993, 16, 17). As considered by Adorno, however, the genre of the essay relates to a specific intellectual framework with the essay, in one summary of his argument, representing 'one of the very few examples – perhaps the *only* possible example – of an unresolved dialectical movement between the two poles of the dichotomy of art and science' (Gualtieri 1998, 50; italics original). The point is that the part of the framework which Adorno emphasises consists almost exclusively of western science and philosophy from the sixteenth century onwards. His reference to the essay as 'accentuating the fragmentary, the partial rather than the total' is followed by a quotation from Georg Lukács on the significance of Montaigne 'ironically' adapting himself to 'the eternal smallness of the most profound work of the intellect in face of life' and highlighting this 'with ironic modesty' by entitling his texts *Essais*; a centre-piece of Adorno's argument, moreover, is that the genre of the essay could be 'interpreted as a protest againt [sic] the four rules that Descartes's *Discourse on Method* sets up at the beginning of modern Western science and its theory' (Adorno 1984, 157-58, 161). Joeres and Mittman have pointed out that women, 'rarely represented in the world of letters at the time of Montaigne and Francis Bacon', could not be expected to 'employ a genre that exuded experience, wisdom, and contemplation, none of which fell within the province of their expected behavior', and that the essay is thus a relatively new genre for women (Joeres and Mittman, 1993, 13). But when they make 'logic' central to their definition of the essay, claiming that '[l]ogic is a vital rhetorical strategy essays use to construct their arguments' (op. cit., 16-17), they do so without problematising, in a gendered context, the significance of the dominant discourse on reason. As Genevieve Lloyd has demonstrated, it is not only the case that 'ideals of Reason' in western philosophy have been defined 'through exclusions of the feminine': as a result of rationality being conceived as 'transcendence of the feminine', the 'feminine' itself 'has been partly constituted by its occurrence within this structure' (Lloyd 1993, 109, 104). In other words, a female writer attempting the genre of the essay would have found herself doubly excluded; and while the chasm separating the genre from a woman's 'expected behavior' has undoubtedly been at least partly bridged since the era of Montaigne and Francis Bacon (Joeres and Mittman 1993, 13), the implicit but close relationship between the genre and the dominant western discourse on reason has remained a potential problem.

During the early phase of Wägner's output with which we are concerned here, there is no doubt that the gendering of reason is an issue in the few texts that can be categorised as essays. In terms of genre categorisation, I have drawn on the basic definition by Joeres and Mittman: 'the essay has at its core an argument that welds its various parts together. Essays make a case for something; they not only present evidence, they also interpret that evidence' (Joeres and Mittman, 16). I also want to foreground the tendency 'to wander around a subject, to investigate various paths toward a point, to enjoy the possibility of digression' (op. cit., 17), along with the corollary that this tendency may add to the blurring of the boundaries of the genre. In the essay, crucially, it is not only the narrator who becomes more prominent as a result, but also the narratee.

The Swedish authority on the genre of the essay, Göran Hägg, whose *Övertalning och underhållning. Den svenska essäistiken 1890-1930* (Persuasion and Entertainment: The Essay in Sweden 1890-1930) appeared in 1978, focused exclusively on volumes of essays and so did not discuss any text by Wägner; what is more remarkable is that despite the fact that his primary material consisted of the work of five male essayists and a single female essayist, he made no attempt to problematise issues of gender. However, in the texts by Wägner from this early period that I have chosen to categorise as essays issues of gender, including the construction of gender, are undoubtedly prominent. The same is true of issues to do with the construction of community – and, by implication, society.

In 1917 Wägner co-edited, with Anna Lenah Elgström and Frida Stéenhoff, a volume entitled *Den kinesiska muren. Rosika Schwimmers kamp för rätten och hennes krig mot kriget* (The Great Wall of China: Rosika Schwimmer's Struggle for Justice and her War against the War). The title alludes to Schwimmer (1877-1948) as one of the leading contemporary women who have 'sökt genombryta den kinesiska mur, som isolerar folken från varandra och gör dem till fientliga horder inbördes' (Elgström, Sahlbom, Stéenhoff and Wägner, 1917, 5) (tried to break through the Great Wall of China that is isolating the peoples from each other and turning them into mutually hostile hordes). Of the ten essays in the volume, Wägner wrote four. With the volume narrating Schwimmer's life with the focus on activism in both the Hungarian and the international women's movement, and more particularly at the Congress at The Hague and in its aftermath, including the attempt in 1915-1916 to set up a structure for continuous mediation, 'Schwimmer' is constructed, in Wägner's essays, as an exceptional female character working in exceptional circumstances. (In the analyses in this section, personal names in inverted commas denote textual constructs.) For obvious reasons, the character of 'Schwimmer' is a rather more complex semantic unit than in the reportage from the Congress at The Hague considered above, and it is possible to discern in these essays all four principles listed by Bal as crucial to the construction of the image of a character: repetition, accumulation, relations to other characters, and transformations (Bal 1999, 125-26). These principles combine to problematise the genderedness of reason as the basis of western civilisation; the urgent need, highlighted by the First World War, for a viable alternative; and the societal implications of such an alternative.

The first of Wägner's essays, 'Katastrofen' (The Disaster), represents 'Schwimmer' in the summer of 1914 as she experiences the outbreak of the First World War in London. While the inclusion of quotations from 'Schwimmer' in combination with the frequent use of the present tense make the representation of the character persuasive and urgent, the most striking aspect is the prominence of the female body and, more particularly, the fusion of body and mind. This representation leaves the reader in no doubt that 'Schwimmer's' efforts to prevent the war from breaking out and then to initiate a process of mediation, required hard thinking, planning, and organisation, but the text emphasises 'Schwimmer's' emotional commitment as the driving force, with the word *hjärta* (heart) as the key word. At a time when many readers would have been familiar with Ellen Key's construction of masculinity and femininity in the complementary terms of the brain and the heart, this essay constructs the character of 'Schwimmer' in terms of a fusion of the two. It is the innovative potential of the fusion of the brain and the heart that is highlighted as Europe on the eve of war has been reduced to a 'hexkittel' (Wägner 1917a, 58) (witches' cauldron), with the war, in 'Schwimmer's' perspective and the narrator's words, 'en följd av att den manliga principen enbart behärskat kulturarbetet' (op. cit., 65) (a consequence of the masculine principle being in sole control of the development of culture). We have encountered this alternative discourse on gender and community/society in texts by Olive Schreiner, Charlotte Perkins Gilman, and Frida Stéenhoff, but a text by Schwimmer in *Jus Suffragii*, the newsletter of The International Alliance of Women, had provocatively described the war as 'den manskapade världens bankrutt' (ibid.) (the bankruptcy of the man-made world), a phrase quoted in this essay. As in some of the reportages from the Congress at The Hague, the narratee is constructed as a key participant in this construction of an alternative femininity; and as soon as the role of the central character's emotional conviction, of her heart, has been foregrounded, the narratee begins to take shape as no less committed to the pacifist effort: 'Tyngdpunkten i hennes [Schwimmers] liv, drivkraften i hennes arbete ha hittills varit tron på möjligheten att forma världen efter *vårt hjärtas* önskan till en mindre hård och orättvis, en lyckligare värld' (op. cit., 60-61; my italics) (The point of gravity in her [Schwimmer's] life, the driving force in her work, have so far been her belief in the possibility of shaping the world, in accordance with the desire of *our heart*, into a world that is less harsh and unjust, into one that is happier). The narratee becomes still more prominent in the second of the essays, 'Erövringen av Amerika' (The Conquest of America), in which the fusion of body and mind is epitomised by 'Schwimmer's' voice, the glimpse of the frankness with which it is able to convey the horrors of war culminating in a direct appeal to the individual listener that insistently engages the narratee too: '[V]ad gör du? – Jag kan ingenting göra. – Jo, du kan det' (Wägner 1917b, 78) ([W]hat will you do? I can't do anything. Yes, you can).

The impact of this alternative construction of femininity is developed briefly in conjunction with an alternative construction of masculinity in 'Underverket' (The Miracle). The story of the cooperation between Schwimmer and Henry Ford (1863-1947) has been told by Anne Wiltsher (Wiltsher 1985, 154-75), and in retrospect questions about this venture are bound to arise, not least because of the approximate coincidence with the introduction of Fordism (which David Harvey has dated to 1914), and Ford's efforts (with Harvey's example dating from 1916) to ensure that 'the "new man" of mass production' would be able to 'live up to corporate needs and expectations' (Harvey 2001, 125, 126). But this is not the place to try to tease out the ideological differences between Rosika Schwimmer and Henry Ford. My focus here is on the representations in Wägner's essay of these two participants in the venture, and in this perspective there is no doubt that their cooperation amounts to something new. In the context of the war with its continuing slaughter a strongly engaged narratee is again constructed: '*Man* kan föreställa sig R. S:s känslor' (Wägner 1917c, 139; my italics) (*We* can imagine R. S.'s feelings); 'Det var *ju* hennes övertygelse' (ibid.; my italics) (*As we know*, she was convinced). The early section of the essay constructs a 'Rosika Schwimmer' haunted by a mounting sense of crisis as president Wilson, expected to head the efforts of the neutral states to initiate a process of mediation, refuses to see her, and against this background the understanding between 'Schwimmer' and 'Ford' emerges as a miracle. 'Schwimmer's' suggestions to 'Ford' are presented in direct speech with a string of imperatives: 'Finansiera en neutral konferens. Men gör mera! Res själv till Europa' (op. cit., 145) (Finance a neutral conference. But do more! Travel to Europe yourself). In a passage in which 'Ford' emerges as a character and not just an actor, his innovative thinking is charted by the narrator, the key term being *förnuftigt* (sensible, rational):

> Och mr Ford lyssnar till detta förslag, han tycker det är *förnuftigt* [...]. Han tänker inte: detta är ett förslag av en våghalsig optimist. Det faller honom icke in, emedan han själv är en man som lyckats på ett fabelaktigt sätt. Han är en människovän, något av en fantasimänniska kanske. (op. cit., 145-46; my italics)

> (And Mr Ford listens to this proposal, he finds it *sensible* [...]. He does not think: this is a proposal by a foolhardy optimist. It does not occur to him, because he himself is a man who has succeeded in a fabulous way. He is a friend of humanity, perhaps a person with quite a lively imagination.)

There is a glimpse here of a new dispensation, one that is based not just on a femininity combining emotion and reason but also on a masculinity constructed in similar terms, with scope not just for reason but for the emotions, the imagination. This essay consistently links to 'Schwimmer's' project the term *fantasi* (imagination), and continues to do so in a conclusion that not only echoes the powerful statement about 'vårt hjärtas önskan' (Wägner 1917a, 60-61) (the desire of our heart) in the opening essay, but that unites humankind in what is constructed as its innermost desire for peace: 'Det var hennes [Schwimmers] övertygelse, att man endast kunde fånga den lidande mänsklighetens fantasi genom att formulera klart och utan räddhåga dess innersta önskan till ett program: avrustning!' (Wägner 1917c, 159-60) (It was her [Schwimmer's] conviction that the only way to capture the imagination of the suffering humanity was to formulate, clearly and without fear, its innermost desire into a programme: disarmament!).

Although Schwimmer's and Ford's joint project failed, this text establishes a space for a collaborative venture based on alternative constructions of femininity and masculinity, with a new, peaceful society as the goal. In the fourth and last of the essays on Schwimmer, her contribution is authorised by means of a quotation, an intertext gesturing towards communities of narratees. '"Se drömmaren kommer där, låtom oss slå honom ihjäl"' (Wägner 1917d, 272) ('Behold, there the dreamer is coming, come and let us slay him') is an approximate quotation from Genesis 37, 19-20 ('Behold, the dreamer cometh. Come now therefore, and let us slay him'), but the biblical allusion was also familiar from a poem by Gustaf Fröding ('Si drömmaren kommer där [...]/kommer och låter oss slå'n!' [behold, the dreamer is coming (...)/come and let us strike him] [Fröding 1902, 88]). While we may be justified in discerning a pointer in the fact that the biblical lines about a male dreamer are applied to a female character, the central metaphor of the final text, that of 'Schwimmer's' perspective on the world as a tree which, although toppled by the outbreak of war, remains alive because its roots are 'sammantvinnade med hennes hjärtas fibrer' (Wägner 1917d, 271-72) (intertwined with the fibres of her heart) and is continuing to send up new shoots, ensures that the fusion of emotions and mind epitomised by the character of

'Schwimmer' remain in focus. 'Schwimmer' did not succeed, but she indicated how and where a new start could be made.

Two years after the publication of the volume in honour of Schwimmer, Wägner contributed to a volume in honour of Ellen Key on her seventieth birthday. According to one source – but not according to the title page – Wägner also co-edited this volume (Claréus 1981, 9). The contributors included, among others, Romain Rolland, Selma Lagerlöf, Havelock Ellis, Georg Brandes, and Hjalmar Söderberg. Entitled 'De tre kraven. Ett kapitel om Ellen Key och kvinnosaken' (The Three Requirements: A Chapter about Ellen Key and the Women's Cause), Wägner's essay has been read as confirmation that the author, despite earlier disagreements, was siding with Key, her position necessitated by the character of the volume (ibid.). I am offering a different reading. This essay engages not just with the division between the body and reason that underpins so much of western civilisation and that determined Key's writing on femininity, masculinity, and the dominant discourse on the family: it also engages with the issue of the feminine as partly constituted by its occurrence within a structure in which, in Genevieve Lloyd's phrase, 'rationality [is] being conceived as transcendence of the feminine' (Lloyd 1993, 104).

Contrary to the reactions to Key's *Missbrukad kvinnokraft* (1896 [the year incorrectly given as 1895, Wägner 1919a, 133]), Wägner's essay suggests that the representation in Key's text of woman as the gender with access to 'mystiska krafter till släktets omdaning och förnyelse' (op. cit., 148) (mysterious powers for the transformation and innovation of the race) has been highly influential:

> Detta är du, detta kan du bli, sade Ellen Key, blott du icke söker spränga ditt väsens gränser, utan söker dig in i dig själv. Mannens erfarenheter, höjder och djup kan du ändå inte nå eller mäta. Söker du likna honom, mister du dig själv. Antingen – eller. Välj. (ibid.)

> (This is you, this you can become, Ellen Key said, as long as you do not attempt to shatter the boundaries of your being but try to find your way into your own self. The man's experiences, heights and depths you still will not be able to reach or measure. If you try to become like him, you will lose yourself. Either – or. Make your choice.)

Texts

The point is that the texts by 'Key', '[h]on, som har så skarp blick för hjärtats och hjärnans konflikter hos den begåvade kvinnan' (op. cit., 156) (she who has such a sharp eye for the conflicts between the heart and the brain in the intelligent woman), and who, in the quotation above, opens up possibilities by engaging the narratee by means of direct discourse as well as direct address, have reinforced the gendered division between the heart and the brain. While surmounting this division at the textual level, these texts with their emphasis on the significance of motherhood and 'natural' areas of work for women have effectively confirmed the connection between the heart and the feminine. As in the case of 'Schwimmer' in the essays discussed above, the bridging of the symbolic roles of the heart and the brain is constructed as fundamental to the contribution of 'Key' too, but the difference is that *the effect* of 'Key's' contribution has been to reconfirm this division rather than to continue bridging it. In urging women to find their way into their selves, *Missbrukad kvinnokraft* has been constructing femininity solely in terms of the heart.

But the narrator of Wägner's text offers an alternative. Wägner's essay gradually brings the professional woman into focus, as in the narratorial comment on the 'Ellen Key' who, as a young child, was playing at being a mother: 'Denna utpräglat kvinnliga och moderliga natur måste ju stå i viss mån främmande för *kvinnornas strävan efter intellektuell utbildning och intellektuella segrar samt ekonomiskt lönande karriärer*' (Wägner 1919a, 133; my italics) (Clearly, the *women's striving for an intellectual education and intellectual victories and careers that would pay a decent salary* must to some extent have been alien to this markedly feminine and motherly character). Contrary to Key's construction of femininity in terms of either – or, the argument developed in this essay constructs femininity in terms of both – and. And against the backdrop of the presentation of *Missbrukad kvinnokraft* as a 'stridsskrift', 'författad efter ensamma kontemplationer' (op. cit., 140) (a polemical pamphlet, written following lonely contemplation), Wägner's text stands out as dialogic, an array of strategies establishing a narratee who is strongly engaged and participatory, a partner in the argument developed by the narrator. The adverb *ju* (clearly, of course) in the quotation above contributes towards the construction of a narratee who is involved and engaged, as does the prominent use of the pronouns *man* (one/you/they/people) and *vi* (we), along with a number of questions such as, 'Vilken är då kvinnornas uppgift [...]? / Jo, svarar Ellen Key [...]' (op. cit., 138) (What, then, is the task of women [...]? / It is, Ellen Key replies [...]). The quotations from 'Key' and from her opponents as well as her supporters add to the dialogic openness of the text, with the alternative epigraph proposed for Key's text, 'ingen kan tjäna två herrar' (op. cit., 137-38) (no man can serve two masters), a quotation from Matthew 6:24, adding to the dialogism of Wägner's text. Wägner's essay, in other words, develops a narrator that foregrounds a construction of femininity which, contrary to that of Key, combines the heart and the brain. The alternative femininity in Wägner's essay is logical and rational and also ideologically committed, the dialogic openness of the text pointing to the significance of networking with other women. In my reading, it is the dialogic exchange running through this essay that allows the narrator to keep the reader in suspense for so long with regard to the meaning of the title of the text; for in what might be perceived as a reversal of the structure of the traditional scholarly article, Wägner's essay only begins to engage explicitly with 'De tre kraven' of the title in the concluding third of the text.

Contrary to the claim that Wägner in this essay is siding with Key (Claréus 1981, 9), I am arguing that this text is in effect developing a narratee with a double pair of spectacles. While there is no doubt as to the significance of the heart in 'Key's' construction of femininity, the narrator establishes an alternative construction of which the narratee, by implication, is also part. The doubleness is in place when the narrator poses a question such as 'Hon [Key] har också fört in kvinnoarbetet på nya banor?' (Wägner 1919a, 147) (She [Key] has also channelled women's work in new directions?); and when the narrator assesses the relevance and impact of the construction of femininity in Key's text:

> Kvinnan kände blott föga igen sig i denna bild. Varken hon själv eller den värld hon levde i stämde med Ellen Keys teckning. Men bilden fascinerade ändå. Den dröjde kvar i minnet och påverkade hennes egen värdering, hennes eget mål. (op. cit., 148)

> (Woman did not recognise much of herself in this image. Neither she nor the world in which she was living corresponded to Key's outline. But the image fascinated her nevertheless. It stayed in her mind and affected her assessment of herself, her own goal.)

This doubleness is particularly marked in the section on 'Key' and the First World War, which contrasts 'Key's' pacifist commitment with her scepticism as regards the efforts of the pacifists: 'Hon hoppades och hoppas väl ännu på hjärtanas förvandling genom lidandet, på att den kränkta moderligheten skulle söka sig sublimare och farligare uttryck än resolutioner och föreningsagitation' (op. cit., 150) (She was hoping and is probably still hoping that the hearts will be transformed by suffering, that the violated motherliness will develop more sublime and dangerous manifestations than resolutions and the agitation of associations).

'Key's' contribution, this essay concludes, has been unique, having achieved a synthesis of the heart and the brain in the sense that her intellectual work has given her a family of readers and admirers, of 'barn över allt i världen' (Wägner 1919a, 155) (children all over the world). But the narrator favours the alternative construction of femininity exemplified by the professional woman and – by implication – the alternative communities emerging as a result of the active contributions of these women. The text reinforces the significance of the economically active woman – and demolishes the corner-stones of Key's construction of femininity at the same time – by expanding, towards the end, on an alternative strand in the women's movement, exemplified by Olive Schreiner and her warnings about women who lack employment lapsing into parasitism; by Charlotte Perkins Gilman (her surname spelled incorrectly) and her argument that housework should be rationalised to give women more time for paid employment; and by Rosa Mayreder and her claim that the notion that women should devote all their energies to the upbringing of their children is mistaken (op. cit., 152-53). While celebrating 'Key', Wägner's essay develops not just a critique but alternative constructions, the emergence of femininity in terms of the heart and the brain dependent on an involvement of the narratee that points towards new communities and, by extension, a new society.

*

The greater complexity of the essay in comparison with the reportage, in combination with my selection of essays, has highlighted the many facets of the central characters in the texts considered above. Constructions of gender are foregrounded in the essays about Rosika Schwimmer and Ellen Key, and the prominent fusion in all five texts of the heart and the brain, which in the binary construction of gender of the dominant discourse were distinctly feminine and masculine respectively, amounts to an innovation and a challenge. Given the history of the essay as a genre steeped in reason and relatively new to women, the representation of both characters as at once heart and brain can also be read as a challenge to and an appropriation of the genre. There is just a glimpse here of a similarly innovative construction of masculinity, the character of 'Henry Ford' in one of the essays about Schwimmer, and the construction of new communities is largely by extension and implication. The complexity of these texts with their affinities with prose fiction, including the construction of the central characters in terms of repetition, accumulation, relations to other characters, and transformations (Bal 1999, 125-26), which here entails the use of for instance direct discourse and direct address to the narratee, makes for narratees who are strongly engaged and thus, by implication, for prominent new communities of readers.

3. Light-Hearted Columns

The light-hearted column tends to be defined as a mixed and transgressive genre. Magnus Fernberg, who has traced the history of the light-hearted column in the Swedish press from the nineteenth century onwards, has pointed to its affinities with both fiction and the daily press, and to its dual aim of entertaining and influencing (Fernberg 2004, 33-36, 5). Birgitta Ney in her study of Lotten Ekman, a woman journalist active during the first decade of the twentieth century and engaged in 'the woman question', has argued that the light-hearted column offered Ekman much greater freedom than the news journalism that dominated her work: 'It would appear that those reflections, opinions, and thoughts that, in her role as a reporter, she felt she had to keep back or at least under control in her news journalism, she was able to express more freely in the form of light-hearted columns or ironical turns of phrase in her articles' (Ney 1999, 78). To what extent, then, does representation in Wägner's light-hearted columns differ from representation in the reportages and the essays, and to what extent can we expect to find alternative constructions of gender and community? We need to approach these questions in the light of Fernberg's observation that the reader is prominent in the light-hearted column and frequently takes on the role of co-creator (Fernberg 2004, 3). How do co-creating readers, themselves forming (gendered) communities, impact on the constructions of gender and community in these texts? And how do these readers relate to the narratees in Wägner's light-hearted columns?

Wägner wrote two series of light-hearted columns. *Klubben* (The Club), written for the weekly *Puck*, was published 8 May – 5 October 1907, and *Fru Hillevis dagbok* (Mrs Hillevi's Diary), written for *Idun*, was published between January 1911 and March 1912. The latter is the more substantial, with individual instalments frequently taking up a full three-column page in *Idun*.

According to Karl Lindqvist, series of light-hearted columns became common in the Swedish press around the turn of the century 1900 (Lindqvist 1980, 88). In Lindqvist's definition, the series of light-hearted columns draws on current events as perceived and commented on by a number of recurring characters (ibid.). In terms of Bal's distinction between actors and characters the series of light-hearted columns, then, tends to operate with 'complex semantic [units]' rather than with mere 'structural [positions]' (Bal 1999, 115) – but, I would add, with scope for a considerable amount of variation. And while the references to current events would have added to the appeal of the series of light-hearted columns at the time, they have of course ensured that these texts quickly lost their relevance. A series of light-hearted columns would also have to be entertaining. Texts categorised as belonging to this sub-genre have commonly been regarded as slight and insignificant, especially if the author, as in the case of Wägner, has also produced texts such as novels.

Ulla Isaksson and Erik Hjalmar Linder have read the series of light-hearted columns from a narrowly biographical perspective. *Klubben*, they claim, is of interest because it combines two types of female characters which they label 'incarnations' of the author (Isaksson and Linder 2003, 121-23), and *Fru Hillevis dagbok* offers insights into the early years of Wägner's marriage to John Landqvist and her work for women's suffrage (op. cit., 205-207). In the context of the present study, *Klubben* and *Fru Hillevis dagbok* are interesting because they constitute a new type of textual space, different from those provided by the reportage, the essay, or the prose fiction. The combination of references to current events and material that is clearly fictitious results in a sub-genre that is conspicuously transgressive, and the element of repetition enhanced by the serial publication foregrounds the role of performativity. Both features are pivotal to the constructions of gender and community.

Klubben (The Club)

The magazine *Puck*, the title echoing the famous *Punch*, was published in Stockholm 1896-1898 and again 1901-1916, and had a distinctly masculine profile. The cartoons focused on gentlemen and military men, while women tended to be depicted as old and/or ugly – or at least this was the case in the year in which *Puck* ran Wägner's series of light-hearted columns. It was quite different from the types of publications with which Wägner was chiefly to be associated during her career; and she was in fact standing in for a colleague at *Puck* at the time (Lindqvist 1980, 87).

According to Karl Lindqvist, to my knowledge the only scholar to have considered *Klubben* in some detail, this text gradually abandons the critique of contemporary society that Wägner was aiming for, in favour of a focus on eroticism and love (Lindqvist 1980, 89-91). It is true that there are aspects of this text and its publication that seem to signal an adaptation to the profile and readership of *Puck*, from the promise in the first instalment of *Klubben* as 'ett slags modern Decameron, fast tamare' (Wägner 1907a) (a kind of modern

Decamerone, but more tame), to the vignette of the four recurring characters, two men and two women gathered around bottles and glasses and with both female characters smoking, and last but not least to Wägner's signature which, uniquely, consists of a drawing of a wasp ready to sting. Everything points to *Klubben* being *risqué*, but this does not mean that the adaptation to the profile of *Puck* is necessarily total. In my reading, *Klubben* is bolder and more challenging than has been observed hitherto.

The meetings of The Club, usually at restaurants in Stockholm, are the focal points of the fifteen instalments, but there are a number of variations with the members, come July, leaving the capital for a hotel in the countryside. Some of the instalments focus on just two of the characters. Whatever the combinations, they are clearly far removed from the dominant discourse on the family. Relationships develop between Fröken Julie (Miss Julie) and the journalist on the one hand, and between Vera and *medicinaren* (the medical student/ physician) on the other; and Lindqvist has contrasted the latter relationship with the former, emphasising that Miss Julie and the journalist 'merely talk' (Lindqvist 1980, 90). But these conversations between the male and female characters are the key feature of this series of light-hearted columns. The foregrounding of dialogue, of many voices in this text which uses the diary format but eschews character-bound narration, enhances the openness of the textual space constituted by each instalment; as Bal has underlined, '[t]he more dialogue a narrative text contains, the more dramatic that text is' (Bal 1999, 60). And when this series of light-hearted columns alludes to current events the instances go well beyond for example the airships which are mentioned in one instalment (Wägner 1907k) and were a central topic in that particular issue of *Puck*. The current events also include issues of gender, with a special emphasis on constructions of femininity. Vera, the *ingénue*, and more particularly Miss Julie, 'kvinnan med ett förflutet, om man fick tro henne själf' (Wägner 1907a) (the woman with a past, if one were to believe her), emerge in terms that problematise the constructions of femininity that were not only predominant in *Puck*, but that were also those of the dominant discourse on gender.

Half-way through *Klubben*, the exasperated medical student/physician who has just had a quarrel with Vera, asks the journalist, '*Hurudana är kvinnorna?*' (Wägner 1907h; italics original) (*What are women really like?*). While the construction of the two female characters in terms of the stereotypical experienced woman and the similarly stereotypical inexperienced one defines them in terms of their relations with men (in relationships that are unambiguously heterosexual), the recurring instances throughout *Klubben* of role-play foreground mimicry and performativity. This is most elaborate in the case of Miss Julie. For not only is her name explained in terms of a reversal of the roles in Strindberg's drama *Fröken Julie* (1888; *Miss Julie*) which famously concludes with Jean sending Miss Julie away to commit suicide: Miss Julie in *Klubben*, by contrast, has stood idly by while a man has shot himself (Wägner 1907l). In the very first instalment, moreover, Miss Julie is introduced as a woman with a passion for beautiful clothes (Wägner 1907a), i.e. the character is constructed in terms of costumes and disguises; and when she writes to the journalist from the hotel, she emphasises how she, born and bred in rural Sweden, has become popular by pretending to be ignorant of life outside the city (Wägner 1907n). In the latter instalment, she also reveals that her real names – so she claims – are Fredrika Amalia (ibid.). I am unable to agree with Lindqvist when he states that Miss Julie is 'the same' from the beginning of this series of light-hearted columns to the end (Lindqvist 1980, 90). On the contrary, it seems to me that Miss Julie can usefully be read in terms of mimicry as defined by Luce Irigaray, according to whom playing with mimesis, for a woman, is tantamount to '[trying] to recover the place of her exploitation by discourse, without allowing herself to be simply reduced to it' (Irigaray 1993, 76). While Miss Julie, as 'the woman with a past' and a modern life-style, might at first sight appear simply to try to emulate the male characters, a reading in Irigarayan terms shows up not just the constructedness of femininity (and, by implication, masculinity), but also, as Miss Julie emerges as the product of role-play, the power relations underpinning the dominant discourse on gender. In *Klubben*, the male characters tellingly gesture towards this connection in the short exchange sparked off by the medical student's/physician's, *'Hurudana är kvinnorna?'* (*What are women really like?*):

– Fråga den, som skapat dem, uppmanade journalisten.
– Ja, men då måste man vara säker på hvem som är den skyldige.
(Wägner 1907h)

('Ask whoever created them,' said the journalist.
'Well, then you've got to be sure who's the guilty one.')

The constructedness of gender in terms of power relations holds the possibility of change. And when Vera announces, in the final instalment, that she is no longer an *ingénue* and that, indeed, her lifestyle now surpasses that of Miss Julie, the significance of the radicalisation of gender represented by Miss Julie is reinforced still further.

As a series of light-hearted columns, *Klubben* represents an ephemeral genre, but as I have tried to demonstrate, the text is considerably more enterprising and interesting than has been observed previously. The adaptation to the masculine profile of *Puck*, in other words, is no more than superficial: *Klubben* is in fact an unusually bold and challenging text to have found its way on to the pages of this magazine.

Fru Hillevis dagbok (Mrs Hillevi's Diary)

Fru Hillevis dagbok (Mrs Hillevi's Diary) was published in *Idun* in 15 substantial instalments between January 1911 and March 1912. Again, this text is characterised by frequent references to current events, for example the death of the poet Gustaf Fröding on 8 February 1911 (Wägner 1911d), the collection towards a gift from the nation to August Strindberg in 1912 (Wägner 1911l; see also Rinman 1967, 141-42), and the award of the Nobel Prize for Chemistry to Marie Curie (Wägner 1911n). The second instalment introduces 1911 as 'Kongressåret' (Wägner 1911b) (the year of Congresses): this was the year when Stockholm hosted the Sixth Congress of the International Woman Suffrage Alliance in June and, in September, the Congress of the International Council of Women. The campaign for suffrage for women and the efforts to improve gender equality in the work place are recurring topics in *Fru Hillevis dagbok*. The main characters apart from Hillevi, middle-class and recently married, are Fanny, her sisterin- law; Madeleine, her cousin; Dr Alva Grat, her former teacher; and Paul, Hillevi's husband and a legal expert holding a government position.

In the character-bound narration of *Fru Hillevis dagbok* there are greater variations with regard to register and style than in *Klubben*, from Mrs Hillevi's private meditations to her coffee shop conversations with Fanny and Madeleine. The instalment about Fröding is a eulogy complete with quotations from Fröding's poetry, while Dr Grat challenges the dominant discourse on gender in contributions at once well-informed and sharp. The narratee constructed by this text is not only up-to-date on current events: s/he is also capable of decoding texts of different types and an alert and sensitive reader of prose fiction. *Fru Hillevis dagbok* is also an unsettled and unsettling text, for while this series of light-hearted columns appeared to have been concluded with instalment No. 14, published on 24 December 1911, an additional instalment was published on 3 March 1912, and since this final instalment was in the form of a drama, the narratee was radically reconstructed in terms of a different genre.

Wägner had a high profile in the Swedish women's suffrage movement and was also Assistant Editor of *Idun* at the time when *Fru Hillevis dagbok* appeared, and there is no doubt that this series of lighthearted columns, published at least initially under a pseudonym (Hillevi), played a role in the context of establishing textual roles and voices. While Wägner wrote in *Idun* under her own name about the Congress of the International Woman Suffrage Alliance in June 1911 and left *Fru Hillevis dagbok* in abeyance throughout the summer (28 May – 17 September), she restricted her writing on the Congress of the International Council of Women to her series of light-hearted columns. In the reading of Isaksson and Linder, *Fru Hillevis dagbok* was designed to appeal to '*Idun*'s "ordinary woman"' (Isaksson and Linder 2003, 206), although Bertil Björkenlid has argued that Mrs Hillevi is in fact quite a complex character (Björkenlid 1982, 235-37). In the context of the present study, *Fru Hillevis dagbok* is interesting in terms of its affinity with prose fiction, with the text constituting textual spaces that problematise constructions of both gender and community. Underpinning the potential of the textual spaces is the effect of serial publication of prose fiction highlighted by Linda K. Hughes and Michael Lund, who have argued that the appearance of women in the literary market in the nineteenth century in combination with the emergence of serial fiction inspired a new type of (female) reader relationship, with serial publication likely to have 'worked to extend female readers' associations of pleasure with renewed and sustained relationships, as they met and came to know characters in part after part' (Hughes and Lund 1995, 145). From a Butlerian perspective, serialisation also reinforces the significance of gender and gendered subjectivity as performative (Butler 2006, 189-93).

Fru Hillevis dagbok offers a neat illustration of the phenomenon that Rachel Blau DuPlessis has termed 'writing beyond the ending', the 'consistent project that unites some twentieth-century women writers across the century' and that involves the 'scrutiny, critique, and transformation' of the romance plot (DuPlessis 1985, 4). In the first instalment Paul, learning of his wife's plan to keep a diary, objects that it is too late: 'Om det varit för ett par tre år sen, då var lifvet väl ganska spännande för dig, *men nu är du gift, pang, och sedan är det inte mera*' (Wägner 1911a; my italics) (If it had been three years ago or so, then I suppose life would have been quite exciting for you, *but now you are married, bang, and that's the end of it*). The dominant discourse on gender is again spelled out at a dinner party at which Mrs Hillevi is lectured by a civil servant who emphasises that 'kvinnan har en gång sitt martyrskap gifvet. Tror ni, min unga fru, att rösträtt och förvaltningsrätt öfver egendom, ansökningsrätt till professur och förhöjd semester kan ta det från henne?' (Wägner 1911g) (woman has had her martyrdom allocated to her once and for all. Madam, do you believe that the right to vote and the right to manage property, the right to apply for professorships and an extended holiday entitlement will relieve her from this?); and the document drafted by a group of upper middle-class women hostile to the campaign for women's suffrage begins: 'Det stora flertalet af kvinnor önska icke bli indragna i det offentliga lifvet, därtill akta de sin uppgift som maka och hemmets vårdarinna alltför högt' (Wägner 1911j) (The great majority of women have no desire to be drawn into public life; they value their duties as wives and preservers of the home much too highly to want to do so).

In the face of these explicit constructions of women as objects, the character-bound narrative of Mrs Hillevi's text provides a series of subject positions for its female characters, the high proportion of dialogue helping to foreground the significance of processes and open-endedness. The position closest to the dominant discourse on femininity is represented by Madeleine, 'den sista sanna kvinnan' (Wägner 1911c) (the last true woman), the phrase an echo of the similarly ironical title of Anne-Charlotte Leffler's (1849-1892) drama *Sanna kvinnor* (1883; True Women); in Madeleine's case, her frustrated expectations of love have reduced her to a tragic figure. A different subject position is represented by Dr Alva Grat, Hillevi's former teacher and a politician and activist in the women's movement. To Hillevi, she is 'den människa, kring hvilken hela arbetet rör sig' (Wägner 1911f) (the human being on whom the entire project is centred), but also someone who 'innerst hvilar i sig själf' (ibid.) (in the last instance relies on her inner strength); and when Alva Grat challenges Paul's misogynism, including his repeated claim that 'Hillevi har det ju bra, som det är' (ibid.) (Hillevi is of course comfortable as she is), she does so knowledgeably and persuasively. A more volatile subject position, at times close to role-play, is associated with Fanny. Getting ready for a party, she can be 'fullkomlig i sin genre, [...] den salta oliven vid alla fester' (Wägner 1911e) (perfect in her genre, [...] the salty olive at all parties); but she also argues for women's rights; and her decision to marry is based on her conviction that all men are much the same: 'Samma deg, kära Hillevi' (Wägner 1911h) (Same paste, dear Hillevi), she tells her sister-in-law over a cup of coffee while they are effectively reducing Fanny's eligible candidates to pieces of pastry.

But it is Mrs Hillevi herself who contributes the most sophisticated problematisation of subject positions, gender, and gendered subjectivity. It is not only the metatextual dimensions of her diary that are highlighted by the instalments devoted to Fröding and Strindberg respectively: in the latter, the discussion arises from readings of

Strindberg quite different from the established ones. Mrs Hillevi's text creates a space for the exploration of gender as constructed; but in line with Suzanne Bunkers's argument that the diary constructs life not as a product but as a process (quoted in Hogan 1991, 98), Mrs Hillevi's diary entries foreground not just 'life' but subjectivity as processual and, indeed, textual. Mrs Hillevi starts writing just an hour or so into the new year, aware not just of the uncertainty of the future but also of her limited perspective of her past:

> Hvar gick jag, hvad ledde mig, hur kom jag dit jag står? Ser jag lugnt och länge tillbaka, då dyker ju milstolparna upp ur töcknet, och jag minns deras skrift. Men hvar är vägen mellan dem, hvar är sammanhanget? Hvart flög mina tankar, skref jag dem på vattnen? (Wägner 1911a)

> (Where did I go, what led me, how did I get to where I am? If I look back, calmly and persistently, then the mileposts will emerge from the mist and I will remember the inscriptions on them. But where is the path between them, where are the connections? In what directions did my thoughts fly, did I write them in water?)

In terms parallel to those in the diary novel *Norrtullsligan*, Mrs Hillevi equates herself with her text. The comparison in the instalment about Marie Curie and the Nobel Prize between radium and that which is unique to each individual, 'ett ämne som fälles ut, icke i laboratoriet, men med omätlig kostnad ur dagarnas mängd i lefvandets mödosamma process' (Wägner 1911n) (a substance that is precipitated, not in the laboratory but at immeasurable cost from the sequence of days in the difficult process of living), might suggest a metaphysical dimension, but the immediate reference is to the significance of the central character, Mrs Hillevi, as a texual construct. The constructedness opens up the possibilities for alternatives and change, with regard to community and society as well as gender; and although *Fru Hillevis dagbok* is a series of light-hearted columns and not a novel in instalments, sections of the text gesture towards the capacity of prose fiction.

Founded in 1887, *Idun* celebrated its first twenty-five years in 1912 and marked the occasion with a series of articles on contemporary Swedish society and culture. One of these was 'Verkliga skäl för kvinnans rösträtt och skenbara' (Genuine Reasons for Women's Suffrage and Apparent Ones), written by Vitalis Norström and published on 18 February 1912. Norström (1856-1916) was Professor of Philosophy at Göteborgs Högskola and a member of the Swedish Academy, and his article, an attack on 'the third sex' (the phrase taken from the title of a novel by the German writer Ernst von Wolzogen, *Das Dritte Geschlecht*, 1899) and its demands for equal rights for women, concluded by likening suffrage for women to a leap into the dark: 'Man *kan* falla på det torra och, om man det gör, *kan* det hända att man inte slår ihjäl sig' (Norström 1912, 103; italics original) (You *may* end up on dry land and, if you do, it *may* be that you won't get killed). For the response to Norström – and in a move that quite literally took the writing beyond the ending – *Fru Hillevis dagbok* was revived, and on 3 March *Idun* published an instalment subheaded 'Tredje könet håller möte' (A Meeting of the Third Sex). Written in the form of a drama, the text focuses on a large group of women including Dr Alva Grat, Fanny, and Hillevi as well as a number of new actors plus anonymous voices, who are having tea and sandwiches following a meeting about a proposal to erect a statue of Fredrika Bremer (1801- 1865), an internationally renowned author and a pioneer in the campaign for women's rights in Sweden. With the name of a hero from Johan Ludvig Runeberg's *Fänrik Ståls sägner* (1848-60; The Tales of Ensign Steel), the iconic text about Finland's struggle against Russia in 1808-09, appropriated for one of the women characters leading the attack on Norström's article, 'Adlercreutz' is asked to read out key passages from his text while Dr Grat as chairperson tries to maintain order among the angry audience. In this hilarious yet serious coda to *Fru Hillevis dagbok*, Norström's arguments are not just deconstructed but demolished, reduced by anonymous voices in the audience to 'det där nonsens' (Wägner 1912a) (that nonsense). Rosi Braidotti has referred to 'the perversely monological mental habits of phallocentrism' (Braidotti 1994, 1-2); and the drama format of the final instalment not only ensures that Norström's monological diatribe is overwhelmed at the textual level, but also reinforces the significance of dialogue and polyvocality throughout *Fru Hillevis dagbok*. When Mrs Hillevi is asked to give the reason why women want suffrage and

Texts

so gets to speak the final line, 'Därför att vi är människor vi också' (Wägner 1912a) (Because we, too, are human beings), her words do not merely summarise the retort to Norström's article but also point towards the problematisation of gendered subjectivity that is such a central dimension of this series of light-hearted columns.

*

The growing prominence of the genre of the light-hearted column in the Swedish press in the early years of the twentieth century needs to be seen in the context of economic, social, and cultural changes which resulted in new categories of readers. It is significant that one of the series of light-hearted columns considered above was published in a magazine with a predominantly male readership, while the other was published in one whose readership was predominantly female.

The series of light-hearted columns analysed here were produced and published prior to the essays discussed in the previous section and prior to the two main clusters of reportages in the section before. These light-hearted columns were written well before the outbreak of the First World War, and so the relevant contexts are national rather than international. But in comparison with for example the reportages on 'Kvinnan som arbetar', published the year after *Klubben*, the series of light-hearted columns distance themselves more emphatically from the dominant discourse on the family. They foreground new constructions of gender, the first within the alternative community of The Club, and the second within the increasingly prominent community of the women's suffrage movement. While the serialisation of both *Klubben* and *Fru Hillevis dagbok* adds to the role of repetition in the construction of the characters, the foregrounding of mimicry in the former and of the significance of character-bound narration in the latter point up the proximity of the genre of prose fiction.

The section that follows offers analyses of six novels published between 1908 and 1920.

4. Prose Fiction

To what extent do works of prose fiction open up possibilities with regard to the constructions of gender and community that are different from those we have encountered in the reportages, the essays, and the series of light-hearted columns? And if they do, what are the effects on the constructions of gender and community? Also, how do the works of prose fiction differ from each other with regard to the constructions of gender and community, given the fact that two of those to be studied here are diary novels and one an historical novel, both of them categories that problematise memory and so have the potential to add new dimensions to the constructions of gender and community? How do the constructions that emerge here relate to the dominant and alternative discourses traced in the previous chapter? Finally, to what extent do my readings with a focus on the constructions of gender and community differ from the existing readings of these novels, and if so, how? According to Conny Svensson, writing in Lars Lönnroth and Sven Delblanc's *Den svenska litteraturen* (1999), *Norrtullsligan* and *Pennskaftet* (1910; *Penwoman*, 2009) are novels about the new professional woman; and *Åsa-Hanna* (1918) steps back from contemporary issues to explore the moral plight of an individual human being. The remaining three novels from this period to be considered here, *Den befriade kärleken* (1919; Love Liberated), *Kvarteret Oron* (1919; District of Unrest) and *Den förödda vingården*, are not mentioned (Svensson 1999, 454-57).

What, then, can these works of prose fiction contribute to the analysis of the issues at the centre of this study? And how do the constructions of gender and community relate to the contexts in which these texts were produced and which included major economic changes, notably the emergence of women in the labour market; the process of democratisation, most importantly the campaign for women's suffrage; and in due course, the First World War and its aftermath?

Texts

Norrtullsligan (The Norrtull Gang)

Wägner's first novel, *Norrtullsligan* (The Norrtull Gang), was written as a serial for the liberal daily *Dagens Nyheter*, where it appeared in eighteen instalments, 3 November 1907 – 2 February 1908. Consisting of seventeen diary entries and one letter, the instalments were published anonymously. In common with *Klubben* and *Fru Hillevis dagbok*, *Norrtullsligan* – the instalments of which, with just three exceptions, have a specific or approximate date – draws on the parallels between the order of events in the story and the period of publication to enhance topicality and relevance. In 1907 the material in Swedish newspapers was still comparatively unstructured, and the actual appearance of the one-column instalments of *Norrtullsligan* in *Dagens Nyheter* was not very different from that of the news items and reportages published on the same page, although the single illustration that accompanied some of the instalments helped to signal a different genre. In a study of New Woman novels published in newspapers, Graham Law has pointed out that the newspapers and journals should not be perceived as mere 'inert receptacles of items of news'; instead, we tend to find examples of 'often complex and volatile interaction between their fictional, editorial, and advertising material' (Law 2001, 18). While I have no space to develop these aspects of the original publication of *Norrtullsligan* here, I do not think there can be any doubt that the destabilisation of genre boundaries, parallel to that in *Fru Hillevis dagbok* published four years later, would have been a significant dimension of the original publication in *Dagens Nyheter*. (Birgitta Holm's analysis of the novel supports this reading; see especially Holm 2002, 159-60.) In addition there are similarities between *Norrtullsligan* and Wägner's series of reportages on 'Kvinnan som arbetar' (The Working Woman), published in *Idun* throughout 1908 and into 1909. The reference by one reviewer of *Norrtullsligan* to the book as 'a series of newspaper articles' (– er –, 1908) would seem to confirm the text's destabilisation of the genre of the novel; and the parallel between *Norrtullsligan* and the reportage has been underlined both by Erik Hjalmar Linder and by Ulla Isaksson and Linder in their biography of Wägner (Linder 1965, 120; Isaksson and Linder 2003, 129). The contemporary relevance of *Norrtullsligan* was highlighted by several reviewers (e.g. von Kræmer 1908, Johanson 1908). Overall, the reception of Wägner's first novel was positive.

Nina Auerbach has characterised the community of women as 'a rebuke to the conventional ideal of a solitary woman living for and through men, attaining citizenship in the community of adulthood through masculine approval alone' (Auerbach 1978, 5). In her analysis of *Norrtullsligan* in the context of women's utopian fiction, Eva Heggestad has argued that the rooms shared by the four female characters who make up the Norrtull Gang serve both as the focal point of a rebellion against the bourgeois way of life and as an 'alternative world' in which the stereotypical gender roles can be turned upside down: 'instead of being condemned to their role as passive objects, [the female characters] are able to assume the role as active subjects' (Heggestad 2003, 90). While there is no doubt that the novel's four female office employees – who constitute a new motif in Swedish literature (Svensson 1999, 454) – are part of a fabula that amounts to a challenge to the dominant discourse on the family and to the constructions of gender and community underpinning this, it seems to me that an analysis in terms of narrative and narration can open up dimensions of this text, especially with regard to gender and subjectivity, that take this radicalism considerably further. As the diary entries of Elisabeth, also known as Pegg, represent the three female characters with whom she is sharing accommodation at Norrtullsgatan in Stockholm – the young and inexperienced 'Baby', Eva who is hoping that her new boss the funeral director will spare her the otherwise obligatory erotic advances, and Emmy who is worn out and ill as a result of years of hard work and low pay – the text narrates the New Women in public as well as in private. In the light of my focus on the constructions of gender and community, the elements and implications of this narration are worth exploring in detail.

For the most part, *Norrtullsligan* is a diary novel, and the combination, in the final instalment, with the epistolary novel, makes for an amalgamation of two methods of telling a story that have been described as 'very closely related' (Romberg 1962, 44). In Bertil Romberg's analysis the diary novel 'gives the author the opportunity of letting the narrator and the reader come up against the action of the novel simultaneously, or at least experience its future happenings with the same degree of uncertainty' (op. cit., 43). To Romberg, there is no doubt that 'the commonest type of diary narrator is the lonely, unhappy human being who cannot attain contact with others and turns inwards upon himself'; and as if to confirm that his gendering of the narrator is not accidental, Romberg – whose seminal *Studies in the Narrative Technique of the First-Person Novel* does not mention *Norrtullsligan* or any other work by Wägner – points to Hjalmar Söderberg's *Doktor Glas* (1905) as the prime Swedish example (op. cit., 44). *Norrtullsligan*, in my reading, is an example of the diary novel functioning quite differently.

Narrated by a character who is both the main protagonist and one of several central characters, *Norrtullsligan* is an instance of the type of narrative voice that Susan S. Lanser has termed 'personal' and described as 'less formidable for women' than authorial voice since a personal narrator 'claims only the validity of one person's right to interpret her experience' (Lanser 1992, 19). However, in my reading this personal voice which, in line with Lanser's subsequent 'sexing' of narrative voices (Lanser 2004, 129) is unmistakably feminine, is at the centre of a narrative project with distinctly political implications (see also Forsås-Scott 2009).

As Suzanne Bunkers has pointed out, diaries embody 'life as *process*, not *product*' (quoted in Hogan 1991, 98; italics original). In the case of *Norrtullsligan* the effect was highlighted by Elin Brandell when the novel appeared as a book, for not only did Brandell claim that virtually all the readers familiar with the text from *Dagens Nyheter*, 'at least our women readers', would sometimes have wondered what happened to the members of the gang beyond the ending of the serial, but she also asked: '[W]ho are in fact the heroines of *Norrtullsligan*, the girls who have no surnames and neither beginnings nor endings to their life stories, but who are nonetheless *as vivid as any four-hundred-page-novel heroine?*' (Brandell 1908; my italics). As Brandell would seem to indicate, the role of language in the construction of life as a process in *Norrtullsligan* is striking. The illustrations range from the narrator's observation, after her first encounter with the articled clerk, that '*De har redan En Man med i romanen*' (Wägner 1908, 10; my italics) (*They've already got A Man in the novel*), which foregrounds the instalments as textual constructions, to Emmy's production, throughout the novel, of a series of wall-hangings, on all of which she embroiders: '*Lär att lida utan att klaga!*' (op. cit., 14, 139; italics original) (*Learn to suffer in silence!*). In *Norrtullsligan* subjectivation is emphatically a process and so highlights a point made by Michel Haar and quoted by Judith Butler: 'The subject, the self, the individual, are just so many false concepts, since they transform into substances fictitious unities having at the start only a linguistic reality' (quoted in Butler 2006, 29). When Pegg narrates a walk with Baby through the centre of Stockholm on a November evening, the constructions of herself and Baby are at once complex and tentative, the linguistic reality emphasised by the fact that the male characters who are the topic both of their conversation and of Pegg's thoughts are, unmistakably, verbal constructs:

> Hon tar min arm och talar, med afbrott endast vid de bättre bodfönstren, om notarien. Han flirtar målmedvetet med henne och har fångat mitt hjärtebarns hjärta. Medan hon talar, går jag och undrar längs hela museikajen, hur det skall sluta. Jag märker nog, att hon tror på tre rum och kök i Vasastan, och jag näns inte säga henne, att jag tviflar. Ju äldre jag blir, dess lättare är det att veta saker och tiga med dem, och mina erfarenheter trugar jag på ingen. Men jag måste småle litet tyst och trött i dimman åt att i Baby iaktta Mig själf, som också en gång icke aktade för rof att gå omkring och tala vidt och skrytsamt och förälskadt om min första Någon. Han var just icke notarie, och den här har smakfullare halsdukar, men någon annan skillnad ser jag inte. (Wägner 1908, 47)

> (She takes me by the arm and talks, pausing only in front of the better-quality shop windows, about the articled clerk. He is flirting with her quite deliberately, and he has captured the heart of my darling child. While she speaks, I am wondering all along the embankment with the museums how this is going to end. I cannot help noticing that she now believes in a four-room apartment in Vasastan, and I cannot bring myself to say to her that I have my doubts. The older I get, the easier it is to know things and keep quiet about them, and I am not forcing my experiences on anyone. But I have to smile silently and wearily in the fog, as I observe in Baby Myself, who in the past thought nothing of telling everyone, and indeed boasting to them, of my love, of my first Somebody. He certainly wasn't an articled clerk, and this one does have a better taste in scarves, but these are the only differences I have been able to spot.)

It is not just the open-endedness of the diary entry that reinforces the significance of subjectivation as a process in this extract. The developing relationship between the two female characters results in resonances between their experience and lack of it, and the implications left to the narratee by a narrator normally reticent about her past add to an involvement that enhances the processual significance of both Pegg's self-criticism and her cynicism regarding men. These New Women are markedly constructions, the tentativeness of their innovatory features reinforced by the fact that their conversation and thoughts unfold while they are walking through Stockholm. Here I discern a link with what Anna Westerståhl Stenport has described, with reference to Anna Branting's novel *Staden* (1905; The City), as 'the concatenation of walking and writing', and which she has summarised as 'a performative city writing' (Westerståhl Stenport 2004, 221). As Birgitta Holm has pointed out, the flat occupied by the members of the Norrtull Gang remains the principal stage (Holm 2002, 153), i.e. the dominant place in the fabula; but the point, in my reading, is that the claim to the freedom of the city is made at all, and made in the form of narrative. The New Women of *Norrtullsligan* are not just insisting on the freedom of the Swedish capital, of public space, as they develop their demands for salaries on which they can survive, for suffrage and citizenship, and for a sexual life of their own: in a space that is effectively new to these female characters, their newness is not just that of the female character who is different from the woman of the dominant discourse on femininity, but that of characters whose construction in terms of language is making their newness limitless.

The political dimensions of the narrative and story of *Norrtullsligan* are reinforced by the focus on what is in fact a community of New Women. Mocking the dominant discourse on the family as effectively as for example Charlotte Perkins Gilman's *Herland*, the New Women of the Norrtull Gang develop their own, quite unconventional celebration of Christmas, with Pegg's young brother Putte as the 'baby Jesus' of the collective of women (Wägner 1908, 94-95). But the sustained ridicule of the wedding of Pegg's bourgeois cousin represents a more elaborate deconstruction of the dominant discourse on the family and the icons of femininity underpinning it. Pegg's narrative in the chapter about the wedding does not focus on the event as such but on her retrospective account following her return to the Norrtull Gang, and this account is anything but coherent: instead the questions and interruptions highlight a dialogism that is further enhanced by Eva's and Baby's quotations of poetry. The stanza by Oscar Levertin (1862-1906, Professor of Literature, author and influential critic), pinpoints the notion of romantic heterosexual love that is systematically torn apart as the members of the Gang want to know if the bride wore an expensive dress, if she was moved to tears, if the food was first-rate, and if Pegg had plenty of champagne. As I have pointed out in another context, there are elements of masquerade in this chapter and elsewhere in *Norrtullsligan* (Forsås-Scott 2004, 92-94), a feature that adds to the prominence of process and performativity. More significant in this context, I think, than Joan Riviere's 'Womanliness as a Masquerade' (1929) – to which Butler devotes several pages in *Gender Trouble* (Butler 2006, 68-73) – is Luce Irigaray's notion of mimicry which I also found to be relevant for *Klubben*:

> To play with mimesis is [...], for a woman, to try to recover the place of her exploitation by discourse, without allowing herself to be simply reduced to it. It means to resubmit herself – inasmuch as she is on the side of the 'perceptible,' of 'matter' – to 'ideas,' in particular to ideas about herself, that are elaborated in/by a masculine logic, but so as to make 'visible,' by an effect of playful repetition, what was supposed to remain invisible: the cover-up of a possible operation of the feminine in language. It also means 'to unveil' the fact that, if women are such good mimics, it is because they are not simply resorbed in this function. *They also remain elsewhere*[.] (Irigaray 1993, 76; italics original)

Significantly, the chapter about the wedding also highlights the narrative basis of mimicry: here Emmy completes the last of the wall-hangings on which she has embroidered, letter by letter, the words *'Lär att lida utan att klaga!'* (*Learn to suffer in silence!*) (Wägner 1908, 138-39; italics original). Following the sumptuous wedding dinner Pegg asks for some of the meagre fare that is all the members of the Gang can afford and declares that, '*Jag vill vara nöjd med mig själf och mitt öde* och min pilsner' (op. cit., 137; my italics) (*I want to be content with my self and my fate* and my lager), her words again highlighting the constructedness and multiplicity of feminine subjectivities that are key features of *Norrtullsligan*. As Ann Ardis has emphasised, the concept of the New Woman amounts to a dismissal of the 'humanistic model of integrated selfhood or "character"', with the New Woman denoting not singleness but plurality (Ardis 1990, 113-14). Wägner's novel illustrates her point.

There are no New Men to take their place alongside the New Women in *Norrtullsligan*. Instead the construction of masculinity, in line with the dominant discourse on gender, consistently reinforces relationships in terms of binarism and power that reduce the female characters to objects. The articled clerk, the son of the widow from whom the four female characters rent their accommodation, takes every opportunity to spy on them, and Pegg notes Eva's crayoned warning on the door-post in the corridor: '*Passera ej vägen, då notarien höres eller synes!*' (Wägner 1908, 12; italics original). (*Do not cross when the articled clerk can be heard or seen!*) The clash between the new constructions of femininity represented by the New Women and the traditional masculinity of the male characters is spelled out by the story's erotic relationships, overwhelmingly heterosexual but complicated by the economic superiority of the male characters. Baby is not just erotically attracted to the articled clerk: his income would free her from a life in poverty. The conflict comes to a head in the case of Pegg, whose meagre salary also has to suffice for her younger brother, and whose boss cultivates an erotic insistence with the capacity to provide her with both financial security and sexual fulfilment within the framework of the dominant discourse on gender. But in what can only be described as a powerful confirmation of the alternative femininities constructed in *Norrtullsligan*, Pegg decides to turn her back on her boss and thus also on her job, indicating her reasons in her final diary entry in which she is thinking of:

mig själf, som skall ge mig af midt i månaden, lönen är *inte* i förskott, och ställa till skandal för att rädda – hvad? – min heder; lydande inte just samvetet, men något obestämdt, som jag kallar själfbevarelseinstinkt. Det är mycket svagt handladt och löjligt, men den enda möjligheten. (op. cit., 172, italics original)

(myself, about to leave in the middle of the month, and I *don't* get my pay in advance, and cause a scandal in order to safeguard – what? – my honour, as I pay heed not exactly to my conscience, but to something that is indeterminate, something that I'd call my instinct of self-preservation. What I am about to do is both weak and silly, but it's my only chance.)

Pegg writes the letter that concludes the novel from a provincial estate where she is helping out with baby twins, feeding the hens and 'trälar värre än om jag vore gift här på gården' (Wägner 1908, 175) (toiling away harder than if I were married on this farm), and this has inspired Eva Heggestad to claim that *Norrtullsligan* ends in a regressive utopia: 'Women need to look back to a pre-industrial society, in which they had considerably greater power and influence over their work' (Heggestad 2003, 96). But in the light of the consistent celebration of the constructions of the New Women in Wägner's text, Heggestad's reading of the conclusion seems neither satisfactory nor logical. The mocking tone of Pegg's letter helps present her seemingly ideal rural life as yet another construction; and given that this life is providing her with an approximation of motherhood (and not just one baby, but twins!) plus hens to look after, I am tempted to read Pegg's new circumstances as an ironic comment on the construction of femininity advocated in texts by Ellen Key (see above, p.71, p.103; Forsås-Scott 2004, 93). The distancing implicit in the ironic narratorial stance would then underline the *impossibility* of any return to the past, making the constructions of the New Women into pointers towards a new future.

In my analysis, then, *Norrtullsligan* does not construct a new society. I disagree with Heggestad's reading of the novel as a feminist utopia, a society of women free from male interference (Heggestad 2003, 85). What the narrative does construct, however, is an innovative community of female characters, a space for processes of feminine subjectivation that are markedly language-based, and that represent the

New Women of *Norrtullsligan* as plural. A reading along these lines calls the binary construction of gender into question, but this dimension is not developed – cannot be developed? – in terms of the male characters. As emphasised by the subheading of the final instalment in *Dagens Nyheter*, 'Ligan skingrad' (Wägner 1908e) (The Gang is Disbanded), the Norrtull Gang is no more by the time Pegg writes the concluding letter to Baby. It has existed long enough to point up not just some of the key aspects of the situation of the new professional women, but also some of the more profound issues to do with constructions of gender in general and of feminine subjectivity in particular.

Pennskaftet (Penwoman)

Like few other Swedish novels of its time, *Pennskaftet* (1910; *Penwoman*, 2009) highlights aspects of the economic, political, and social conditions in Sweden around 1910, with a special emphasis on the process of democratisation in general and on women's suffrage in particular. This is a novel about a young female journalist and her friends and supporters in the campaign for women's suffrage. In this novel, the New Women are contrasted to more elaborate constructions of the dominant discourse on gender. But they are also explored in the context of new communities and, more importantly, in the context of radical – but hitherto neglected – problematisations of gender and subjectivity.

Unlike *Norrtullsligan*, *Pennskaftet* is narrated by an external narrator, and more specifically by the heterodiegetic-extradiegetic type whose sex, according to Lanser's classification, is normally unmarked (Lanser 2004, 129), as is indeed the case in *Pennskaftet*. At the same time, the text includes a considerable proportion of direct dialogue (as Horace Engdahl has suggested, the novel could easily be turned into a drama [Engdahl 2003, xii-xiii]), and it is also virtually free from the 'maxims' which, in the analysis of Lanser, can play a key role in enhancing narratorial authority (Lanser 1992, 17). Indeed, the novel's opening sentence, which indicates a generalisation that subsequently turns out to be unmistakably gendered, can be read as a pointer towards a problematisation of narratorial authority: 'För den, som en gång hållit af en stationsinspektor, finns det helt visst angenämare sätt att tillbringa sin dag än att säfligt fara fram genom Sverige med ett persontåg.' (Wägner 1910, 5) (For a person who was once in love with a stationmaster, there are most certainly more pleasurable ways of spending the day than being carried across Sweden at a leisurely pace on a stopping train [Wägner 2009, 9]). As it becomes apparent that the seemingly gender neutral 'den, som' (a person) and the next paragraph's 'man' – similarly gender neutral in Swedish – (a person/one/she/someone) refer to Cecilia, a schoolteacher who, moreover, is interpreting her situation following her fiancé's desertion of her in terms of the dominant discourse on the family and so regards herself as irredeemably sullied, gender and narrative authority are problematised in a context of gender and power. At the same time there is no mistaking the narrator's closeness to a character such as Cecilia, whose focalisation effectively becomes that of the narrator as Cecilia's past is outlined in the second paragraph. This closeness turns out to extend to all the female characters engaged in the campaign for women's suffrage and becomes conspicuous in the public settings of a Stockholm which these female characters are striving to make their own, to live and work and move around in on the same conditions as men (see Forsås- Scott 2003b, 209-10). The constructions of new communities that result from the suffrage campaign and which are underpinned by leafleting, public speaking, and other aspects of an election campaign along with the wait, in a public square, for the election results, combine to make the claim for a share in the public spaces more emphatic and politically charged than in *Norrtullsligan*. The narratee is constructed in this context of gendered radicalism, party to the insights and ambitions of a group of female characters who are not only calling the dominant discourses on gender into question but have embarked on the task of changing them. The engagement of the readers is spelled out in Barbro Alving's summary of the reception of the novel's New Woman: she 'was accepted and liked and disarmed many [readers]' (Alving 1968, 128).

Texts

The dominant discourses on the family and gender are rolled out in the chapter representing dinner-time in the boarding-house where Penwoman is living along with other single professionals and occasional visitors to the capital. The single professionals are predominantly male, *en route* to their roles as husbands, fathers, and family breadwinners. They represent a relatively broad range of professions: the chief cashier, the editor, the clerical officer, the trainee architect. The professional range of the female characters is restricted to the teacher from the opening chapter, the journalist, and 'författarinnan, fröken Anderson-Jublin' (Wägner 1910, 30) (the authoress, Miss Anderson-Jublin [Wägner 2009, 24]). Having internalised the dominant discourse to the extent that she has effectively assumed responsibility for her fiancé's treatment of her and withdrawn into total isolation, Cecilia clearly does not share the ambitions of the other professionals around the table; and the role of the dominant discourse on the family is confirmed by the other two female guests, the sister of the landlady and her daughter.

As one of many positive reviewers, the critic Klara Johanson highlighted the impact of Penwoman as 'a real human being': 'Alive and warm and eager, hotfot from some rushed journalistic assignment, she comes running into the novel' (Johanson 1910). Her observation can be seen to highlight the role of subjectivation as a process in the novel. In *Pennskaftet* this process is more conspicuous than in *Norrtullsligan* because it involves a problematisation of gender. Penwoman is both the female character who is having to negotiate the unwanted approaches of men as she makes her way home from the editorial office late at night, and the more ambivalently gendered character spotted one afternoon by the clerical officer 'midt ibland *en hop andra gatpojkar*, som samlats kring ett slagsmål' (Wägner 1910, 28; my italics) (in *a crowd of other street urchins* who had gathered round a fight [Wägner 2009, 23]). But *Pennskaftet*'s problematisation of gender does not stop here.

In an essay first published in 1986, Joan Wallach Scott has described the connection between 'gender', meaning 'the social organization of the relationship between the sexes', and 'gender' in its grammatical sense as 'both explicit and full of unexamined possibilities'. The explicit connection she has in mind refers to languages that categorise nouns as either masculine or feminine, while the unexamined possibilities arise from the fact that 'in many Indo-European languages there is a third category – unsexed or neuter' (Scott 1988b, 28-29). Elaborating on Scott's observation, Yvonne Hirdman has pointed out that 'the possibilities of the Swedish language with both non-neuter and neuter can no doubt provide material for [the development of] utopian dimensions' (Hirdman 1987, 206). It is precisely these dimensions that Wägner's text is exploring, although as far as I know this important aspect of the novel has gone unnoticed until now.

In modern Swedish, nouns have one of two grammatical genders, neuter or non-neuter, with nouns referring to human beings usually non-neuter and the exceptions conspicuous because there are so few of them (Hultman 2003, 48-49). But the affectionate name given to Barbro Magnus, the central character in Wägner's novel, is remarkable in that 'Pennskaftet', literally 'the pen-holder', is grammatically neuter. As the reference is to a character, i.e. the meaning is 'animate', the pronoun in this case should have been *hon* (she) (op. cit., 49). But this text, developing a technique that is not immediately translatable into English, frequently foregrounds the *grammatical* gender of the central character. (In the examples that follow, my translations deviate slightly from the published version to illustrate my point, with the published version in square brackets.) In Chapter II, as the guests in the boarding-house are waiting for Penwoman, there are references to her in terms that are grammatically neuter: 'hvar är Pennskaftet? [...] *Det* har väl mycket att göra som vanligt' (Wägner 1910, 27-28; my italics) (where's Penwoman? [...] *It*'ll be busy as usual, I expect [where's Penwoman? [...] She'll be busy as usual, I expect (Wägner 2009, 23)]). The feature is reinforced in the reflections of the trainee architect at the point when he has just invited Pennskaftet out for a meal: 'Pennskaftet var *sött*, och att *det* samtidigt var *trefligt* att vara tillsamman med, stämde precis med hans erfarenhet om omoraliska familjeflickor' (Wägner 1910, 62; my italics) (Penwoman was pretty, and the fact that *it* was also fun to be with exactly matched his experience of the less moral among girls from good homes [Penwoman was pretty, and the fact that she was also fun to be with exactly matched his experience of the less moral among girls from good homes (Wägner 2009, 45)]). Here the Swedish adjectives *sött* and *trevligt*, the -t endings necessitated by the neuter gender of the noun/name, reinforce the gender anomaly. This slippage in Wägner's text between signifier and signified initiates a radical deconstruction of the male – female binary, a binary that in the reading of Hélène Cixous defines the 'solidarity between logocentrism and phallocentrism' and that is thus fundamental to western thought (Cixous and Clément 1987, 65). Susan S. Lanser, referring to the rejection in Romance languages and in German of 'simple gender associations between sign and referent', has argued that these languages construct 'a *sex*/gender dynamic which [...] is already in some sense "queer"' (Lanser 2004, 126; italics original). This grammatically based queering of the sex/gender dynamic is investigated in Wägner's novel. And however conspicuous the grammatically neuter central character, it is significant that the queering is not confined to it. Here is Cecilia reflecting on a question from one of her new friends in the suffrage movement: 'Cecilia [...] undrade hur *den* var skapad, som denna afton *var karl till* att gå och glädja sig öfver sin kommunala valbarhet, men det gjorde *hon*' (Wägner 1910, 148; my italics) (Cecilia [...] wondered *what sort of person* it could be, who *was man enough* to spend an evening like this rejoicing that *she* could stand in local government elections, but *this woman* was doing just that [Wägner 2009, 98]). In this sentence the gender neutrality of the determinate pronoun 'den' (the person) is complicated by an idiomatic phrase couched in the masculine, 'var karl till' (was man enough), the power implications of which are momentarily heightened (the possessive pronoun *sin* does not define the gender of 'the person') by the paradox arising from the combination of the phrase with the notion of municipal elegibility – hardly a novelty for Swedish men, but granted to women in 1909 – only to be radically undercut by the reminder that the reference throughout has been to a female character, 'hon' (she). Trying to keep up with this balancing act and thus becoming party to the ironic implications, the narratee shares in the process as the dominant discourse on gender is called into question and agency is distinguished from domination.

One of the effects of the destabilisation and deconstruction in *Pennskaftet* of the male – female binary is the pinpointing of the dominant discourse on gender. In a chapter such as the one about dinner-time in the boarding-house, the performativity of gender is foregrounded as a result. According to Judith Butler, performativity should be understood 'not as the act by which a subject brings into being what she/he names, but, rather, as that reiterative power of discourse to produce the phenomena that it regulates and constrains' (Butler 1993, 2). In Chapter II of *Pennskaftet*, the predominance of conversation and discussion, most of it in the form of direct speech, has the effect of making the reiterative power of discourse highly prominent, given that the focal point throughout is Penwoman. In this chapter the character is introduced, is overtly referred to in terms that are grammatically neuter, and is even asked, by a male adversary, whether it would not prefer to be a man. (Penwoman's response, ' – Nej, men skulle inte ni?' (Wägner 1910, 40) (No, but wouldn't you? [Wägner 2009, 31]), has the effect of making her adversary leave the room.) It is Miss Anderson-Jublin who brings up the topic of women's suffrage at the dinner-table, and by reiterating a number of the standard arguments against suffrage for women, she and the landlady's sister, married to a deputy judge, demonstrate the power of the dominant discourse. It is by their feminine charm, not by suffrage, that women can achieve what they want; it is not a matter for women how the men are running the country; and women simply do not need suffrage: 'Ställning i samhället har vi gudilof genom våra män, inflytande har vi indirekt genom våra söner, om vi vill ha det, och till att sköta våra affärer har vi våra snälla bankdirektörer' (Wägner 1910, 33-34) (We have our position in society through our husbands, thank God; we have influence indirectly, through our sons, if we want; and to manage our affairs we have our kind bank managers [Wägner 2009, 27]). In drawing on a range of familiar arguments (including Ellen Key's point about mothers achieving influence via their sons), these female characters, constructing themselves as subservient to men in every respect, illustrate the reiterative power of the dominant discourse on gender. The male characters repeatedly demolish the argument for suffrage for women and reinforce the dominant discourse on gender. In the opinion of the editor, women should attend to their duties in the home rather than interfere in matters they do not understand, and should they get the right to vote, they would vote like their husbands anyway. When the chief cashier asks Penwoman whether she wouldprefer suffrage or a new hat, the clerical officer reinforces the point by declaring that it is 'förbannadt oestetiskt och missklädsamt att rösta' (Wägner 1910, 38) (damned unaesthetic and unbecoming to vote [Wägner 2009, 30]). Again, these male characters bring into focus the reiterative power of the dominant discourse on gender as they insist on constructing women as objects for whom suffrage would be a mere new accessory. As their arguments highlight, the construction of masculinity hinges on a position of total superiority that is reiterated in every respect, economically, politically, socially, and intellectually. But this position of power is undercut by the fact that the male characters leave the room one by one rather than continue their arguments with Penwoman; and as the chapter concludes with the clerical officer denouncing Penwoman to the trainee architect for her moral laxity, this confirmation of the power of the dominant discourse on gender – in which female characters who do not fit in easily find themselves with a slur on their moral standards – simultaneously points up the hollowness of the masculine position.

What is the effect, then, of the destabilisation and deconstruction of the male-female binary in terms of the construction of the character of Penwoman? Who is she – or rather, it – in the context of the dominant discourse on gender? In line with Ann Ardis's reading of the New Woman as plural, Horace Engdahl in his introduction to *Pennskaftet* has pointed to the multiple identities of the New Woman (Engdahl 2003, viii). The text constructs the central character as a journalist, as Cecilia's close friend, as a suffragist, as a prostitute when she is taken for her friend Klara, as the guest of Baron Starck at his estate, as the lover of the trainee architect with whom she shares a cottage during the summer, and as a fallen woman to whom the family of the trainee architect refuses access when he becomes seriously ill. The riddle of identities, Princess Charlotte – Penwoman – Klara (Wägner 1910, 60, 140-42, 303-305), contributes to highlighting the significance of Penwoman's multiple identities, which ensure than she never remains in any of the boxes constructed by the dominant discourse on gender. Contributing to profiling the types of femininity accommodated by the dominant discourse, she is at the same time the focal point of multiple femininities.

The other effect of the novel's destabilisation and deconstruction of the male-female binary is a process of change. I have referred above to the significance of conversations, of dialogue in the form of direct speech in *Pennskaftet*, and while this dialogism can confirm the power of the dominant discourse, as my analysis of Chapter II above has demonstrated, it can also, as is apparent from the same analysis, point the way towards change. An interesting example is the long discussion in Chapter IV between Penwoman and the trainee architect, Dick, as they are having a meal at a restaurant. Here the characters' constructions of each other also shift and change, as the following extract exemplifies:

– Tycker ni, att jag är skenhelig, frågade hon.
– Åja, kanske litet, sade han, men det är mycket klädsamt hos er. Pennskaftet suckade.
– Jaså, det är resultatet af att jag på ett artigt och lojalt sätt velat låta er förstå, att man inte löser säsongkort till mig, som till operan eller varmbad. Och jag säger det ju inte till er utan skäl, som ni nog vet.

Han svarade, att det visste han visst inte, det var då det sista han hade tänkt, och att han tyckte bättre om både operan och varmbad. Men långt ifrån att bli förlägen, skrattade hon åt honom, och till sist måste han medge, att hon hade rätt.

– Ja, inte kunde jag veta, sade han buttert. Hvarför skall ni segla under så falsk flagg? Låta tala om er som ni gör.

– O, det är en slags okonstlad njutning jag har. Det är för resten ett utmärkt sätt, att få veta, hvad manfolken går för.

Han fick plötslig känsla af att ha fallit igenom i en examen. (Wägner 1910, 67-68)

('So you think me hypocritical?' she asked.
'Well, perhaps a little,' he said, 'but it's very becoming.'
Penwoman sighed.
'So that's what happens when I politely and loyally try to point out to you, that people can't take out a season ticket for me as if I were the opera house or the hot baths. And I've every reason for telling *you* this, as you well know.'
He replied that he most certainly did not know that; it was the last thing he had thought, and anyway he much preferred both the opera and the hot baths. But far from being embarrassed, she laughed at him, and in the end he had to admit she had been right.
'Well how was I to know?' he said morosely. 'Why must you sail under such a false flag? Let people talk about you as they do?'
'Oh, it's just a simple pleasure I allow myself. And, incidentally, an excellent way of finding out what men are like.'
He had a sudden sense of having failed an examination. [Wägner 2009, 48])

Initially Dick appears to be in charge, relying on his rule-of-thumb construction, in line with the dominant discourse on gender, of women as either moral or immoral, and convinced that Penwoman's mockery of him is a façade. At the same time, Penwoman's speeches distance her from any clichés, problematising her subjectivity by contrasting her with institutions such as the opera and the hot baths, and so puzzling Dick who accuses her of sailing under a false flag. In this extract, Penwoman gains total control and demolishes Dick's initial constructions of relations of gender and power, contributing at the same time to the new constructions of gender that are at the centre of this text. When, at the end of their meal, she prepares to leave him, it is Dick who asks to accompany her, 'så att jag också får lära mig litet om de nya kvinnorna' (Wägner 1910, 72) (so I get a chance to learn about the new women [Wägner 2009, 50]), a process that is to continue through much of the narrative and that also will involve the deconstruction of Dick.

Unlike in Wägner's previous novel, the process of change in *Pennskaftet* extends via new communities to the outline of a new society. The starting-point is the summerhouse that Penwoman and Dick share in the Stockholm archipelago, with a more expansive new community emerging when a contingent of Penwoman's friends in the suffrage movement settles at a nearby house to prepare a national rally and the forthcoming election campaign. Here the women in the suffrage movement work long days in an atmosphere of harmony and optimism, and at the rally Penwoman makes her first public speech, Dick joins the campaign for women's suffrage, and a gentleman, realising that Penwoman has 'planer på att förändra världens utseende' (Wägner 1910, 228) (plans to transform the look of the whole world [Wägner 2009, 151]), is converted to the cause. The destabilisation and deconstruction of the male-female binary centring on the character of Penwoman are fundamental to these changes; and this radical problematisation of the gender binary continues to underpin the scene in which a new community – and perhaps indeed society – becomes most palpable, the wait in a Stockholm square for the results of the local elections with the group of suffragists in the midst of the throng as one of 'de allra starkast laddade energicentra' (Wägner 1910, 266) (the most charged of those energy cores [Wägner 2009, 174]).

The destabilisation and deconstruction of the gender binary of the dominant discourse extends to sexuality. As Bertil Björkenlid has pointed out, the relationship between Penwoman and Dick was perceived by leading figures in the Swedish campaign for female suffrage as deeply damaging to the movement (Björkenlid 1982, 248-50). Seen in the context of the emphasis in the movement on the kind of solid respectability calculated to enhance the acceptability of the campaign's demands, the reaction was hardly surprising. What is surprising is that Björkenlid, more than seven decades after the original publication of *Pennskaftet*, insists on reading the novel in the context of the suffrage campaign only. As I have demonstrated, *Pennskaftet* offers a far-reaching problematisation of the construction of gender, and it does so in terms that highlight the significance of performativity. Here 'sex' can also be read in Butlerian terms, i.e. 'no longer as a bodily given on which the construct of gender is artificially imposed, but as a cultural norm which governs the materialization of bodies' (Butler 1993, 2-3). As Butler has repeatedly emphasised, this cultural norm is heterosexual, and the sexual relationship that so worried some of the readers of *Pennskaftet* in

1910 is clearly heterosexual. In my reading, however, this relationship is further profiled against a same-sex relationship. While there may be a hint of an erotic relationship between Pegg and Baby in *Norrtullsligan*, there are elements of the relationship between Cecilia and Penwoman, defined by Isaksson and Linder in terms of mother and daughter (Isaksson and Linder 2003, 169), that suggest an intimacy that is erotically charged. The key event occurs one evening when Penwoman visits Cecilia in her new flat, only to find that her friend has fallen asleep in the midst of writing an article about suffrage and is lying on her sofa 'med ansiktet uppåtvändt och en stor kudde i famnen, hvars lena siden hon tryckte mot sin kind. Lampskenet föll öfver alla de bedröfvade nätternas linjer i hennes lilla ansikte, som utan dem skulle varit ungt och vackert' (Wägner 1910, 117) (her face turned up and a large cushion in her arms, its smooth silk pressed to her cheek. The lamplight fell on all the lines that nights of sorrow had etched on her small face, which but for them would have been young and beautiful [Wägner 2009, 79]). Penwoman's involvement with both her friend and the suffrage movement crystallises in the feeling which inspires her to write for Cecilia the remainder of the article:

> Hon tog pennan, orden tycktes marschera upp vid tonerna af en festmarsch, med en rysning af glädje kände hon, hur det strömmade likt floder af eld genom hennes högra hand ned i pennan. När hon hunnit till sin signatur, reste hon sig plötsligt, gick bort till Cecilia och gömde sitt heta hufvud i en flik af hennes morgonrock. (Wägner 1910, 119)
>
> (She took up the pen, the words seemed to come trooping up to the tones of a celebration march; with a shiver of joy she felt a flowing sensation run like rivers of fire through her right hand and down into the pen. When she reached the signature, she rose suddenly, went over to Cecilia and burrowed her hot head into a fold of her dressing gown. [Wägner 2009, 80])

In my reading the context, Penwoman's feelings as she writes, and her concluding intimacy with Cecilia all contribute to making the erotic connotations of this scene unmistakable. Moreover, Penwoman soon declares that she would not mind living with Cecilia, and not long afterwards it becomes clear that she is actually doing so, at least at times (op. cit., 102, 114).

In the final chapter of the novel, just before her marriage to Dick, Cecilia gives to Penwoman a gold pendant with opals and then leaves Penwoman sitting in bed with the gift: '– Mitt hjärtas älskade, sade hon. Och somnade med smycket tryckt mot sitt hjärta' (Wägner 1910, 324) ('My heart's beloved,' she said. And fell asleep with the pendant pressed to her heart [Wägner 2009, 211]). As both Horace Engdahl and Ebba Witt-Brattström have pointed out, it is unclear whom Penwoman is addressing: might this be Dick? or Cecilia? or the suffrage movement? or, possibly, her unborn child? or, in Witt-Brattström's phrase, 'herself as a narcissistic woman of original wholeness' (Witt-Brattström 2004, 10; Engdahl 2003, xv)? Neither commentator, however, has related this ambivalence to the scene immediately before in which Penwoman, reduced to 'den lilla nakna hvita grodan i duschbaljan' (Wägner 1910, 320) (the naked little white frog in the tub [Wägner 2009, 209]), is given a bath by Cecilia's housemaid and uses the opportunity to learn 'hvad de olika kroppsdelarna heter på köksspråket, så att jag vet, när jag skall gå ut på torget och köpa mat' (Wägner 1910, 320) (what all the different parts of the body are called in kitchen talk, so I know when I have to go to the market to buy food [Wägner 2009, 208]). When Penwoman learns, on her own body, about the locations of the thymus (sweetbread) and the ribs (Wägner 1910, 320), the slippage between signifier and signified that I have shown to be pivotal to the narrative of this novel is finally problematised in terms of the body. As Butler has underlined, the body is in no way prior to the sign, but '[t]his signification produces as an *effect* of its own procedure the very body that it nevertheless and simultaneously claims to discover as that which *precedes* its own action' (Butler 1993, 30; italics original). For all the differences between Butler's analysis and Patricia Waugh's use of the concept of 'self', Penwoman's final words, couched as they are in terms of love, can also be read as pointing towards constructions in terms of what Waugh has called 'self-in-relationship' (Waugh 1989, 13-14), and thus towards a future based on boldly different constructions of both gender and community and, by implication, society.

Åsa-Hanna

The eponymously titled *Åsa-Hanna* (1918), a historical novel that highlights some of the economic changes that were beginning to transform rural Sweden in the second half of the nineteenth century, has long been regarded as Wägner's masterpiece. In Erik Hjalmar Linder's influential history of literature, *Fyra decennier av nittonhundratalet* (Four Decades of the Twentieth Century), 1949, *Åsa-Hanna* was given more space than any other text by Wägner and, in the second edition (1965), a unique section of its own (Linder 1949, 90-106; Linder 1965, 118-30). In their biography, first published in 1977, Isaksson and Linder expressed few reservations about labelling the novel 'the best or even the only basis of E[lin] W[ägner]'s purely artistic reputation' (Isaksson and Linder 2003, 239). The first version of the novel, *Vansklighetens land* (The Perilous Land), was serialised in *Idun* from the end of July 1917 to January 1918 and published in a cheap edition in 1917 in *Iduns romanbibliotek* (*Idun*'s novel library), with Bonnier publishing the second version under its definitive title in 1918 and a third version in 1946, the latter in conjunction with the release in that year of a film based on the novel. The analysis that follows is based on the second version, which is the one that has been reprinted from 1947 onwards.

In *Den svenska litteraturen*, Lars Lönnroth and Sven Delblanc's authoritative history of Swedish literature, Conny Svensson has developed the status of *Åsa-Hanna* in terms of the absence of contemporary issues (the place and time of the story are rural Sweden in the final decades of the nineteenth century) and the focus on the central character and 'her struggle to remain a good human being' (Svensson 1999, 457). My reading turns that of Svensson on its head by foregrounding presence, not absence: *Åsa-Hanna* is an historical novel – the first by Wägner – and as Peter Middleton and Tim Woods have reminded us, 'literary texts might be significant forms of contemporary historicism, in which shifting senses of the pastness of the past – its location and the mechanisms whereby it is maintained and transmitted – are explored in ways that are not available in other discursive modes' (Middleton and Woods 2000, 36). Set in the past, the story of *Åsa-Hanna* pivots on memory – 'a means of overcoming the limitations of the human condition as it is understood in contemporary culture, by making the past appear once again in the present, despite its temporal, and possibly spatial, distance' (op. cit., 21) – by setting against each other two versions of the past of Frans Adamson, shopkeeper in the Småland parish of Ljungheda, and his family: either he is innocent, as concluded by the judge who has recently acquitted him (Wägner 1918, 64), or there is substance to the local gossip about the criminal past of Franse and his family. As the character of *Åsa-Hanna* marries with the ambition of turning her husband into a better human being and instead finds herself safeguarding the dark secrets of her new family in Mellangården, the story foregrounds the relevance of the past while also highlighting key issues about the family, gender, domination, and agency. This story, moreover, contrasts the community represented by the parish of Ljungheda, complete with parishioners and institutions representing moral and ethical safeguards such as the Law and the Lutheran State Church, with the alternative community represented by the gossip that is ubiquitous in the narrative of this novel. In my reading *Åsa-Hanna* launches a radical problematisation of phallogocentrism, i.e. the conjunction of phallocentrism – 'a system that privileges the phallus as the symbol or source of power' (Moi 1985, 179) – and logocentrism. From a perspective of gender the text explores the significance of both the Law and the Lutheran State Church, with the critique of the Church, moreover, implicitly linked to the quartercentenary of Luther's publication of his theses, an event commemorated in Sweden in the autumn of 1917, during the period when the first version of *Åsa-Hanna* was serialised. But the text also points towards an alternative community and, in the last instance, towards a new community of readers.

The prominence of the Law stems partly from the criminality of Åsa-Hanna's new family, but intertwined with this is the status of women in marriage, illustrated by examples ranging from the character of Åsa-Hanna who, shortly before her wedding, realises what is implied in her mother's dictum, 'hustrun får allt bli som gården' (Wägner 1918, 93) (it is up to the wife to become like [the family at] the farm), to the midwife who, in a reversal of the gender roles of the dominant discourse, is the one who supports her husband (op. cit., 293). The status of women in marriage was a key issue at the time when the novel appeared, being studied by a pan-Scandinavian committee in preparation for the introduction of new marriage legislation. In the chronotope of *Åsa-Hanna*, the parish of Ljungheda in the province of Småland in the second half of the nineteenth century, the Lutheran State Church also has a central position, and the role of the Church is reinforced not just by the prominence of characters such as the Dean and his family along with other ministers of the Church, but again by the problematisation of the position of women in marriage.

The words of ministers of the church constitute the most striking examples of phallogocentrism in *Åsa-Hanna*. When, early in the novel, Åsa-Hanna's devout mother seeks the assistance of the Dean to overcome the religious crisis in which she finds herself, the confession that takes place constructs the characters in terms of a relationship of gender and power determined by the office of the Dean:

> – Men då tillsäger jag mor Katrina, svarade prosten efter något betänkande, myndigt förlitande på sin auktoritet, att det inte är så. Det förkrossade hjärtat är redan förlåtet. Håll fast om Jesu kors och se upp mot Honom, som hänger där för våra synder. (Wägner 1918, 31)

> (But then I tell you, Mother Katrina, the Dean said after some reflection, magisterially relying on his authority, that that is not how it is. The heart that is contrite has already been forgiven. Hold on to the cross of Christ and look up to Him who is hanging there for the sake of our sins.)

It is not just the narratorial addition, 'myndigt förlitande på sin auktoritet' (magisterially relying on his authority), that underlines the position of the Dean but also, of course, his access to and use of the Word of God as a means of intervening in the lives of his parishioners. The Law Officer is the text's other major focus of phallogocentrism, with the respectability of the married Åsa-Hanna ultimately aimed at this representative of the Law:

> På hennes bykar funnos inga dolda fläckar att dölja, hennes gardiner voro alltid uppdragna, hennes dörrar aldrig låsta, hennes ögon voro alltid klara,

kring hennes mun fanns inga rynkor att läsa i, hennes hand darrade aldrig, då det kom ett brev med okänd handstil, hon flög inte till, när det ropades: länsman kommer! (op. cit., 141-42)

(On her washing, there were no secret stains to hide, her curtains were always open, her doors never locked, her eyes were always bright, around her mouth there were no lines to read, her hand never trembled when a letter with unfamiliar handwriting arrived, she never gave a start when someone called out: the Law Officer is coming!)

As early as her wedding day, Åsa-Hanna has learnt to keep a close eye on the reactions of the Law Officer, and what is arguably the text's most prominent example of phallogocentrism is the stern speech the Dean delivers to the newly-weds with the Law Officer among the guests. Here the power spheres of the Dean and the Law Officer coincide as the Dean lectures Åsa-Hanna and Franse on 'all världslig rikedoms fåfänglighet och snara, om välmågans och välmaktens usla tomhet, där inte den skinande fläckfria hedern fanns, om människans jämmerliga irring och blindhet, som icke inser vad som är det enda nödvändiga' (op. cit., 106) (the vanity and trap that worldly riches are, on the wretched emptiness of prosperity and wealth unless based on gleaming, spotless honour, on the miserable confusion and blindness of the human being who does not understand the one thing necessary). The Dean's monologue, replete with biblical vocabulary and phraseology, pinpoints the moral code of the Lutheran State Church in terms of the salvation of the individual human being, but it also serves as a reminder of the binary construction and hierarchisation of gender that are fundamental to Lutheranism.

How, then, does the text handle the phallogocentrism foregrounded by the story and the language of *Åsa-Hanna*? While the third version of the novel ends with Åsa-Hanna in command and the Law Officer knocking on the door, presumably to arrest her husband (Wägner 1946, 294), the second version would seem to confirm the dominance of phallogocentrism as the plot ends with Åsa-Hanna succumbing to her husband who tells her that '*du ska få tiga och arbeta*' (Wägner 1918, 418; italics original) (*I'll make you shut up and work hard*). It is this ending that Holger Ahlenius, editor of *Valda skrifter* (Selected Works) by Wägner, claims to be the 'most convincing from a psychological and artistic point of view' (Ahlenius 1950, 19). But does the novel, then, simply reinforce phallogocentrism? No, it does not. A reading that focuses on the constructions of gender and of relationships of gender and power in terms of narration and language can profile *Åsa-Hanna*, a novel with a reputation for being unproblematic from a (gender-) political point of view, as a radical critique of phallogocentrism and a text that opens up possibilities of change in terms quite different from those we have encountered in the previous novels.

To begin with the text, the ministers of the church and the Law Officer may indeed epitomise phallogocentrism in *Åsa-Hanna*, but it is also worth noting that gossip plays a prominent role in this novel; indeed, gossip is more prominent here than in any other work of prose fiction by Wägner. The minimal definition provided by Patricia Meyer Spacks in her seminal study of gossip is 'idle talk about other persons not present'; but as Spacks has pointed out, this definition in fact covers a broad spectrum, from gossip as 'distilled malice' to gossip as 'a function of intimacy' (Spacks 1985, 26, 4-5). I do not believe there is much point in attempting to categorise the gossip in *Åsa-Hanna*, but what I find interesting and relevant is Spacks's argument about the 'subversive implications both of literal gossip and of its printed transformations': gossip as a phenomenon, she writes, 'raises questions about boundaries, authority, distance, the nature of knowledge; it demands answers quite at odds with what we assume as our culture's dominant values' (op. cit., 12). In the fabula of *Åsa-Hanna* power is economic, social, and ecclesiastical, with the effects fused in terms of gender and the family. But the foregrounding of phallogocentrism helps profile power in terms of text, and this is also where the prominence of gossip in this novel, along with the links between gossip and fiction highlighted by Spacks, become crucial. 'Fiction', according to Spacks,

> reveals more clearly what didactic texts only hint: that gossip, 'female talk,' provides a mode of power, of undermining public rigidities and asserting private integrity, of discovering means of agency for women, those private citizens deprived of public function. It provides also often the substance and the means of narrative. (op. cit., 170)

The parishioners of Ljungheda exchange news, or gossip, whenever they get a chance to meet, whether this is on the road, in the grocery at Mellangården, or after church on a Sunday. The two key conveyers of gossip in Ljungheda are Koke-Martina, early on the housemaid at the Dean's but also the character who takes on the cooking and baking for weddings and funerals and so is able to amass a huge amount of information about the parishioners; and Lydia Liljelund, the midwife whose profession brings her inside many of the farms and cottages of the parish. In being a parish where 'allting spörjs' (Wägner 1918, 105) (everything gets around), Ljungheda is hardly exceptional, but given the prominence of phallogocentrism in the story, the effect of the no less prominent polyphony of gossip is to call into question, to undermine, and to challenge. In the rural Swedish community of the second half of the nineteenth century constructed in *Åsa-Hanna*, political democracy is still non-existent, and so the significance of gossip in the text revolves not just around gender but also around class. Ironically, the extent to which gossip in this text constructs and deconstructs characters and, to quote Spacks, provides 'the substance and the means of narrative' (Spacks 1985, 170), becomes most conspicuous in the chapter about the election of a Rector to succeed the Dean, a chapter in which Koke-Martina also plays a leading role as the key figure in what becomes known as 'käringpartiet' (Wägner 1918, 331) (the old women's party). Dismissing the narrative about the intrigues surrounding the election as 'unwarranted detail', Staffan Björck would seem to find sections of this part of the novel superfluous (Björck 1968, 207-208); but these sections are of course prime examples of the manipulation of the fabula into a story, and as Bal has pointed out, it is 'basically at this level that suspense and pleasure are provoked, and that ideology is inscribed' (Bal 1999, 79). As the parish annexed to Ljungheda takes the opportunity to get rid of their much-disliked minister only to have Ljungheda overturn the result, the power of the parishioners is briefly highlighted. Indeed it is reinforced as the disliked minister dies, devastated by the course of events, his demise exposing both his greed and his craving for power as he is found to have disinherited the wife and children he has made to starve, bequeathing his wealth to the parishioners who made him their Rector for a day. Although the eventual result of the election turns out to hinge on the manoeuvring of one of the young ministers (who smartly eliminates his main rival by means of 'ett samtal av en cigarrs längd' [Wägner 1918, 335] [a conversation the length of a cigar] and ensures that his engagement to the bishop's daughter is announced just before the decisive round of voting), the role of gossip throughout the election episode has not just helped pinpoint the significance of phallogocentrism in this text but has also had the effect of radically problematising it, foregrounding an alternative community in the process.

In Spacks's analysis gossip, '[m]ore insistently than other forms of conversation [...] involves exchange not merely, not even mainly, of information, and not solely of understanding, but of point of view' (Spacks 1985, 21-22). With phallogocentrism so prominent in *Åsa-Hanna*, gossip plays a key role in paving the way for alternative focalisations. Lydia Liljelund, the midwife, tells an outrageous story about the meanness of the much-disliked minister, describing to Åsa-Hanna and her mother how, while assisting the minister's wife in childbirth, she was involved in a continuous struggle with him as he tried to deprive the two women of firewood for the stove and paraffin for lighting (Wägner 1918, 155-58). Here the focalisation of the midwife determines the construction of the minister, her version problematising the significance of phallogocentrism. The protagonist, Åsa-Hanna, turns out to play a key role as an alternative focaliser, one instance being the chapter entitled 'Ugnsrakan' (The Oven-rake) in which alternative focalisation is similarly bound up with gossip. Married just seven weeks previously and busy baking bread, Åsa-Hanna is reflecting on her husband and in-laws in the light of the rumours and gossip about her new family:

> Hon mindes någon dunkel historia från sin barndom, att Fransa farfar dött på så sätt att di inte stämt blon i tide på honom. Och hon hade hört något om att gamle Adam, Fransa far, blev misstänkt för att ha handlat med flit och inte i okunnighet, fast han blev frikänd vid tinget. Hon hade inte vidare tänkt på de där gamla historierna, som folk mest glömt nu mera, det kan så lätt komma ut rykten, det ser man bäst på vad di kunde sätta ihop om Franse och Stina Snabb. (Wägner 1918, 126)

(She could remember some vague story from her childhood, that Franse's grandfather had died because they hadn't staunched the blood in time. And she'd heard something about old Adam, Franse's father, how he'd been suspected of having done it deliberately and not out of ignorance, although he'd been freed by the district court. She hadn't thought any further of those old stories which people nowadays had mostly forgotten, rumours get out and about so easily, you see that from what people had made up about Franse and Stina Snabb.)

With Franse having married Åsa-Hanna, with the blessing of the Lutheran State Church, to help ward off the rumours about his family's past, the construction of the character of Åsa-Hanna is more prominently linked to gossip than that of any other character. But as Spacks has pointed out, the function of gossip can also be subversive (Spacks 1985, 12), and it is the subversive dimensions that dominate as Åsa-Hanna's focalisation initiates a process of subjectivation. Middleton and Woods use the term 'regeneration' for the combination of external narration and free indirect discourse and describe its function as that of creating 'the sense of closely rendered observer memories' (Middleton and Woods 2000, 89); but in *Åsa-Hanna*, I would argue, the prominent use of free indirect discourse and free indirect thought assumes a new significance in the passages directly connected with Åsa-Hanna's struggle to emerge as a subject. While in the quotation above the borderline between external narration of the omniscient variety and free indirect discourse is difficult to define, the use of dialect words and phrases would seem to suggest free indirect thought. Examples are the genitive 'Fransa' and phrases such as 'att di inte stämt blon i tide' (that they hadn't staunched the blood in time) and 'vad di kunde sätta ihop' (what people had made up). Several reviewers of the novel were critical of this use of dialect outwith direct speech, one of them even accusing Wägner of having failed to pay sufficient attention to her text (Bergstrand 1918; see also Lindblad 1918, Österling 1918). Staffan Björck has written more positively on the use of dialect in the free indirect discourse in *Åsa-Hanna*, arguing that the dialect elements make such passages more lively and colourful (Björck 1968, 124), but he has made no attempt to develop his findings.

Texts

Shlomith Rimmon-Kenan has defined one of the functions of free indirect discourse as the enhancement of 'the bivocality or polyvocality of the text' (Rimmon-Kenan 1988, 113). In other words, free indirect discourse can be seen as distilling in narrational terms one of the key effects of gossip. Moreover free indirect discourse, according to Rimmon-Kenan, 'may promote an empathetic identification on the part of the reader' (op. cit., 114), a point elaborated by Kathy Mezei who has approached free indirect discourse in the context of 'the conflict between conventional gender roles and [...] the resistance to traditional narrative authority in which a masterly male subject speaks for and over the female object of his gaze', and has found that the 'undecidability inherent in the structure of FID [free indirect discourse] makes it an appropriate space for the complicated interchange between author, narrator, character-focalizer, and reader' (Mezei 1996, 66, 67). If we accept the linkage highlighted by Spacks between reading novels and participating in gossip (Spacks 1985, 22), the prominence in Åsa-Hanna's process of subjectivation of free indirect discourse/free indirect thought thus also helps pinpoint the involvement of the narratee and foreground that of the reader.

In the passage from the novel quoted above, the opening phrases of the first three sentences, 'Hon mindes någon dunkel historia från sin barndom' (She could remember some vague story from her childhood), 'Och hon hade hört något om att' (And she'd heard something about), 'Hon hade inte vidare tänkt på' (She hadn't thought any further of), are narrated by the external narrator. But the ways in which each of these sentences develop indicate that free indirect thought then takes over. In the first two sentences, the dialect genitive 'Fransa' signals the shift, with a series of dialect forms following in the first, and what is arguably a colloquial phrase, 'ha handlat med flit' (having done it deliberately), in the second. In the third sentence, the chief indicator of free indirect thought is the syntax, with the last two clauses, constructed as complete sentences, tagged on as in the spoken language: 'de där gamla historierna, som folk mest glömt nu mera, *det kan så lätt komma ut rykten, det ser man bäst på vad di kunde sätta ihop om Franse och Stina Snabb*' (my italics) (those old stories which people nowadays had mostly forgotten, *rumours get out and about so easily, you see that from what people had made up about Franse and Stina Snabb).* In the context of the prominent phallogocentrism of the novel, this complexity and potential of free indirect thought is crucial to the text's destabilisation of the dominant discourse on gender and to Åsa-Hanna's process of subjectivation. The examples that follow come from the chapter entitled 'Lågan' (The Flame), in which Åsa-Hanna at last confronts phallogocentrism in the shape of the Law Officer.

At this point in the story, Åsa-Hanna has been married for a number of years and is the mother of three children. As part of the safeguarding of the family secret, she has helped ensure that her father-inlaw and her mother-in-law have died without getting the opportunity to confess to the murder of Franse's grandfather. But when her husband strikes up a relationship with the wife of her childhood friend Magnus and initiates an attempt to acquire his farm while Magnus is in the United States, Åsa-Hanna's efforts to thwart her husband seem to bring her ever closer to unravelling the family secrets. It is the advice from her uncle, Anders Petter, that she do so, which Åsa-Hanna is turning over in the following passage:

> För resten, var det väl inte så alldeles tvärsäkert, fast Anders Petter sagt det, att det var hennes plikt att ange sin man och sig själv och vanära sina barn? Vad gick det egentligen för nöd på dem? Var det någon som lärde dem något ont? På den frågan svarade hon helst icke. Den saken står ju inte förlivet, tänkte hon. Men det gör Magnusa sak. (Wägner 1918, 359-60)

> (Anyway, it probably wasn't absolutely certain, although Anders Petter had said so, that it was her duty to report her husband and herself and bring disgrace on her children? Weren't they well enough off? Did anyone teach them evil? That question she preferred not to answer. There is no particular hurry about the matter, she thought. But about Magnus's business, there is.)

Here the free indirect thought may largely take the form of questions, yet its effect in authorising the character of Åsa-Hanna is emphatic. Constructing Åsa-Hanna as the subject, these questions not onlychallenge the relations of gender and power on which the régime in Mellangården has been based: by implication, the critique also points up the relations of gender and power in the Lutheran State Church, which has sanctioned Åsa-Hanna's marriage into a family of notoriously bad reputation and, as the Dean's wife has admitted as early as Åsa-Hanna's wedding day, left her 'att på egen hand reda upp sitt öde' (op. cit., 107) (to sort out her fate on her own). It is this Åsa-Hanna, the character whose emergence as a subject has been precipitated by means of focalisation and free indirect thought, who determines, still in the chapter called 'The Flame', to speak to the Law Officer so as to prevent her husband from depriving Magnus of his farm. For the first time, Åsa-Hanna openly confronts the phallogocentrism that has been the motor of the story. The trappings of this phallogocentrism are to some extent peeled away as Åsa Hanna's initial focalisation conveys the image of 'lagens ansikte' (the face of the Law) on this occasion, in the middle of the afternoon, bearing on its left cheek 'det välkända mönstret efter länsmanskans soffkudde' (the familiar pattern of the sofa cushion made by the Law Officer's wife), and as the direct speech of their conversation pinpoints the patronising tone of the Law Officer in his reference to Åsa-Hanna and her rival as 'brunetten och blondinen' (Wägner 1918, 363, 365-66) (the brunette and the blonde). Significantly, the Law Officer attempts to brush aside the first part of Åsa-Hanna's story: '– Jag tror fru Adamson brukar läsa romaner' (It seems to me you're in the habit of reading novels, Mrs Adamson); and when Åsa-Hanna raises the topic of the murder of her husband's grandfather, the Law Officer attempts to dismiss it as '[s]åna gamla historier' (op. cit., 365, 367) (old stories like that), i.e. gossip. In this sequence, gossip punches holes in the official narratives as, moreover, one of the representatives of phallogocentrism tries to equate events that do not fit into this narrative with 'novels'. The full significance of Åsa-Hanna's revelations is pinpointed when, a few hours after her confession, the Law Officer turns up outside her home and invites her to retract, emphasising not only her responsibilities towards her family but also his readiness to overlook what he construes as an over-hasty statement by a wife temporarily upset by the infidelity of her husband: 'Tänk bara hur det skulle gått, om hon inte träffat på en human och erfaren karl, som gränat i tjänsten och sett varjehanda och lärt sig att en får lov att ta det lugnt och försiktigt *för att inte vända rent opp och ner på samhället*' (op. cit., 377; my italics) (Just imagine what might have happened if you had not come across a man who is kind and experienced, who's grown grey in the service and who's seen all sorts of things and who's learnt that one has to do things calmly and prudently *so as not to turn society upside-down*).

As Åsa-Hanna returns to the family and home she has jeopardised by rebelling against the dominant discourse on the family, exposing the significance of phallogocentrism in the process, she is rewarded by a glimpse, as the sun is about to set, of the heavenly city of Jerusalem. With her realisation that a flame of the celestial light is now burning inside her, the free indirect thought recurs:

– Vad hetade väl denna här lågan, som kom så oförtänkt te me i mitt djypa elände och mörker? Jag kan inte kristna na, för jag var inte känder me sådan eld förr. Men hon måtte ändå va en gnista av en gnista av det himmelska ljuset? Och fast hon är så liten, att hon inte skulle märkas däruppe i Staden, vars ljus är Lammet, så synes hon me stor här, där hon har så mö mörker att skina imot. (Wägner 1918, 373)

(What was the name of this flame, which came so unexpectedly to me in my deep misery and darkness? I'm unable to christen it, because I haven't known such a fire before. But I think it must be a spark of a spark of the heavenly light? And although it's so small that it wouldn't be noticed up there in the City, whose light is the Lamb, it seems big enough here where it's got so much darkness to shine against.)

In an analysis of *Åsa-Hanna* published more than two decades ago, I made what I now think is rather heavy weather of the biblical allusions and quotations in the text, arguing that these were prominent enough to enable us to read the novel as structured on the basis of the Bible (Forsås-Scott 1986). I now regard it as more meaningful to read the biblical vocabulary and quotations in terms of intertextuality. What I have in mind is the kind of significance of intertextuality that Michael Worton and Judith Still have summarised in the following terms:

On the one hand, there is phallic monologism or the illusion of unity and self-sufficiency. On the other hand, there is liquefaction, the vehicle of passion – even madness, polyphony, the receptive object penetrated by other voices and so on. The latter pole has been admired, but, more particularly, feared for many centuries. We would argue that it can be read as a figure of 'femininity', of that particular 'other' to *the same*. (Worton and Still 1990, 30; italics original)

In what is arguably the novel's most radical example of the deconstruction of phallogocentrism, the biblical allusions and quotations are decontextualised and put to new and different uses in the construction of Åsa-Hanna as a subject. Åsa-Hanna's husband may indeed threaten her, on one of the final pages of the novel, with the phrase '*du ska få tiga och arbeta*' (Wägner 1918, 418; italics original) (*I'll make you shut up and work hard*); but as I have attempted to show, a reading in terms of narration and language with an emphasis on the role of free indirect discourse/free indirect thought as a key factor in the process of subjectivation, makes the notion of Åsa-Hanna '[shutting] up' a contradiction in terms. And given the connection, highlighted by Spacks, between the participation in gossip and the reading of novels, with the focus on the '*subversive implications* both of literal gossip and of its printed transformations' (Spacks 1985, 12; my italics), the fact that *Åsa-Hanna*'s prominent narratee has been party to this process throughout is crucial. Reading, as Middleton and Woods have reminded us, is itself 'a practice of memory, because texts are forms of prosthetic social memory by which readers increase and correct their own limited cognitive strengths and participate in a public memorial space' (Middleton and Woods 2000, 5). In a Sweden that was not just being transformed by industrialisation and urbanisation but that was also in the midst of a process of democratisation, including the campaign for female suffrage, the historical novel *Åsa-Hanna*, while problematising the dominant discourses on gender and community, clearly also points ahead, for textual memory, as Middleton and Woods have underlined, also looks forward: 'It not only empowers societies to manage territories and plan for the future, it also contains a promise that this can be a democratic process' (ibid.).

As I have tried to show, Wägner's best-known novel is considerably more radical than previous readings have allowed.

Den befriade kärleken (Love Liberated)

The serialisation of Wägner's next novel, *Den befriade kärleken* (Love Liberated), began in late 1918, the year in which *Åsa-Hanna* was published, and by the end of 1919, she had published two new novels, *Kvarteret Oron* (District of Unrest) as well as *Den befriade kärleken*. Dismissed by the reviewers, *Kvarteret Oron* has since been reprinted and even turned into a television serial, and the novel's representation of Stockholm in the immediate aftermath of the First World War has been much praised (see e.g. Isaksson and Linder 2003, 269-72). Following a lukewarm reception, *Den befriade kärleken* has remained a neglected text. According to Wägner's biographers, this novel should be read in the context of what they perceive as Wägner's growing commitment to Christianity (op. cit., 263-68). My readings of these two novels challenge the standard ones, and my starting-point, in both cases, is the prominence in the texts of the First World War. While there are traces in both of the linkage between masculinity and femininity and war and peace respectively, in other words the pattern we have encountered in Schreiner and Gilman, and in some of Wägner's reportages and essays relating to the war, the problematisation of gender and power in texts by Frida Stéenhoff, for example in 'Feminismens moral', strikes me as a more relevant point of reference with regard to *Den befriade kärleken* and *Kvarteret Oron*. *Den befriade kärleken*, which is largely set in Stockholm, and *Kvarteret Oron*, which combines a provincial setting with a setting in the capital, develop the impact of the war on a bold and experimental scale, and it is on the implications of this approach for the texts' explorations of the constructions of gender and community that I shall focus here.

In volume 2 of *No Man's Land*, entitled *Sexchanges*, Sandra M. Gilbert and Susan Gubar analyse the pivotal significance of the First World War in the context of gender and literary modernism. According to Gilbert and Gubar, 'many women writers recorded drastic revisions of society that were [...], directly or indirectly, inspired by the revolutionary state in which they were living'; more specifically, a number of women writers, including Virginia Woolf, 'explored the political and economic revolution by which the Great War at least temporarily dispossessed male citizens of the primacy that had always been their birthright, while permanently granting women access to both the votes and the professions that they had never before possessed' (Gilbert and Gubar 1989, 264, 263). Sweden remained neutral throughout the First World War, and the linkage familiar from e.g. the British context between the women's war effort, including access to new professions, and the granting of suffrage for women is largely irrelevant. Yet it is in the context of the First World War, as encapsulated in Nina Macdonald's lines, 'All the world is topsy-turvy / Since the War began' (quoted in Gilbert and Gubar 1989, 263), a trope familiar from my analysis of the reportages from Vienna in 1920, that I am going to read *Den befriade kärleken* and *Kvarteret Oron*, demonstrating the extent to which this hitherto neglected perspective helps highlight the significance of the constructions of gender and community in these texts, with a special emphasis on the relations between gender and power in terms of agency as well as domination.

As I have mentioned in the section on the cultural context above, *Den befriade kärleken* was serialised in the conservative weekly *Vecko-Journalen* (The Weekly Journal) (Praktupplagan), 1 December 1918 – 23 March 1919. The instalments appeared among photographs of German soldiers returning home, of the unfolding revolution in Germany, and also of working-class unrest in Sweden; and this context would undoubtedly have enhanced the significance of the upheavals made prominent in the text of the novel. Narrated by an external narrator who is omniscient and gender neutral, *Den befriade kärleken* in fact has two parallel stories which gradually merge, and which radically problematise the dominant discourse on the family. Contrary to my perspective back in 1983, I no longer regard one of these stories as more important than the other (Forsås-Scott 1983). Instead I want to argue that they can usefully be read in the light of Bal's point about narratological analysis as 'a dialectic back-and-forth between speculation and verification', with the interrelations between the two stories foregrounding in this text what Bal has termed 'a chance to "talk back," to complicate or even counter what we had assumed, or tend to wish to see confirmed' (Bal 1999, 126).

One of the stories focuses on the dominant discourse on the family in the sense that it revolves around a married couple consisting of Filip, a celebrated poet with his sights on membership of the Swedish Academy, and his wife and muse Andrea. The other story introduces an alternative discourse. Mikaela, Filip's foster-sister, is not only unmarried but runs an alternative community in the shape of a home offering former prisoners, all of them male, support to adapt to a life in freedom. She even has the audacity to point out that: ' – Det är inte mycket [...] men alltid ett surrogat för matriarkatet, för det är jag, som styr' (Wägner 1919b, 20) (It's not a lot [...] but at least it's a substitute for matriarchy, for I'm in charge).

The radical construction of Mikaela and her ex-prisoners talks back and challenges the construction of Filip and Andrea in terms of the dominant discourse on the family. The role of performativity is further highlighted by Mikaela, who describes the transformation of her clients into 'gentlemen' as a creative enterprise (Wägner 1919b, 23). But then the First World War breaks out, the world is turned upside down, and performativity and its implications are more starkly profiled. Filip is in South Africa seeking new inspiration, and following an investigation into his relations with a German family, he is detained in Cape Town. Here the officer in charge underlines the now inferior position of the famous Swedish poet by poking fun at him for his surname, Mr Humble, and a Swedish businessman confirms his lowly status by employing him as a secretary (op. cit., 76, 80). In the meantime Andrea, having devoted months to writing to Filip and waiting for him, constructs a new existence for herself within the framework of a new type of community, one of the religious sects thriving on the apocalyptic sentiments whipped up by the war; and given that 'Guds barns äldste' (the Elders of God's Children) have a female character, Dorkas Olsson, as one of its leading figures and go on to prepare the newly converted Andrea for a career as a missionary in Africa, the reversal of the power relationship that originally characterised Filip's and Andrea's marriage is soon complete. Mikaela, on the other hand, is forced out of her business and her house by one of her gentlemen turned war-time profiteer; interestingly, he is the brother of Dorkas Olsson. With Mikaela's relationship with another of her gentlemen becoming increasingly close at the same time she, in a development that is the reverse of that of Andrea, moves from a position of power in terms of agency towards integration into a seemingly conventional heterosexual relationship. The war, in other words, facilitates the kind of abrupt reversals that demonstrate that gender and relations of gender and power are performative and in a state of flux. Commenting on Nina Macdonald's line about all the world being 'topsy-turvy / Since the War began', Gilbert and Gubar have argued that 'the reverses and reversals of no man's land fostered the formation of a metaphorical country not unlike the queendom Charlotte Perkins Gilman called Herland' (Gilbert and Gubar 1989, 263); and for all the differences of the project in *Den befriade kärleken*, there are distinct parallels with Gilman's novel in terms of the foregrounding and exploration of relations of gender and power as economic, political, social, and cultural constructions.

Throughout, the textuality of the convoluted story is prominent, although the significance of the use of language is not investigated in anything like the detailed ways we have encountered in *Pennskaftet* or *Åsa-Hanna*. The counterpoint of the text of the novel is the output of Filip, whose celebrations of his muse Andrea have established his reputation and whose 'En landsflyktings sånger' (The Songs of an Exile), posted from South Africa, offer Andrea 'en slags smekmånad med hans dikter' (Wägner 1919b, 98) (a kind of honeymoon with his poems). While Dorkas Olsson destabilises Andrea's role in Filip's writing by underlining, once she has seen the poet's latest volume, 'att man endast ska dyrka Gud och inte människor' (op. cit., 118) (that you should worship only God and not human beings), the new collection of poetry that appears on the day Filip takes his seat in the Swedish Academy has a title that signals the status quo: it is called *Den fångna kärleken* (op. cit., 278) (Love Incarcerated). It is Mikaela who challenges the author, her now famous brother, by asking: 'Kan du inte nu älska oss allesammans, hela världen, och leva och dikta för oss?' (op. cit., 304) (Can't you now love us all, the whole world, and live and write poetry for us), and pointedly suggesting that his next book be titled – like the novel we are reading – *Den befriade kärleken* (Love Liberated) (ibid.). At one level, these points can be read as a critique of the Swedish Academy for continuing to sanction, despite the war, texts as irrelevant as Filip's poems. More importantly, Mikaela's question indicates that in a world turned upside down, an extensive enquiry into constructions of gender and relations of gender and power such as that provided by the novel entitled *Den befriade kärleken* is a key step towards new communities and a better future.

Kvarteret Oron (District of Unrest)

Kvarteret Oron (District of Unrest) is a diary novel, and the entries cover a period of six months from 1 December [1918] to 27 May [1919]. Unlike *Den befriade kärleken*, *Kvarteret Oron* has some explicit references to the topsy-turvy world, from the title to the narrator's summary of how the war has affected Europe, 'nämligen att utarma, demoralisera och vända upp och ner på det' (Wägner 1919c, 19) (namely to pauperise it, demoralise it and turn it upside down). Most conspicuous, however, are the references to one of Wägner's earlier novels. The fact that the reviewer of *Kvarteret Oron* in the daily *Ny Tid* noted that Wägner's work so far had revolved chiefly around female suffrage and the situation of women office workers (–m, 1919), indicates that by 1919, Wägner had an authorial profile that was sufficiently distinctive for it to be evoked for textual purposes. For while the reviewer in *Ny Tid* argued that the references to the suffragists and the office workers served as a mere framework for the plot of *Kvarteret Oron* (ibid.), I want to take the implications of these references a step further. In *Kvarteret Oron* the references to categories of characters familiar from Wägner's earlier work – and the chief point of reference, in my reading, is her best-known diary novel, *Norrtullsligan* – help reinforce the anomaly of the main character who, uniquely in Wägner's novels so far, is not a hard-working, (lower) middle-class New Woman but a member of the aristocracy. In a topsy-turvy world, *Kvarteret Oron* highlights the significance of textuality by turning one of Wägner's best-known novels upside down.

The dominant discourse on the family is swiftly demolished in *Kvarteret Oron* as Brita Ribing, the character-bound female narrator, introduces herself as a twenty-seven-year-old widow, until recently the wife of Henrik Ribing who has died an alcoholic, and the mother of a young boy who is mentally handicapped as a result of his father's drinking habits (Wägner 1919c, 8-11). As Brita Ribing migrates from her role as a self-supporting single woman to her role as the relative of a wealthy uncle and aunt living in one of Stockholm's most exclusive areas and back again, her text constructs her as the epitome of a revolutionary era, of a world turned upside down: 'Ingen, som denna förmiddag mötte mig på vägen till diplomatstan, där farbror har en villa vid Djurgårdsbrunnsviken, kunde trott om mig annat än att jag var en dam av solida ekonomiska villkor och lyckligt lottad på alla vis' (op. cit., 16) (No one who met me this morning as I made my way to the Diplomatic Quarter where my uncle has a villa by Djurgårdsbrunnsviken, would have thought that I was anything other than a lady enjoying a solid financial situation and privileged in all respects). Not unlike Pegg's diary entries in *Norrtullsligan*, Brita Ribing's similarly processual writing contributes to foregrounding the constructedness and complexity of feminine subjectivity. Indeed, Brita Ribing's reflections, during a church service, on her family coat of arms and her maiden name, Gyllensting ('golden stab' or 'golden stitches'), spell out the linkage in this novel between text and subjectivity:

> Mitt namn hade förändrat utseende och blivit något helt annat, en söm av gyllene styng på ett mullmörkt kläde. *Varje dag var ett styng, och när dagarnas rad var slut, skulle man få tillfälle att se vad för slags mönster jag åstadkommit i livet.* (op. cit., 44; my italics)

> (My name had changed its appearance and become something quite different, a seam of golden stitches on cloth dark as the earth. *Each day was a stitch, and when the sequence of days was completed, people would be able to see what kind of pattern I had achieved in my life.*)

While her wealthy peers emphasise the complexity of Brita Ribing's subjectivity as they tell her to 'sluta upp med den där envisa nycken att bli självförsörjande och leka proletär' (Wägner 1919c, 181) (give up those stubborn fancies to be self-supporting and play at being a member of the proletariat), the fabula offers her the opportunity to rise above these wealthy peers too so that, for a limited part of its duration, Brita Ribing is effectively constructing herself in terms of three levels of society, taking it for granted that the triumphal arch and the crowd outside the church are in her honour rather than in that of the King of Sweden. Destabilising the relationship between signifier and signified by playing with the issues of feminine subjectivation and relations of gender and power and so highlighting the significance of performativity and masquerade, *Kvarteret Oron* develops a take on these matters that is more frivolous and arguably more provocative than in any of Wägner's previous novels. The exceptional power of Brita Ribing is based on the discovery of a cellar full of bottles of spirits, hoarded by her late husband in anticipation of a total ban on the sale of alcohol. (The introduction of a total ban had been enjoying increasing support in Sweden throughout the 1910s and was to become the subject of a referendum in 1922 [Carlsson 1968d, 24-28].) The existence of the alcohol helps generate some astounding twists of the story as Brita Ribing hatches plans to salvage it from the executors as a means of protecting the financial future of herself and her son, but her exploitation of her asset also turns into a series of acts of economic and communal reconstruction, made all the more poignant by the fact that they take place in a revolutionary era. At a time when milk, butter, and meat are scarce, Brita Ribing exchanges some of her bottles of spirits for food which she distributes among the self-supporting women and other poor neighbours in Stockholm (Wägner 1919c, 76-82). And when she allows provincial estate-owners to buy alcohol from her cellar, it is on condition that they accept with each bottle 'en liten, liten proletär' (op. cit., 46) (a teensy-weensy proletarian), her tactics securing summer holidays for 100 city children (ibid.). Her support of a scheme that would allow every officer in the Swedish army to buy a share of the alcohol (op. cit., 100-101), could be construed as an attempt to immobilise the defence of the country, but this pacifist implication is not developed. There is no doubt, however, that the cellar full of alcohol enables Brita Ribing to construct a series of glimpses, however fantastic, of a remodelled society based on alternative constructions of gender and community. But this window of change is a narrow one, just sufficient for the alternatives to become visible; and as Brita Ribing decides to marry the new owner for the sake of gaining access to the estate that continues to mean so much to her, she discovers that her fiancé, a captain in the army, has sold it. As Brita Ribing is again locked into the dominant discourses on gender and community, including the familiar hierarchical constructions of masculinity and femininity, the reader is left pondering the remarkable patterns that her diary entries have created in constructing her life of words.

Den förödda vingården (The Ravaged Vineyard)

While largely well received (e.g. Bergman 1920, S.R.O. 1920, Anon. 1920, 826-27), *Den förödda vingården* (1920; The Ravaged Vineyard) has subsequently become one of Wägner's most neglected novels. Isaksson and Linder have written it off as a mere 'sketch-book', with most of the material having its 'equivalent in reality' (Isaksson and Linder 2003, 289, 290), in other words in the encounter with Vienna represented in the series of reportages in *Dagens Nyheter* in the early months of 1920. The Swedish contexts – economic, political, social, and cultural – outlined above are largely irrelevant here; but the fact that we are dealing, in the reportages and the novel respectively, with closely related material developed in different genres makes an analysis of the novel all the more urgent in the context of the present study.

The text of *Den förödda vingården* focuses on Rut Malmfelt, a young Swedish woman, who travels to Vienna in January 1920 to work for an aid project. The other main characters are Hans von Turnheim on whose card his titles, 'friherre' (Baron) and 'kapten' (Captain), have both been crossed out (Wägner 1920o, 29); Gisela Zimmermann, a journalist on *Wiener-Presse*; and Jones, a British journalist. Issues of representation emerge as a central aspect of the narration of this externally narrated novel, and these also have a key impact on the construction of the narratee.

While Wägner's reportages about Vienna highlight their immediacy, the novel's narrative about Vienna comes complete with prominent instances of intertextuality which, in line with an observation made by Middleton and Woods, can contribute to foregrounding social memory (Middleton and Woods 2000, 81). The novel has an epigraph, a stanza from the poem 'Dolores di Colibrados' by Gustaf Fröding. In line with the first of the functions distinguished by Genette, this epigraph elucidates and justifies the title of the novel (Genette 2001, 156-57). The stanza includes the line 'förödd är en vingård med ädelt vin' (Fröding 1902, 121) (ravaged is a vineyard with noble wine), and the title of the novel pivots on the phonetic parallel between Wien, the form for Vienna also used in Swedish, and the poem's homophonic *vin*, 'wine', with the ravaged vineyard of the poem turning into an allusion to the Vienna ravaged by shortages of food and fuel in the wake of the First World War. But in this epigraph, which ends with the celebration of 'en skön och en stolt ruin' (ibid.) (a beautiful and a noble ruin), there is also, as I shall demonstrate, an element of Genette's second function: the epigraph comments on the text of the novel, 'whose meaning it indirectly specifies or emphasizes' (Genette 2001, 157). The opening chapter, moreover, is entitled 'Skapelsen' (The Creation), the narrative linking the title to Haydn's oratorio and also to the ambitions of Rut who is about to join the project in Vienna (Wägner 1920o, 10, 14). But the title of the opening chapter also draws attention to the novel as an artefact, and more specifically to the significance of narration and representation in the text. What is narrated here, how is it narrated, and what are the effects?

The contrast between the realistic representation of the opening chapter and the disjointed images of the two following ones, 'Sirapen' (The Treacle) and 'Film' (Film), could hardly be greater. A tree walks along the quay by the Danube, followed by a huge bundle of twigs. Waves of treacle suddenly cover a street, and the bundle of twigs appears in the middle. In 'Film', at the Last Judgement Vienna style, a court is trying children who have stolen to alleviate their hunger. In a case of glaring juxtaposition, this part of the narrative contrasts with that of the remainder of Chapter Three, about the selection of suitable examples of suffering for the making of a film for British audiences.

In *The Theatre of the Absurd* Martin Esslin has argued that the 'sense of metaphysical anguish at the absurdity of the human condition' had resulted in 'the open abandonment of rational devices and discursive thought' in the drama of writers such as Beckett, Adamov, Ionesco, and Genet (Esslin 1970, 23-24). *Den förödda vingården* cannot be labelled absurdist, but the collage of powerful, disjointed, and often puzzling images, especially in Chapters Two and Three, represents a radical break with the opening chapter and, indeed, with Wägner's previous prose fiction. Add to this the facts that characters in Bal's sense of 'complex semantic [units]' are interspersed with actors, mere 'structural [positions]' (Bal 1999, 115), and that some of these actors – just as in for example some of August Strindberg's (1849-1912) expressionist drama – are not individualised beyond labels such as 'den blinde' (the blind man), 'portvakten' (the door-keeper), and 'klippfisken' (the split cod), and it becomes obvious that the narrative of this novel draws on aspects of modernist writing to represent the disintegration of a community, a new version of a world turned upside down.

What conclusions can we draw about the construction of gender in the dismantled community of *Den förödda vingården*? While Gilbert and Gubar have argued that a number of women writers at the time of the First World War 'covertly or overtly celebrated the release of female desires and powers which that revolution made possible' (Gilbert and Gubar 1989, 263-64), there is no equivalent in *Den förödda vingården* of the experimental foregrounding of feminine agency that I have traced in *Den befriade kärleken* and *Kvarteret Oron*. Although it is true that the novel's Swedish charity workers, most of whom are female, have power thanks to their access to money and food, this power is hardly developed in the story. Instead the text highlights the constructedness of gender and, more particularly, of gender boundaries by means of a character such as the fifteen-year-old boy who has had to take on the roles of both breadwinner and housewife so as to be able to support his siblings and, even more strikingly, the character Rut first encounters in the children's court and who 'såg ut som en förklädd gosse, tunn och mager med kortklippt hår, herrhatt, krage och kravatt' (Wägner 1920o, 31) (looked like a boy in disguise, thin and worn with short hair, a man's hat, collar and tie). '[D]et finns inte i hela Wien en person, som kan mer nöd än jag' (op. cit., 46) (In the whole of Vienna, there is not a person who knows more about suffering than I do), claims

Gisela Zimmerman, the female journalist who looks like a boy in disguise, and the construction of whom would seem to indicate that in the face of suffering on this scale, traditional gender distinctions may become marginal, perhaps even out of date.

The dismantled community of *Den förödda vingården* is chiefly constructed in terms of a handful of characters and a number of actors. The dominant discourse on the family is comprehensively deconstructed by the case of the fifteen-year-old family breadwinner-cum-housewife whose father is dead, whose mother has lapsed into apathy, whose nine-year-old sister is the size of a two-year-old, whose youngest sibling is similarly disfigured by starvation, and whose home is a room with a packing case and some rags. Unlike the English film about the situation in Vienna, this text does not censor the suffering; and there are many examples of how wounds physical and psychological, along with hunger, bitterness, cold, and anger are reducing the functions of the novel's citizens of Vienna and thus adding to the chaos of their community.

But in this work of prose fiction in which, as the making of the film illustrates, representation is power and in which, moreover, two of the key characters are journalists, the text also provides space for the development of new relationships. New relationships can be synonymous with bridge-building, as illustrated by the box of provisions Rut has her mother send to her landlady, and by the relationships between Gisela Zimmerman and Mr Jones and Rut and von Turnheim respectively. But the most remarkable example, at once pinpointing and crossing boundaries, occurs at the very end when Gisela, trampled at a demonstration and left with injuries she has no chance of surviving, is assisted by Rut in committing suicide. Afterwards von Turnheim watches Rut arrange Gisela's head on the pillow:

> Han såg henne göra denna handling och kom med ens ihåg henne sådan hon var första dagen, hur tafatt hon kommit och bjudit honom bröd på gatan. Han mindes henne dansande, han såg henne tydligt sådan han en gång gått förbi henne, medan hon tittade i bodfönster.
> – Lille broder! viskade hon.
> – Hur mäktig och underbar kärleken, tänkte han. (Wägner 1920o, 172)

(He saw her carrying out this act and suddenly remembered her as she had been on the first day, how awkwardly she had come and offered him bread in the street. He remembered her dancing, he saw her clearly as she had been once when he had passed her while she was looking in a shop window.
'Little brother,' she whispered.
How powerful and wonderful is love, he thought.)

Hans von Turnheim is eventually forced out of his nihilism by his love of Rut. But this final sequence is just as much about the relationship between Rut and Gisela. Just like the concluding words of *Pennskaftet*, those of Rut are ambiguously addressed, with the potential to embrace all those present along with others beyond this circle. It is in this sense of identification, which eventually transcends the binary construction of gender (Rut's address to Gisela is 'Lille *broder*' [my italics; Little *brother*]), that the personal relationships in this novel culminate; and it is these relationships, along with the subject positions they provide, that emerge as the basis of a new and better community.

To summarise my findings about the construction of gender and community in the reportages relating to Vienna and the novel respectively, the trope of the-world-upside-down is a fundamental aspect of the narratives of both types of text. But unlike the novels *Den befriade kärleken* and *Kvarteret Oron*, the narratives of which also foreground this trope, the texts relating to Vienna in 1920 do not offer space for experimentation with the trope and its implications: here the trope is the key dimension of the communities constructed by the narratives and, in the novel, of the characters too. The chief consequence is boundless suffering. While the sequences of modernist narration in *Den förödda vingården* represent a significant change, both in the context of the realist narration elsewhere in the novel and in the context of the realism of the novels analysed previously, it is the prominence of suffering, in the reportages as well as in the novel, that has the effect of putting the spotlight on the construction of new communities rather than on the construction of gender. A string of narrative devices, exemplified by the frequent use of the indefinite pronoun *man* (one/you/they/people) in the reportages and the range of subject positions offered by the characters in the novel, help construct the narratees as the participants of narratives that are about participation; and the foregrounding of boundary-crossings and bridge-building creates a momentum in both categories of text, in sharp contrast to the static celebration of the proud and noble ruin of the novel's epigraph. In both the reportages and the novel, the development of the trope of the world upside down offers new beginnings. The question is how the new communities will be constructed, and to what extent they will involve a reconstruction of gender too?

*

The novels discussed here were published during a period of extensive economic, political, social, and cultural change in Sweden. As I have tried to demonstrate, a comparison between constructions of gender and community in these works of prose fiction and in the reportages, essays, and light-hearted columns considered earlier in this chapter is clearly fruitful, with the most obvious difference with regard to the novels being the extent of gender experimentation and gender political critique. While according to the standard histories of literature issues of gender begin to fade away after *Norrtullsligan* (1908) and *Pennskaftet* (1910), I have been able to demonstrate that gender is central to the stories of all the novels considered here with the exception of the very last, *Den förödda vingården* (1920). An analysis of the constructions of gender in these novels also points up the significance of alternative communities. Among the most conspicuous examples of experimentation and critique are the deconstructions of gender, at the level of grammar, in *Pennskaftet*, which strengthen the significance of the New Women and the new communities of the text; and the demolition of phallogocentrism in the form of the Law and the Lutheran State Church in *Åsa-Hanna* (1918), with the constructions of the community of the parishioners in terms of gossip and the subjectivity of the central character chiefly in terms of free indirect thought and free indirect discourse both foregrounding the significance of narrative. The trope of the-world-upside-down in some of the prose fiction relating to the First World War as well as in the reportages from Vienna in 1920 is linked to comprehensive investigations into constructions of gender in terms of domination and agency in novels such as *Den befriade kärleken* (1919) and *Kvarteret Oron* (1919), while in the reportages from Vienna and in *Den förödda vingården* the economic, political, and social collapse of the city brought on by the war and its aftermath has made the construction of alternative communities not just urgent but crucial to a more peaceful future.

In the majority of the novels investigated here the narrator is external, with only *Norrtullsligan* and *Kvarteret Oron* exemplifying character-bound narration, but as I have demonstrated processes of subjectivation are prominent in both categories, from Åsa-Hanna's narrative transition from object to subject to Brita Ribing's process of writing herself in the diary entries that make up *Kvarteret Oron*. While the narratives of all these novels leave the dominant discourse on the family far behind, the alternative constructions of femininity are only rarely complemented by new constructions of masculinity, with Dick in *Pennskaftet* and Mikaela's partner in *Den befriade kärleken*, Mr Törnros, among the few examples. Much more important, as I have emphasised, are the constructions of alternative communities. Reaching well beyond the group of self-supporting women in *Norrtullsligan* or the members of the women's suffrage movement in *Pennskaftet*, these alternative communities are also prominently textual, with narratives that emphatically engage the narratees by means of for example dialogue, free indirect discourse or irony, also having the effect of foregrounding communities of readers.

Chapter 5:
Gender, Community and the First World War

In an overview of the texts by Wägner analysed in the previous chapter, the shift emphasised by critics who have foregrounded the novels, notably Linder (1965) and Isaksson and Linder (2003), from a focus on women in contemporary society in the early texts to a focus on ethical/religious issues in relation to the individual character in the later ones, is no longer visible. What stands out is instead the watershed constituted by the First World War. Wägner's reportages, essays, light-hearted columns, and prose fiction were produced and consumed in a Sweden undergoing rapid changes, economically, politically, socially, and culturally, but in a bird's-eye perspective of all the texts analysed above, the international dimensions are as important as those relating to Sweden in a state of transformation. The prominence of the First World War and its consequences added to the deconstruction of the dominant discourse on the family and contributed to highlighting alternative constructions of both gender and community. The war enhanced the significance of the struggle for women's suffrage as an international movement and also reinforced the role of new organisations such as the Women's International League for Peace and Freedom and Save the Children as trans-border, alternative communities.

We have seen how an early series of reportages such as the one about women in employment (1908-09) constructed categories of women in economic and social roles, some of them quite new and others less so, and with an emphasis also on the alternative communities constituted by their professional associations. The light-hearted columns dating from more or less the same period implied a greater emphasis on the transformative potential of the textual space, with the diary format of series such as *Klubben* (1907) and *Fru Hillevis dagbok* (1911-12) contributing in this analysis to highlighting constructions of gender in terms of performativity, with the emphasis on role-play helping to bring out the significance of power in terms of domination for the constructions of gender while also providing space for agency. The deconstruction of the dominant discourse on the family was prominent in early novels such as *Norrtullsligan* (1908) and *Pennskaftet* (1910), with the radical problematisation of gender in terms of grammar, the queering of the text, a most remarkable feature of the latter.

The First World War gave a new impetus to the explorations of constructions of gender and community, the earliest example being the reportages relating to the Women's International Congress at The Hague in spring 1915. Here new constructions of gender and community were bound up with efforts to achieve a ceasefire and a lasting peace, but while much of the rhetoric at the Congress would appear to have polarised constructions of gender by equalling femininity with peace and masculinity with war, Wägner's reportages, as we have seen, tended to tone down or avoid this type of essentialist construction. In a similar vein the essays from 1917 on Rosika Schwimmer, the Hungarian feminist pacifist, foregrounded as fundamental to her project the fusion of body and mind – at a time when the influential texts of Ellen Key, to take but one example, emphatically polarised gender by constructing masculinity in terms of the brain and femininity in terms of the heart. In one sense the novels from the period 1917-19 continued the experimentation with constructions of gender and community that we have encountered in early novels such as *Norrtullsligan* and *Pennskaftet*, but with the war (and its aftermath) adding key dimensions. The deconstruction of phallogocentrism in *Åsa-Hanna* (1918) and the foregrounding of the process of feminine subjectivation that was exemplified by the central character (and that also added to the prominence and engagement of the narratee), emerged in the chronological context of the production and reception of the novel as related to inequalities of gender and power underpinning the war. With regard to novels such as *Den befriade kärleken* (1919) and *Kvarteret Oron* (1919), the role of the texts as spaces for experimentation was unmistakable, with the dual stories of the former and the diary format of the latter highlighting the changeability, the topsy-turviness resulting, in immediate terms, from the war and its aftermath but offering exceptional opportunities for explorations of gender, power, and agency. We have also seen how the character-bound narration of *Kvarteret Oron* and the diary form have reinforced the construction of femininity in terms of performativity and masquerade. In *Den förödda vingården* (1920), the novel representing life in Vienna in the immediate aftermath of the war, the experimental function of the textual space was enhanced by a number of modernist features. But in a parallel to the reportages relating to Vienna during the same period, the text of the novel focused on the collapse of a community/ communities. In the novel, however, gender was arguably less insignificant given that the construction of new and alternative, more peaceful communities was rooted in relationships between individual characters, and here binary constructions of gender were also complemented by an indication of a same-sex relationship.

In other words, my feminist poststructuralist approach has helped show up dimensions of these texts that make the constructions of gender and community bolder, more comprehensive, and more innovative than noted previously. According to the literary histories, the contributions in terms of gender of Wägner's novels from this period (and the focus has been on the novels only) have been to introduce women characters in new economic, political, and social roles, as in *Norrtullsligan* and *Pennskaftet*. Rosi Braidotti has defined as 'the best way out of the dichotomous logic in which Western culture has captured sexed identities' that of '*[working] them through*':

> Working through the networks of discursive definitions of 'woman' is useful not only in what it produces as a process of deconstruction of female subjectivity but also *as process*, which allows for the constitution and the legitimation of a gendered female feminist community. (Braidotti 1994, 200; italics original)

By studying the broad range of Wägner's texts, I have shown not just how prominent these processes are, but also how radical they can be. Given these findings, what can we expect to find in the analyses of texts from 1922 onwards?

Part II.
New Communities: A New Society?
1922-47

Chapter 6:
Contexts

1. Economic

During the period beginning in 1922, Swedish women had the right to vote in national elections, and a growing proportion of them was also in paid employment. But as Ulla Wikander has pointed out, the relationship between women's suffrage and full citizenship on the one hand and their increasing participation in the labour market on the other is a complex one (Wikander 1999, 140-47).

In Lennart Schön's analysis the 1920s, along with the preceding decade, amounted to a second cycle of investment based on the economic renewal that had been taking place during the years 1890-1910, with 1930 marking the beginning of the second phase of the industrial breakthrough in Sweden (Schön 2000, 273). Sweden in the 1930s emerged as both affluent and highly successful (Therborn 1988, 29), the nation's prominence celebrated in the American journalist Marquis Childs's *Sweden: The Middle Way* (1936). To Childs, there was no doubt that Sweden was a 'machine civilization', with 'proportionately more telephones, more electrical devices, more motor cars in Stockholm than in any other European city' (Childs 1936, 21). The economic crisis of the early 1920s had been short, lasting from 1920 to 1922, but its effects had been far-reaching. The crisis had marked a watershed in the nation's development from an agricultural to an industrial economy, with Swedish farmers hit particularly hard by the economic downturn. The differences between urban and rural areas had become increasingly pronounced as a result, with the young women in particular leaving the rural areas (Schön 2000, 297-301). Also, a range of institutions that were to play major parts in the new phase of the development of modern Swedish industrial society gained in strength and influence in the wake of the crisis, including a number of leading companies and the groups owning them (notably the Wallenberg family), plus the banks, the state, and the local authorities (op. cit., 293-96, 299-301). The 1920s Swedish economy was characterised by competition and rationalisation, but also by new products, expanding markets, and a considerable amount of long-term investment (op. cit., 304-305).

While Schön has emphasised the significance of the expansion of 'kvinnornas arbetsmarknad' (the women's labour market) in the 1920s, the job categories listed confirm the gendered segregation of the labour market: women worked in nursing, education, and domestic service, in the clothing industry and in the food industry (Schön 2000, 320-23). The introduction of assembly-line production and taylorism, which replaced relatively complex tasks with several simplified ones, made women workers increasingly attractive in the labour market. Referring to the European context, Wikander has traced the origin of the linking of women workers and rationalisation to the First World War when women's contribution to the labour force, although extensive, was nevertheless regarded as exceptional (Wikander 1999, 157-58). In peace time, the employment of lower-paid women workers was a means of keeping costs down. In Wikander's analysis, the gendered division of labour became an integral part of the industrial and capitalist processes of transformation taking place in Europe throughout the first half of the twentieth century (op. cit., 143).

The conflicts surrounding the legislation introduced in 1923 to give Swedish women access to the majority of public-service posts have been seen as illustrating both the gendered division of the labour market and key elements of the discursive foundations underlying this division. In the provocative phrase of Greta Wieselgren, author of a major study on women's access to public offices in Sweden, the equality achieved by the introduction of suffrage for women 'was of the same kind as that in the presence of Our Lord and caused just as little irritation'; it was the legislation of 1923 that constituted 'the high threshold' (Wieselgren 1969, 246). Lydia Wahlström used a battery of statistics, quotations, and references to underpin her account of the haggling over salaries and pensions that preceded the implementation of the legislation in 1925 and demonstrated how women, irrespective of whether the comparison concerned salaries, pensions or technical ability, were trapped by the notorious mismatch between apples and pears (Wahlström 1933, 213-43). In theory, the legislation granted women equal access to most public-service posts and made no distinction between unmarried and married women, but as Wahlström has pointed out, the notion underlying the delaying tactics and the continuing discrimination was that of the man as the family breadwinner (op. cit., 236). In Wikander's analysis the First World War – like the Second World War – reinforced the myth of the happy family, not just in Sweden but throughout Europe, and had the effect of returning women to a nostalgically idyllicised home whose focal point was the mother as a symbol of security (Wikander 1999, 159-61). The dominance of this discourse, according to Wikander, was fundamental to the growing gender segregation characterising the Swedish labour market in the 1920s. The notion of the 'housewife contract', i.e. the tacit definition in Swedish social democracy of women as home-makers which, in Yvonne Hirdman's periodisation, characterised the decades from the 1920s to 1960 (Hirdman 1996, 209-14; see also Hagemann and Åmark 2004, 190), amounts to a closely related reading. However, the work of Renée Frangeur on the struggle in Sweden during the interwar years for married women's right to paid employment has demonstrated that Wikander's and Hirdman's periodisations are totalising to an extent that is in fact misleading (Frangeur 1998).

Following the election in 1932 and the formation of a Social Democratic government headed by Per Albin Hansson, the construction of *folkhemmet* (the home of the people) was initiated. Resulting in very high levels of unemployment, the Depression in Sweden had also been epitomised by the disintegration of the business imperium of the tycoon Ivar Kreuger. Against this background the government introduced its new economic policy, according to which the active role of the state would ensure both long-term planning and greater security for the citizens (Schön 2000, 331-32). As a result the Swedish economy achieved a rate of growth in the 1930s and 1940s higher than that of any other country in the world (op. cit., 334). The three leading sectors were transport, industry, and the public sector (op. cit., 336-38), underpinned by the rapid expansion of hydroelectric schemes. The relations between trades unions and the employers' organisation were regulated by the Saltsjöbaden agreement of 1938, which reinforced the economic stability.

2. Political

During the 1920s Sweden had a succession of Conservative, Liberal, and Social Democratic governments. Following the election to the riksdag in 1932, the Social Democrats became dependent on the support of the Farmers' Union, and between 1936 and 1939 these two parties formed a coalition government. The new coalition formed in December 1939 consisted of Social Democrats, members of the Farmers' Union, Liberals, and Conservatives and governed Sweden throughout the Second World War, and was then succeeded by a Social Democratic government. There were no women members of any of these governments before 1947, when Professor Karin Kock became a minister without portfolio and, the following year, Minister of National Economy.

Throughout this period, the proportion of women in the *riksdag* remained very small indeed. The *riksdag* had 150 members in the First Chamber and 230 in the Second Chamber, and out of this total of 380 there were just 5 women in 1922, a figure that then went down to 4 before rising to 6 in 1933 and 10 in 1937 (Östberg 2000, 70). In percentages, this works out at figures ranging from 1.1 to 1.6, with a climb to 2.6 in 1937. Women constituted no more than 5 per cent of the members of the *riksdag* by 1941, and 7 per cent by 1947 (Palme 1969, 63).

In a study of women in Swedish politics during the interwar years, Kjell Östberg has concluded that politics remained a masculine preserve. While the political parties had separate women's associations, some of them dating from before the introduction of suffrage for women, the new interest in these associations among male politicians that Östberg has traced was wholly focused on the women as voters (Östberg 2000, 65-66). The women's associations also influenced public opinion and functioned as pressure groups, but with regard to 'issues of importance to women': 'In common with a number of other women's organisations, they were important fora in which central sections of the emerging welfare policy were being formulated and in which the actual construction of these was begun' (op. cit., 66). But the parameters of the women's associations of the political parties were set by men: as Östberg has pointed out, *Frisinnade kvinnors riksförbund* (The National Association of Liberal Women), which refused to accept such parameters, also failed to survive (ibid.). In 1931, the Association was transformed into *Svenska kvinnors vänsterförbund* (The National Association of Women on the Left), an organisation designed to bring together women's groups whose political commitment was left of centre. In local government, very few women were involved, and while committees covering matters such as child welfare and poor relief tended to include token women, women tended to be absent from committees covering finance and planning (op. cit., 70). In Östberg's reading, women were systematically excluded from both national and local politics, and in an illuminating chapter he demonstrates the pervasiveness of the discourse on politics as masculine, to the extent that 'the women's inadequate awareness of the importance of participating in political work [...] was blamed on the women themselves and became a central element of their self-image' (op. cit., 91). Drawing a parallel with the introduction of suffrage for men in 1909 and the comprehensive and relatively smooth integration of the labour movement into Swedish politics, Östberg is unable to discern any similar desire to involve women in politics: 'Rather than working out solutions to the problems in the form of training and integration, the differences between women and men were turned into fixed entities' (op. cit., 97). In other words, the tendency to reinforce gender differences in the labour market that we have traced above would seem to have been even more marked in the field of politics. As a result there was a proliferation of women's organisations in Sweden in the 1920s and 1930s, with many of them emerging from employment and professionalisation and others springing up in fields such as philanthropy, religion, temperance, and pacifism; and these organisations form the focus of the second half of Östberg's study.

Hjalmar Branting (1860-1925), who had been elected to the Second Chamber in 1896 and become the chairperson of the executive committee of the Social Democratic Party in 1907 and Sweden's first Social Democratic Prime Minister in 1920, was strongly committed to international cooperation, disarmament, and peace. An advocate of Swedish membership of the League of Nations, he was elected to the Council of the League of Nations in 1923. But few shared Branting's interest in international politics, and during the interwar period no foreign-policy issues appeared in party manifestos or in election campaigns in Sweden (Olsson 1968, 144). A handful of journalists played an important role in adding to the general public's awareness of international issues. One of these was Elin Wägner who wrote in *Tidevarvet* about European politics and disarmament. However, the most influential of these writers was Fredrik Böök, well-established as a literary critic and subsequently a Professor of Literature (1920-24) and a member of the Swedish Academy. Reporting chiefly from Germany and Central Europe, he gradually became increasingly sympathetic towards the Nazis (ibid.).

3. Social

In a chapter on class and culture in Sweden during the interwar period, Jonas Frykman and Orvar Löfgren have emphasised the fact that the very idea of 'the home of the people' was based on the notion of 'a democratic state consisting of citizens with a strong sense of social responsibility'. In this perspective, they have concluded, the interwar years marked a period when the individual human being '[emerged] from the collective to [be nationalised] as a citizen' (Frykman and Löfgren 1985, 137). They do indeed use the verb *förstatligas* (be nationalised). Without going into their justifications for the term, I am highlighting it here as a pointer towards a social context which, unlike the social context in the period 1907-21, was characterised by a high degree of state intervention.

Sweden had a population of 5.9 million in 1920, rising to 6.2 in 1935 and 7 million in 1950 (Sköld 1968, 120). The birth-rate recorded in 1934 was the lowest in the world. In *Nation and Family* (1945), the substitute for an English version of Alva Myrdal and Gunnar Myrdal's *Kris i befolkningsfrågan* (1934; The Demographic Crisis) (Myrdal 1945, vii), Alva Myrdal has summarised the impact of *Kris i befolkningsfrågan* (albeit with an unfortunately chosen noun). The book, she wrote,

> first served to bring to general attention the fact not only that a decline in total population was impending but also that such a decline was destined to take the form of an incessant and self-perpetuating liquidation [sic] of the people. Next it succeeded in making people realize that the practical problem of averting that fate involved social reforms creating a new foundation for the institution of the family. The scheme of social reforms outlined was well in line with the reforms for social security and increased welfare launched by the dominant political party, the Social Democrats, and so immediately entered the domain of practical politics. (op. cit., 27)

Irrespective of whether the demographic crisis is explained in terms of a long-term decline in the birthrate (op. cit., 48-54), or as a result of cramped and inadequate housing (50 per cent of the housing stock in Swedish towns consisted of flats of two rooms or less in 1933 [Frykman and Löfgren 1985, 16]), the quotation above gives an indication of the level of state intervention with which the crisis was tackled. Two government commissions were appointed following the publication of *Kris i befolkningsfrågan* (see Hatje 1974); indeed, the appendix to *Statens offentliga utredningar* (The Swedish Government Official Reports) 1938: 19, 'Yttrande med socialetiska synpunkter på befolkningsfrågan' (Observations with Social-Ethical Perspectives on the Demographic Crisis) had the title 'Kvinnornas kris' (The Women's Crisis) and was signed by Elin Wägner along with Rut Grubb, a doctor, and Ruth Gustafson, a member of the *riksdag* (see Gustafson, Grubb and Wägner 1938, 236-50). The solution to the crisis, both as advocated by the Myrdals in *Kris i befolkningsfrågan* and as developed by the government commissions, was to reform the family and, more especially, the family in relation to the state. One cluster of measures centred on antenatal and maternity care, financial support for new mothers, and health-care for children; while another centred on housing as 'the very frame of the home, which determines the life of the family', and involved an extensive programme for the construction of modern, well-organised, and spacious housing, the overall aim being 'the remaking of society for children' (Myrdal 1945, 232). The education of the citizens was a central plank of this programme, and here *Riksförbundet för sexuell upplysning* (The National Organisation for Sexual Education), which had been launched in 1933 with the working class along with the rural population as its main target groups (Frykman and Löfgren 1985, 56-57), also made an important contribution. However, other significant elements of the welfare state were only introduced after the Second World War, such as old-age pensions (1946), child benefit (1947), and health insurance (1955).

4. Cultural

In many respects, it is possible to trace during the period 1922-47 the continuation and expansion of developments in the cultural sphere that we discerned during the period 1907-21. This is true of areas such as education, the book market and books, and the press. But there are also major new developments during what is essentially the interwar period. Swedish literature during these years was characterised by the emergence of 'proletarian writers', authors who came from a working-class background, and by the introduction of modernism. A mass medium such as the press was complemented, from 1925, by radio broadcasting which then expanded rapidly. At the same time, the popularity of the cinema continued to grow.

Education

Throughout the 1920s and 1930s, the period of compulsory schooling was extended. The compulsory system was complemented by vocational training, which also saw a moderate expansion during this period (Wallberg 1968, 256). But while there was a considerable increase in the proportion of each year group going on to the *realexamen*, roughly the equivalent of the GCSE, with the proportion of girls passing the *realexamen* also rising from just over one third in 1920 to just under half in 1950 (Kyle and Qvist 1974, 75), this was not true of the *studentexamen*, the equivalent of A-levels and the requirement for university entrance. In 1920 just over 2 per cent of each year group passed the *studentexamen*, with less than 20 per cent being women (Wallberg 1968, 254; Kyle and Qvist 1974, 75). Following the opening of the state upper secondary schools to women in 1927, there was a marked increase in the proportion of women passing the *studentexamen* in the 1930s and 1940s; but by the beginning of the 1950s the proportion of the year group was still just 6.5 per cent, and the major expansion of upper secondary education in Sweden only began in the 1960s (Wallberg 1968, 254). Throughout the interwar period, only a very small proportion of each year group would go on to higher education. In 1920, the figure was no more than 1.5 per cent, with about 10 per cent of the students being female. There was an increase in the number of students in higher education in the 1940s and then a rapid rise, with the major expansion of higher education beginning in the 1960s (op. cit., 257-58). The proportion of women also grew, reaching close to 40 per cent in 1966 (op. cit., 258).

Books

With improvements in education and, from the mid-1930s, economic circumstances, the reading public also expanded. The number of authors publishing fiction grew during the interwar years, a time when film and radio also offered new opportunities to publish, with a notable increase in the proportion of writers from the lower middle class and the working class: in the 1940s, writers from these categories constituted 39 per cent of those getting their first book published (Svedjedal 1993, 585). As Pia Lamberth has found, there was a considerable increase in the number of women writers, up from 200 active women writers in 1900-1909 to 700 in 1940-1949 (Lamberth 1991, 32-33). But gender equality remained a distant goal, and as Johan Svedjedal has pointed out with reference to the interwar period, 'the men retained their position at the centre of literature

– often by placing each other there by means of reviews, grants and references' (Svedjedal 1993, 586). And, one might add, literary histories: Edith Södergran (1892-1923), the pioneering modernist poet in Norden, was only brought in from the margins with the publication of Volume 3 of *Nordisk kvinnolitteraturhistoria* (1996; The History of Nordic Women's Writing), in which the emphatic opening chapter is devoted to her work (Witt-Brattström 1996a).

In a survey of Swedish women's writing in the 1920s, Margaretha Fahlgren, Yvonne Hirdman, and Ebba Witt-Brattström have highlighted the prominence in many of these novels of conflicts arising from the sexual freedom of the New Woman. Marika Stiernstedt (1875-1954), whom Wägner knew well, explored in her women characters the tensions between erotic desire and the craving for greater independence (Fahlgren, Hirdman and Witt-Brattström 1996, 377). Kristina Fjelkestam in a pioneering study has mapped the representations of the New Women in Swedish prose fiction by women during the interwar years: the flapper, the mannish lesbian, and the companionate wife (Fjelkestam 2002). And in response to the group of male working-class modernists which emerged in the late 1920s and inspired the definition of the female body in terms of landscape and scenery that was to recur throughout the 1930s, a number of women writers problematised the relationship between women characters, the earth, and eroticism. As Witt-Brattström has pointed out, several of these novels criticise the proprietary masculine perspective on the feminine body and the earth while developing, at the same time, an ambivalent position with regard to eroticism (Witt-Brattström 1996b, 390-91). As we shall see, the relationship between women characters and the earth is central in many of Wägner's texts from the 1930s and 1940s, but usually in the context of more wide-ranging problematisations of the construction of gender and community. Witt-Brattström has also demonstrated the extent to which the work of Moa Martinson (1890-1964) constitutes a series of challenges to the male modernists (Witt-Brattström 1988).

Overall, aspects of gender were more prominent and explicit issues in Swedish literature in the 1920s and 1930s than in the two previous decades, and it is to this potentially more polarised context that we need to relate Wägner's texts from this period.

Press and Radio

The expansion of the Swedish press that we traced in Chapter 2 culminated at the beginning of the 1920s, when there were more independent dailies in Sweden than at any time before or after this period (Hadenius and Weibull 2003, 57). *Tidevarvet*, the radical weekly launched in 1923 by a group of women who were members of the National Association of Liberal Women, appeared at the very end of this period of expansion; and for all its innovative significance, *Tidevarvet* struggled financially throughout much of its thirteen-year lifespan.

Radio broadcasting began in Sweden in the 1920s. *AB Radiotjänst* (The Swedish Broadcasting Corporation) was established in 1924 and began broadcasting on 1 January 1925 (Hadenius and Weibull 2003, 164-65). In the periodisation of Stig Hadenius and Lennart Weibull, the years 1925-39 constituted the establishment phase, with the real breakthrough for radio broadcasting occurring during the Second World War, when a third daily news broadcast was introduced and very high proportions of those who had radio sets were tuning in on a regular basis (op. cit., 167-70). During the decade 1945-55, radio broadcasting was the dominant medium in Sweden, with television introduced in 1955.

Drama and Film

It is possible to talk of a new era in Swedish theatre from around 1920, pioneered by directors such as Per Lindberg and Olof Molander, and developed from the 1930s by Alf Sjöberg and from the 1940s by Ingmar Bergman. The building of new theatres in some of the major cities attracted new audiences, as did the launch of radio drama in 1925. Wägner wrote a couple of works for the stage, one of them a collaborative effort, but she did not succeed in getting any of these works performed. She was more successful with her dramas for radio, and her radio dramas performed in 1930-34, six in all (the last of these a collaborative work), will be considered in the section on radio drama below.

Wägner also retained her interest in the rapidly expanding medium of film. The first Swedish sound film was made in 1929, but in 1923 Wägner's *Norrtullsligan* had formed the basis of a silent film scripted by the author Hjalmar Bergman. As I have pointed out in a comparison of the novel and the film, the latter shows up the tendency of the medium of film to stereotype the female characters, with even Elisabeth reduced to an erotic object and marriage held up as the most desirable goal for a woman (Forsås-Scott 2004, 88-92). A film based on Wägner's novel *Vändkorset* (1935; The Turnstile) was made in 1944, and in 1946 the film *Åsa-Hanna* was released, the script having been written by Barbro Alving.

To sum up, the most important aspect of the economic, political, and social developments in Sweden during this period was the realisation of the Social Democratic 'home of the people'. Yet parallel with this there was a marked and sometimes growing gender segregation, in the labour market and in politics; and as will become apparent in Chapter 7 below, there is a persuasive argument according to which the notion of 'the home of the people' was indeed based on the traditional pattern of male breadwinner plus housewife. However, there was a considerable increase in the number of women writers during this period, and although a new medium such as radio, along with film, would seem to have had a conservative impact on constructions of gender, there is no doubt that prose fiction played a major role in problematising issues of gender and sexuality throughout the period 1922-47.

The following chapter explores constructions of gender and community during this period in terms of dominant and alternative discourses on citizenship.

Chapter 7:
Discourses: Citizenship

As we have seen, there was a number of significant developments with regard to the rights and agency of women in Sweden during the period 1922-47 with reforms such as the new Marriage Code, access to public service posts, and the introduction of maternity benefit and legislation banning the dismissal of women on the grounds of pregnancy or marriage. In the interwar period women in Sweden also formed organisations 'in virtually all areas of life: political associations, associations for housewives, professional women, women in industry and in trades unions, associations for the liberation of women, for peace and freedom, and for social issues of all kinds' (Björk 1999, 13). The framework was the newly democratic Swedish state which, from 1932 onwards, was being transformed into a welfare state, the *folkhem*. As Anders P. Lundberg has pointed out, the concept of 'the home of the people' has been central to determining 'the understanding of community and national integration' in twentieth-century Sweden (Lundberg 2005, 64). But the proliferation of women's organisations in the 1920s and 1930s would seem to indicate a need for smaller and gender-specific communities; as Gunnela Björk has underlined, these organisations provided women with educational opportunities, gave them the chance to formulate questions for which there were no audiences elsewhere, and enabled them to meet 'women who were active in party politics and who functioned as conduits to the political public sphere' (Björk 1999, 297).

Before we can move on to the constructions of gender and community in a range of texts by Wägner from the years 1922-47, we need an outline of the constructions of gender and community current during this period. I have chosen to scrutinise these through the prism of citizenship. The introduction, just before the beginning of this period, of democratisation and suffrage helped highlight discourses on citizenship; the training of the newly enfranchised women to take on their rights and responsibilities as citizens became important projects for women's organisations covering the entire political spectrum; and for the Social Democrats constructing the welfare state, citizenship became a key concept. The dominant discourse on citizenship was redefined somewhat in response to the conditions prevailing during the Second World War, but these redefinitions were no more than temporary.

T. H. Marshall in 'Citizenship and Social Class' (1950) divided citizenship into three parts or elements: civil, political, and social. The civil element was composed of 'the rights necessary for individual freedom – liberty of the person, freedom of speech, thought and faith, the right to own property and to conclude valid contracts, and the right to justice'; the political element was defined as 'the right to participate in the exercise of political power, as a member of a body invested with political authority or as an elector of the members of such a body'; and the social element was synonymous with 'the whole range from the right to a modicum of economic welfare and security to the right to share to the full in the social heritage and to live the life of a civilised being according to the standards prevailing in the society' (Marshall and Bottomore 1992, 8). Each of the elements of citizenship was linked to a specific century, the civil element to the eighteenth, the political element to the nineteenth, and the social element to the twentieth century (op. cit., 10). The elements were also dependent on each other, the political one on the civil one, and the social one on the political one. Marshall's analysis has been criticised for being ethnocentric and Anglocentric (Siim 2000, 27), and as has frequently been pointed out, it was also gender blind (see e.g. Björk 1999, 16).

In the outlines that follow of dominant discourses on citizenship in Sweden in the period 1922-47 and of one alternative discourse, Marshall will serve as the theoretical starting-point, but the work on gender and citizenship done over the past few decades by historians and theorists will ensure that Marshall's model is repeatedly problematised and challenged. I will draw on the work of the Danish sociologist Birte Siim and also on that of the Australian ecofeminist philosopher Val Plumwood.

1. Dominant Discourses

In spring 1928, at a time when the Liberals were in government, Per Albin Hansson, Chair of the Social Democrats, gave a speech in the *riksdag* entitled 'Folkhemmet, medborgarhemmet' (The Home of the People, the Home of the Citizens), 'perhaps the most famous piece of rhetoric produced by a Swedish Social Democrat' (Karlsson 2001, 460). Hansson began by evoking the sense of community fundamental to the good home:

> The good home does not know of anyone who is privileged or neglected, of favourites or step-children. In it, no one is looking down on anyone else, no one is trying to gain advantages at the expense of anyone else, the stronger does not oppress and rob the weaker. In the good home there is equality, consideration, cooperation, helpfulness. (Hansson 1982, 227)

Pointing out that society had often been perceived in terms of liabilities and rights, Hansson emphasised the significance of consideration for others. The realisation of the good home in society at large would have to focus on the dismantling of the barriers currently separating the citizens. In political terms, the citizens had indeed achieved equality, but in social terms, they were still living in a class society, and in economic terms in 'a dictatorship of a minority' (ibid.). Rejecting the notion of a socialist revolution, Hansson hailed paid work as 'the most important source of wealth and culture' (op. cit., 229). But the concepts of master and servant would have to be abandoned, with the introduction of industrial democracy necessary to complete the process of democratisation that had already taken place in political terms (op. cit., 230-31). The realisation of 'the home of the people' would also necessitate a considerable expansion of provision for the unemployed, the sick, and the old. Hansson based his outline of 'the home of the people' on the decisive redistribution of wealth, achieved by means of pay, taxation, changes to the inheritance laws, and nationalisation (op. cit., 232-33).

Mikael Hallberg and Tomas Jonsson have suggested a link between the introduction of female suffrage and the emergence of the rhetoric developing the notion of 'the home of the people' (Hallberg and Jonsson

1993, 26-29); but while the popularity of this rhetoric in the mid-1920s, across almost the whole of the political spectrum, is emphasised in Jonsson's subsequent doctoral thesis about the ideology of the Social Democratic Party 1911-1944, the link with the introduction of female suffrage is no longer made. Here, Jonsson has instead related this rhetoric to the ideological transformation that the Social Democratic Party underwent in the 1920s, the aim being to turn it into 'the people's party' (Jonsson 1998, 241). The concept of citizenship became the crucial link between 'the home of the people' – a phrase first used by Per Albin Hansson in 1925 – and 'the people's party' (op. cit., 221, 241). Jonsson has highlighted the significance, from the mid-1920s onwards, of the concept of social citizenship in Swedish Social Democratic ideology. Based on the notion of the rights of all citizens, this concept made it possible to define the interests of the workers as identical with those of society as a whole (op. cit., 272). The speech Hansson gave in spring 1928 was a neat illustration as it foregrounded the importance of dismantling the class society and bringing all citizens together in 'the home of the people'. But the emphasis was wholly on inequalities of class, not on inequalities of gender.

For an outline of the construction of feminine citizenship in Sweden during the inter-war period, I shall draw in the next few paragraphs on the overview provided by Gunnela Björk in her study of women as collective political actors in Örebro during the period 1900-1950. Although Björk's emphasis is on what she labels political citizenship she also, still following Marshall's categories, covers civil citizenship and social citizenship in her introductory overview (Björk 1999, 13-28). In one respect, however, my categorisations will differ from those of Björk. As has been pointed out, Marshall's model failed to take into account women's relation to wage work (Siim 2000, 15). While Björk has preferred to outline the situation of women on the labour market under the heading civil citizenship (Björk 1999, 20), I have preferred to follow Siim who has categorised 'economic rights on the labour market' together with social welfare rights (Siim 2000, 17).

Marshall's list of the rights that together make up the civil element of citizenship, 'liberty of the person, freedom of speech, thought and faith, the right to own property and to conclude valid contracts, and the right to justice' (Marshall and Bottomore 1992, 8), shows up considerable differences between the masculine and feminine versions of the civil element in Sweden during the interwar period. The granting to women of legal independence had been a drawn-out process, with the husband's guardianship finally abolished by the Marriage Code of 1921, but the husband remained the guardian of the children, his nationality determined that of the wife and the children, and the wife had to take the husband's surname (Björk 1999, 18). Björk has also highlighted the differences with regard to men's and women's rights over their bodies, emphasising the threats and violations to which women have traditionally been subjected, including the notion of the husband's 'marital rights', plus the effects of legislation against contraceptives and abortion (ibid.). In the light of Marshall's model which constructed the civil element of citizenship as a prerequisite for the political element, it is thus clear that the introduction of the remaining aspects of the political element, genderequal suffrage and eligibility in local elections (1918), and women's suffrage and eligibility to the *riksdag* (1919), resulted in a political citizenship the basis of which was quite different from that of male citizens, with the differences particularly marked in the case of married women (op. cit., 20-23). However, the bars to the right to vote that were to remain in place until 1945 (dependence on poor relief, being under guardianship, bankruptcy) affected many more men than women; and as Björk has emphasised, the notion that those who were 'dependent on a person or on society should not have suffrage runs all through the discussions about suffrage and bars to suffrage during the first half of the twentieth century' (op. cit., 22). Finally the social element of citizenship, related by Marshall to the welfare state, was in effect also based on differing constructions of gender, with the combination of male breadwinner and housewife as the norm and welfare rights linked chiefly to paid employment and income, and to a lesser extent to motherhood (op. cit., 24). With regard to paid employment, major gender differences were to remain throughout the period with which we are concerned. Up to the introduction of the new Marriage Code in 1921, a married woman in theory had to ask her husband's permission to take up paid employment (op. cit., 19).

Women remained barred from public service posts until 1925 and from state upper secondary schools until 1927; and the gendered divisions on the labour market continued to impact on the social element of citizenship (ibid.). They do so to this day.

Per Albin Hansson's speech of 1928 set out a vision of the welfare state that was to begin to be realised from 1932 and that was quickly to achieve international fame, in part thanks to Childs's *Sweden: The Middle Way* (1936). But as indicated by the sketch above of what was arguably going to emerge as the dominant discourse on citizenship during the period 1922-47, the Swedish welfare state, famed for its equality, remained riven with gendered divisions. Yvonne Hirdman has quoted from a speech by Arne Eriksson, a delegate at the Social Democratic Party conference in 1972, whose retrospective view of the gendering of the welfare state was clearly intended to be positive:

> I am thinking of the circumstance that the man has worked in the Party and the organisations, in local politics, the trades union and so on, while the woman has had the greater responsibility for the home and the children. On this basis we have built a well-functioning democracy of which there has been virtually no equal. Of course this state of affairs has involved sacrifices for both husband and wife in the family, but it has been a division of labour with a purpose. The role of the wife in this context deserves to go down in history. Her achievement has been heroic. Thanks to her work, she has enabled her husband to make a concentrated contribution to the life of the organisations. (quoted in Hirdman 1996, 210)

Hirdman has analysed gender in the Swedish welfare state in contractual terms, describing the period 1930-60 in terms of *husmoderskontraktet* (the housewife contract). She has defined 'contract' as 'an invisible relation, a received, culturally inherited "agreement", a kind of (enforced) connection between two entities' (Hirdman 1990, 78). The basis of 'the housewife contract' was the majority interpretation of what Hirdman has termed *en hushållsdemokrati* (a household democracy): the men would be responsible for the big household, the state; and the women for the small one, the individual home (Hirdman 1996, 209). Hirdman has described the emergence of the housewife contract as 'a (hidden) historical compromise between women and society/the state': while a new type of social policy was created, focused on the home rather than the workplace, women were allocated a tripartite political dimension, 'as political subjects (to a very limited extent), as implementors or a kind of political intermediaries, and as objects' (Hirdman 1990, 86). The result was 'a peculiar combination of modernity in terms of form and conservatism in practice: in new, modern and functional homes the housewife was to bring up the new and more numerous generation as good citizens' (ibid.).

Hirdman's summary of the final report by the 1935 government commission on the demographic crisis, set up in response to Gunnar and Alva Myrdal's book *Kris i befolkningsfrågan* (1934), illustrates her argument about the housewife contract. As young couples and families were offered loans towards housing costs, they should also be offered guidance on suitable housing and furnishings. Here Hirdman has pointed to the influence of Ellen Key (Hirdman 1993, 153) and her advocacy of 'beauty in the home'; but the guidance outlined by the committee aimed very much further and included the household economy, diet, cookery, and clothing. These recommendations constructed the housewives as key actors, tellingly separating them from the married women who were also in employment, as in a heading quoted by Hirdman: 'The position of mothers working in the home. The *problems* of married women in employment' (op. cit., 155; my italics). In Hirdman's analysis, the norm of the housewife was the Swedish Social Democratic solution to the growing gender conflict, and more specifically the expansion of masculinity, that had been an integral part of modernity (op. cit., 13-14, 156). While deviations from the norm were permitted, Hirdman has read the decision by a majority of the members of the government commission to recommend assistance to families in the form of cash rather than food and clothing as further evidence of the norm of the housewife: constructing the housewife as competent and well-informed, the cash support also confirmed the political desire to raise her self-esteem (op. cit., 157-58).

In Hirdman's periodisation, 'the housewife contract' in Sweden was followed around 1960/65 by *jämlikhetskontraktet* (the equality contract), which in turn was followed by *jämställdhetskontraktet* (the equity contract) from around 1980 onwards (Hirdman 1990, 89-104). All three contracts exemplify what Hirdman has termed 'the stereotypical gender contract' or 'a gender order', characterised in her reading by the binary contrast and hierarchical relationship between masculinity and femininity (Hirdman 2001, 88-90, Hirdman 1990, 78-80). While Hirdman's analysis in terms of gender contracts has been highly influential, it has also been extensively criticised. Gro Hagemann and Klas Åmark in a comprehensive critique, first published in 1999, have highlighted the problems caused by Hirdman's repeated insistence on the gender order as generally applicable, by the rigid determinism and structuralism resulting from this, by the vague definition of 'contract' in her model, and by the lack of space in this model for individual contributions (Hagemann and Åmark 2004).

While it seems to me that Hirdman's concept of 'the housewife contract' can provide us with a preliminary map as we navigate the construction of gendered citizenship in Sweden during the period 1922-47, it is also obvious that the concept is in no way sufficient. The sociologist Margareta Lindholm in a comparative study of the thought of Alva Myrdal and Elin Wägner in the 1930s (1990), has a background chapter on women's citizenship on which I will draw as a means of modifying and problematising Hirdman's analysis. Lindholm has investigated the journals of a number of leading women's organisations with a special emphasis on the meaning of female/feminine influence on society as indicated by terms such as *ansvar* (responsibility) and *självständighet* (independence) (Lindholm 1990, 77). In doing so, she has put the spotlight on the continuing role of communities that were gendered female, in other words communities which, as Joan Wallach Scott and Gunnela Björk among others have pointed out, had the paradoxical effect of reinforcing the gender differences they were wanting to overcome (Scott 1998, 169-75; Björk 1999, 298).

In *Morgonbris*, the journal of the Social Democratic Women's Organisation (which had been founded in 1920), Kaj Andersson during her period as editor, 1932-36, highlighted the relationship between home and industry, and more especially the role for industrial production of the expertise of women as home-makers; however, the

Discourses: Citizenship

perceived basis of women's influence subsequently shifted, from the home to social policy (Lindholm 1990, 89). A series of articles from 1937 argued for the necessity of equal pay and women's political representation (op. cit., 94-95), and in terms that were highly critical of the Social Democratic Party, one of these articles drew a parallel between the dissatisfied women and the working class that had recently succeeded in its struggle for equality (op. cit., 95). Overall, according to Lindholm, there was a strong emphasis in *Morgonbris* on the significance of the participation of women in the development of the new, democratic society (op. cit., 98).

While the National Alliance of the Swedish Housewives' Association, which had been founded in 1919 and began to publish a magazine for its members in 1925, profiled itself chiefly as an organisation for housewives (Lindholm 1990, 99), there are interesting parallels between the construction of feminine citizenship in this magazine and in *Morgonbris*. With the education of the housewives for their responsibilities as citizens a key principle, the National Alliance of the Swedish Housewives' Association joined forces with other women's organisations working to expand the political representation of women (Lundh 1944, quoted in Lindholm 1990, 99), and argued that the questions facing the female citizens were the same irrespective of whether they were housewives or in paid employment (Lindholm 1990, 99-100). The members' magazine foregrounded the role of new technology and scientific advances for household management and the education of children; and by the mid-1930s the National Alliance of the Swedish Housewives' Association, just like the Social Democratic Women's Organisation at this time, was highlighting the significance of women's leadership with regard to production as well as consumption (op. cit., 101). With their homes managed more efficiently, women would have more time to develop their roles as citizens in a wider social context (op. cit., 102).

Unlike the two women's organisations just discussed, *Yrkeskvinnors riksförbund* (The National Alliance of Professional Women) was established in 1935, bringing together a number of local associations as late as 1937 (Lindholm 1990, 108). The organisation highlighted women's rights in the labour market, including women's access to fields of employment traditionally perceived as masculine (op. cit., 108-09). Women's problems in combining marriage and employment were discussed more extensively in the two magazines published by this organisation than in those of the Social Democratic Women's Organisation and the National Alliance of the Swedish Housewives' Association, and with regard to the role of modern housing and the rationalisation of housework there was an emphasis on the positive impact on marriage as well as the children: 'The new woman was her husband's fellow-worker, not his housekeeper' (op. cit., 110).

Lindholm's findings suggest that the concept of 'the housewife contract' is of relatively limited usefulness for an analysis of the construction of feminine citizenship in Sweden in the 1930s. While, in a couple of the women's organisations Lindholm has studied, a preoccupation with the role of the housewife is conspicuous, the emphasis was not just on these women citizens as the managers of modernised households, but also on their significance as active contributors to the new society that was emerging, especially in the area of social policy. Alternatively, the modernisation of housework was a prerequisite for women's contributions in the labour market.

I read the work of Alva Myrdal during this period as radicalising the dominant (Social Democratic) discourse on the gendered construction of citizenship to such an extent that we are justified in perceiving Myrdal's contribution as adding a new strand to the dominant discourse – a strand, however, that did not come to full fruition until after the period with which we are concerned here. Myrdal (1902-1986) was a social scientist who would go on to work for the United Nations, Unesco, and the Swedish Delegation for International Disarmament in Geneva; in the 1930s she was involved in the development of education for pre-school children and headed Stockholm's Socio-Pedagogical Training College between 1936 and 1948. Myrdal's texts blend a scientific and a political rhetoric (Lindholm 1990, 192); and it is the fact that Myrdal was one of the social engineers who helped initiate the transformation of Swedish society in the 1930s (Hirdman 1993, 92-175) in combination with her special interest in the situation of women that makes her contribution relevant here. But with her contribution the emphasis shifts, from the actual communities constituted by the various women's organisations surveyed above to the emerging 'home of the people'. For the outline that follows, I am drawing chiefly on the chapter about Myrdal in Lindholm's comparative study of Myrdal and Wägner and on some of Yvonne Hirdman's work on Alva Myrdal.

The basis of Myrdal's analysis of the situation of women was the socialist interpretation developed by Engels and Bebel (exemplified in the present study by the work of Olive Schreiner and Charlotte Perkins Gilman); and her conclusion in *Nation and Family* (1941) was that '[t]he feminine sex is a social problem. Whether a woman is young or old, whether she is married or not, whether a wife works or not, she is likely to be a problem' (Myrdal 1945, 418). Industrialisation had radically changed the significance of the family, especially in economic terms, thus leaving modern society with 'the maladjusted family', notably the wife and children, as an irrational and ineffective remnant of the past (op. cit., 4-7). The solution, as advocated in Alva Myrdal and Gunnar Myrdal's study prompted by Sweden's declining birth-rate, *Kris i befolkningsfrågan* and developed by two government commissions set up in the wake of this study, was to reform the family, and more especially the family in relation to the state. The 'task of our generation', Alva Myrdal wrote in *Nation and Family*, would be to:

> reintegrate the family in the larger society. [...] we should reconsider in a realistic and cautious manner the division of functions between the family household and the national household and induce such changes in this division as may best preserve the fundamental values of our cultural heritage in a period of structural economic and social changes. [...] The family reforms will [...] introduce national profit and investment motives in addition to the motives of democratic justice and humanitarian sympathy. They will lift social policy to the level of social planning. (op. cit., 6-7)

Yvonne Hirdman has used the phrase 'teknisk darwinism' (technical Darwinism) to encapsulate the advanced social planning advocated by the Myrdals: only a surge in the birth-rate would safeguard the maximum use and development of new engineering and technology

(Hirdman 1993, 120). But it was this social planning that would pave the way for women to enter employment and regain their position in society (Lindholm 1990, 213). Hirdman's illustrations include Alva Myrdal's plans for collective housing, as well as her plans for the collective education of children, the result of which would be 'desirable social [individuals]' (Hirdman 1993, 109, 111). Alva Myrdal also envisaged that husbands and fathers would take greater responsibilities for the home and the children. In *Nation and Family* she stressed the importance of making 'marriage and even parenthood a more equal partnership, as it was in the agrarian society' (Myrdal 1945, 120); but as Lindholm has pointed out, a section reinforcing this point is to be found in the Swedish version only (Lindholm 1990, 214-15).

Alva Myrdal's summary of the implications for women of the Swedish approaches to the demographic crisis has often been quoted: 'The old debate on married women's right to work was turned into a fight for the working woman's right to marry and have children' (Myrdal 1945, 403). This 'fight', however, was to be a lengthy one. Myrdal went on to develop and strengthen her argument in a book co-written with Viola Klein and published in 1956, the title of which speaks for itself: *Women's Two Roles: Home and Work*. But as Gunhild Kyle has pointed out, some of Myrdal's arguments, including her emphasis on the need to reconstruct the roles of fathers as well as mothers, only became prominent in the Swedish feminist debate of the 1970s (Kyle 1980, 363). The construction of the new society that the social engineers began to plan in the 1930s was certainly a long-term project.

This project, moreover, was interrupted by the Second World War. The programme of social reforms was brought to a halt in 1938; and the civil element of citizenship was restricted by the imposition of official censorship during the war (Molin 1974, 255-88). In a pattern familiar from the First World War, the new war contributed to foregrounding the role of women as household managers (Lindholm 1990, 95-115). At the same time, the Liberal Margit Wohlin, writing in 1940 in the journal of the National Association of Professional Women, did not hesitate to hail the total war as a phenomenon that would bring about equality between women and men (op. cit., 114). In a move that could be seen to develop the 1930s project of modernising housework, *Hemmens forskningsinstitut* (The Home Research Institute) was established in 1944 'to work for a systematic rationalisation of the working conditions in the Swedish homes' (quoted in Lövgren 1993, 146). As Hirdman has pointed out, the war could also be perceived as the 'final eruption of irrationalism' (Hirdman 1993, 176), and as soon as the allied forces began to achieve some successes, the detailed planning of the Swedish welfare state was again under way. But while the planning of the 1930s had focused on developing the competence of the citizens, the planning of the 1940s focused on democracy, and more specifically on developing what Uno Åhrén, writing in 1945, termed 'a democratic model of the human being, for whom freedom and independence [...] combined with a sense of social responsibility' (quoted in Hirdman 1993, 177).

2. An Alternative Discourse

The ideological unity underpinning the planning of the modern Swedish welfare state may well appear to have been total; but there were also cracks and fissures that could provide seedbeds for alternatives (Domellöf 2003, 122, n. 1). The most important of these alternatives was *Föreningen Frisinnade Kvinnor* (The Swedish Women's Liberal Association). In 1923 this Association became *Frisinnade Kvinnors Riksförbund* (The National Association of Liberal Women) and following the splitting of the Liberal Party in the same year, the National Association became increasingly independent. Also in 1923, a leading group of women in the National Association launched a weekly newspaper, *Tidevarvet* (1923-36), and two years later *Kvinnliga medborgarskolan* (The Women Citizens' College) at Fogelstad (1925-54). The development of the concept of citizenship in the National Association (replaced in 1931 by *Svenska Kvinnors Vänsterförbund*) [The Association of Swedish Women on the Left]) and also in *Tidevarvet* and at Fogelstad offers insights into constructions of gender and community – and, indeed, society – that differ radically from those defined by the dominant discourses on citizenship. Given that Elin Wägner was a key figure in the Swedish Women's Liberal Association, the National Association of Liberal Women, and the Association of Swedish Women on the Left as well as in *Tidevarvet* and at Fogelstad, an outline of the constructions of gender and community as formulated by this alternative discourse on citizenship is a prerequisite for the analyses of Wägner's texts that follow. As a result of her extensive involvement, Wägner wrote a number of relevant texts about the Associations (including political programmes), *Tidevarvet*, and Fogelstad; to steer clear of circularity I have, as far as possible, avoided these in the outline that follows. There is a shortage of comprehensive academic studies of the Associations, *Tidevarvet*, and Fogelstad (although Irene Andersson is now working on a study of the Associations); and so my outline is based on the somewhat piecemeal studies that exist, along with pamphlets and other relevant material from the period.

Ada Nilsson, a doctor who like Wägner played a leading role in the Associations, in *Tidevarvet* and at Fogelstad, has emphasised the difference between the *laisser-aller* of traditional liberalism and the Swedish Women's Liberal Association: the women who agreed, in January 1922, on the significance of the contribution of the individual human being and on the responsibility of the human being for society at large, were '*perfectly clear about the fact that the forms of social life* [...] *[would] have to undergo radical changes*' (Nilsson 1940, 68; italics original). The programme adopted by the National Association of Liberal Women in 1923 – which, as Elisabeth Tamm emphasised, took its starting-point in cooperation between women and men (Tamm 1923) – included demands such as improved provision for mothers and children, better housing, and better education, and so anticipated the plans drawn up by the Social Democrats a decade or so later. But the subdivision on 'Arbetslivet' (Working Life) began with a section on the importance of spiritual/intellectual work, 'Det andliga arbetet', and concluded with a section on the need for far-reaching changes to the ownership of land; and the subdivision on 'Samhällslivet' (Social Life) dealt chiefly with the significance of peace, between social classes and between nations (Anon., 1923a). Showing up the limitations of Marshall's model and contrasting starkly with the constructions of gender and community and, by extension, society that we have encountered above, the programme of the National Association of Liberal Women was that of a political women's organisation whose members were using their recently granted citizenship as a platform for the radical remodelling not just of Swedish society but of the world at large: rooted in justice and thus freed from economic speculation and inequality, this new world were to revolve around *'respect for life in all its forms and differences'* (Nilsson 1940, 113; italics original). The statement by the National Association of Liberal Women issued ahead of the elections to the Second Chamber of the *riksdag* in 1928 reinforced much the same points, with the addition of sections on unemployment and on free trade (Anon., 1928). The pamphlet published ahead of the elections to the Second Chamber in 1932 foregrounded five areas: the economy and the land issue; health; education; men's and women's equal rights to employment and equality in legal terms; and peace (Anon., 1932). By this time, the National Association of Liberal Women had been replaced by the National Association of Women on the Left, whose aim was to work for 'an enlightened and responsible democracy, for the development and solution of social issues in radical terms, for everybody's equal right to employment, and for everybody's equal status before a court of law' (quoted in Kellgren 1971b, 173). The new Association, which brought together groups as well as individuals, was not party political (Nilsson 1940, 156). In the wake of Hitler's *Machtübernahme* in 1933, Social Democratic women joined; and the struggle against re-armament and fascism that dominated the 1930s culminated in 'Kvinnornas vapenlösa uppror mot kriget' (The Women's Unarmed Revolt against War), which secured the support of approximately 20,000 women in Sweden and sent a delegation arguing the case for peace based on justice and solidarity to the League of Nations in Geneva (Anon., 1935; see also Wägner 1935b, Andersson 2001, 183 240, and below, pp.245-48).

Andrea Andreen (1888-1972), a physician who became the Chairperson of the National Association of Women on the Left in 1947, has described the period 1938-46 as one of intense activity for *Radikala Föreningen* (The Radical Association), a Stockholm-based group belonging to the National Association of Women on the Left (Andreen

1964, 17). But she has not highlighted the fact that when the Radical Association met in February 1940 to debate 'Omistliga värden' (Indispensable Values), the published summary amounted to an outline of a new world. The summary began by underlining the importance of the financial assistance given to pregnant women and new mothers (threatened by cuts due to the expanding defence budget) and by criticising the war-time restrictions on the freedom of expression; but the major section dealt with peace, formulating a cultural critique that was not only gendered but – far ahead of its time – also environmentalist. Envisaging a new world in which 'the effaced authority of women would again become a stabilising element ensuring an overall balance' (Anon., 1940), this summary included the demand that every human being re-examine her/his relationship with the earth. The ruthless exploitation of the earth was neither acceptable nor useful for humankind; and, it was argued, '[t]he white race [had] suffered enormous damage as a result of its subjugation of other races, a subjugation that [had] allowed it to exploit without hindrance peoples who may well have a wiser and more respectful attitude to the earth than has the white race' (ibid.). Dismissing moves towards centralisation, standardisation, and incorporation, the summary advocated an entirely new type of social organisation, consisting of small units that together would form a *'world agreement without forcible means and without a superstructure'* (ibid.; italics original).

'Omistliga värden' is a remarkable document which has not received the attention it deserves. While the Swedish Women's Liberal Association, the National Association of Liberal Women, and the Association of Swedish Women on the Left had foregrounded a construction of feminine citizenship characterised by an emphasis on activism, on the significance of the individual human being, and on the role of women's solidarity, along with a society in which justice would be the foundation of equality and peace, the summary of the discussion held by the Radical Association in 1940 developed these positions in universalist terms, outlining what can only be referred to as a post-colonialist deconstruction of power along with a concept of the self that anticipated what Val Plumwood, theorising from a feminist ecological perspective, was to term in 1993 the 'self-in-relationship' (Plumwood

1993, 154). (Although the term is identical to that used by Patricia Waugh in 1989, Waugh's perspective does not include ecology; see Waugh 1989, 13-14.) With small units underpinning a new type of social organisation, there are marked similarities between this programme and Frazer and Lacey's 'dialogic communitarianism' with its emphasis on democracy, a relational theory of the self, and the placing of 'questions of both public goods and the institutions needed to support them, and the ideal of collective life based on mutual acceptance and recognition, at the heart of politics' (Frazer and Lacey 1993, 203). However, in Sweden in 1940 only a small minority of women would have shared ideas of the kind formulated in 'Omistliga värden'; and, far ahead of its time as it was, the call made in 1944 by what had then become *Sveriges Radikala Kvinnoförbund* (The National Association of Radical Women) for gender equality in the *riksdag*, county councils, and local authorities, with one woman and one man in each post (Anon., 1944, 7; see also Wägner 1944), also failed to attract much attention. Overall, the National Association of Women on the Left suffered a sharp decline during the Second World War (Clayhills 1991, 478), although the Association survived to join in 1946 the newly formed Women's International Democratic Federation (Andreen 1964, 25-29), whose programme included peace by democracy, i.e. full political, economic, legal, and social rights for the women of the world, and peace for the sake of the children, i.e. the opportunity for the children of the world to grow into physically and mentally healthy, harmonious, and happy adults (Andreen 1947). With the realisation of the Swedish welfare state in a context of rapid economic progress from 1945 onwards, the 'indispensable values' defined by the Radical Association in 1940 would no doubt have seemed unfashionable and irrelevant.

How radical, then, was the political weekly *Tidevarvet*, launched in 1923 by the National Association of Liberal Women to be edited in accordance with its programme (Nilsson 1940, 75), yet never, as Lena Eskilsson has pointed out, its mouthpiece (Eskilsson 1991, 125)? According to the declaration in the first issue, 'everything concerns women and their opinions concern everybody'; and the weekly was aiming to be 'a meeting place, an arena, in which men and women as equals' were to strive for 'a liberal way of thinking' and for its application 'in social life and legislation' (Anon., 1923b). How, then, was the concept of citizenship developed in *Tidevarvet*, and what conclusions can we draw from this regarding the constructions of gender and community?

A tabloid, usually consisting of six or eight pages, *Tidevarvet* was published between November 1923 and the end of December 1936. A group of women on the executive committee of the National Association of Liberal Women also played leading roles in *Tidevarvet*, with Wägner as the editor from the summer of 1925 until the end of 1927 and on the editorial board from November 1923 until December 1932 (Forsås-Scott 1999, 21-22). At its peak, the weekly had close to 3,000 subscribers (Eskilsson 1991, 111).

The paper attracted a wide range of contributors, men as well as women, including prominent political commentators, authors, critics, theologians, and physicians. Ragna Kellgren, who has edited a volume with material from *Tidevarvet*, has written about the 'intensity with which the various contributors [communicated], about key issues, with the readers' (Kellgren 1971b, 15); and the now crumbling pages are still very much alive with expertise, commitment, and a strong sense of urgency. (*Tidevarvet* is available on microfilm and can now also be read on DVD.) *Tidevarvet* covered Swedish politics, including debates in the *riksdag* and the work of government commissions, as well as politics in the other Nordic countries, but it also provided extensive coverage of European politics including disarmament, the latter largely thanks to Wägner. The paper also carried articles on topics such as ethics, religion, industrial work, education, health, the demographic crisis, and the situation of women past and present, while at the same time devoting space to literature, theatre, and art, and to short stories as well as serialised novels. According to the declaration in the first issue, *Tidevarvet* was not aiming for a division of its material into distinctive fields, as there was 'no woman's world separate from man's world, just as [there was] no world of literature, art, drama, religion or speculation separate from the world of politics and society. There is only one single world of the spirit' (Anon., 1923b).

The ambitious coverage in this weekly produced and, to a large extent, written by women, amounted to a strong statement about the significance of feminine citizenship. Elisabeth Tamm, writing in 1926, underlined the duty of the women citizens to insist on the same standards of justice in public life as in private life (in Kellgren, 1971a, 54); while an anonymous text from 1927 reminded women that their silence and absence were underpinning many of the shortcomings of Swedish society at the time (quoted in op. cit., 64-65). A text published in the wake of the agreement in 1927 on public service salaries which, according to the anonymous author, showed a determination to 'reduce and curtail the opportunities and income of women, both in the civil service and the local authorities', emphasised the need for concerted and responsible action: 'it is up to women to make things different. No emotional outbursts! No noise! But *different*. And definitely *different*. If the men do not want to make space for women, the women will have to secure space for themselves' (quoted in op. cit., 62; italics original). While the role of the women citizens in creating a different type of society was often referred to, the specificity of this contribution gradually became clearer, partly as a result of the deteriorating international situation. An anonymous text from 1924 warned against the idea that women would merely become 'useful for simpler tasks' when what was required was 'a new assessment, a new content, a new politics' (quoted in op. cit., 25). When the Nobel Peace Prize for 1925 was awarded to the British Foreign Secretary Austen Chamberlain and the Vice President of the United States General Dawes, and the Peace Prize for 1926 to the French and German Foreign Ministers, Briand and Stresemann, Elisabeth Tamm argued that the award of peace prizes at that particular time did not make sense: 'What have these four men done to promote peace?' (quoted in op. cit., 58). Peace, Tamm emphasised, was about creating a new attitude among the general public: 'It is the moral and ethical outlook of the peoples that has to be transformed' (quoted in op. cit., 59). A text published in 1928 attacked capitalism (quoted in op. cit., 72), and a text that appeared in 1931 linked capitalism to foreign policy and the consequences of the Versailles Treaty in particular, instead arguing the case for justice and mutual understanding (quoted in op. cit., 117-18). The foregrounding of the defence of democracy from 1933 onwards included an anonymous text according to which the foundations of democracy ought to be a new policy on the distribution of land in combination with the freeing of spiritual/intellectual life from state monopolies (quoted in op. cit., 156), and an article by Andrea Andreen-Svedberg in which she contrasted the political mass movement she had experienced in Germany in the summer of 1933 with a 'humanity' consisting of individuals with distinct personalities and the capacity to think independently and take responsibility for their actions (quoted in op. cit., 157). A text headed 'Den nya politiken' (The New Politics) and published in 1935 rhetorically dismissed liberalism, socialism, and communism only to outline the way forward in terms of a combination of all three:

> A *liberalism* subordinate to a societal ideal [...], the right and freedom of the individual, but not at the expense of the many! A *socialism* that truly gives to the individuals this right, but simultaneously safeguards the joint interests of the whole! A *communism* without dictatorship, in other words a kind of liberal communism, that safeguards the rights of all. (quoted in op. cit., 172; italics original)

The Women's Unarmed Revolt against War, a major project in *Tidevarvet* in 1935, combined active, responsible citizenship with social and political solidarity and justice, and so highlighted the argument underpinning *Tidevarvet*, i.e. that women had a unique contribution to make to a world in which everything was of equal concern to men and women. Overall, *Tidevarvet* is a remarkable example of both the deconstruction of the gender roles of the dominant discourses, and the creative potential of an alternative textual space. While the deconstruction of the society of the dominant discourses was less radical than in a text such as 'Omistliga världen' (published four years after *Tidevarvet* had ceased to appear), the prominence of justice, land reform, and peace pointed to a society quite different from the one being put together at the same time by the Social Democrats.

In 1935 Honorine Hermelin, the Head of The Women Citizens' College at Fogelstad throughout its existence (1925-54), defined the aim of the College as that of providing 'a breathing space in this world of isolation behind divisive walls – walls between classes, opinions, occupations, political parties – so that at the College you would, if possible, be able to take a deep and free breath simply in your capacity

Discourses: Citizenship

as a human-being-and-citizen' (Hermelin, H., 1956, 203). An article in *Tidevarvet* in February 1925 which introduced the first courses at the College under the heading 'Kvinnlig medborgarbildning' (Education for Feminine Citizenship) emphasised the need to establish connections between society and the home, with those working in the home learning to relate their contribution to society as a whole, and those employed outside the home learning to relate their contribution to the value and care of the individual human being. The syllabus would centre on social studies and the study of human nature, and the College would strive to bring together students from as wide a range of backgrounds as possible (Anon., 1925b). The formal announcement of the courses offered in 1925, which dominated the front page of the same issue of *Tidevarvet*, encapsulated the aim of the work of the College in a phrase that has subsequently become famous: 'to relate to each other the work of the hand, the brain and the heart' (Anon., 1925a).

Based on the model of the folk high-school, the Women Citizens' College was residential. It normally offered three courses per year, in spring, summer, and autumn. The two key areas of study, in which history and psychology played prominent roles, were complemented by oral presentations and essay writing. An imaginary local authority which provided the course participants (the term *kursdeltagare* denoted both students and teachers) with the opportunity to engage in extensive role play soon became renowned; and the evening gatherings at which individual participants spoke without preparation about experiences at home or at work, were clearly significant from both an educational and a social point of view (see Björkman-Goldschmidt 1956a, 141-62). On the whole, the organisers succeeded in their ambition to attract women from different walks of life to the courses at Fogelstad: while teachers constituted the biggest category, the second biggest was women working in the home and women working in industry (Eskilsson 1991, 196). The lists of course participants in the commemorative volume published in 1956 contain 1,706 names. The College also attracted participants from other countries, initially chiefly from the Nordic countries, but gradually from other European countries too and occasionally from as far afield as the United States (Björkman-Goldschmidt 1956a, 208-31). As early as 1925, former course participants set up an organisation, *Fogelstadsförbundet* (The Fogelstad Association), which met annually at Fogelstad and continued to function until 1981 (Clayhills 1991, 119).

Located at the estate of Fogelstad, which was owned by Elisabeth Tamm and situated some distance south-west of Stockholm, the Women Citizens' College became a meeting-place for women intellectuals (although men occasionally gave lectures too), with female members of the riksdag, authors, journalists, actors, artists, musicians, and composers participating in the courses (Eskilsson 1991, 190). Elsa Björkman-Goldschmidt, a journalist and author involved in the work of the College, has described it as 'a one-off school whose living water had not yet turned icy in the deep-freeze of regulations' (Björkman-Goldschmidt 1956b, 69). The College received no state support and so was free to develop its own syllabus; and while one consequence is the absence of reports by external assessors, there is on the other hand a wealth of archival material including lecture notes, essays, and daily minutes to provide detailed insights into the work of the College. Much of this material, available in KvinnSam at Göteborg University Library, has not yet been explored, and I shall continue to base my outline on published sources.

One course participant who returned to Fogelstad again and again spoke of the interesting and remarkable people she invariably encountered there: only gradually did she realise the extent to which the unique environment was impacting on the course participants. The result, she pointed out, was greater respect and understanding for her fellow human beings in general (Hermelin, C., 1956, 117). Ragna Kellgren, who also returned to the College, has described the atmosphere as one in which the spiritual and the material merged: 'The bread shone. The ground was as exquisite as the soul. The soul of a human being shone through the body, a whole together' (Kellgren 1973, 213). Other reactions concerned the restraint of the teachers, with the course participant in question realising only after some time that a more categorical position would have deterred the more reserved participants: 'This is how shy people are, I realised. You learnt to respect the individuality of others – but you also understood what effort this involved on the part of the teachers' (Hermelin, C., 1956, 117). In a promotional leaflet from 1939 Honorine Hermelin, summarising her experiences of the 45 courses in which she had participated so far, focused on what she called 'the miracle', the moment when a course had become a whole, when 'a new harmony [had] emerged from a multitude of differences, when a new insight with a new living language [had] come into being' (Hermelin 1939). Referring to the unique environment and the different backgrounds of the participants, Hermelin wrote of the courses as inspiring that which was 'characteristic, creative, brave and unique in the individual human beings' and so giving these human beings 'the strength to create a new community':

> And it is this, I have learnt from the Citizens' College, that is the point or the depth in which citizenship as such is rooted, in which the individual human being becomes aware of her or his own, living, political responsibility and so actually becomes brave enough to tackle social tasks in real life. (ibid.)

The responsible, knowledgeable and creative female citizen was clearly at the centre of the activities at Fogelstad; and with regard to the construction of gender, there are thus direct parallels with the National Association of Liberal Women and the Association of Swedish Women on the Left and *Tidevarvet*. It is more difficult to be equally specific with regard to the constructions of community – and society. Taking her cue from the title of an anonymous article about the College published in *Tidevarvet* in 1929, Lena Eskilsson has called her book about the Women Citizens' College *Drömmen om kamratsamhället* (The Dream of the Society of Comrades), and she has contrasted the role of the family model in much utopian thinking with the role of the circle of friends or comrades for the visions of society developed at Fogelstad (Eskilsson 1991, 209). Arguably, the absence of a coherent societal ideal was more marked in the case of Fogelstad than in the case of either the Associations or *Tidevarvet*: the focus was more on the women who would create a new future and less on the new future as such.

*

I am going to sum up my findings regarding discourses on citizenship using Birte Siim's categorisations of feminist theories of citizenship as a starting-point. The dominant discourses in Sweden in the period 1922-47 with their emphasis on the construction of feminine citizenship within the framework of marriage, exemplified by Per Albin Hansson's speech in 1928 and texts by the Myrdals, chiefly by Alva Myrdal, from the 1930s onwards, can be read at least in part as illustrating the patriarchal hypothesis propounded by Carole Pateman. In her analysis, the marriage contract is fundamental to women's oppression as it subjects the individual woman to her husband's control. 'Heterosexual relations', Pateman writes, 'do not inevitably take the form of mastery and subjection, but free relations are impossible within the patriarchal opposition between contract and status, masculinity and femininity. The feminist dream is continuously subverted by entanglement with contract' (Pateman 1997, 187-88). Pateman's model, however, clearly is not sufficient. Alva Myrdal's contributions in particular can in part be read in terms of the model Siim has labelled the maternalist-communitarian one, and which is most prominently represented by the work of Jean Bethke Elshtain. In Siim's summary, Elshtain interprets 'the family, women's responsibility "as mothers" and their preoccupation with "immediate concerns"' not as a barrier to women's political participation but rather as the basis of their political role (Siim 2000, 34). In terms that echo some of the ideals underpinning the Swedish welfare state, Elshtain has argued for a redefinition of the dichotomy private – public, with the private spheres 'bearing their own intrinsic dignity and purpose tied to moral and aesthetic imperatives, all the textures, nuances, tones and touches of a life lived intimately among others', while the public world 'must nurture and sustain a set of ethical imperatives, including a commitment to preserve, protect, and defend human beings in their capacities as private persons, and to allow men and women alike to partake in the good of the public sphere on an equal basis of participatory dignity and equality' (Elshtain 1981, 351). But however innovative the society that was being constructed on this basis in Sweden, its range was strictly limited by the national borders. While Sweden had been an active member of the League of Nations since its inception in 1920, no foreign policy issues appeared in any party political manifestos or Swedish election campaigns throughout the entire interwar period (Olsson 1968, 144).

While the limitations of Marshall's model of citizenship are apparent from any gendered perspective, they are particularly conspicuous in the context of my alternative discourse, constituted by the National Association of Liberal Women and the Association of Swedish Women on the Left, the weekly *Tidevarvet*, and the Women Citizens' College. Although there are arguably elements here that bring Elshtain's maternalist-communitarian model into focus, we need, as I have indicated, to go beyond the types of feminist theory of citizenship categorised by Siim if we want to try to pinpoint the constructions of gender and community – and, by extension, society – emerging from this alternative discourse on citizenship. Val Plumwood has defined the 'self-in-relationship' or 'relational self' as giving 'an account of the non-instrumental mode, which includes respect, benevolence, care, friendship and solidarity', underlining that such a non-instrumental conception of relationship to the other is an important ingredient in 'ecological selfhood' (Plumwood 1993, 154-55). The women active in the Associations, writing in *Tidevarvet*, and participating at Fogelstad would of course not have used a term such as 'ecological selfhood', but Plumwood's concept clearly highlights relevant elements. In a subsequent work she has written on both land ownership and spirituality in terms akin to those underpinning the alternative discourse outlined above, with the deconstruction of 'the rationality of monologue' – 'termed monological because it recognises the Other only in one-way terms' (Plumwood 2002, 19) – and the construction of ecofeminist alternatives which constitute her project in *Environmental Culture: The Ecological Crisis of Reason*, having distinct affinities with the projects of the Associations, *Tidevarvet* and Fogelstad. As I have emphasised, the construction of community in *Tidevarvet* and at the Women Citizens' College has much in common with Frazer and Lacey's 'dialogic communitarianism', but another recent theory such as Plumwood's on ecological selfhood helps foreground the extent to which the sense of ethical responsibility so prominent in the texts constituting this alternative discourse had global implications.

Chapter 8:
Texts 1922-36

This chapter covers a wide range of texts from the period 1922-36. The first section focuses on journalism in the form of a small selection of opinion pieces. I then move on to a text that poses major challenges in terms of genre categorisation, *Från Seine, Rhen och Ruhr. Små historier från Europa* (From the Seine, the Rhine and the Ruhr: Anecdotes from Europe) from 1923, and from there to the radio dramas, six in all, performed 1930-34. The last section offers analyses of four novels.

1. Opinion Pieces

With the formal introduction of citizenship for women in Sweden in 1919/1921, the problem of gender equality was commonly regarded as having been solved. However, as we have seen in Chapter 7, the introduction of suffrage for women was also followed by public discussions and disagreements on the constructions of both gender and community and, by extension, society. This is one of the reasons why, when making a selection from Wägner's journalism from the period 1922-36, I have chosen from the category that can be labelled opinion pieces. Wägner's regular journalistic forum for almost the whole of this period was the weekly *Tidevarvet*, the source of four of the five texts analysed below.

David Randall has defined one distinctive type of opinion piece, the editorial, in terms that are applicable to the opinion piece more generally. Such texts, he writes, should not be 'a series of wilful assertions laid upon each other': instead editorials should offer 'a fresh point of view', should 'contain sufficient elements of background and analysis to make them understandable to those who have not read the story(ies) they are based upon', and should be 'arguments constructed as tightly as a wellwound spring' (Randall 2000, 205). While Randall's definition is a useful basis for my analyses, the texts I have selected range well beyond the strict boundaries of the editorial. Indeed, *Tidevarvet* may well have inspired some innovative developments of journalistic genres – although this type of investigation is well beyond the scope of the present study. Wistrand has highlighted the many different facets of Wägner's work in *Tidevarvet* (Wistrand 2006, 81-158).

As we have seen in Chapters 6 and 7 above, women in Sweden during the interwar period achieved a higher public profile than ever before, participating in local and national politics, playing a more important role in the labour force, and organising on an unprecedented scale, while at the same time being subjected to both gender segregation and gender discrimination. How, in this dynamic setting, are gender and community constructed in the opinion pieces by Wägner selected here, and how do these constructions relate to the constructions of gender and of community that emerged from my survey of discourses on citizenship above? How do Wägner's texts relate – and respond? – not just to the construction of femininity in terms of what Yvonne Hirdman has labelled 'the housewife contract' and to the alternative promoted by Alva Myrdal, but to the emphasis on the individual as adaptable to the social engineering project developing in Sweden in the 1930s? And in the light of the new Swedish welfare state taking shape, what kinds of community – and, indeed, what kind of society – are being constructed in Wägner's opinion pieces? Finally, what kinds of narratee emerge from these texts, and how are these engaged? The Swedish social engineers of the 1930s were constructing the individual human being in scientific terms, as illustrated by Gunnar and Alva Myrdal's *Kris i befolkningsfrågan*; but might those of Wägner's opinion pieces that use a spectrum of registers and metaphors construct more manyfaceted narratees and thus be more sophisticated in terms of what Norman Fairclough has termed 'coherence', the positions they set up for interpreting subjects (Fairclough 2006, 83-84, 134-36)? These are the key questions underlying my analyses of the selected opinion pieces that follow.

'Liv eller död' (Life or Death) was published in what was only the second issue of *Tidevarvet*, on 1 December 1923. The text was given a prominent position, with the first few paragraphs taking up the fifth and final column on page 1 (the rest of the text appeared on page 2) and thus balancing the material in the first column, which reiterated the aims of *Tidevarvet* as stated, in the same space, the previous week.

A mere four years after the Versailles Treaty, 'Liv eller död' holds up as an imminent threat a new and much more devastating war: 'Om Europa vill begå självmord, finns det nämligen nu alldeles utomordentliga möjligheter därtill' (Wägner 1923a, 1) (For if Europe is wanting to commit suicide, the opportunities for doing so now are exceptionally good). Not only is the existing peace based on fear: the rapid development of air warfare is paving the way for total war. 'En effektiv stridsberedskap betyder ett hänsynslöst användande av den moderna teknikens alla hjälpmedel med tårgaser, dårgaser och bacillprojektiler. Det blir kemisternas och farmakologernas krig' (op. cit., 2) (To be efficient, readiness for action will be tantamount to the ruthless use of all the means of modern technology, such as tear gas, gas that drives its victims insane, and projectiles loaded with germs. This will be the war of the chemists and the pharmacologists). Terms such as *försvar* (defence) and *värnplikt* (conscription) (the Swedish word literally means 'duty to protect') are no longer adequate and are deconstructed in this text; their replacements, according to the narrator, should be 'vetenskaplig stridsberedskap' (scientific preparedness for war) and 'folkets offerplikt' (the people's duty to make sacrifices) respectively (ibid.). The total war is threatening communities and societies with total destruction, and Europe is facing the prospect of being reduced to 'en grushög' (ibid.) (a pile of ruins).

As humankind faces these extreme threats everybody, the narrator points out, has a duty to make a stand. Here the narrator, who has become an increasingly prominent *jag* (I), declares that the total pacifism that is the logical conclusion of her argument represents her own position and neither that of *Tidevarvet* nor of the National Association of Liberal Women. While this declaration opens the way for further back-up of some of the claims made in the text – 'fyra års iakttagelser i Europas *post bellum*' (Wägner 1923a, 2) (four years of observations in Europe's post bellum) – it also helps to highlight the relative insignificance of the narratee in this fact-laden text. The threat of total war also contributes to marginalising the significance of gender, and the linkage of men with warfare that we encountered in some of the texts from The Hague in 1915 is dismissed here as out of date. The 'spridda grupper' (ibid.) (scattered groups) working for peace in both Germany and Britain are non-gendered in this text, and the figure symbolising the pacifist efforts is Gandhi.

In contrast to 'Liv eller död', 'En negerstat i staten' (A Negro State within the State), published just a week later, constructs the state in terms of deepening gender divisions. Indeed, these divisions are given racial – and arguably also post-colonial – proportions as the oppression of women is paralleled with the oppression of blacks.

The argument of 'En negerstat i staten' pivots on the power relationship between the white man and marginalised or absent Others. The text, however, deconstructs this opposition, its multitude of facets adding up to an innovative textual space in line with the aim of *Tidevarvet* – as stated by the 'visible narrator' (Bal 1999, 18) of this piece – to be 'något annat än en fristående dambilaga utan huvud' (Wägner 1923b, 6) (something other than a separate women's supplement without a main paper). The text consists of three parts: an opening section dominated by direct speech; a fact-laden middle section with a character-bound narrator; and a concluding poem, four stanzas in Swedish translation from a work by the American author Sarah Cleghorn (1876-1959). While I have once categorised this text as an essay (Forsås-Scott 1999, 37), I now believe it is more rewarding to read it as an innovative opinion piece, the registers of which construct a narratee of considerable complexity. This narratee is not just engaged by the rational argument of the narrator but also by the rhetorical features, the metaphors, and the imagery of this text.

With its foregrounding of anonymities, the opening paragraph is neutral in terms of relations of power:

> En afton i somras vandrade en fransyska och en svenska tillsammans i en bokskog, som sträckte sig ner mot Stora Bält. Emellan sig hade de ett sällsamt Något, som stundom bara var en Röst, stundom då skogen glesnade något mot havet var en Röst och en vit skjortkrage. (Wägner 1923b, 1)

(One evening last summer a French woman and a Swedish woman were walking together in a beech wood that extended down to The Great Belt. Between them they had a strange Something which sometimes was just a Voice, sometimes, when the wood thinned somewhat towards the sea, a Voice and a white shirt collar.)

In direct speech, the Voice begins to detail the rich cultural heritage of the blacks, their current oppression, and their desire to contribute to world culture, only to have the parallels with the women's movement spelled out to him by the two female characters. The agreement by these three characters on the destructive impact of the white man belongs in the post-First-World-War context in which the grip of the old imperial powers was weakening and the blacks in the United States had become more vociferous in their demands for full civil rights; but their agreement also anticipates a post-colonial understanding of the relationship between gender and race. 'Can the subaltern speak?' Gayatri Chakravorty Spivak was to ask in a famous article published in 1985; and this is the question that the characters in this text along with the visible narrator are effectively formulating. It is this perspective and the consistency with which it is developed that makes the argument of 'En negerstat i staten' so provocative and so far-reaching, flying in the face as it does of the notion – stated in the text by an anonymous male philosopher – that women at the time had developed a separatist agenda.

Towards the end of the first part of the text the narrator piles up examples of the racial ghettoisation of American society; and it is the factual details and thus the persuasiveness of this pattern that give such weight to the survey in the second part of the text of the situation of women in Sweden in the wake of the granting of full citizenship. While acknowledging the progress women have made, the character-bound narrator singles out the dangers of a system that continues to insist on the separateness of women, demonstrating that even the achievements of the New Woman have effectively become worthless: 'De unga flickorna tro sig mycket frigjorda, emedan de få röka eller låta bli, dricka sprit eller låta bli, gifta sig eller låta bli efter egen smak. Men ett osynligt stängsel bygges omkring dem' (Wägner 1923b, 5) (The young girls believe they are very liberated because they are free to smoke or not, drink alcohol or not, marry or not, just as they please. But an invisible fence is being built around them). With the power of the white man intact, Swedish society is becoming ghettoised in terms of gender just as American society has become ghettoised in terms of race; and the women who should have added 'något av sin personlighet och sina synpunkter' (op. cit., 6) (something of their personalities and their points of view) and so helped reinvent Swedish society are being left in isolation and frustration – stranded, in effect, in communities with nothing but negative features. While the prominent linkage of women and blacks holds out the promise of a more extensive political struggle, the challenging form of this text and thus its coherence in Fairclough's sense (Fairclough 2006, 83-84, 134-36), is no less bold. The concluding stanzas from Sarah Cleghorn's poem focus on the extent to which the slaves and the blacks through their very absence have shaped the history of the United States and, indeed, the soul of the white man; but in the last instance the absences, racial and/or gendered, at the forefront of this text are challenged by its new community of interpreting subjects.

Signalling the prominence of intertextuality in its title, 'Lysistrates och fredens timma' (The Hour of Lysistrata and of Peace) was published in *Dagens Nyheter* on 11 January 1935. In a new Swedish translation, the drama by Aristophanes had had its first performance at the Dramatic Theatre in Stockholm on 16 November 1934; but just as prominent an intertext here is Alva and Gunnar Myrdal's *Kris i befolkningsfrågan*, which had appeared in December 1934. In formulating a response to the Myrdals' book, Wägner's opinion piece foregrounds feminist pacifism, both in terms of intertextuality and in terms of a psychological analysis.

Kris i befolkningsfrågan had singled out fundamental changes to the functions of the family as the key to tackling the crisis: 'A shared place to live, shared leisure and the elusive, subtle personal relationship – these factors, in our opinion, are constitutive of the family, and they will last. But not so the private running of households, individualistic parental authority, or the wife's confined course of life' (Myrdal, A. and Myrdal, G. 1934, 319). In Wägner's opinion piece, the Myrdals are only referred to explicitly as instances of economists and sociologists who have tried to relate motherhood to the political economy of modern society, but their much-debated book is clearly one of the main platforms for the development of the argument. Along with the Myrdals, the text also refers to the Norwegian psychologist Ingjald Nissen (1896-1977), whose *Seksualitet og disiplin* (1934; Sexuality and Discipline) – of which Wägner owned a copy with a dedication from the author – problematised what he regarded as the static relationship between 'the worship of masculinity' and feminine inferiority (Nissen 1934, 9-10); but it is the juxtaposition of Aristophanes's comedy from 411 BCE and the Myrdals' book, published just a month before Wägner's text, that forms the main intertextual basis on which the argument of this opinion piece is developed.

The character-bound narrator of 'Lysistrates och fredens timma' announces from the start that the demographic crisis will be represented in this text as 'en kvinnornas kris med all den ensidighet och förkortning som därav blir följden, men detta med berått mod, eftersom man i en artikel kan ha rätt att lägga tonvikten på synpunkter som annars löpa fara att glömmas bort i den allmänna diskussionen' (Wägner 1935a) (a women's crisis, with all the one-sidedness and abridgement that follow; this, however, is quite deliberate since in an article one may be entitled to emphasise perspectives that otherwise risk being forgotten in the general debate). With the 'actional component', the 'force' (Fairclough 2006, 82) of this text a prominent feature, tentative phrasing and rhetorical questions engage the narratee in the radical proposal that the Swedish demographic crisis is the result, not of a rebellion led by a modern Lysistrata, but of the unconscious reactions to childhood memories, social attitudes, and the current situation by 'fruarna och fröknarna Anderson, Johanson, Bergström och Lindström, som utgöra den kompakta massan av vårt folks kvinnor i barnproducerande ålder' (ibid.) (the Mrs and Misses Anderson, Johanson, Bergström and Lindström, who make up the mass of women of fertile age in our country). These women certainly will not point up the cause of the crisis: 'det är dem fjärran att påstå att männen fela, lika fjärran att bruka sin makt och träda fram för att styra' (ibid.) (it is far from them to claim that the men are wrong, just as it is far from them to use their power and come forward to take charge). Developing an argument that would seem to expand that of Mathilde Vaerting, the narrator goes on to claim that men have consistently over-valued their own capacity while under-valuing women, and that the marginalisation of women in society has resulted in 'utvecklingen' (progress) being deprived of 'en justerande och reglerande faktor' (ibid.) (a correcting and regulating element): 'Männen ha format och omformat samhället, absorberade av att utnyttja planeten och kämpa med varandra om bitarna av den' (ibid.) (Men have shaped and re-shaped society, absorbed by the task of exploiting the planet and fighting each other for the pieces). Here the positive connotations of 'progress' are demolished by an outline of civilisation as masculinist and thus preoccupied not just with warfare but also with the exploitation of the environment. In the Swedish context, this represents a remarkably early pointer towards an ecofeminist position.

The foregrounding of a women's rebellion that is 'omedvetet eller nätt och jämnt medvetet' (Wägner 1935a) (unconscious or barely conscious) helps to focus a psychological perspective on gender inequality, with the reasons for the demographic crisis spelled out here including the recollections of the women of child-bearing age both of the situation of their own mothers, often bringing up many children in conditions of abject poverty, and of 'minnet av krig och hotet om krig' (ibid.) (the memory of war and the threat of war). The latter point is reinforced by another intertext, Matthew 24:19 about the conflicts that will be part of the end of the world: 'And woe unto them that are with child, and to them that give suck in those days!'. Unemployment and the threat of unemployment is another reason, while the difficulties experienced by many women combining paid employment and marriage is a third. Linking into her argument a reference to a text by the Norwegian feminist writer Camilla Collett (1813-1895), the narrator emphasises that middle-class women are also suffering due to 'det maskuliniserade samhällets brist på vaksamhet' (ibid.) (the lack of vigilance of the masculinised society) with regard to the situation of women and children. With a strategy familiar from some of the reportages from the Congress at The Hague in 1915, this text appropriates military vocabulary to exemplify the refusal of Swedish women to bear children, a strategy that is clearly designed to enhance the significance of the women's refusal, but that also has the effect of disarming the original vocabulary. Although the construction of gender in this opinion piece is binary, with the division in terms of warfare and motherhood echoing texts by Wägner from the First World War, the rich array of intertexts in combination with the force of this piece construct a narratee who is not just prominent but gender neutral, and who is key to the new society that can be glimpsed at the end: 'De fordringar kvinnorna satte upp om fred mellan folken och en nyorganisering av samhället, som skulle bli så mycket lättare om inte krigshotet längre förryckte allt, de skulle kunna få en oerhörd tyngd – om de ställdes' (ibid.) (Demands made by women for peace between the peoples and a new organisation of society, which would be much easier if the threat of war did not distort everything, these demands could acquire great weight – if they were made.) In the reading developed in this opinion piece, in other words, the demographic crisis was not just the result of the economic and social problems women in Sweden were experiencing, as the Myrdals were claiming, but of a deep sense of psychological alienation; and the bold linkage between the demographic crisis and the threat of war was underpinned by Vaerting's analysis of gender in terms of power.

The text entitled 'Vad tänker du, mänsklighet?'(Humankind, What are You Thinking?) initiates in its very title the construction of a textual community that is even more extensive than that of the previous text. Published in *Tidevarvet* on 7 September 1935, this was the speech Wägner had made a few days previously at a public meeting known as 'Kvinnornas representantmöte Ned med vapnen i alla länder' (The Meeting of the Women's Representatives: Down the Weapons in All Countries), one of the climactic points of the 1935 Swedish women's anti-war campaign 'Kvinnornas vapenlösa uppror mot kriget' (The Women's Unarmed Revolt against War). Irene Andersson has described *Tidevarvet* as 'a platform and a stage' for this campaign (Andersson 2001, 184); and *Tidevarvet*'s account of the meeting at which the speech was made, consisting of 75 elected representatives of the 20,000 women who had signed the petition, was published in tandem with Wägner's text (see Hermelin 1935). Andersson has likened the organisation of the campaign to those of the *folkriksdagar*, the people's parliaments working for general suffrage in Sweden in the late nineteenth century; and as she has also pointed out, the issue of the distribution of spending on military resources and on social policy initiatives respectively, which became pivotal to the campaign, had in fact engaged Swedish liberals and social democrats since the beginning of the twentieth century (Andersson 2001, 238-9). What made the campaign distinctly different in the Swedish context was the gender-based political message (op. cit., 239). In Wägner's text, the gendering of the argument is prominent from the start, linking femininity to peace and masculinity to war with an insistence that we have not encountered in my selections from her journalism since the texts from The Hague in 1915.

'Vad tänker du, mänsklighet?' begins by contrasting an episode from the old border confrontations between Danes and Swedes during which the Danes burned a Småland village yet spared a dwelling housing a woman in childbirth, with the duties facing the modern soldier involved in a war that has become total: 'Hans uppgift blir att förvirra, förgifta, förbränna mänskliga hem där gamla dö, där barn födas, där människor gå i sin dagliga gärning' (Wägner 1935b, 3) (His task will be to derange, to poison, to burn down the homes of human beings in which old people are dying, children are being born, human beings are going about their daily work). In a much elaborated version of the reference in 'Liv eller död' to the risk of Europe being reduced to 'a pile of ruins' (Wägner 1923a), 'Vad tänker du, mänsklighet?' relates communities epitomised by everyday life to the threat of comprehensive destruction. And with a question that appropriates the kind of rhetoric familiar from the texts from The Hague in 1915, the narrator asks, 'Hur kan en man av kvinna född förmås till något sådant?' (Wägner 1935b, 3) (How can a man born of woman be persuaded to do something like this?), only to answer her own question by explaining modern soldiering in terms of a contemporary version of slavery and posing a new question that reinforces the parallels with the rhetoric used twenty years previously: 'Är det inte skam för Europas kvinnor att de ingenting gjort för att befria sina söner ur detta förtryck?' (ibid.) (Is it not a disgrace for the women of Europe to have done nothing to free their sons from this oppression?).

Texts 1922-36

The changed circumstances have given questions such as these a new urgency. Strengthening the argument with facts, the narrator illustrates with a quotation from the British Prime Minister (Baldwin), according to whom '"[d]et enda försvaret är angrepp, vilket betyder att vi måste döda kvinnor och barn fortare än fienden, om vi önskar rädda oss själva"' (ibid.) (the only defence is attack, which means we have to kill women and children faster than the enemy does if we want to save ourselves); with details of the new duties of the housewife as she prepares her home for fire and gas attacks from the air; and with the situation of the mother of the soldier training for air warfare:

> Kan hon säga honom att visserligen är det ett ohyggligt brott att gå lös på försvarslösa människor med eld och gift, ett brott som straffar sig grymt på den som begår det. Men, min gosse, gör du det i krig, då är det rätt, då uteblir följderna och du räddar din själ. Jag tror inte att det går att säga så. (ibid.)
>
> (Can she say to him that it is true that it is a hideous crime to attack defenceless human beings with fire and poison, a crime the consequences of which will most certainly find out the person who commits it. But, my son, if you do it in war then it is right, then there will be no consequences and you will save your soul. I do not think one can argue like this.)

As indicated by a number of the quotations so far, this text uses tactics to engage the narratee and underpin a more extensive community of the type familiar from some of the earlier journalism, ranging from rhetorical questions and questions-and-answers to the prominent use of the inclusive *vi* (we), to intertextuality in the form of quotations, and the deconstruction of a key phrase, in this case 'försvar för land och frihet' (Wägner 1935b, 3) (defence of the nation and of freedom). But there are a couple of new features too. Here we encounter, for the first time in the texts by Wägner selected in this study, the device that was to become prominent in the pamphlet *Väckarklocka* (1941), namely the more insistent exhortation to the narratee that consists of the italicisation of crucial phrases, for example, with reference to air warfare, '*Europa gick därmed in i ett källarskede av sin ärorika historia*' (ibid.; italics original) (*Europe thus entered a basement phase of its glorious history*).

Following an account of how Stockholm is being prepared for aerial bombardment, the narrator, using *vi* (we) to highlight the support of the women who have joined the campaign, addresses the official in charge directly, combining this address with the use of italics: '*här finns en mänsklig faktor som stryker ett streck över era kalkyler!* [...] Räkna inte med kvinnorna som krigsrobotar!' (op. cit., 4; italics original) (*there is a human factor here that will annul your calculations!* [...] Don't count on women becoming war robots!). Here the basis for the involvement of the narratee is clearly one of strength: unlike twenty years previously, women in Sweden have the right to vote, and the campaign against war has attracted the support of 20,000 of these women. The success of the campaign is not just a pointer towards 'hur dåligt det nya källar- och cementskedet passar oss människor' (op. cit., 5) (how badly the new basement and concrete era suits us humans), but also an indication of the fundamental aspirations of humankind: 'Människor vilja leva, sträva för sig och de sina, andas fritt, se utan fruktan mot himlen' (ibid.) (Human beings want to live, to work for themselves and for their nearest and dearest, to look without fear towards heaven). While the gulf between femininity and masculinity is to some extent bridged at the rhetorical level in this text, the contention that women have a unique contribution to make to a more peaceful world is underlined by the summary of the aims of the campaign:

> Dess uppgift är att på bredast möjliga front kämpa mot det fega accepterandet av kriget, riva upp den falska tryggheten, ställa människor inför verkligheten, slåss mot denna nya befästning av våra hem som om vi vore tillbaka i medeltiden, opponera mot att vi dras in i krigsmaskineriet, söka komma själva krigssystemet till livs. (ibid.)

> (Its task is to fight, on the broadest front possible, against the cowardly acceptance of war, to tear up the false sense of security, to make human beings face reality, to fight against this new fortification of our homes as if we were back in the Middle Ages, to oppose the fact that we are being dragged into the machinery of war, to get at the very system of war.)

Pivotal to the argument in this opinion piece, then, is a community of women, 'vår rörelse' (op. cit., 4) (our movement), in opposition to a society – Swedish society, western society – preparing for war.

Texts 1922-36

With 'Två landskap' (Two Landscapes), the demands for peace and a new organisation of society referred to in the previous text have become quite specific. Subtitled 'Ett resebrev' (A Travel Letter), 'Två landskap' appeared on the front page of *Tidevarvet* on 8 August 1936, next to an article about the Spanish Civil War and the possibility of interventions by other European countries, including Mussolini's Italy and Hitler's Germany. By contrast Wägner's text (which, like 'En negerstat i staten', I have once categorised as an essay [Forsås-Scott 1999, 46] but now prefer to read as an innovative opinion piece) begins as a travelogue with the character-bound narrator representing life at Bad Fusch, in the Alps near Salzburg, and outings on the newly built Glocknerstrasse. Here the focus on aspects of the scenery stands out. The rich vegetation on the south side of the Alps turns out to consist of communities of tiny plants which nevertheless play a key role in helping to reduce erosion on the huge mountains, and the ubiquitous water illustrates a similar conjunction of small and great:

> dropparna som spruta upp i vita, vilda kaskader, flyta strax därpå ihop i en tung vattenmassa, vilket inte hindrar dem att kort därpå, när ett hinder möter som de måste ta var för sig, skiljas igen och komma ut som hela, runda och oskadda individer ur den kollektiva massan, i vilken de strax åter skola uppgå. (Wägner 1936, 4)

> (the drops bursting up in white, wild cascades soon after come together and form a single, heavy body of water, which does not prevent them from separating again when they encounter an obstacle that they have to negotiate on their own and emerging as complete, rounded and undamaged individuals from the collective mass of which they will again become part soon afterwards.)

But then this evocative travelogue comes to a halt, leaving the narratee in a limbo:

> Jag föreställer mig att någon, i varje fall redaktören av Tidevarvet, har läst så här långt i min beskrivning. I så fall har hon hela tiden undrat hur detta kan hänga ihop, eftersom hon väntat en artikel om en konferens i Salzburg. Till detta kan jag då endast säga att, bitte, jag har hela tiden skrivit om konferensen i Salzburg. (ibid.)

(I imagine that someone, at least the editor of *Tidevarvet*, has read this far into my account. If so, she has been wondering what this has been about, since she had been expecting an article about a conference in Salzburg. All I can say is, *bitte*, I've been writing about the conference in Salzburg all along.)

The interpretation of the text so far, the reading of it as a travelogue, is called into question, the narratee is foregrounded by means of direct address ('ni kan när som helst [...] fara till Bad Fusch' [ibid.] [you can travel, at any time (...), to Bad Fusch]), and the visible narrator uses a rhetorical question to spell out the central symbolism of the narrative so far:

> Har jag inte kanske skrivit om den region som är alltings början, där förvandlingen från moln till regn och vattendrag försiggår, där små kraftlösa källor födas som växa, förenas med andra, flyta ihop och bli en livgivande, hejdlös kraft? Men det är ju precis den region där vi måste mötas, då vi vilja tala på våra olika tungomål om en framtid som skulle kunna medföra att kvinnorna tillträdde sitt medregentskap i världsförloppet. (ibid.)

> (Have I not written about the region where it all begins, where the transformation from clouds into rain and water courses is taking place, where small powerless springs emerge that grow bigger, unite with others, merge and become a life-giving, unstoppable force? But this is exactly the region in which we have to get together when we want to speak in our different languages about a future that might include the access of women to their joint governance of the course of the world.)

As I have pointed out in a Swedish context, the use of the plural form of the first-person personal pronoun, *vi* (we) has the effect of embracing not just the readers of *Tidevarvet* but also women more generally, with the inclusion of the narratee in the construction of the new world that follows – and where the pronoun is repeated – being particularly significant (Forsås-Scott 1999, 48). The same feature is to be found in some of the texts of Virginia Woolf (Allan 1993, 135).

But the new world that emerges in this opinion piece is totally inclusive, 'en värld där rovdriften med jordens rikedomar, däri inbegripna skogar, djur och människor' (Wägner 1936, 4) (a world in which the ruthless exploitation of the wealth of the earth, including forests, animals and human beings) has ceased, and where life is the ultimate value. This new world has a world government and a world court, both respected by all nations who have equal numbers of female and male representatives in both. This new world does not have a military army but a workers' army in which work of all kinds is shared equally and carried out together, allowing the individual citizen to leave this army 'inte som psykisk och fysisk invalid, utan med rikare krafter och färdigheter och med existensminimum säkrat för hela livet' (ibid.) (not as a mental and physical invalid, but with greater strength and abilities, and with a minimum level of subsistence secured for the rest of his/her life). In this new world, motherhood is voluntary and an integral part of the citizens' contributions to society, all children have equal rights, and one gender no longer '[skriver] lagar för det andra utan att begripa vad det [är] frågan om' (ibid.) ([writes] laws for the other without understanding what it [is] all about). In this new world, there are no wars.

The references to Women's Organisation for World Order, whose conference had just taken place in Salzburg, appear only towards the end of the text, and the gendered reading of the mounting problems of the world – 'det ena könet dignar under ett övermäktigt ansvar och det andra förtvinar utan att bruka sina krafter' (Wägner 1936, 4) (one gender is being weighed down by an excessive responsibility while the other is withering without using its powers) – is ascribed to the members of this organisation. Yet, as I have pointed out in my Swedish analysis, Wägner's opinion piece represents a marked toning down of the gender contrasts that are so prominent in a WOWO document such as the programme preserved in the collection of Wägner's friend Flory Gate (1904-1998) in Göteborg University Library (Forsås-Scott 1999, 49; see also Andersson 1993, 15-16). Leaving the Social Democratic welfare state taking shape in Sweden at this time far behind, Wägner's opinion piece which so prominently engages the narratee, builds bridges between individuals, between women and men, and between human beings and living others, as the basis for a new way of living on this earth that is not just peaceful but that also constitutes a radically new understanding of the environment and humankind's dependence on it.

To sum up, this selection of opinion pieces, the first two of which date from 1923, just a few years after the granting of full citizenship to women in Sweden, explore constructions of gender in terms of imbalances of power that are becoming deeper and deeper, with consequences that are becoming increasingly momentous. While explanations for this imbalance are sought in the work of theorists such as Vaerting and Adler, the emphasis in the opinion pieces selected here is on war and peace. New communities consisting of pacifists are prominent in some of these texts, and 'Vad tänker du, mänsklighet?' foregrounds an alternative community consisting of the 20,000 Swedish women who have signed a petition against war. Implicit in this alternative community is a concept of citizenship as involving responsibilities that are not just national but global. The preponderance of narrators who are visible in the sense defined by Bal (Bal 1999, 18), in combination with narratees whom complex narrative structures and shifting registers frequently construct as multi-faceted, helps foreground the interrelations and innovation needed to build new communities, and the programme outlined in 'Två landskap' is nothing less than a blueprint for a new world. Although the threat of war sometimes has the effect of marginalising gender, as in 'Liv eller död', the contributions of women play a prominent role in some of the alternative communities that emerge here. But as in 'Två landskap', these communities can also reach beyond social structures centring on humankind to embrace all living beings. The environmentalism or, indeed, ecofeminism for which some of these texts argue is not only ahead of its time but also involves a concept of citizenship based on responsibilities that are global.

2. *Från Seine, Rhen och Ruhr (From the Seine, the Rhine and the Ruhr)*

Like the reportages from Vienna in 1920 and the novel *Den förödda vingården* published in the same year, the volume that appeared in 1923, *Från Seine, Rhen och Ruhr: Små historier från Europa* (From the Seine, the Rhine and the Ruhr: Anecdotes from Europe), drew on Wägner's travels on the continent in the wake of the First World War. However, the premises were different. While Wägner had travelled to Vienna early in 1920 primarily to report in *Dagens Nyheter* on the suffering of the population in the aftermath of the war, she travelled on several occasions to Germany, and to the occupied areas in particular, in 1921-23. In February-March 1921 she travelled with a minister in the Swedish State Church, Gunnar Vall, with whom she had been commissioned by *Förbundet för kristet samhällsliv* (The Society for Christianising Social Life) to report on conditions in the occupied Rhineland; and in November 1922 she travelled, again in the Rhineland, with the English Quaker Marion Fox to prepare a report for the Women's International League for Peace and Freedom which was holding a conference at The Hague in December (Isaksson and Linder 2003, 298-303, 348-49). While the former trip resulted in a published report and there are reportages by Wägner about the 1922 conference at The Hague and other aspects of her travels, the volume she published following her travels in 1921-23 was not a novel like *Den förödda vingården*. Neither was it a collection of reportages, nor a travelogue. The reception of the volume – which was positive – showed almost as many genre labels as there were reviewers, and the problems with genre categorisation may well have contributed to the marginalisation of *Från Seine, Rhen och Ruhr*. In Linder's *Fyra decennier av nittonhundratalet* (1949; Four Decades of the Twentieth Century), the volume was mentioned in a single sentence with the texts neutrally described as *skildringar* (accounts) (Linder 1949, 99); and the same laconic sentence recurred in the second, much expanded edition (Linder 1965, 126). Isaksson and Linder devoted two pages to the book, inevitably approaching it in mainly biographical terms, and negotiating the problem of genre by referring to 'columns [that coalesce] into an impressionistic prose poem' (Isaksson and Linder 2003, 352-53). Most recently Birgitta Wistrand has characterised the volume as a 'collection of short stories'; strangely, however, she combines this categorisation with the claim that all the texts have the same narrator and that this narrator, moreover, is identical with Elin Wägner (Wistrand 2006, 213-18).

In my reading of *Från Seine, Rhen och Ruhr* it is not the genre issue *per se* that emerges as important, but rather the persistent foregrounding of narrative and narration. As the subtitle emphasises, these are 'Anecdotes from Europe', and the volume effectively consists of series or chains of narratives, of stories told by characters in the texts and stories based on what the narrators, visible in the sense defined by Bal (Bal 1999, 18), claim to have seen, heard or read, with the blurred boundary towards fiction sometimes becoming quite prominent: 'Jag återger här hans historia, *så gott jag kan*' (Wägner 1923c, 77; my italics) (Here I will retell his story *to the best of my ability*). The nouns *historia* (story), *berättelse* (story, narrative) and *anekdot* (anecdote) are high-frequency words in this volume, consistently highlighting the metatextuality of *Från Seine, Rhen och Ruhr*.

But as the texts in this volume repeatedly emphasise, stories can have a range of functions. The very first text contains a remark about the effect on the people (the French in this case) of being made to 'se händelserna genom pressens glasögon och få dem tillrättalagda och förklarade för sig av politikerna' (Wägner 1923c, 9) (see the events through the spectacles of the press and have them elucidated and explained by the politicians); and the text about cases of rape in the occupied areas provides examples of the use of narratives for political propaganda as well as for personal gratification (op. cit., 141-45). The texts in *Från Seine, Rhen och Ruhr* distance themselves emphatically from these types of use of narrative. While Ricoeur has pointed to the double sense of the term 'history', the fact that it has 'designated for at least two centuries, in a great many languages, both the totality of the course of events and the totality of narratives referring to this course of events' (Ricoeur 1988, 102), the texts in Wägner's volume not only highlight this semantic coincidence but also begin to prize it apart. Referring to the French occupation of the Ruhr province in 1923 as the major political event of that year and comparing it to other decisive historical events such as the fall of Carthage or the fall of Napoleon, one of Wägner's texts emphasises the fact that despite what may seem to be the total predominance in 1923 of the confrontation between France and Germany, there were other courses of events too, some of them quite different:

> Men många trådar spändes även då mellan andra fästen än utrikesministerier och krigsministerier, högkvarter och front.
> Det är inte heller så, att huvudskeendet drar med sig alla andra skeenden i samma riktning. Var och en, som tänker efter, kan dra fram samtidiga händelseförlopp, som syfta åt helt annat håll, drivna av krafter, rakt motsatta dem, som ledde detta. (Wägner 1923c, 31)

(But even then many threads were spun between points of attachment other than Foreign Offices and Ministries of War, headquarters and fronts.
Nor is it the case that the main course of events pulls all other courses of events in the same direction. Anyone who reflects on this can think of simultaneous courses of events that aim in quite a different direction, driven by forces quite contrary to those governing the main course of events.)

At a time when the international community was demonising Germany in the wake of the First World War and supporting the action taken by the French government, the textual space of *Från Seine, Rhen och Ruhr* facilitates alternatives, with the majority of the prominent narratives clearly driven by forces quite contrary to those governing the main course of contemporary political events. A model referred to in several of these texts, and one that I read as a model for the volume as a whole, is that of the communication between Quakers, based on the notion of the significance of the individual human being. As explained in one of these texts, a key aspect of this communication consists of the copying of letters or parts of letters:

> Man tror inte det är möjligt i vår tid förrän man själv sett det, att i den utsträckning som sker bland kväkarna nyheter kunna cirkulera genom brev och avskrifter av brev. Och inte bara nyheter utan även yttre och inre erfarenheter, ord av uppmuntran, av godhet, som, sända från en vän till en vän, skickas vidare till nästa att göra samma tjänst. (Wägner 1923c, 108)

> (Until you have seen it for yourself, you do not think it is possible in our day and age for news to circulate via letters and copies of letters to the extent that happens among the Quakers. And not just news but also outer and inner experiences, words of encouragement, of goodness which, having been sent from one friend to another, are sent on to the next to do the same service.)

Indeed, the volume contains a text which purports to be an extract from a letter to a named friend of the narrator of this text; and it is not just the alleged origins of 'La Sainte Chapelle' that illustrate the points made about the mode of communication of the Quakers, but also the symbolism of the text. Hidden away in the Palais de Justice in the middle of Paris and with only the thin golden spire revealing its existence, La Sainte Chapelle, its interior shimmering with the multi-coloured light from the stained glass windows, becomes a symbol of 'den avsides världen' (op. cit., 96) (the world apart), which is not aware of itself and whose inhabitants do not all know each other: 'De finnas, som leva i ensamhet och främlingskap, ända till dess de finna någon, som känner igen dem som medborgare. Denne känner alltid en annan, och så är gemenskapen bildad' (ibid.) (There are those who live in loneliness and as strangers, until they find someone who recognises them as citizens. This person always knows someone else, and thus a community is formed). This world apart is to be found in the midst of the other one, sharing with it 'de dagliga ödena och de nattliga farorna' (op. cit., 97) (the daily fortunes and the nightly dangers), but being one of its citizens clearly bears no comparison to being a citizen of Germany or France or, for that matter, Sweden, in 1923. The references in these texts are to citizenship across national borders, to membership of a new type of community; and although the Quaker mode of communication serves as a model, the new type of community clearly is not limited to Quakers but has the potential to embrace all those to whom 'den enskilda människan har ett värde' (op. cit., 109) (the worth of the individual human being matters).

I read the collage of texts that makes up *Från Seine, Rhen och Ruhr* as an integral part of the project to build a new type of community based on an alternative concept of citizenship. Here I believe the thought of Mikhail Bakhtin can help clarify the significance of the texts of the volume with their strong emphasis on narrative and narration. As Michael Holquist has pointed out in *Dialogism: Bakhtin and his World*, the self in Bakhtin's work emerges as a 'multiple phenomenon' consisting of a centre, a not-centre, and the relation between the two (Holquist 1991, 29). The most important of these, the relation, is 'never static, but always in the process of being made or unmade' (ibid.). And as Holquist has also pointed out, a relation is of course also 'a *telling*, a narrative' (ibid.; italics original). The short, multi-faceted texts in Wägner's volume which, as the title indicates, range from narratives set in France to narratives set in the occupied parts of Germany, spin threads between a multitude of selves and others, French, German, English, Swedish and beyond, effectively illustrating what Holquist has termed 'a cardinal assumption of dialogism', namely that the cognitive space of every human being is 'coordinated by the same I/other distinctions that organize my own' (op. cit., 33). The key symbol of this significance of Wägner's text is the subterranean world of the Ruhr, the myriad passageways that constitute an alternative network of communication, and that have enabled French soldiers to exchange their uniforms for the clothes of German coal miners:

> Hur underbart att tänka, då man möter arbetarmassorna på väg hem, att bland dem, svarta som de förrymda slavarna, som sökte skydd och gömsle i nordstaterna undan sina ägare, dölja sig fransmän, som hellre dela tyskarnas arbete, faror och möda och ta sin extra risk på köpet än stå kvar under den franska trikoloren. (Wägner 1923c, 188)

> (How wonderful to think, when one meets the masses of workers on their way home, that among them, black as the escaped slaves who were seeking shelter and hide-outs in the North away from their owners, Frenchmen are hiding who prefer to share the toil, danger and effort of the Germans and to accept the additional risk, rather than to remain under the French tricolour.)

The many selves in the kaleidoscope of narratives that make up *Från Seine, Rhen och Ruhr* become a textual community, their affinity crystallised in the phrase '*Ich kenn die Läut*' (Wägner 1923c, 250; italics original) (I know the people), used in 'De utvisade' (The Exiles) to introduce the first-person narrator and her colleague to a group of exiled Germans, but resonating throughout the entire volume. This community also embraces the narratees – for given those genre variations that I have not attempted to specify, there are clearly differences between the narratees constructed in a text such as 'En dröm' (A Dream) with its affinities with the essay and prose fiction, and a text such as 'Ovädret över Bochum' (The Storm over Bochum) with its many affinities with the reportage. The marked genre variations emphatically discourage any notion of a single narrator. The concluding text, 'Om Rhen och Main' (About the Rhine and the Main), explicitly discourages the identification of any single narrator with

Elin Wägner. Dated and signed by the anonymous '*Författaren*' (op. cit., 274; italics original) (*The Author*), not by the name of the author, this text, significantly, also contains a section about this narrator's efforts to remove from the manuscript all instances of the first-person singular of the personal pronoun, *jag* (I), 'som man plockar tråckeltrådarna ur ett färdigt handarbete' (op. cit., 273) (as one removes the tacking-thread from a completed piece of needlework). Although 'Elin Wägner' does appear as the name of the character-bound narrator in one of the texts (op. cit., 207), this is three-quarters of the way into the volume, at a point when the narrators have clearly become so many and so many-faceted that it is possible to play with the name. Like the different narratees, the different narrators are involved in the construction of an innovative textual space in which relations, in the dual sense of the word, predominate. The penultimate text, 'Vägen och vinsten' (The Path and the Gain), with its optimistic suggestion that the passive resistance in the occupied Ruhr might mark the beginning of 'en folkens befrielsekamp mot militarismen' (op. cit., 263) (a struggle by the peoples to liberate themselves from miltarism), explicitly links back to some of the early texts about pacifism in France, e.g. 'Ungdom' (op. cit., 17-27) (Youth), a feature that helps to foreground the significance of the distinctive textual space of *Från Seine, Rhen och Ruhr*.

According to Ulla Isaksson and Erik Hjalmar Linder, a German friend of Wägner's was hoping to find a German publisher for the book (Isaksson and Linder 2003, 356). *Från Seine, Rhen och Ruhr* appeared in Swedish in May 1923. Just six months later, Adolf Hitler gained prominence as the leader of Germany's fledgling National Socialists as the failed *putsch* in the Bürgerbräukeller in Munich took place on 8-9 November. Wägner's book was not translated into German or into any other language.

With regard to the construction of gender in this volume, we may feel justified in attempting to draw parallels with the reportages from Vienna in 1920 and the novel *Den förödda vingården* from the same year, texts about which I concluded that issues of gender tended to be overshadowed by the emphasis on the suffering of the people/the characters. In the collage of texts that constitutes *Från Seine, Rhen och*

Texts 1922-36

Ruhr, gender is more prominent, but in terms that are as kaleidoscopic as the texts in the volume. An early text such as 'Ungdom' (Youth), about the young Frenchmen prepared to refuse military conscription, signals the impact of power irrespective of gender; and a few of the portraits of female characters in this volume are distinctly negative, such as that of the aristocratic German lady in one of the areas occupied by the *entente* who is having to house a Belgian family in her attic flat (Wägner 1923c, 148-53). But there is also a long section, more or less in the middle of the volume, of texts arranged under the heading 'Om kvinnorna' (About the Women). There are arguments here about the need for women to become less dependent on 'låneord från det manliga ordförrådet' (op. cit., 124) (loanwords from the masculine vocabulary) and find their 'egen form för det ljus, den kraft som är i dem' (op. cit., 135) (own form for the light, the power they have in themselves). While there are no specific details about this new form, perhaps the fact that the section headed 'Om kvinnorna' like no other section in the volume bridges and combines the material about France on the one hand and Germany on the other, points up this low-key volume as a whole as a feminine project. But the construction of gender in terms of the equating of masculinity with war and femininity with peace which we have encountered in texts by Wägner relating to the First World War and also in some later texts, is not relevant to *Från Seine, Rhen och Ruhr*.

As for the construction of community, the texts as such with their network of relations, of narratives, are key to the foregrounding of individual characters and thus to the outlining of alternative communities. The concluding sentences of 'La Sainte Chapelle' spell out the contrast with the existing system:

> Det är som om de, som sköta om rörelsen i världen, arbetade under ett jättelikt missförstånd i fråga om vad verklighet är.
> Verklighet, det är människornas, mänsklighetens förnyelse, dess vilja och duglighet och glädje att leva. Att betänka verkligheten, det är att spara och skydda den kraft, genom vilken den ena generationen stiger upp ur den andra för att fortsätta och fullkomna dess arbete. I den strid som nu föres mellan system, maktgrupper och klasser är bara en faktor bortglömd och lämnad ur räkningen, och det är människan. (Wägner 1923c, 98)

(It is as if those in charge of what is happening in this world were working under the thrall of a huge misunderstanding of what reality is.

Reality, that is the regeneration of human beings, of humankind, its desire and capability and joy in living. To take reality into account is to safeguard and protect the force through which one generation emerges from the other to continue and complete the work of humankind. In the struggle now raging between systems, powerful groups and classes, only one factor has been forgotten and left out of account, and this is the human being.)

Produced at a time of momentous significance in European politics, *Från Seine, Rhen och Ruhr* with its short and varied texts involving the frequent blurring – and questioning – of the boundary between nonfiction and fiction as well as the foregrounding of metatextuality, stands out among the texts explored so far in this study as an unusually clear-cut example of 'a collective or group creative process', one of the phrases used by Alastair Fowler to define genre (Fowler 1997, 277). While gender is constructed in binary terms, the linkage between masculinity and war on the one hand and femininity and peace on the other, so prominent in some of the texts from the Congress at The Hague in 1915 and also in some of the opinion pieces from the 1920s and 1930s, is not relevant here. These are texts in which the representation of alternative communities also emerges as a means of forging such communities, the Quaker model of communication between fellow human beings threading together these texts with their representations of characters of various nationalities, of meetings and encounters, of conversations, exchanges, and understanding.

3. Radio Drama

In comparison with Wägner's prose fiction, the drama for radio has attracted little attention. In Linder's *Fem decennier av nittonhundratalet*, Wägner's contribution to radio drama is mentioned neither in the section on Wägner's output nor in the section on drama for radio (Linder 1965, 1:118-30, 2:107-36); and in its successor, *Den svenska litteraturen*, Birgitta Steene's very short section about drama for radio and television

1920-1995 deals only very briefly with the former medium (Steene 1999). In their biography of Wägner, Ulla Isaksson and Erik Hjalmar Linder refer in passing to just two of the radio dramas, *Credo* (1934) and *Spinnerskan* (1941; The Spinster), the former co-written with Ragnar Hyltén-Cavallius and drawing on much the same material as the 1927 novel *De fem pärlorna* (The Five Pearls), and the latter subsequently reworked as the title story of Wägner's final collection of short stories which was published in 1948 (Isaksson and Linder 2003, 432, 443, 403). The most extensive explorations consist of the pages in Gunnar Hallingberg's *Radioteater i 40 år* (1965; Forty Years of Radio Drama) and his doctoral thesis *Radiodramat. Svensk hörspelsdiktning – bakgrund, utveckling och formvärld* (1967; The Radio Drama: Its Background, Development and Structure with Reference Mainly to Radio Playwriting in Sweden), plus a chapter by Margareta Wirmark in a *festschrift* that appeared in 1987.

But although Wägner's output for radio is not extensive – it consists of five short dramas broadcast in 1930 and 1931 in addition to the two longer dramas mentioned above – this work is certainly worth exploring. The medium was a new one, and in the context of this study, Wägner's drama for radio is worth investigating for this reason alone. As Karin Nordberg has pointed out, radio broadcasting was the first mass medium to cover the length and breadth of Sweden, with the monopoly of *Radiotjänst* (The Swedish Broadcasting Corporation) ensuring that the programmes on offer were more or less identical across the country (Nordberg 1998, 14-15). But with the technology originally having been used by the military and the merchant navy, there was a distinctly masculine dominance in early Swedish broadcasting, with women struggling to gain an influence during the 1930s, a decade during which the programme makers tended to focus on women chiefly in their roles as mothers and educators in the home (op. cit., 35, 40, 320-21). Yet, as Nordberg has also emphasised, radio broadcasting was simultaneously providing a new forum for women's voices and 'women's topics', helping to bring these out of the ghettos of the women's magazines (op. cit., 323). When radio broadcasting began in Sweden in 1923, the number of listeners was 40,000; by 1937, the number of licences had risen to 1,000 000.

Gunnar Hallingberg's pioneering volumes on Swedish radio drama provide an indispensable context for Wägner's contributions. As Hallingberg has emphasised, early Swedish radio drama was strongly influenced by stage drama with Per Lindberg, in charge of the newly-formed Department of Drama at the Swedish Broadcasting Corporation 1929-31 and the director with whom Wägner was to work most closely, having many years' experience as a theatre manager and director of stage drama in both Stockholm and Göteborg (Hallingberg 1967, 58-61). Hallingberg, however, does not regard Wägner's contribution to radio drama as in any way significant: implicitly basing his conclusion on a distinction between literature and 'tendentious' texts, he finds that she was interested in the medium mainly as 'an opportunity to trot out ideas' (op. cit., 123). Yet just a page or two previously he would seem to have contradicted this claim with his argument that the concerted efforts by *Radiotjänst* to recruit six authors, including Wägner, as radio dramatists by providing them with free radio sets, were driven by a desire to involve authors representing 'a perspective on culture embraced by the majority' (op. cit., 118-19, 121-22). Margareta Wirmark on the other hand is convinced that the drama written by Wägner, of which the drama for radio constitutes a major part and in which Wirmark also includes film scripts, is substantial enough to provide material for a doctoral thesis (Wirmark 1987, 335). With regard to the five short radio dramas from 1930-31, Wirmark highlights the contemporary relevance, the prominence of women characters representing a range of social classes, the witty dialogue, and the prominent moral stance (op. cit., 341).

In the context of the present study, the key question inevitably concerns the constructions of gender and community in Wägner's radio drama, including any differences in comparison with the other genres under investigation here. Given my periodisation of the material, I shall analyse the five short dramas, *Barnjungfrun* (1930; The Nursemaid), *Tre åldrar* (1930; Three Ages), *En helgonlegend* (1930; A Legend), *Han som blödde* (1931; He who Bled) and *Sjömansbruden* (1931; The Sailor's Bride), along with *Credo* (1934). My analyses are based on the original manuscripts available in the archives of *Radiotjänst*. There are very few recordings of radio drama

Texts 1922-36

from this early period (Hallingberg 1965, 296), and given the focus of my study, I have made no attempt to take into account the directors' decisions as indicated in their copies of the texts.

The stories of Wägner's five short radio dramas from 1930 and 1931 all revolve around female characters, but in contexts that tend to emphasise the construction of gender, usually as a result of the foregrounding of radio drama as theatre and performance. While aspects of power in terms of both domination and agency are more or less prominent as part of these constructions of gender, the distinctive characteristic of these radio dramas is the growing significance of the medial space, with the implications this also has for the role of the listener. In Wirmark's reading, the settings are mundanely realistic, 'a hotel, an exhibition, a café' (Wirmark 1987, 342). But as has been emphasised by Tim Crook, radio drama has a unique capacity to construct imaginative spaces, the emergence of which is also dependent on the listener's involvement:

> Radio's imaginative spectacle presents a powerful dynamic which is rarely prioritised by alternative electronic media. By giving the listener the opportunity to create an individual filmic narrative and experience through the imaginative spectacle the listener becomes an active participant and 'dramaturgist' in the process of communication and listening. This participation is physical, intellectual and emotional. (Crook 1999, 66)

In several of my analyses above, I have pointed to the significance of dialogism in Wägner's texts; as is clear from Crook, radio drama offers new versions of dialogism. While all five dramas are set in Sweden in or around 1930-31, the growing prominence of the medial space contributes to highlighting not just the specificity of the space constructed by the sounds emanating from the radio set and thus also the fact that the characters and their gender are part of this construction, but the engagement of the listener/dramaturgist too. In the majority of these dramas, it is this engagement that forms the implicit basis of new communities.

The first three of Wägner's radio dramas were broadcast under the heading 'Kvinnans kvart' (Fifteen Minutes for Women), an item which

Per Lindberg had introduced in 1929 and characterised as a forum for 'the secrets of the hearth and of vanity' (quoted in Hallingberg 1967, 70). As Wirmark has pointed out, Wägner was to protest against this categorisation of her radio dramas in a letter to Lindberg dated 14 March 1931, and the two dramas broadcast in 1931 appeared without the heading (Wirmark 1987, 339-40). However, even prior to Wägner's explicit protest, her contributions to 'Kvinnans kvart' would certainly have constituted challenges to the programme item as characterised by Lindberg.

The waitress who is the symbolic 'nursemaid' of the title of Wägner's first radio drama, broadcast on 25 February 1930, turns on their head conventional notions of both gender and class. Not only is her thorough professionalism backed up by financial knowhow and personal savings, but her experience, perceptiveness, and wisdom become crucial for an architect in a state of crisis following a professional blunder as well as for the architect's ignorant wife. As Signe, the waitress, demolishes Mrs Axelson's traditional understanding of masculinity and femininity and makes her realise the importance of a career of her own, Mrs Axelsson's reference to the prospect of wearing the black dress of a waitress, 'Det blir som en maskerad' (*Barnjungfrun*, 15) (It's going to be like a fancy-dress party), crystallises the significance not just of gender constructionism but of performativity throughout this drama.

While an alternative community emanating from the new understanding between the two female characters is at best implicit in *Barnjungfrun*, it is at the forefront of *Tre åldrar*, set at the exhibition of modern life that was taking place in Stockholm in the summer of 1930 and broadcast on 3 June. At the exhibition, according to an article by Wägner published in spring 1930, 'the outlines of daily life and of the Swedish home' would emerge 'in amazingly new forms' (Wägner 1930, 1); and it is in this context of radical social innovation that the story of *Tre åldrar* brings together three characters representing different constructions of femininity yet constituting a family community: the anonymous grandmother who spends her time making lace in a small provincial town; her daughter Anna who owns a beauty parlour; and Birgit, the granddaughter and niece, who has turned her back on what she perceives as the bourgeois ideals of the older generations and advocates and practises both social equality and sexual freedom. With the innovative and modernist yet temporary housing and furniture of the exhibition enhancing the theatricality of the setting, the costumes and appearances of the three female characters are similarly highlighted, from the grandmother's old-fashioned clothing with its exquisite lace to her daughter's fashionable suit and young Birgit's trousers. With both femininity and social class so prominently constructed, the exhibition with its mass-produced housing, furniture, and household equipment is effectively propelling forward the radical social changes for which Birgit and her friends are working: 'det är det stiliga och flotta med den moderna riktningen som man ser här på utställningen, att dom gör vad dom kan för att befria en från mödan att skaffa stora inkomster' (*Tre åldrar*, 11) (this is what's so smart and swell with the modern trend you see here at the exhibition, that they're doing what they can to free you from the effort to make a lot of money). Providing a framework for new communities, for alternatives to the traditional family community represented by the three female characters, the exhibition has opened the door to the transformation of society that Birgit perceives as not just necessary but as the duty of her generation: 'Det är vi som har ansvaret för vår egen och hela världens framtid' (op. cit., 13) (It's we who're responsible for the future of ourselves and the whole world).

En helgonlegend, broadcast on 29 December 1930, refers in more general terms to the context beyond the drama in the sense that the darkness of winter is also an element of the setting. Here, however, the transformations taking shape in the distinctive space established by the broadcast words operate at a less concrete level, with the listener becoming more prominently engaged. Mrs Brant and her engineer husband have married recently and settled in the far north of Sweden, where the darkness of a winter without snow turns out to be so total that Mrs Brant cannot make out a single detail when she looks out in the morning and so sees no point in opening the curtains (*En helgonlegend*, 2). In the exceptional, intimate space that emerges as a result Mrs Brant, pregnant and dressed in white, also assumes exceptional dimensions: 'vet du vad *jag* trodde först, när jag såg dej så vit och ljushårad under ljuskronan, jag trodde du var en av de saliga' (op. cit., 4; italics original) (d'you know what I believed when I first saw you all white and fair-haired under the chandelier, I thought you were a blessed spirit), says a poor old woman who has rung the doorbell. While the story of this drama revolves around the theft of a tablecloth, embroidered 'med hela förlovningskärleken kvar' (op. cit., 10) (with all the love from our engagement still alive) by Mrs Brant for her fiancé, it is the construction, significance, and impact of this female character, in her specific medial space, that are at the centre of *En helgonlegend*. When the old woman shows Mrs Brant her stolen tablecloth as the prize in a lottery, she buys all the remaining lottery tickets rather than claiming her property back, explaining to her husband that taking as her model St. Athanasius who got a thief to return a stolen book, she too has wanted to be 'ädelmodig intill vanvett' (op. cit., 8) (magnanimous to the point of madness). The table-cloth is indeed returned to her. Here any social transformation is initiated at the personal level as Mrs Brant's private conversations, addressed to a second-person singular *du* (you) which shifts from the foetus in her womb to the anonymous addressee of a dream and then to God as she prays for the old woman to be influenced by her magnanimity (op. cit., 3-4, 6, 9), inevitably involve the listener too. The basis of this new community is not practical and concrete, as in *Tre åldrar*, but ethical and moral.

The central character in *Han som blödde* (broadcast on 8 May 1931) is 'Andra friherrinnan' (The Second Baroness), and with her predecessor, 'nu fru Karlson' (*Han som blödde*, 1) (now Mrs Karlson), also appearing in this radio drama, the construction of class as well as gender is highlighted from the beginning. On this occasion, however, the realism combines with an element of fairy-tale or legend akin to that established by the medial specificity of *En helgonlegend*. As the Second Baroness makes her way through a tiny gate in the wall surrounding the policies and old manor house once owned by her husband's family but now the property of Mr Anderson, the contractor in charge of the town's cleansing service, she enters a unique space. Thanks to her initiative an old misunderstanding is cleared up, the social hierarchy represented by the Second Baroness on the one hand

and the parvenu Mr Anderson on the other is deconstructed, and in a symbolic gesture Mr Anderson begins to tear down the barbed wire along the top of the wall, cutting his hand in the process. The implications of his action are spelled out to him by the Second Baroness: 'Ni var lika glad som jag över den mänskliga gemenskapen mellan oss. Det gör en sällsamt lycklig att bryta ner mångåriga murar. Det skulle bara ske oftare. Livet skulle jämt vara sånt som det är i dag' (op. cit., 12) (You were as glad as I was at the spirit of community uniting us as human beings. To break down age old walls makes one uniquely happy. But it should happen more often. Life should always be as it is today.) With the unique medium of the radio allowing the spirit of community to extend to the listeners, this radio drama offers the embryo of a new society based on a spirit of community with the capacity to bring human beings together, no matter how different they may be.

The last of these short radio dramas, *Sjömansbruden* (broadcast on 26 September 1931), opens with Lina, the central character, in a busy café at a railway junction. Here the foregrounding of communication in conjunction with Lina's marked absent-mindedness contribute to the specificity of another medial space that engages the listener in a process that effectively turns into a private confession. A sailor who enters the café turns out to be a colleague of Lina's fiancé and just back from the Far East, and from him she learns that the young man whom she has recently rejected after ten years had in fact been planning to marry her on his return to Sweden. On one level the communication between them has not worked, with disastrous consequences, but on another, he influence has persuaded him to change his habits, making Lina conclude that 'Kärleken förtröttas inte. Men jag förtröttades' (*Sjömansbruden*, 8) (Love doesn't tire. Yet I did.). Constructing gender in binary terms, this radio drama problematises communication as the basis for the construction of communities rather than any community as such.

When *Credo*, the radio drama about violence and Quaker-inspired pacifism in the border region between Germany and France in 1923 24, was broadcast in October 1934, Wägner had already made extensive use of the material. It had been central to the plot of *De fem pärlorna*

(The Five Pearls), the novel she had published in 1927 and which will be discussed below (see below, pp.278-83); the novel had been preceded by a shorter version that had been serialised in *Tidevarvet*, also in 1927. Together with the theatre and film director Ragnar Hyltén-Cavallius, she had subsequently written a film script based on the same material, but although there are synopses in both German and French in the Wägner archive, no film was ever made (Isaksson and Linder 2003, 432; Wirmark 1987, 342). Alongside the version for radio, Wägner and Hyltén-Cavallius had been working on a version for the stage, but despite the fact that the Dramatic Theatre in Stockholm had wanted to perform the play and a contract had been signed in August 1935, the drama was never staged (Wirmark 1987, 342).

The radio version has some features pointing up the affinity with a drama for the stage, most importantly the division into five acts (using three different settings), plus the list of *dramatis personae* which, with its total of 23 characters (a list that omits the Doctor), 13 of whom are named, is a distinctly long one for this medium: Hallingberg's calculations based on the 126 radio dramas published in *Svenska radiopjäser* (Swedish Radio Dramas) 1945-1966 gave an average of between 6 and 7 (Hallingberg 1967, 240). But at the same time, *Credo* is a drama that foregrounds the specificity of the medium. While Margareta Wirmark, following Erik Hjalmar Linder, has highlighted the autobiographical origins of this radio drama and offers a wholly realistic reading of the text (Wirmark 1987, 342-43), *Credo* in fact quickly establishes a space beyond that of everyday life, a symbolic space akin to that which we have encountered in *En helgonlegend*, which adds to the dimensions and resonances of the elements of the story. Thus the heavy rucksack with which Credo's aunt arrives in the opening scene calls forth comparisons with the burden of sins carried by Bunyan's Pilgrim (*Credo*, 2); the notion that Credo has a mission as a Quaker and may in fact be perceived as 'Guds budbärare' (op. cit., 11) (God's messenger) gives this story an aura of the legend; and the symbolism of the setting of the final act, 'Vid ett färjställe vid Rhen' (op. cit., title page) (At a ferry crossing on the Rhine), is spelled out aurally and verbally as a distant rumbling accompanies the words spoken to Credo by her uncle:

Texts 1922-36

Lyssna, Kate! Än är det tyst och tomt på den här gamla stridsplatsen. Ett ögonblick är den övergiven, och historien håller andan. Men om du lyssnar noga, ska du höra, hur folk kommer från öster och väster – för att mötas här omkring en segrare. Hör du bilar och motorcyklar och trampet av fötter på båda sidor om stranden? (op. cit., 72)

(Listen, Kate! This old battle ground is still quiet and empty. For a moment it is deserted, and history is holding its breath. But if you listen carefully, you will hear people coming from the east and the west – to gather here around a victor. Can you hear cars and motor cycles and the tramping of feet on both sides of the river bank?)

While the symbolism of the setting and the story is clearly crucial to the wider international relevance of the drama about Credo, the dimensions of her mission obviously go far beyond any notion of national citizenship. This drama represents an example of world citizenship enacted on the European stage where the First World War had originated less than a decade previously, and where the defusing of new conflicts is of paramount importance. To what extent, then, is gender of significance in this context, and how, first of all, is gender constructed in this drama? Is it possible, in addition, to discern the construction of new communities, of a new society?

The exiled ruler of Pfalz is an old warrior, a colonel bearing the name of the Roman god of war, Martius. His headquarters, the rear building at a hotel where he is shielded from his enemies, is a hive of political activity focusing on violent means as Martius and his inner circle plot to kill Kark, the usurper, and thus retake Pfalz. In other words, the linkage between masculinity, violence, and war is more emphatic in *Credo* than in any other text by Wägner studied so far, with the exception of some of the texts relating to the Congress at The Hague in 1915 and some of the opinion pieces from the 1920s and 1930s. But unlike Martius, Credo effectively plays a multiplicity of roles: as a young American Quaker, she has come to Pfalz to run a Quaker home for children orphaned by the First World War (*Credo*, 6), but when the drama begins she is Martius's secretary and, she says, also his Foreign Secretary (op. cit., 10). She is also the niece of the Quaker couple, James and Mary Nevins. Central to Credo's Quaker mission, however, is the fact that she and Martius are in love. The hotelier's wife provides a crude construction of femininity in terms of erotic conquest as she tries to persuade Credo to go to bed with Martius as a means of enhancing his prowess as a warrior: 'Låt honom besegra er i kväll. Lär honom att han ännu är en man som kan segra över kvinnor. Då tror han också att han rår på själva ödet' (op. cit., 15) (Let him conquer you tonight. Teach him that he is still a man capable of conquering women. Then he'll believe that he can take on fate itself). But while the love between Credo and Martius is certainly crucial to the plot, the constructions of gender turn out to be rather more complex. As Credo persuades Martius to postpone the planned murder of Kark for five days, she is by no means the archetypal female character reduced to merely influencing the man she loves: not only is she intending to turn to politicians in Paris and London for assistance in solving the Pfalz crisis, but she has to take immediate action and travel to Speyer and personally avert the killing of Kark, a project during which she turns out to risk being raped as well as murdered. Just as importantly, Martius is transformed by Credo's love and determination, declaring to the wife of the hotelier just before he is assassinated by Kark's henchmen that 'Kärlek och ädelmod är också en politisk linje' (op. cit., 64) (Love and magnanimity also make a political line).

Given that conventional constructions of gender are not just problematised but also radically modified by the story of this drama, can we then also claim that a new community emerges in *Credo*? Wirmark has summarised the message of the radio drama in the words spoken by Credo at the end, 'Man får inte skicka andra i döden. Man får på sin höjd dö själv för sin tro!' (*Credo*, 75) (You mustn't send others to their deaths. At most, you can die yourself for your belief!), words also used by Wägner to pinpoint the 'idea' of the drama (Wirmark 1987, 343). It is of course true that the postponement of the murder of Kark secured by Credo has paved the way for the assassination of Martius. But in another respect Credo succeeds, for Kark and his supporters flee when the news of the attack on Martius spreads, and as the dying Martius is carried towards the border, he is heading a crowd of citizens returning to their province by peaceful means, the beginnings of a new community. In this radio drama, which was performed the year after Hitler had come to power, there is still space for the initiative of the individual citizen, and for all the tentativeness of the alternative community, this is clearly based on peace and love.

*

Wägner's drama for radio, including the longer play she co-wrote with Ragnar Hyltén-Cavallius, certainly tore apart the construction of women as mothers and educators in the home that predominated in Swedish radio broadcasting in the 1930s. With prominent female characters developed in public settings – the sole exception is Mrs Brant in *En helgonlegend* who assumes the proportions of a saint – these six texts all problematise the dominant discourse on gender as they foreground female characters in professional roles and/or as the initiators of ethical transformations. While the constructedness of gender is frequently enhanced by an emphasis on role-play and performativity, the uniqueness of the medial space of radio drama with the listener/dramaturgist as a key participant is highlighted in a number of these dramas, most prominently in *Tre åldrar*, *En helgonlegend*, and *Credo*. The conspicuous social divisions signalled in several of these dramas in class terms point towards a gradual bridging of differences. Although *Credo* is unique in having a central female character who is a Quaker, both *En helgonlegend* and *Han som blödde* also emphasise the role of ethical transformations in underpinning new communities.

4. Prose Fiction

How, then, are gender and community constructed in the prose fiction of this period of major economic, political, social, and cultural changes which included the beginnings of the project to build 'the home of the people'? At a time when the dominant discourses on gender and community in Sweden began to fuse in a welfare state project founded on a traditional construction of gender, some of the opinion pieces and especially texts such as *Från Seine, Rhen och Ruhr* engage with international politics in the aftermath of the First World War and effectively construct citizenship in terms of involvement across borders and boundaries. The radio drama similarly focuses on the building of new communities, with the intimate and suggestive potential of the new medium in focus in the five short dramas studied here, while the five-act *Credo*, set on the contemporary European stage, explores the role of alternative constructions of gender in the emergence of a community bringing about peace.

I have chosen to analyse four novels from this period. The place of the fabula of *Den namnlösa* (1922; The Anonymous Woman) is a Småland vicarage (indeed, the parish bears the same name as that in one of Wägner's earlier novels, *Åsa-Hanna*), but as I shall show, the apparent seclusion of the place only enhances the wider relevance of the constructions of gender and community. The story of *De fem pärlorna* (1927; The Five Pearls) has obvious similarities with *Credo*, the radio drama broadcast in 1934, but the narrative of the novel problematises and expands the constructions of gender and community. *Dialogen fortsätter* (1932; The Dialogue is Continuing) was contemporaneous with the Social Democratic election victory that marked the beginnings of the Swedish welfare state, but with its dismantling of the dominant discourse on gender this text points far beyond 'the home of the people' and towards a new type of international community. Finally one of Wägner's most neglected novels, *Mannen vid min sida* (1933; The Man at My Side), a character-bound narrator's travelogue from Spain in 1933, turns out to be an exceptionally interesting example of the significance and potential of textual space involving bold radicalisations of the constructions of both gender and community.

Den namnlösa (The Anonymous Woman)

In the context of Susan S. Lanser's argument that sex, gender, and sexuality are significant categories of narratological analysis (Lanser 2004), Rakel Ljunghed, the character-bound narrator in Wägner's novel *Den namnlösa* (1922; The Anonymous Woman), might at first sight seem to be too obvious an illustration to merit much discussion. Indeed in *Romanens formvärld* (1953), Staffan Björck's influential study of the narrative of the Swedish novel, Rakel Ljunghed is singled out among the character-bound narrators in Wägner's novels and most emphatically categorised with regard to sex and gender: 'here [in *Den namnlösa*] the first-person narration is highly motivated and its resources well utilised, *perhaps overdone, you occasionally say to yourself when faced with distracting feminine deviations*' (Björck 1968, 52; my italics). Björck's sexism is of course inexcusable. But it is certainly true that Rakel is a prominent narrator, an instance of a specific version of the narrator, in Bal's phrase 'a "visible" narrator' (Bal 1999, 18). Most conspicuously, perhaps, she foregrounds herself by addressing both her diseased heart and God (e.g. Wägner 1922, 11-12, 89-90). In addition, the sequential ordering of her story is more complex than suggested by the critic Klara Johanson, who claimed in a letter to Wägner that the plot 'is taking place [...] as it is being expressed' (Johanson 1953, 119). Rakel's narration in fact contains extensive instances of retroversion, notably in Chapters 2, 5, 11 and 14; and the recollections, memories, and reflections help expand her narratorial presence. She has a preference for profiling herself as someone in control: '– Jag är en sådan människa [...] som alltid borde komma i en liten flickas väg, när hon tänker fara till Nässjö eller någon annan sjö i oktober' (Wägner 1922, 10) (I am the kind of person [...] whom a little girl should always encounter when she is thinking of going to Nässjö or some other lake in October). Rakel steps in, arranges, interprets, and tells the truth – her interference and frankness justified, she argues, by the fact that she has not got long to live (op. cit., 113). In Lanser's schema of narrative voices the personal one, of which this clearly is an example, is characterised by its relative lack of narrative authority, given that 'a personal narrator claims only the validity of one person's right to interpret her experience' (Lanser 1992, 19). Rakel Ljunghed's repeated claims to narratorial authority – reinforced by her efforts to guide and control the story – problematise Lanser's analysis in interesting ways, and I shall return to these.

Lanser has also contrasted the narrow range of the personal narratorial voice with the 'broad powers of knowledge and judgment' of the authorial voice, that of the external narrator (Lanser 1992, 19). The rural Småland vicarage that is the place of this narrative might at first sight seem to reinforce this narrowness – but this reading is mistaken. Rakel Ljunghed's narration and the story that unfolds both firmly relate the vicarage to a wider and war-torn European context. An occupational therapist, Rakel has spent the previous fourteen years working abroad, some of them in a hospital treating victims from the trenches of the First World War (Wägner 1922, 18). The anonymous woman of the title describes to Rakel how she was raped and then raises the issue of the credibility of her narrative, drawing an explicit parallel with the claims by German women that French soldiers have been committing rape in the areas of Germany occupied in the wake of the war (op. cit., 131). And Georg, who is the son of the vicar and training to become a doctor, and who not only has experience from war-time hospitals but is also likened by Rakel to the victims she has treated (op. cit., 18), turns out to have brought the war straight into the vicarage: the attacks he has begun to suffer, and which have split his personality and threaten his future, take the form of loud, angry, and often physically violent confrontations with an imaginary enemy, invariably a German woman. While Rakel has simply been asked to return home by her brother, the vicar, who has given her no explicit reason, the fact that she brings with her the sick anonymous woman whom she has found on the train and then encounters her sick nephew in the vicarage turns her into a catalyst – albeit with less control than she might claim to have – and makes her narration resonate with issues to do with gender and power, with relationships and community, and with war and peace.

Virtually the entire narrative of *Den namnlösa* takes place in a well-defined administrative community, the Småland parish of Ljungheda, in which the parish church and the vicarage are the focal points, both of them with Elias, the vicar, in charge. He receives and counsels his parishioners, admonishing the daughter of Åsa-Hanna (a character recalling Wägner's earlier novel) to remain in her unhappy marriage (Wägner 1922, 254-57); he conducts the funeral services, including that of his servant Niklas (op. cit., 224-29); and, most importantly, his sermons draw the members of his parish and beyond to Ljungheda church every Sunday – including, on this occasion, Rakel:

Det var första gången överhuvud, som jag såg honom på fars och morfars predikstol. Efter så många år hade församlingen icke tröttnat på honom, den hade fyllt upp den stora kyrkan med hjälp av en del folk från angränsande socknar. Antingen de voro unga och raka eller krumma av arbete och år, voro de alla så stilla i kyrkan. Och här och där i bänkarna lyste ett ansikte som ljus i en julotta. (op. cit., 68)

(For the first time ever, I saw him in my father's and grandfather's pulpit. After all those years, his parishioners had not tired of him, they had filled the big church with some assistance from people of neighbouring parishes. Whether they were young and upright or bent by toil and years, they were all so quiet in church. And here and there in the pews, a face was shining like a candle at an early service on Christmas Day.)

And the construction of Elias Ljunghed's authority by language goes beyond the conventional parameters: as he preaches about 'själens gemenskap med levande Gud' (op. cit., 70) (the communion of the soul with the living God), he is the representative of the Word of God.

But if the authority of the vicar is emphatically constructed in terms of language, so of course is that of his sister, the narrator. Her narration highlights a community that partly overlaps with that headed by her brother, yet differs in the sense that the vicarage with its characters is the focal point, with the prominence of both direct speech and indirect discourse in combination with the narrator's reflections also making this a narrative community, a community of many voices. And contrary to the representation of Elias's parishioners in church on a Sunday, the community in the vicarage, as I have indicated above, does not emerge as a harmonious one. While the references to the First World War and its aftermath are conspicuous with regard to characters such as Georg and the anonymous woman, the key issues profiled by Rakel's narration of the community of the vicarage are those of gender and of gendered relations of power. As a result of Rakel's narration, the centrality of these issues then continues to reverberate in the communities well beyond the vicarage.

It could be argued that *Den namnlösa* provides an early illustration of Yvonne Hirdman's notion of 'the housewife contract': the vicar's wife, Helena, who for many years has been running the vicarage, usually full of boarders preparing for their confirmation and with only

Niklas to help out in the kitchen, has as her remaining ambitions to stay in her post until the end and to have 'överansträngning' (Wägner 1922, 50) (overwork) as the cause of death on her death certificate. As Rakel's narration reaches across the faultlines in the vicarage, it represents a vicar's wife who combines a deep respect for her husband's mission in life with the refusal to walk to church with him on a Sunday; the couple, moreover, turn out to sleep at opposite ends of the vicarage (op. cit., 145, 27). Rakel's narration also draws parallels between Helena and her mother, the latter a frustrated and spiteful widow of a minister, and highlights the possibility of the characters merging with each other: 'Om man ville eller ej, måste man söka likheten och darra för utsikten, att den skulle bli större' (op. cit., 32) (Whether you wanted to or not, you had to look for the similarity and tremble at the prospect of it becoming greater).

If the narrator's representation of the relationship between the vicar and his wife can be read, at one level, as a critique *avant la lettre* of 'the housewife contract', the representation of Niklas reinforces the constructedness of both gender and gendered relations of power. Rakel does not elaborate on the reasons why Niklas has never been able to do his military service, till the soil or get married (Wägner 1922, 222); but working as a maid in the vicarage, he belongs at the very bottom of the hierarchy headed by the vicar, defining himself as a mere 'tynt [...] som gör kvinnfolkasysslor' (op. cit., 165) (sissy [...] who is doing women's tasks). Rakel's initial label for this male character with black stubble all over his face and a big kitchen apron is 'grotesk' (op. cit., 22) (grotesque), but the old widow's bullying of him reinforces the constructions of gender and power in terms of sexuality as she refers to him as 'en snöping' (op. cit., 81) (a castrated person), and the representation of him in death, 'med sitt sydländska utseende, som han fått gud vet varifrån, kanske av en zigenare någonstädes borta i släkten' (op. cit., 199-200) (with his southern appearance, stemming from God knows where, perhaps from a gipsy far back in his family), adds an element of race.

Rakel's narration allows the narratives about both Helena and Niklas to reverberate in the novel's central account about gender and gendered relations of power, that of the anonymous woman of how she was raped. The anonymous woman explains the years of illness she has suffered subsequently as caused by this violation of her body (Wägner 1922, 127); but the dismantling of her subjectivity is most emphatically rendered in her narrative about her recurring dream of being turned into a snake:

> jag drömde att jag var en orm, som krälade på sin buk i stoftet. Men jag hade en människas huvud. Det var för resten mitt eget huvud, om du vill veta detaljer. Hela tiden försökte jag hålla det högt, så att jag inte skulle bli för smutsig och nerstänkt i ansiktet. Men försök att tänka dig att vara så nära jorden med sin mun och sina ögon. En riktig orm avskyr inte att kräla på marken, men jag var så olycklig, jag försökte resa mig, men det var ju löjligt och gick förstås inte. Jag var ju sån. (op. cit., 120)

> (I dreamed that I was a snake, crawling on my belly in the dust. But I had the head of a human being. It was my own head, if you want to know the details. All the time I was trying to hold it up, so that I wouldn't get dirty or splash my face too much. But try to imagine being so close to the earth with your mouth and your eyes. A real snake doesn't hate crawling on the ground, but I was so unhappy, I tried to get up, but that was silly and of course I couldn't do it. This was how I was.)

While the narrative of the anonymous woman is mediated by Rakel and thus also by the close relationship that develops between these two characters, the issues of gender and power are rendered much more starkly in Rakel's accounts of the attacks suffered by her nephew, Georg. For unlike Isaksson and Linder, I do not read the representations of Georg's attacks as realistic descriptions of a patient suffering from a split personality (Isaksson and Linder 2003, 321). Georg's attacks define gendered relations of power in the sense that he is striving to control the imaginary woman. But Rakel's narration also highlights the effects of this ongoing struggle for control: Georg is regarded as being ill, his status is undermined, and his future career is under threat.

Character-bound though Rakel's narration is, it emphatically admits these and other characters into the story, working across the conflicts that separate a number of them and providing them with plenty of space, notably in the form of dialogue in direct speech. Strikingly, there are sections of dialogue in this novel in the form of dramatic dialogue, with the name of the speaker followed by a colon and her or his speech; such sections occur repeatedly in the long night-time conversation during which the anonymous woman reveals to Rakel that she has been raped (Wägner 1922, 121-23, 129-30, 135, 138-39). In addition to Rakel's voice, then, the voices of a number of the other characters also become prominent in her narration; and the significance of this dialogism is reinforced by the letters which make up most of Chapter 11, towards the end of the novel, and which are letters to Rakel from Georg, from the anonymous woman, and from Helena (op. cit., 268-74). Given that Rakel also fails in her efforts to control and guide the story, with even her own supposedly terminal condition ceasing to be a threat in this narrative that 'talks back' (Bal 1999, 126) to an unusual extent, the community that her narration represents is conspicuously new. For contrary to the claims made by Isaksson and Linder, this is not a novel about 'the mystery of [...] relinquishment' (Isaksson and Linder 2003, 321), even if Rakel refers to the concept. In *Den namnlösa* the young woman and the young man, sick though they are, fall in love with each other, and as the anonymous woman lies dying, even the vicar and his wife seem to begin to overcome the distance between them (Wägner 1922, 338). Susan S. Lanser has pinpointed the relatively limited narratorial authority of the character-bound narrator (Lanser 1992, 19), and in *Den namnlösa* this limited narratorial authority effectively becomes a tool for the narrative deconstruction of the phallogocentrism that the vicar represents. Bound up not just with the Lutheran church but also with militarism, phallogocentrism is not just sidelined but dismissed by the narrative of this novel which so emphatically opens up an alternative space for a community characterised by love and peace.

De fem pärlorna (The Five Pearls)

The novel that Wägner published in 1927 has similarities with *Från Seine, Rhen och Ruhr* (1923) in the sense that the story explores national conflict and pacifism in the wake of the First World War. But with its narrative about military occupation, assassination, and reconquest, and with the soldier Sebastian Martius and a young American Quaker, Kitty Nevinson, as the central characters, the story of *De fem pärlorna* (The Five Pearls) makes for a more urgent problematisation of military conflict and pacifism. While some reviewers were untroubled by the names given to the countries involved – Vinland (Wine Land), Slättland (Land of Plains) and Treves – and able to read the novel in terms of the tensions between France and Germany at the time (e.g. Bolander 1927, Söderhjelm 1927), others dismissed the novel, including influential critics such as the author Sten Selander who wrote scathingly of 'pacifism and the romantic notions of a maid' (Selander 1927), and Fredrik Böök, Professor of Literature, who argued that the 'political mass convulsions and the revolutionary scenes' appeared 'lifeless and thin; it is all too meagre and dry for illusion to be achieved', and that Wägner with this novel had entered uncharted waters and 'lost her bearings' (Böök 1927).

In *De fem pärlorna* we do not have a character-bound narrator, as in *Den namnlösa*, but an external one; to be more specific, the narrator in the novel under discussion here is heterodiegetic-extradiegetic, in other words 'absent from the story he [sic] tells' (Genette 1995, 244-45) and, although fictitious, included in no diegesis but 'on an exactly equal footing with the extradiegetic (real) public' (Genette 1994, 84). According to Susan S. Lanser, the sex of this type of narrator is normally unmarked (Lanser 2004, 129). How, Lanser asks, is the reader then likely to gender this type of narrative voice (op. cit., 131)?

In my reading, there is no doubt that the narrator in *De fem pärlorna* is masculine. At the opening of the novel, the narrator highlights Martius, the exiled soldier laying plans that combine military and sexual conquest (Wägner 1927, 5); and the sequence in which Kitty, more commonly known as Credo, views some of the scenery of Vinland not just in terms of the female body but in terms of her own, is managed by a masculine narrator who makes her see the landscape through the eyes of her lover:

> Hon förstod att han måste älska dalens öppna famn och den blottade jordens röda skimmer under morgonens silverblåa slöja. Hon förstod vilken komplimang han avsett, då han sagt att hans barndoms landskap liknade henne. (op. cit., 6)

(She understood that he could not but love the open bosom of the valley and the red lustre of the bared earth beneath the silver-blue veil of the morning. She understood what a compliment he had intended when he had said that the landscape of his childhood looked like her.) This is also a narrator who uses 'maxims', the extrarepresentational acts that Lanser has highlighted as crucial to establishing narratorial authority (Lanser 1992, 16-17), and some of these highlight military expertise, such as 'Ingen anförare i världen tycker om att köra in i en lugn by, där han väntar en bösspipa bakom varje gardin, och bakom varje husknut en man med en handgranat' (Wägner 1927, 88) (No captain likes to drive into a quiet village where he expects the barrel of a gun behind every curtain, and a man with a hand grenade round every house-corner), or 'Om en befälhavare fattat beslut att en aktion ska uppskjutas i fem dagar, blir det honom angeläget att ordern går fram till ort och ställe, oavsett om de skäl som ligga till grund för beslutet äro högst tvetydiga' (op. cit., 179) (If a commander has decided to postpone an action for five days, it will be important to him that the order to do so reaches its destination, no matter how ambiguous the reasons on which his decision has been based).

To my knowledge the issue of the gendering of the narrator in *De fem pärlorna* has not previously been discussed (but see Forsås-Scott 2009), but in light of Lanser's claim about the gender of the external narrator normally being unmarked, I am tempted to assume that hostile critical reactions such as those of Selander and Böök may have been caused, at least at one level, by the perceived incongruity between the gender of the author and that of the narrator.

According to Lanser's classification of narrative voices, *De fem pärlorna* is an example of 'authorial voice': the narrative situation is heterodiegetic, public and, as we have seen, self-referential in its use of 'maxims' which attract attention to the narration as such (Lanser 1992, 15-17). In addition, then, this narrator adds to his authority by profiling himself as distinctly masculine. But in a pattern familiar from *Den namnlösa*, this narrator also opens up the narration to the other characters. There is plenty of dialogue in the form of direct speech in *De fem pärlorna*, but the characters are also brought to prominence by means of free indirect thought, and by shifts in focalisation. And these features, significantly, become increasingly conspicuous, creating a contrast between the authoriality of the masculine voice at the beginning of the novel, and the gradual deconstruction of this authoriality as the other characters become more and more prominent.

The passage about Martius's and Credo's visit to the theatre on New Year's Eve illustrates the shift in a nutshell. Credo has just discovered that Cark, the usurper of Vinland, is due to be killed the following evening; moreover, her protests against the plan have been fruitless. In the ancient Indian drama being performed on the stage, a servant is trying to prevent a man from being hanged for a crime he has not committed, only to discover that his protests also fall on deaf ears:

> Credo gömde ansiktet i sina händer, och Martius, hela tiden medveten om varje hennes rörelse, lade armen om hennes skuldra och drog henne till sig.
> – Han blir ändå räddad, viskade han tröstande, du kan gärna se upp.
> Men hon såg inte upp. Den fattige, usle dragarens klagan och förbannelser hade väckt ett sällsamt eko i hennes själ. Var inte hans raseri och vanmakt hennes raseri och vanmakt? Hon var som han det tillbakavisade vittnet. (Wägner 1927, 167)

(Credo buried her face in her hands and Martius, conscious all the time of her every movement, put his arm around her shoulder and pulled her close to him.
'He will be saved all the same,' he whispered reassuringly, 'you may just as well look up.'
But she did not look up. The outcry and curses of the poor, miserable coolie had struck a strange echo in her soul. Were his fury and powerlessness not her fury and powerlessness? Like him, she was the rejected witness.)

In the first half of this passage, both characters are observed from outside by the narrator, who is highlighting bodily movements and direct speech while also privileging the insight into Martius: 'hela tiden medveten om varje hennes rörelse' (conscious all the time of her every movement). But there is no comparison between this narratorial comment and the effect of the prominence given to Credo's thoughts in the second half. The novel's masculine narrator, who has appeared to be in such close agreement with Martius, the character who not only counts generations of soldiers among his ancestors but who is wholly preoccupied with his plans to eliminate the usurper and retake Vinland, is making space for the thoughts of the female central character, and these thoughts are formulating a protest against Martius's plans in terms of gender and gendered relations of power. The challenge that *De fem pärlorna* poses to the narratee does not stem merely from the story, in which the last-minute reprieve for Cark offers his men the opportunity to strike first so that Martius, when he eventually heads the return to Vinland, is dying: even more significant is the fact that in this narrative the alternatives to warfare and military conquest are given increasing amounts of space. Kristoffer, an old soldier who has taken orders all his life yet assists Credo in preventing the assassination of Cark, sets out to her in direct speech the revolutionary impact of his action (op. cit., 242-43); and Martius, in a page-long letter to Credo, spells out the effects of the upheaval that the reprieve for Cark is causing: 'Jag har aldrig förr ruinerat mig så fullständigt med en gåva till en kvinna' (op. cit., 216) (Never before has a gift I've given to a woman bankrupted me so completely).

The engagement of the narratee, alert to the different voices and the community the majority of them gradually form, is central to this novel's project of constructing a new community. The destruction of a community is epitomised by the appearance of the government building in the occupied capital of Vinland, originally designed as a monument to civic pride: Credo finds the classical columns covered in swear-words, the floor full of dirt and rubbish, and the main guard half asleep along the walls among bundles of food and jars of wine, mandolins, packs of cards, and guns waiting to be cleaned (Wägner 1927, 244). The new community emerges around the dying Martius and consists of the exiled inhabitants of Vinland who join him for what becomes a peaceful return to their country. Founded on peace, this community has an international framework in the Society of Friends represented by Credo's aunt and uncle and, most importantly, by Credo herself. At a time when the dominant discourse on feminine citizenship in Sweden was revolving around the duties of the housewife, *De fem pärlorna* focused on a female central character capable of taking political action in an international context and directly influencing issues of war and peace. When, on the final page of the novel, Credo prepares to testify in court about the political role of the love between her and Martius, the foundations of the new community that have been given increasing prominence in the narration are about to be spelled out in public.

Dialogen fortsätter (The Dialogue is Continuing)

Dialogen fortsätter appeared on 1 November 1932, less than six weeks after the formation of the Social Democratic government that was to begin the task of tackling a range of economic and social problems and turning Sweden into 'the home of the people'. Given that Wägner's novel investigates Swedish society at the time with a focus on key issues such as the demographic crisis, gender, class, war, and peace, it might conceivably have caused a debate in the press. But there was no debate. The 4,200 copies – a low figure for a novel by Wägner – printed in November and December were not followed by a new edition; the novel was not republished in the series of selected works 1950-54; and the second-wave feminists who began to take in interest in the novel in the 1970s were unsuccessful in their efforts to have it reprinted. In the context of the present study, my earlier reading with reference chiefly to Greek mythology (Forsås-Scott 1996, 177) is not relevant, and the same is true of Gunilla Domellöf's closely related but more expansive reading (Domellöf 2001). Bibi Jonsson has read *Dialogen fortsätter* mainly in terms of motherliness, matriarchy, and love (Jonsson 2001, 309-39).

In this novel of 400 pages, one chapter has become comparatively well known, the one in which four members of the county council, all of them male, meet to decide on the stream-lining of maternity care while leaving a delegation of eight women waiting outside to make their opinions known. (Indeed, this chapter would appear to be the only part of the novel known to Conny Svensson, author of the section on Wägner in Lönnroth and Delblanc's *Den svenska litteraturen*, with Svensson convinced that it is Chapter I [Svensson 1999, 457]; in fact, it is Chapter V.) In the context of the present study of the constructions of gender and community, the chapter provides as good an illustration as any, with the relations of gender and power in terms of domination represented by the story reinforced by the voice of the narrator. For all the differences between Mr Andersson and Mr Jansson, both of them members of the *riksdag*, and between Count Moll and the Leader of the County Council, 'en slags broderlig likhet' (Wägner 1932, 67) (a kind of brotherly similarity) becomes apparent as they prepare to receive the delegation of women,

> ty de utgjorde en liten avdelning av den mandatmakt som alltjämt är den största synliga makten i världen. De konstaterade det inte just nu, men deras verksamhet skulle inte ha varit dem så självklar, om de inte vilat i det trygga medvetandet att hundratusen andra små avdelningar arbetade samtidigt med den. [...] Längre bort [...] arbetade hemligt eller öppet andra grupper av vita män med större avgöranden och större maktområden men även dessa voro Anderssons och Janssons bröder. (op. cit., 67-68)

(because they constituted a small unit of the mandated power which still remains the biggest visible power in the world. They did not establish it at this very moment, but they would not have taken their activity for granted if they had not been resting assured that a hundred thousand other small units were simultaneously at work. [...] Further away [...] other groups of white men were working secretly or openly with bigger decisions and bigger domains of power, but these, too, were Andersson's and Jansson's brothers.)

Using the term 'mandatmakt' (mandated power; the Swedish term dates from 1924 and a document about the League of Nations), and referring to 'grupper av vita män' (groups of white men), the narrator who is boldly – and presciently – analysing relations of gender and power in terms of colonial rule clearly is not just female but feminist. I do not think there can be any doubt that this narrator contributed to *Dialogen fortsätter* receiving one of the most vitriolic reviews of a text by Wägner ever written, the critique in which Holger Ahlenius dismissed the very notion of opposition between women and men as 'idiotic', and also took a swipe at 'the repugnant publication *Tidevarvet*' (Ahlenius 1932). It is not just possible but likely that the profiling of the novel's narrator as both female and feminist has played a part in the marginalisation of *Dialogen fortsätter*.

The notion of the 'mandated power' of men becomes pivotal to the narrative and narration of *Dialogen fortsätter* as this text embarks on a deconstruction of phallogocentrism that is far more comprehensive and radical than the one we have encountered in either *Åsa-Hanna* or *Den namnlösa*. Making her first – and last – speech in the Second Chamber of the *riksdag*, Kristina Ring specifies the range of this phallogocentrism: 'här sitter riksdagen, här ligger lagboken, där står kyrkan' (Wägner 1932, 398) (here sits the *riksdag*, here lies the copy of the code of laws, there is the Church). Having become a member of the *riksdag* following the death from a heart attack of one of the members of the County Council meeting about maternity care, Kristina resists the objections of her former husband, himself a member of the First Chamber – 'Du kommer att göra ett fiasko, stackars barn, som ingen före dig' (op. cit., 156) (You'll be a fiasco, poor child, like no one before you) – and is greeted by fellow members of the *riksdag* determined to control her voting. Yet she succeeds not just in making her voice heard, in direct speech, but in destabilising the entire edifice constructed by the *riksdag* and by extension the society for which it legislates, and she does so with her demand that mothers and children be placed at the centre of a new society: 'vi måste ha en värld dit kvinnorna nänns sätta sina barn' (op. cit., 400) (we have to have a world in which women dare to have children). Significantly the law is epitomised by the trial of an abortionist, Mrs Persson (abortions were illegal in Sweden at this time), with the harshness of the judge explained in terms of the need to replace 'fruktan för helvetet och Gud' (op. cit., 292) (the fear of hell and of God) which, the judge claims, used to underpin women's commitment to motherhood, with fear of the police. But again, the cracks in the edifice are glaringly obvious, the examples ranging from the exploitation by the female office workers in Nils Erik Cronberger's firm of solicitors of the legal skills they have picked up, to the article in which Märta, the solicitor's sister, is arguing that women's refusal of motherhood is tantamount to war against a system constructed by and for men (ibid.). Nils Erik's and Märta's father, finally, represents the Lutheran State Church and does not hesitate to highlight the unique authority that allows him to act as a minister 'in persona Christi' (op. cit., 191). When his service on Epiphany is broadcast, the artist who happens to be listening in his studio reacts instinctively to the control of his voice: 'Den slog emot honom genom radion med en sådan makt och myndighet att Hallind lade bort cigarretten utan att tänka därpå och tog ner benen ur soffan' (op. cit., 214) (Via the receiver it struck him with such power and authority that Hallind automatically put his cigarette aside and took his legs down from the sofa). But again phallogocentrism is deconstructed as Anselm Cronberger's service inspires the feminist pacifist work that Hallind designs for the *riksdag*: a fresco of the Madonna and Child wearing gasmasks.

But *Dialogen fortsätter* is also a novel in which new and alternative communities are constructed. While the feminist narrator is undoubtedly omniscient, she is certainly not foregrounding her authority, and there is generous space here not just for dialogue in the form of direct speech, free indirect discourse, and free indirect thought, but also for intertexts such as 'Morgonrodnans fana svajar' (Wägner 1932, 54) (The banner of the sunrise is flying in the wind), a line from a poem by Viktor Rydberg (set to music by the composer Elfrida Andrée [1841-1929], this had become a popular song at the Women Citizen's College at Fogelstad [Björkman-Goldschmidt 1956a, 90]), and an extract from the gospel (Wägner 1932, 214). As the narrative constructs a collage of voices and thus a narratee at once receptive, well-informed, and engaged, some of the novel's intertexts and fictitious quotations point up a range of alternative communities. The article that Kristina Ring's son Torkel has cut from the paper is not about customs duty on potatoes, as his father assumes: the reportage on the reverse, the quotations from which take up half a page in the novel, is about the activities of the young war resisters whom Torkel has joined and whose network is rewriting his father's map from the First World War (op. cit., 260-61, 272-73). Ivar Ficke, the son of a book-keeper who once worked for Torkel's father, is a member of this network and Torkel's close friend; but Ivar's poem – which extends over two and a half pages – is a celebration of his girlfriend Sara and the feminist community to which she belongs, with an emphasis on the potential of this community to turn the existing social order upside down (op, cit., 379-81). But the most striking of these alternative communities is the meeting about gender and the labour market, with the venue consisting not of a room but of 'blott några kubikmeter sönderspjälkat utrymme som blivit över då arkitekten ritade sitt gotiska rådhus' (op. cit., 198) (just a few cubic metres of split-up space left over when the architect designed his neo-Gothic town hall), and with Märta Cronberger specifying its significance: 'Det här är bara en bivuak utanför portarna till en stängd stad. Man inrättar sig!' (op. cit., 200) (This is just a bivouac outside the gates of a closed city. We're having to adapt!). Märta's speech to this gathering, a page and a half of direct speech, demolishes the notion that women and men should work together to improve the situation of women and denounces not just contemporary Swedish society but the western world as a whole as masculinist as well as capitalist and militarist:

> Männen är inte våra försvarare.
> Männen är inte våra försörjare.
> Deras blodlystna nationalgudar borde inte vara våra gudar.
> Deras ledare som böjt knä för Baal och Moloch borde inte vara våra ledare.
> *Tyvärr äro de det!* (op. cit., 204-205; italics original)
>
> (The men are not defending us.
> The men are not providing for us.
> Their national gods, clamouring for blood, should not be our gods.
> Their leaders, who have knelt in front of Baal and Molech, should not be our leaders.
> *Unfortunately they are!*)

Märta Cronberger's feminism becomes even more provocative as she equates the marginalisation of women in Sweden with that of blacks, describes herself to her lover Johan Hallind as a 'hysterisk vit kvinna med negroid uppsyn' (Wägner 1932, 223) (hysterical white woman with Negroid features), and makes him refer to the bivouac meeting as 'ett negermöte' (ibid.) (a Negro meeting). With her curly black hair Sara Svart ('Black'), who has met Märta Cronberger at a 'bildningskurs' (op. cit., 53) (educational course) and elevated her to her ideal, effectively epitomises Swedish women as black, a dimension which raises the issue of a postcolonial approach to *Dialogen fortsätter*. While Sweden by the early 1930s had not been a colonial power since Finland became part of the Russian empire in 1809, the aftermath of the First World War, and more especially the work of the League of Nations from 1919 and Gandhi's campaign against the British Empire in India which had begun in the same year, had brought colonialism to the forefront of international politics. And similarly, while the population of Sweden in the early 1930s was largely white European, the demands of blacks in the United States for citizen rights had begun to gain prominence after the war (Franklin and Moss 1994, 354-60). Ania Loomba has pointed out that colonialism does not have to emanate from outside of a country or a people but 'can be duplicated from within', and she has referred to Jorge de Alva and his argument that many people living in both once-colonised and once-colonising countries 'are still subject to the oppressions put into place by colonialism' (Loomba 2007, 16, 17). With regard to *Dialogen fortsätter*, Sweden's colonial past is insignificant in comparison with the references to international events and world politics at the time; indeed, it is Sweden's detachment from the problems of colonialism and decolonisation that makes Märta Cronberger's inistence on their relevance to white Swedish women so provocative. But however uncompromising her analysis of the position of white women, in Sweden and in the western world as a whole, Märta eventually declines the offer from the preacher Signe Dufva to accompany her to India and the new possibilities this vast community has to offer. While the dissolution of the Second Chamber of the *riksdag* has been engineered by Kristina Ring's former husband and his conservative colleagues to stop her demands for demilitarisation in their tracks (Wägner 1932, 367, 388), the elections coming up hold out the promise of a new community and thus a – more fruitful – continuation of the dialogue about gender, domination, and agency brought into focus in this novel.

Mannen vid min sida (The Man at My Side)

Published in October 1933, *Mannen vid min sida* (The Man at My Side) was well received, with the positive reviews appearing in papers representing the full political range, from *Arbetet* on the left (Bergstrand 1933) to the liberal *Dagens Nyheter* (Bolander 1933) and the conservative *Svenska Dagbladet* (Lindqvist 1933) and *Nya Dagligt Allehanda* (Erdmann 1933). But the novel did not make it into the standard histories of literature, and as a result it has received very little critical attention. Isaksson and Linder, who have taken Wägner's own outline of the mixture of genres – 'a hybrid between novel and travelogue, philosophy, all in one' (quoted in Isaksson and Linder 2003, 470) – as an indication of the relative insignificance of the text, have read the novel chiefly in autobiographical terms: 'Everything that Elin Wägner, the alert tourist in Spain, had read, seen, been told and experienced has cheekily and casually ended up on the pages, and this certainly makes for a lively read' (op. cit., 471). While Bibi Jonsson's attention to this text in her study of the utopian scheme in Wägner's novels of the 1930s is most welcome, Jonsson's focus on the search for the Great Mother (Jonsson 2001, 277-79) is not relevant for the present study. I also want to distance myself from my earlier, rather rigid reading in terms of European politics and feminist pacifism (Forsås-Scott 1991), and instead highlight the novel's multi-faceted textual space in terms of freedoms and possibilities for the explorations as well as the constructions of gender and, in particular, community. I also want to draw attention to Bal's reminder about a traveller in narrative 'in a sense always [being] an allegory of the travel that narrative is' (Bal 1999, 137).

European and world politics in the first few decades of the twentieth century constitutes the prominent context of the character-bound narration of Karin Hall, a freelance lecturer who travels to Spain in spring 1933 to gather material for her talks in provincial Sweden. There are references in her narrative to the Algeciras Conference (Wägner 1933, 49, 53), in other words the conference that was arranged in 1906 to solve the First Moroccan Crisis, and the outcome of which was to add to the international tensions that led to the First

World War. Staying at a hotel in Algeciras, she overhears three Englishmen 'som diskuterade om de borde uppskjutit världskriget eller ej och som undrade hur mycket fortare de möjligen kunde vunnit det, om de börjat 1906' (op. cit., 49) (who were discussing whether they should have postponed the World War or not, and who were wondering how much more quickly they might have won it if they had started in 1906). While passing through Hamburg on her way to Spain, Karin Hall finds herself in the midst of a political confrontation and succeeds, she is later informed, in capturing on film 'de sista levande kommunisterna i samlad aktion på öppen gata i Tyskland' (op. cit., 67) (the last living communists taking action in a body in public in Germany). And from Mrs Bertram Roden, an Englishwoman who has been playing a leading role in the Women's Army Auxiliary Corps during the World War, she learns that the next war is likely to begin very soon (op. cit., 162).

In this context of international political high tension Karin Hall, the narrator, represents herself as naive, helpless, and insignificant. Having established her reputation with lectures about museums and looking around for new topics, she travels to Spain on the advice of Mr Karlson, chair of the Good Templars' study circle in Bjurnäs by the Arctic Circle, with the aim of buying postcards and taking some photos with which to continue to attract audiences (Wägner 1933, 16-18). Having reached Algeciras, Karin Hall appears to be losing control as 'en liten vinddriven djinn från de gäckande andarnas land på andra sidan Medelhavet fått tag i mig och börjat leka med min existens' (op. cit., 41-42) (a little wind-driven djinnee from the land of the mocking spirits on the other side of the Mediterranean had got hold of me and begun to play with my existence); and discussing towards the end of her travelogue the mounting crisis in Europe with some new acquaintances, she claims – in English – that 'I am of no consequence whatever' (op. cit., 264).

By consistently constructing herself as inadequate and inconsequential, the narrator is in effect pointing up the significance of the narrative space which she, according to the fiction, is putting together. Introducing in an essay dating from 1937-38 the word chronotope as a term for 'the intrinsic connectedness of temporal and spatial relationships that are artistically expressed in literature', Mikhail Bakhtin explained that the word, literally 'time space', was 'employed in mathematics, and was introduced as part of Einstein's Theory of Relativity': 'What counts for us is the fact that it expresses the inseparability of space and time (time as the fourth dimension of space)' (Bakhtin 1994, 84). The trope of the-world-upside-down, central to my readings of novels such as *Den befriade kärleken* (1919) and *Kvarteret Oron* (1919), clearly is not adequate as we approach *Mannen vid min sida*, but as I have pointed out in my earlier study of the text, the theory of relativity certainly is (Forsås-Scott 1992, 102). However, it now seems to me that Bakhtin's chronotope opens up far more helpful perspectives. For in *Mannen vid min sida* it is not only Karin Hall's encounter with a fellow traveller with the ability to '[vända] upp och ner på det självklara' (Wägner 1933, 118) ([turn] the obvious upside down) that conjures up a prominent chronotope that includes, in the midst of the North African soukh, 'tidens träd med sin vida krona av samtidigt existerande tideräkningar. Somliga voro gamla, somliga voro nya, i detta träd var år 10 ett lika riktigt tal som år 10,000 eller 1933' (ibid.) (the tree of time with its wide crown of concurrent ways of calculating time. Some of these were old, others were new, in this tree the year 10 was just as correct as the year 10,000 or 1933). Karin Hall also refers to Edward Macmaster, with whom she strikes up a relationship, as 'Adertonhundratalet' (op. cit., 127) (the Nineteenth Century); and the American Jew whom she encounters on several occasions, Gratey Black Montrose/Grete Schwarz Rosenberg, is at once young and a million years old (op. cit., 245, 114-15). And when Karin Hall and Macmaster explore Seville together, it is the presence of the city's great past that inspires her sense of ecstasy:

> genast vi började vår vandring den blommande sköna vårmorgonen, var det som om en kontakt slutits mellan staden och mig, och dess gångna århundraden ledde sin oerhörda anspänning och triumf upp genom mina lemmar. Det var inte något enstaka konstverk som åstadkom detta, inte den mest utsökta guldmosaik eller det skönaste arkitektoniska perspektiv, ingen detalj av den förbryllande rikedomen och inte heller dess helhet. Nej, vad som försatte mig i extas tror jag var att de kulturer och raser som blommat här, som kämpat, sökt överglänsa och utrota varandra och smält

samman i nya föreningar, ännu stå kvar i sina dramatiska ställningar från det stora skådespelets tid. (op. cit., 133)

(as soon as we began our walk this blossoming, beautiful spring morning, it was as if a connection had been established between the city and me, with its past centuries conveying their immense exertion and triumph up through my limbs. It was not an individual work of art that had this result, not the most exquisite gold mosaic nor the most beautiful architectonic perspective, no detail of the bewildering abundance nor its entirety. No, I believe I was moved to ecstasy by the fact that the cultures and races that had blossomed here, that had fought each other, struggled to outdo and annihilate each other and fused into new combinations, still remain in their dramatic positions from the era of the great drama.)

The constitution of this chronotope in terms of many different centuries and cultures in interaction with each other within the boundaries of the nation known in 1933 as Spain is strikingly represented in the chapter entitled 'Röster' (Voices). Following the day's experiences in Seville and halfway between wakefulness and dreaming, Karin Hall is continuing to hear the voices she has been listening to during the day, and on the model of parts of the night-time conversation between Rakel Ljunghed and the anonymous woman in *Den namnlösa*, these voices are represented in the form of direct speech, as characters in a drama in dialogue with each other. Here saints, painters, a prior, a black slave, posterity, the Madonna in Montserrat, Mr Bertram Roden, Macmaster, Karin Hall as 'I', a queen, a king, the Duchess of Alba, Theresa of Avila, the Inquisition, and the cathedral in Seville all engage in dialogue, confirming both the range and the potential of the chronotope of this narrative.

How, then, is gender constructed in this narrative space which, to apply the words of Middleton and Woods, not only enables readers to 'participate in a public memorial space' but, as textual memory, 'also looks forward' (Middleton and Woods 2000, 5)? With unusual clarity, this narrative shows up gender as a cultural construction dependent on changing discourses and relations of power. While Andreas, Karin Hall's ex-husband, participates in his role as an authority on international civil law in a conference about the nationality of married women (Wägner 1933, 33, 208), he is continuing his private quest for what he terms 'la grande femelle', provocatively outlined by his ex-wife in physical and, indeed, animal terms: 'en fjärilsvingad kossa med stora juver, en näktergals tunga och en kattas grace' (op. cit., 39) (a cow with the wings of a butterfly and a big udder, the tongue of a nightingale and the grace of a she-cat). Macmaster may be an ageing man who has made his fortune from sweets, but to the inhabitants of North Africa his very shadow assumes the shape of 'stora slagskepp, bombplan och kulsprutevagnar' (op. cit., 78) (big battleships, bombers and vehicles with mounted machine-guns). Even more strikingly, the female characters in this narrative cover an immense spectrum, from Theresa of Avila to Karin Hall who claims to be 'of no consequence whatever' (op. cit., 264), from Mrs Bertram Roden with her considerable military experience and far bolder military ambitions to the North African women, 'starka, härdade och sköna' (op. cit., 98) (strong, hardy and beautiful), who are responsible for cleaning the streets in the soukh: 'De sopade gödseln av gatorna och tömde den i renhållningsåsnornas sidokorgar med oförliknelig kraft och behag' (ibid.) (They swept the dung off the streets, emptying it with incomparable strength and grace in the side-baskets carried by the donkeys assisting with the cleansing).

And how is community constructed in this chronotope that seems to be transgressing all conceivable limits? Indeed, is the concept meaningful, given the scope of the narrative space of this novel? I certainly believe it is, but in a version which, unlike the communities we have traced in Wägner's texts so far, comes close to that which the anthropologist Victor W. Turner has named 'communitas'.

Mannen vid min sida is a work of prose fiction, and the present study clearly is not an anthropological one. But there are aspects of Turner's well-known study of *The Ritual Process* which, it seems to me, can help us get a clearer idea of that which is specific to the narrative of this novel, a text quite unique in Wägner's prose fiction. As Turner considers rites of passage he introduces the concept of liminality, explaining that '[l]iminal entities are neither here nor there; they are betwixt and between the positions assigned and arrayed by law, custom, convention, and ceremonial' (Turner 1969, 95). It is possible to read Karin Hall's travelogue as an extended example of liminality, and a number of the binary oppositions that Turner lists as a means of defining 'liminality contrasted with status system' are relevant to the reading of the bold chronotope of Wägner's text that I have been outlining here, including transition/state, totality/partiality, homogeneity/heterogeneity, equality/inequality, anonymity/systems of nomenclature, and – given that the international financial crisis temporarily leaves Macmaster penniless – absence of property/ property, absence of status/status (op. cit., 106). In Turner's analysis, communitas is contrasted to structured society, with communitas emerging as 'a matter of giving recognition to an essential and generic human bond, without which there could be *no* society. Liminality implies that the high could not be high unless the low existed, and he who is high must experience what it is like to be low' (op. cit., 97; italics original).

It is the context constituted by the international political tensions of 1933 that gives the communitas emerging in *Mannen vid min sida* its significance. While in my earlier analysis of this novel I highlighted the role of the love between Karin Hall and Macmaster as the antidote to the extreme version of a patriarchal system represented by Hitler's Germany (Forsås-Scott 1992, 103), I now find it more meaningful to read the relationship of Karin Hall and Macmaster in the context of the communitas that the chronotope of the narrative makes so palpable. The relevant instances go beyond the chapter called 'Röster' (Voices) to include passages such as Karin Hall's version of the fairytale from the soukh, the one beginning 'Det var en gång en kvinna från en liten stad i det fjärran landet Sverige som vandrade omkring och råkade kliva över i en annan tideräkning' (Wägner 1933, 126) (Once upon a time there was a woman from a little town in the distant country Sweden who was wandering about and happened to step across into a different chronology); and the discussion about democracy, power, and freedom in the penultimate chapter, the one that brings together an anonymous Spaniard, his anonymous wife, Germano Black, Grete Schwartz Rosenberg, Mr Bertram Roden, and Karin Hall, and which, in the narrator's phrase, exemplifies the kind of discussion 'som kunde hållas var som helst, där människor ännu voro i stånd att diskutera' (op. cit., 261) (that could be held wherever people were still able to discuss).

Swedish literary histories place considerable emphasis on the *beredskapslitteratur* (literature of preparedness) of the 1930s and early 1940s, texts by writers such as Pär Lagerkvist, Eyvind Johnson, and Vilhelm Moberg that denounced fascism and defended democracy, freedom, and humanism. To my knowledge, *Mannen vid min sida* has never been categorised as an example of literature of preparedness. Is this because classical Greece, as in Lagerkvist's 'Hellensk morgondröm' (A Morning Dream in Hellas), was the perceived origin of key western values, with the Spain and Africa of Wägner's text alien and puzzling in this context? Is it because the textual space of *Mannen vid min sida* is doing so much more than formulate a programmatic defence of democratic values? Or because the sub-genre of the travelogue has been perceived as too lightweight for the text to be categorised as an instance of literature of preparedness? Or is it because the narrator is female? (With reference to the last question it is worth pointing out that Karin Boye's novel *Kallocain* [1940], to my knowledge the only text by a woman writer to make it into the category of literature of preparedness [see e.g. Brandell 1967, 304], has a male narrator.)

As I have attempted to demonstrate, *Mannen vid min sida* is an extraordinary example of the significance and possibilities of the textual space, the narrative juxtaposing constructions of gender and community in terms that not only formulate critiques but that also pave the way for innovations.

*

With a democratised Sweden and the emerging 'home of the people' as the immediate context, these four novels, then, critique conventional constructions of gender and outline new communities that range across boundaries and borders. The aftermath of the First World War and the threat of a new war underpin the narratives of all four novels, and it is within this framework that texts such as *Den namnlösa* and *Dialogen fortsätter* carry out their extensive investigations into phallogocentrism, and texts such as *De fem pärlorna* and *Mannen vid min sida* place their central characters in complex and volatile international contexts. With regard to the full range of texts explored in this chapter, in other words the opinion pieces, *Från Seine, Rhen och Ruhr*, and the radio dramas as well as the prose fiction, it is the variations and interrelations between these texts that stand out. As I have shown, communication is a prominent issue in a number of the texts from this period, with communication across borders and boundaries also requiring new channels of communication.

In the following chapter, we shall relate these findings to texts from 1937-47.

Chapter 9:
Texts 1937-47

The contexts of this period of a decade were overshadowed by the Second World War. But after a hiatus in the first few years of the war, the project of building the Swedish welfare state was resumed in the early 1940s and so continued to reinforce the dominant discourses on gender and community. The alternative discourses on citizenship that we have traced throughout the 1920s and the first half of the 1930s were becoming increasingly marginal: while the Women Citizens' College at Fogelstad continued to operate, the work of the Association of Swedish Women on the Left was inevitably obscured by the war, and *Tidevarvet* had ceased publication in December 1936.

In this chapter I am analysing six texts from this period. While the last three are works of prose fiction, all of them novels, the first three would seem to have little in common except for the fact that they were produced and published within the space of four years, 1939-43. So what are the connections, then, between *Väckarklocka* (1941; Alarm Clock), which I am tentatively categorising as a pamphlet; *Tusen år i Småland* (1939; A Thousand Years in Småland), which combines history writing with a travelogue; and the two-volume biography *Selma Lagerlöf* (1942-43), and what do these texts contribute to the key issues of this study, the constructions of gender and community?

1. *Väckarklocka (Alarm Clock)*

Written and published during the Second World War, Wägner's *Väckarklocka* was intended, according to one authority, 'to set off a counter-movement, against war, violence and oppression, for a peaceful and respectful co-existence', with Wägner's critique of civilisation having the potential to 'alter the power structure between the sexes, and [...] change the way human beings inhabit the earth and co-exist with each other and the environment' (Leppänen 2005, 17, 18). The text has sometimes been compared to Rachel Carson's *Silent Spring* (1962) (see e.g. Isaksson and Linder 2003, 588).

Katarina Leppänen in her doctoral thesis about *Väckarklocka* has surveyed the attempts to categorise the text in terms of genre, arguing that the genre is in fact indeterminate (Leppänen 2005, 35, 18). In an earlier analysis of *Väckarklocka* which I based on the surviving manuscripts and proofs, I used Ottar Grepstad's genre definitions in *Det litterære skattkammer* (1997; The Literary Treasury) to categorise *Väckarklocka* as a pamphlet, and more specifically as an example of the *debattbok*, a book designed to stimulate debate, that was to become prominent in Sweden in the 1960s and 1970s (Forsås-Scott 2003a, 28-35). As I have signalled with my references to Alastair Fowler in the opening chapter of this study, including his reminder that 'the character of genres is that they change' (Fowler 1997, 18), I now prefer a more fluid approach to the concept of genre than that offered by Grepstad. Consequently the genre categorisation of *Väckarklocka* will emerge from my analysis rather than provide a pre-existing box for the text. But as preliminary markers for my analysis I want to point to the loose definition, by two Swedish scholars, of the function of the pamphlet as that of 'rousing public opinion' (Ledin and Selander 2003, 110), along with a couple of lines from the back of the edition of *Väckarklocka* in the series of classics published by Bonnier (2007), according to which Wägner in this book is 'inviting the reader to dialogue, debate, and reflection on issues that still remain desperately urgent today in our globalised world'.

How, then, was *Väckarklocka* received when it was published in November 1941, at a time when the Second World War had been raging for more than two years and Adolf Hitler seemed unstoppable? Contrary to the claim by Erik Hjalmar Linder, *Väckarklocka* was by no means greeted with 'embarrassed silence' (Linder 1978, 11); but it is true to say that two of the key issues raised in the text, war and peace, and the environment, tended to be marginalised by the reviewers (Forsås-Scott 2007, 16-18). The reviewers were chiefly preoccupied with the text's treatment of gender roles and the implications of this in the context of Swedish society at the time. Some indication of the range of the public debate caused by *Väckarklocka* can be gauged from the contrast between on the one hand two articles headed 'Den borttappade yrkeskvinnan' (The Disappearance of the Professional Woman) in which Karin Kock, Professor of Economics, attacked as reactionary the text's treatment of women's roles (Kock 1942a, Kock 1942b), and on the other a reportage from a meeting about *Väckarklocka* arranged by the Fredrika Bremer Association in January 1942, at which 'the most distinct signal of the evening' was the demand that women, 'with new self-esteem', should step forward 'as the representatives of the homes and require that the homes be placed in the midst of society' (Zweigbergk 1942). A new edition of the text in 1978, when the ground had been prepared by second-wave feminism as well as the preoccupation in Sweden with environmental issues, caused a heated debate (Forsås-Scott 2007, 21-23), but this falls outside the scope of the present study.

The two most substantial studies of *Väckarklocka* are the three chapters in Isaksson and Linder's biography of Wägner and the doctoral thesis by Leppänen mentioned above. While Isaksson and Linder devote a considerable amount of space to the text, providing generous quotations and a particularly detailed analysis under the heading 'Kvinnornas glömda historia' (The Forgotten History of Women) (Isaksson and Linder 2003, 562-74), their reading remains closely linked to Wägner's biography. Leppänen's reading is refreshingly different as she relates *Väckarklocka* to a European feminist context and approaches it in relation to works by Rosa Mayreder, Mathilde Vaerting, and Johann Jacob Bachofen, as well as the activities of the Vienna-based Women's Organisation for World Order. In *Väckarklocka*, Leppänen argues, the notion of a 'matriarchal past' is no more than 'a backdrop to Wägner's political theory' and a device to tackle the tendency of history to '[limit] our ability to think differently' (Leppänen 2005, 100). Leppänen locates the text's key contribution in the field of ecofeminism, with '[b]oth "women" and "nature" [becoming] politicised categories defined in relation to other political categories such as "citizen" and "state"', and Wägner effectively an 'until recently, mainly unknown forerunner' of late twentieth-century and early twenty-first-century ecofeminists such as Susan Griffin, Vandana Shiva, and Karen Warren (op. cit., 212).

The analysis that follows takes its starting-point in perspectives on the text quite different from those developed by either Isaksson and Linder or Leppänen. I am not interested in the text as a series of direct, reliable statements defining Elin Wägner's political opinions and ideological positions. In line with my approaches to other texts considered in this study, I do not read the narratorial 'I' as synonymous with Elin Wägner. My focus is on the narrative space of *Väckarklocka* which, in the context of this study, is unique in its complexity. For this is an intricate web of narrative, including anecdotes, along with quotations, including some in verse and a few in foreign languages plus, indeed, references to texts and textual material considered previously in this study. The marked dialogicity of the text is enhanced by passages in italics, lists of key points, and numerous questions, including questions combining into what effectively becomes exchanges with the narratee; as I found in my earlier study of *Väckarklocka*, these features became more prominent as the work on the manuscripts and sets of proofs proceeded (Forsås-Scott 2003a). In this many-faceted, open, and dynamic textual space the narratorial 'I' becomes a character-bound narrator, no more.

In the web of narrative of *Väckarklocka*, constructions of gender are clearly relevant in several different contexts. How, first of all, does gender relate to the narrator, to what extent is the narrator gendered, and how? Secondly, how does gender relate to the narratee and, beyond the narratee, to the readers, the audience? Does this narrative address specific categories of readers, and if so, who are these, and what means does the narrative employ, and with what effects? And to turn, finally, to the construction of community, what kinds of communities are constructed, how are they constructed, and what are the implications of these constructions?

Defining the project of *Väckarklocka* in the opening pages, the narrator also begins to construct her gender along with her political-ideological position. With the Second World War raging around 'vårt land' (our country), the narrator in setting out the purpose of her narrative foregrounds personal pronouns to signal her identification with 'kvinnorna' (the women) central to this project: 'Mitt [uppsåt] var att ge ett bidrag till kvinnornas självprövning, en analys från min synpunkt av *vårt* läge, hopsummering av *våra* svårigheter och möjligheter, *våra* drömmar och planer för framtiden' (Wägner 1941, 6; my italics) (My [purpose] was to make a contribution to the women's self-examination, an analysis from my perspective of *our* situation, a summary of *our* difficulties and possibilities, *our* dreams and plans for the future). This feminine narrator quickly profiles herself as highly critical of contemporary – Swedish? – society, from a feminist perspective:

> *Kvinnorna har högsta anledning att ta under omprövning huruvida inte det mesta de accepterar som självfallet och böjt sig för som oundvikligt, verkligen också är självfallet och oundvikligt. Detta betyder att granska det samhälle vi lever i och den ställning och hållning vi intar där.* (op. cit., 6-7; italics original)
>
> (*Women have every reason to re-examine whether most of what they accept as natural and have bowed to as inevitable, is indeed natural and inevitable. This means scrutinising the society in which we are living, and our position in and attitude to it.*)

Significantly the series of images with which the narrator illustrates the claim that western civilisation is on a permanent war-footing – the tractor that is as capable of ploughing the land as attacking the enemy, the factory that can produce silk stockings as well as bombs, the aeroplanes that can carry bombs as well as those wounded by the bombs – culminates in a narratorial position that goes well beyond a feminist-pacifist one: 'människornas frihet och lycka har kommit att betyda *herraväldet över jorden*. Detta erövrarmål, som allt mer kommit att bestämma utvecklingens hållning, har inte tålt att några gränser bestod för människan' (op. cit., 13; my italics) (the freedom and happiness of humankind has become synonymous with *the mastery of the earth*. This conquerors' goal, which has increasingly determined the attitude to progress, has not tolerated any limits for the human being). In the context of the opening pages of *Väckarklocka*, the resonances of the phrase 'herraväldet över jorden' (the mastery of the earth) are unmistakable, with the compound *herravälde* consisting of *herre* meaning 'master', plus *välde* which means 'power' and is connected with *våld*, 'violence'. The position that this feminine narrator assumes is not just feminist and feminist pacifist: at this point, it is also ecofeminist.

The ecofeminist position is reinforced in a section of *Väckarklocka* that constitutes a scathing critique of the resolutions that had been adopted at the Women's International Congress at The Hague in 1915, in other words the resolutions presented in texts by Wägner published in *Idun* soon after the Congress – texts, moreover, which I have analysed in Chapter 4.1 above. In *Väckarklocka*, the resolutions adopted at The Hague are criticised for their lack of radicalism and for their underlying assumption that life after the First World War would continue along much the same lines as before, with empires remaining in place albeit accepting the existence of the League of Nations, and with 'infödingar' (natives) and women managed in a 'humaniserat kolonialsystem' (Wägner 1941, 203) (humanised colonial system). There is a connection here between the image of western civilisation as a machine – 'Vi vill förbättra maskineriet, se till att det fungerar mera gnisselfritt än förut' (op. cit., 202-203) (We want to improve the machinery, make sure it functions with fewer grating noises than before) – and the perspective in the resolutions on the natural resources and the environment: 'Begäran att naturtillgångarna skall fördelas rättvist tyder på att blott alla får vara med om den hänsynslösa och planmässiga utsugningen av jorden så är allt gott och väl' (op. cit., 203) (The demand for the natural resources to be shared fairly indicates that as long as everybody is allowed to take part in the ruthless and methodical impoverishment of the earth, everything is fine). At this point in the narrative, the narratorial ideological position has been expanded in terms of 'min grupp' (my group) or 'vår grupp' (op. cit., 187) (our group), the configuration credited with the 'som man kan tycka enkla [upptäckten] att varenda samhällsfråga kunde granskas ur kvinnlig synpunkt och därmed komma i ny belysning' (op. cit., 186) (the seemingly elementary [discovery] that every issue in society could be scrutinised from a feminine perspective and so appear in a new light). 'Systemet' (The System) that is being criticised in *Väckarklocka* is capitalist and militarist, and against this the

Texts 1937-47

narrator sets the interrelatedness of key issues such as education, the distribution and use of land, the demographic crisis, and pacifism. A summary towards the end of the penultimate chapter which not only reinforces the gendering of the narrator but also illustrates the programmatic force of this text with, I would argue, its prominent focus on rousing public opinion, is worth quoting at length:

In en värld
där maskinmässig produktion och destruktion synes vara det enda viktiga,
där arbetare och soldater tar ut sina krafter vid produktions- och destruktionsmaskinerna,
där ärelystnaden är inriktad på att förstöra tingens grundegenskaper för att få fram främmande egenskaper,
där framtidsplanerna för efterkrigstiden går ut på höjd produktion av människor och varor,
där jorden alltjämt behandlas med en fräckhet utan like,

i denna världen kan man därför tänka sig en rörelse mot huvudströmmen. Även om förslaget inte går ut på något märkvärdigare än att kvinnorna med vetenskapens hjälp – eller till vetenskapens hjälp, det kommer på ett ut – börjar granska och pröva vad som bjuds dem av andliga och materiella konfektionsvaror och med jorden som hjälpkälla och till jordens skydd i detalj efter detalj gör sig oberoende av systemet de råkat in i. (op. cit., 317)

(In a world
in which mechanical production and destruction appear to be all that matters,
in which workers and soldiers get exhausted by serving the machines of production and destruction,
in which ambitions are focused on destroying the fundamental qualities of objects so as to achieve qualities that are alien,
in which the plans for the future of the post-war era amount to an increase in the production of human beings and goods,
in which planet earth is still treated with an unprecedented effrontery,

in this world it is thus possible to conceive of a movement against the mainstream. Even if the proposal does not amount to anything more remarkable than that women with the help of science – or in order to help

303

science, which comes to much the same thing – begin to scrutinise and test what they are being offered in terms of spiritual and material ready-made goods, and with the earth as their source of help and for the protection of the earth make themselves independent, in one detail after another, of the system in which they have found themselves.)

To what extent, then, does the feminine, feminist, feminist-pacifist and – as we have found – ecofeminist narrator in *Väckarklocka* construct a gendered narratee, how is any gendering of the narratee achieved, and what conclusions can we draw, beyond the narratee, about the gendering of the reader?

In the opening pages of *Väckarklocka* there is a series of caveats and, indeed, apologies from the narrator for the simplifications necessitated by the urgency of the issues involved, and one of these explicitly concerns men as well as women: 'Det kommer att verka som om jag i min envishet att se forntid, nutid och framtid ur kvinnornas synpunkt alldeles glömde bort att män och kvinnor är i samma båt' (Wägner 1941, 7) (It will appear as if, in my insistence on seeing the past, the present, and the future from the women's perspective, I am forgetting completely that men and women are in the same boat). But it has to be said that the narrative of *Väckarklocka* offers relatively few instances of named men in positive contexts; along with a handful of Swedish pacifists and ecologists plus the Danish theologian Vilhelm Grønbech, these include Aldous Huxley, Lewis Mumford, the historian and philosopher Gerald Heard, Ehrenfried Pfeiffer (a disciple of Rudolf Steiner), D. H. Lawrence (with initials reversed), and Mahatma Gandhi (op. cit., 280-81). The feminist narrator prominently constructs the narratee as feminine, and often in opposition to masculinity as in the following passage where *vi* (we), the personal pronoun in the first person plural, links the narrator and the narratee:

> Vad som utmärker *oss alla* på vilket stadium *vi* än befinner *oss*, är att *vi* inte tillräckligt genomträngts och skakats av det historiska faktum att här bryter ut en världskonflikt mellan männen av oöverskådliga följder utan att kvinnorna som icke är i krig med varandra, kunnat göra något för att hejda den. [...] *Vi* märker inte vilken medveten och omedveten oförskämdhet som ligger i att *vi* inte tillfrågas om någonting varken före, under eller efter dessa världskrig. *Vi* kränks inte tillräckligt i *våra*

samveten över *vår* overksamhet och maktlöshet, ty *vi* anser dem självfallna. *Vi* tänker inte på att om *vi* håller denna inställning ända till slutet, kommer den nya världen att gestaltas utan hänsyn till *oss*. (op. cit., 22-23; my italics)

(What is characteristic of *us* all, irrespective of what stage *we* are at, is that *we* have not been sufficiently permeated and shaken by the historical fact that a world conflict, the consequences of which are impossible to anticipate, breaks out between the men while the women, who are not at war, have not been able to do anything to stop it. [...] *We* do not notice the conscious and unconscious insolence in the fact that *we* are not consulted about anything either before, during, or after these world wars. *Our* consciences are not outraged enough at *our* passivity and powerlessness, because *we* consider them natural. *We* do not reflect on the fact that if *we* retain this attitude to the end, the new world will take shape without *us* being taken into account.)

But as I shall show, *vi* (we) in *Väckarklocka* can also expand far beyond a feminine narratee. Indeed, an early example is to be found in the account in the opening chapter of the preparations in the narrator's home village for Mother's Day, which include the mothers facilitating their children's celebrations of them the following morning. Significantly, the prominent role of gender in this example is quickly sidelined: 'En sådan kväll hade man anledning betänka att livet ingalunda är ett rov som den starke erövrar från den svage' (op. cit., 12) (On an evening like that, one has reason to reflect on the fact that life certainly is not a booty that the stronger captures from the weaker). As a result of this expansion of the symbolism of Mother's Day, *vi* (we) in the following sentence clearly includes male as well as female narratees: '*Vi* bär oss åt som om *vi* glömt att mötet med svagheten hos den starkare utlöser lust att skydda och bevara' (ibid.; my italics) (*We* are behaving as if *we* had forgotten that the encounter with weakness in the person who is the stronger triggers a desire to protect and preserve).

While at first sight the narratee in *Väckarklocka* may appear to be more or less consistently feminine, a reading that the reception has also reinforced, the narrative does in fact from the very beginning construct narratees that are not just feminine but frequently also masculine and sometimes indeterminate with regard to gender. This effect is strengthened as the notion of femininity is destabilised and multiplied throughout the text. The notion may appear solid enough in an early sentence such as: 'Jag anser ett genombrott av *det kvinnliga inflytandet* nödvändigt för att återställa jämvikten' (Wägner 1941, 30; my italics) (I consider a breakthrough of *the feminine influence* necessary for the balance to be restored). A statement such as this one will have contributed to the definition of Wägner's position on feminism as a prominent instance of essentialist 'difference feminism'; but we do not have to get far into *Väckarklocka* to realise that the text is asking us to read 'women' and 'femininity' in many different senses. For the instances here, offered to the readers as possible points of identification, range from a group consisting of Swedish housewives and women in paid employment via a women's study group active in Vienna prior to 1938 to peasant women in Crete, women members of the Yugoslav community for the organisation of work and property known as the *zadruga*, and women getting together in Småland for a *skäktegille*, a communal and celebratory scutching of the flax (op. cit., 31, 43, 71, 113-15, 306-309). These more or less contemporary instances are interspersed with references to a wealth of female characters who have achieved prominence in history, among them Freydis in *Eirik Raude's Saga*, the goddess Nerthus in Tacitus's *Germania*, Hrosvita, Hildegard of Bingen, Theresa of Avila, St. Bridget of Sweden, Jeanne d'Arc, and Ellen Key (op. cit., 109-11, 111-12, 130-31, 133, 153). Paradoxically, these multiple constructions of 'woman' and 'femininity' culminate in the chapter focused on the housewives, 'Elden har överlevt natten' (The Fire Has Survived the Night). In this chapter the many-faceted knowledge along with the instincts and skills of the housewives, in part illustrated by the example of Mother Joad in Steinbeck's *The Grapes of Wrath* (1939), are consistently connected to 'gammal tradition' (ancient traditions), to the extent that 'det berömda uttrycket: Küche, Kinder, Kirche' (the famous expression: Kitchen, Children, Church) is held up as encapsulating 'alla livets väsentligheter' (op. cit., 246) (all that matters in life). In the debate about *Väckarklocka* in *Dagens Nyheter* in 1979 Barbro Backberger, referring to the last two of these short quotations, claimed that Wägner was 'striking [...] a blow' for Nazism

(Backberger 1979); but it only takes a moderately attentive perusal to realise that the text in no way supports this kind of reading. In line with the appropriation of war-like vocabulary in pacifist contexts in, for example, some of Wägner's texts relating to the Women's International Congress at The Hague in 1915, the Nazi slogan is appropriated in *Väckarklocka* and deconstructed in a very different context. Turning to Yvonne Hirdman's periodisation, the informal agreement termed 'husmoderskontraktet' (the housewife contract) was firmly established in Sweden by the time Wägner wrote *Väckarklocka*; but in Wägner's text, by contrast, the relationship between the individual home and 'systemet' (the [political and social] system) is a dynamic and potentially revolutionary one:

> På vilket område vi än prövar oss fram, finner vi en motsatsställning mellan hemmen och det system de inrutats i. [...] Men om frihet och demokrati inte *kan* bestå utan många små levande verksamma enheter, och hemmen under nuvarande förhållanden inte kan vara dessa enheter, då är det nuvarande systemet inte ett bra system, och vi måste förklara krig däremot. (op. cit., 255; italics original)
>
> (In whatever field we explore, we find an antithetical relationship between the homes and the system they have been boxed into. [...] But if freedom and democracy cannot survive without a multitude of small, living, active units, and the homes under current conditions *cannot* be these units, then the present system is not a good one, and we have to declare war against it.)

This is provocative language, and the challenge was more pronounced when *Väckarklocka* was published in 1941, with the Second World War raging and neutral Sweden, despite the temporary interruption, in large measure synonymous with the Social Democratic project and more particularly with the construction of 'the home of the people'. This project is adding resonances to the discussion in *Väckarklocka* of the role of the individual homes and the significance of the housewives. In line with the gender indeterminacy of the narratee and the multiplicity of 'women' and 'femininity' traced above, the construction of the narratee in 'Elden har överlevt natten' (The Fire Has Survived the Night) can embrace both masculine and feminine as in the following question, in which '*väldiga mänskliga möjligheter*' (*huge human possibilities*) is gender neutral, and *vi* (we) reaches far beyond 'we women' to include the citizens not just of Sweden but of the western world: '*Har vi verkligen råd att låta väldiga mänskliga möjligheter rinna bort oanvända bara därför att utvecklingen händelsevis och slumpvis format till en sorts hem där de inte kan utvecklas till sin fulla kapacitet?*' (op. cit., 227; italics original) (*Can we really afford to let huge human possibilities drain away unused just because progress has accidentally and haphazardly formed a kind of home in which they cannot develop to their full capacity?*)

The quotation above illustrates some of the grammatical and typographical features – in this case the inclusive *vi* (we), the provocative question, and the italicisation – that contribute not only to making *Väckarklocka* unique among Wägner's texts but also to highlighting narratees who are frequently gender neutral, or perhaps rather masculine as well as feminine. As I have found in my study of the manuscripts and proofs of *Väckarklocka*, it is not only the case that the proportion of italicised lines increases markedly in the final one third of the text, but the sequence (1) manuscripts, (2) proofs, (3) published text also shows that the practice of italicising sections of the text becomes more frequent (Forsås-Scott 2003a, 31). And it is significant that a series of ecofeminist points on one of the final pages of the book culminates in an italicised sentence claiming that 'försiktighet, hushållning och vård är det rätta sättet att handskas med naturen' (respect, thrift, and care is the right way to handle nature) that foregrounds 'människan' (the human being, humankind) and so constructs the narratee as both masculine and feminine: '*På den linjen ligger vägen till återupptäckt av vad som egentligen var människans uppgift på jorden bredvid den att sörja för sitt eget släktes framgång och försörjning*' (Wägner 1941, 336; italics original) (*In this direction is the path to rediscovering humankind's actual task on this earth along with that of catering for the progress of and provision for their own species*). The arrangement of sections of the text in the form of lists is also more common in the published version than in the first manuscript (Forsås-Scott 2003a, 32); and in an example such as the long section beginning 'I en värld' (In a world) quoted above there is again a marked gender neutrality, with the scope of the issues –

militarism, capitalism, and the exploitation of the environment – effectively marginalising the genderedness of the narratee.

A further significant aspect of the construction of the narratee in *Väckarklocka* is the inclusion in the narrative of a considerable number of quotations. As Judith Still and Michael Worton have pointed out, intertextuality engages the reader and, they continue with reference to Montaigne, 'it is the reader who thereby founds [...] the text of the *Essays*' (Still and Worton 1990, 11). There are well over 100 quotations clearly marked as such in *Väckarklocka*, virtually all of them in place in the manuscripts. They range across poetry, drama, and prose; they are mostly in Swedish but occasionally in English and German; and they cover western culture from ancient hymns to the Mother Goddess to contemporary Swedish social debate, with occasional intertexts from oriental cultures too. The reader – or perhaps even the narratee – who 'founds' the text of *Väckarklocka* by engaging in this dialogism is largely gender neutral. The same is true of the narratee constructed by the text's numerous questions. 'The essence of the *question*', Hans-Georg Gadamer has emphasised, 'is to open up possibilities and keep them open' (Gadamer 2003, 299; italics original); and there is clearly a link between his point and the fact that the questions, as I have found, become more frequent in the final one-third of *Väckarklocka* (Forsås-Scott 2003a, 36). As we have seen, the engagement of the narratee is often reinforced by means of the use of pronouns, and these not only include the personal pronoun *vi* (we) which, as in the quotation above beginning *'Har vi verkligen råd att låta väldiga mänskliga möjligheter rinna bort oanvända'* (*Can we really afford to let huge human possibilities drain away unused*), embraces all citizens in western civilisation, but occasionally also *Ni*, the second-person plural, polite address 'you', and much more commonly the indefinite or quantitative pronoun *man* (one/you/they/people), familiar in the present study from as far back as some of Wägner's reportages from the Congress at The Hague in 1915. Adding to the effect of the frequent questions, these pronouns reinforce the engagement of the narratee/s in a text whose openness increases gradually yet markedly, and in a list of questions such as the following, there can be no doubt that the pronoun *man* is contributing to constructing masculine as well as feminine narratees:

Kan man tro på människorna?
Kan man lita på de skapande krafterna?
Kan man lita sig till sanningens makt att tära sig igenom? (op. cit., 190)

(Can one believe in humankind?
Can one trust in the creative powers?
Can one trust in the power of truth to force its way through?)

In *Väckarklocka*, the frequent construction of the narratee as masculine as well as feminine is integral to the text's feminist dialogicity, a feature of the kind which Lynne Pearce has also read with a focus on the narratees (Pearce 1994, 105-108). But of particular relevance here is the work of Anne Herrmann who, in a comparative study of dialogism in Virginia Woolf and Christa Wolf, shows how Wolf in a 'Selbstinterview' about her novel *Nachdenken über Christa T.* (1968) within the interview format with its questions and answers uses personal pronouns in the first person plural – familiar from *Väckarklocka* – to refer not just to the narrator and the narratee but also 'to the questioner and respondent of the interview, and to the participants in a socialist society' (Herrmann 1989, 77). Our exploration of the gendering of the narratees in *Väckarklocka* has contributed to pinpointing a dialogism that similarly opens up alternatives (Forsås-Scott 2003a, 39-40), which can of course also be extended to involve the readers of the text.

How, then, is community constructed and what kinds of community are constructed in this text that combines such a markedly feminine and feminist narrator with narratees that can be feminine, or masculine as well as feminine, or indeterminate with regard to gender? Any answers to these questions are necessarily linked to the prominence of narrative and (textual) memory which also enhances the metatextuality of *Väckarklocka*; and before I proceed to the more specific issues about community, I shall outline the aspects to do with narrative and memory in the text on which any such analysis has to be based. In the section of the chapter 'Elden har överlevt natten' that tells the story of the women's traditional skills in nomadic and agricultural societies, the narrator problematises the conjunction of narrative, memory, and power in terms that resonate far beyond this specific account. The women who knew how to gather, prepare, and preserve edible plants and combine these into a nutritious diet, how to produce and gather fibres that could be spun and woven into clothing and other textiles, and how to provide basic health care, would also have passed on their vital knowledge 'med all den auktoritet varav de var mäktiga' (with all the authority of which they were capable):

> Men auktoriteten minskade och samtidigt minnet av det långa experimenteringsskedet och dess förvärv. Det blev väl också mindre och mindre tid till den grundliga undervisningen i berättelsens form, ju kortare de gemensamma arbetsstunderna blev. Det lönade sig allt mindre och mindre att berätta ju färre åhörarna blev. (Wägner 1941, 237)

> (But their authority diminished and with it the memory of the long period of experimentation and its achievements. There was probably also less and less time for solid education in the form of story-telling the shorter the joint periods of work became. It made less and less sense to tell these stories the fewer the listeners became.)

The narrative of *Väckarklocka* includes many different stories, but one of the most prominent clusters tells the stories of a matriarchal system preceding that which this text terms patriarchal (Wägner 1941, 78). In Katarina Leppänen's reading matriarchy merely 'works as a backdrop to Wägner's political theory' (Leppänen 2005, 100), but I would like to highlight the fact that the concept is also relativised by the narrator. For not only is 'moderåldern' (literally, the mother age) described as 'oändlig och mångfaldig i sina uppenbarelseformer' (limitless and multiple in terms of the forms in which it appears) and chronologically elastic in the sense that the transformation into patriarchy 'kan ha skett år 1400 före Kristus på Kreta och 1/1 1906 i en av de indiska staterna' (Wägner 1941, 78) (may have taken place 1400 BC in Crete and on 1 January 1906 in one of the states in India): the wealth of stories that make up the narrative of *Väckarklocka* contributes significantly to the destabilisation of what may at first sight appear to be a classic example of a grand narrative. One example of such a story prominently combining narrative and memory is the one I have referred to above, tracing ancient traditions underlying the skills and attitudes of the modern housewife. Peter Middleton and Tim

Woods analyse memory and literary texts from a postmodern perspective, yet with reference to *Väckarklocka* I find useful their reminder that postmodernism is 'haunted by the new popular culture of memory', with the past now being 'widely believed to depend upon memory, personal and social, traumatic and repressed, involuntary and planned' (Middleton and Woods 2000, 82). Much of the narrative of *Väckarklocka* is about the repression of memory, whether personal, social, traumatic, involuntary, or planned. As Middleton and Woods have also underlined, 'reading itself is a practice of memory, because texts are forms of prosthetic social memory by which readers increase and correct their own limited cognitive strengths and participate in a public memorial space' (op. cit., 5). When *Väckarklocka* establishes a public memorial space it is by telling history differently, but doing this using so many stories and constructing narratees of such a wide range that even the potentially controversial notion of matriarchy becomes integral to the textual memory which, in the phrase of Middleton and Woods, also 'looks forward': 'It not only empowers societies to manage territories and plan for the future, it also contains a promise that this can be a democratic process' (ibid.).

It is in this context that the reader of *Väckarklocka* encounters the many communities to which the text refers, from the rural village in Småland to the women's study group active in Vienna prior to 1938, from the monastery to the Yugoslav *zadruga*, but with the family and more specifically the mother and child at its core (Wägner 1941, 52). The highlighting in *Väckarklocka* of affection as 'det första sociala bindemedlet' (the original social glue) and the narrative linkage of women with 'växtplatsernas hemligheter, trädens och örternas hemligheter' (op. cit., 53) (the secrets of the habitats, the secrets of the trees and the plants), along with the narrator's insistence on the survival of traces of some of these elements in the work and attitudes of modern Swedish housewives who combine responsibility for their families in their homes with a key political role, establishes a connection with the early twenty-first-century political system that Rosi Braidotti has labelled rhizomic and described as a 'scattered, weblike system [...] which defies and defeats any pretence at avant-garde leadership by any group' (Braidotti 2006, 7-8). While Braidotti's postmodern form of humanism which 'stresses the interdependence of self and others, acknowledges contingency and values responsibility' (op. cit., 120) is clearly relevant to the environmental contextualisation of a range of communities constructed in *Väckarklocka*, Braidotti's key concept of *zoe*, 'the affirmative power of life, [...] a vector of transformation, a conveyor or a carrier that enacts in-depth transformations' (op. cit., 109), may appear to be less so; it is certainly different from that of ecological feminism or ecofeminism, which Braidotti defines with Karen Warren as 'an umbrella term which captures a variety of multicultural perspectives on the nature of the connections *within* social systems of domination between those humans in subdominant or subordinate positions, particularly women, and the domination of nonhuman nature' (Warren 1994, 1; italics original). However, as I move on to an analysis of the most important construction of a community in *Väckarklocka*, the narrative in the final chapter, 'Molnfödelse' (Cloud Birth), about the meeting of a group of friends and their planning for a new world, I am keen to keep the concept of *zoe* in focus.

The central section of the chapter focuses on some 'strängt arbetande stadsbor' (Wägner 1941, 324) (hard-working city dwellers [Wägner 1997, 49]) who, in the winter of 1940, are spending a weekend with a friend in a cottage in the country:

> Inom en ring av ljus och värme och fred satt vi där och talade om framtiden. Vi vände upp och ner på många ting, sista kvällen gällde det begreppet levnadsstandard. Folk med nedskurna inkomster och ökade utgifter borde här företa en omvärdering i god tid, tyckte vi. (Wägner 1941, 324)

> (We sat there in a circle of light and warmth and peace, talking about the future. We chewed over many things; on the last evening, the subject was the concept of the standard of living. We felt that people with reduced incomes and increasing expenditure should undertake a reassessment in good time. [Wägner 1997, 49])

Not only is this a narrated community, with the personal pronoun *vi* (we) helping to integrate the anonymous participants, and with anecdotes, the occasional instance of direct discourse, and numerous instances of diegetic summary and indirect content paraphrase (Rimmon-Kenan

1988, 109-10) engaging the narratee in the discussion: this also becomes an example of a community whose members are inspiring each other, a creative community where suggestions and ideas give rise to ever bolder suggestions and ideas. Their starting-point, moreover, is the concept of the standard of living, fundamental to the Social Democratic project of building the *folkhem* (the home of the people) and defined by the Social Democrats in purely economic terms, one example dating from a few years after the publication of *Väckarklocka* being the public conversation between a dozen political figures (11 men and 1 woman) arranged in October 1947 by *Sveriges socialdemokratiska ungdomsförbund* (The Social-Democratic Youth of Sweden) and published in 1948 as *Vår levnadsstandard* (Our Standard of Living). How, then, does the community that emerges in the final chapter of *Väckarklocka* define the concept of standard of living?

At the top of their list they place clean fresh water, followed by bread made from 'säd som vuxit på frisk jord – frisk betydde här att den varken fick vara sur eller övergödd, att den skulle vara full av liv och så ren, att man kunde smaka på den' (Wägner 1941, 325) (grain that had grown in healthy soil – healthy here in the sense that it should be neither acidic nor over-fertilized, that it should be full of life and so clean that one might sample a taste of it [Wägner 1997, 50]). The friends add top-quality milk, meat, and vegetables from nearby farms and growers and, with reference to the exploited workers on the Californian fruit farms, the requirement that as consumers, they should be able to demand a minimum standard for those working in food production. They go on to list silence, clean air, the right to follow in their lives the rhythm of the seasons and the rhythm of night and day, few but high-quality possessions, and spacious living accommodation with direct access to the ground and room for both guests and tools. They also include 'något att leva för' (Wägner 1941, 329) (something to live for [Wägner 1997, 51]), by which they mean tasks that can be followed through from beginning to end, work that can 'foga sig [naturligt] in i de större sammanhangen och harmoniera med andra människors strävan och välfärd' (Wägner 1941, 329) (fit naturally into a wider context and harmonize with the efforts and well-being of other people [Wägner 1997, 51]). They add a fixed place of abode and, to crown their list, 'att kunna få vara med dem man tycker om' (Wägner 1941, 331) (being able to be with the people you like [Wägner 1997, 52]). Given this outline of a new world put together by the group of friends in *Väckarklocka*, the concept of the standard of living is effectively sidelined by that of quality of life, values that cannot be measured in money, although the term only appeared in English in 1943 and in Swedish as recently as 1968. And what is interesting here is not just the breadth and depth of these radical plans, but the features of the kind of community they imply. Defining the criteria for an ecofeminist moral epistemology, Braidotti has highlighted

> a commitment to communities that goes beyond classical communitarianism and has a richer understanding of what an enlarged community could be. The very terms of constitution of a community are questioned and not merely the web of interests that hold them together. Communities of choice get the priority, especially those based on friendship or affinity. An even higher moral priority is given to 'oppositional communities' which challenge dominant ways of thinking and being in the world and provide resistance to sexist, racist, heterosexist and speciesist biases. (Braidotti 2006, 114)

By any standards, the community that emerges in the final chapter of *Väckarklocka* is a good example of an ecofeminist or even an oppositional community, quite different from the community of 'the home of the people' that was taking shape in Sweden when the book appeared. This bold construction was not obvious to the majority of Swedish readers in the early 1940s; but on the other hand the sheer number of subsequent editions makes it clear that the capacity of this text to rouse public opinion by means of its broad and multi-faceted narrative, its typographical devices to emphasise key points, and its constructions of the narratees as participants in the discussion, has continued to engage new generations of readers in Sweden and beyond. I am continuing, in other words, to read *Väckarklocka* as a pamphlet, but with an emphasis on the openness and ongoing effects of the genre. And as I have demonstrated with regard to the construction of gender, this text in fact combines a narrator who is feminist, feminist pacifist, and ecofeminist as well as feminine with narratees who are not just plural but who can be feminine, and sometimes masculine as well as feminine, or sometimes gender neutral. In my reading this openness, these possibilities are fundamental to the text's construction of community, and in particular to the resonances and implications of the community that emerges in the concluding chapter. It may well be that this narrative openness – in a text that has often been held up as a key example of gender essentialism – has contributed to attracting new generations of readers. And there can hardly be any mistaking the prominence of gender balance and of a construction of community grounded in the interrelationship between humankind and the environment as '[i]dealet' (the ideal) is formulated in the penultimate chapter:

> *en värld, framsprungen ur samarbete mellan män och kvinnor, en värld där rörelse och jämvikt är riktigt avpassade mot varann, liksom hjärnornas och händernas arbete, en värld som uppvisar den rätta blandningen av samfundsgemenskap och individuell frihet, vördnad för livet och mod att riskera det för en god sak, jordförbundenhet och himmelslängtan.* (Wägner 1941, 298; italics original)
>
> (*a world that has emerged from cooperation between men and women, a world in which movement and balance are properly adjusted to each other just like the work of the brains and the work of the hands, a world that shows the right mixture of social community and individual freedom, respect for life and the courage to risk it for a good cause, affinity with the earth and desire for heaven.*)

Reinforced by a number of textual and typographical features the radicalism of *Väckarklocka*, then, is not just feminist and feminist-pacifist: as I have shown, the text also anticipates major aspects of the ecofeminism that has emerged over the past few decades.

The text to be considered next was written a couple of years earlier and is very different: the narrative thread would make it possible to categorise *Tusen år i Småland* (A Thousand Years in Småland) as a travelogue, but this is also a history of part of Småland, and other genre labels are arguably relevant too. What, then, can this text add to our study of the constructions of gender and community?

Texts 1937-47

2. Tusen år i Småland *(A Thousand Years in Småland)*

In 1933 the publisher Wahlström & Widstrand had launched a series of books about Swedish provinces. The parameters of the series had been outlined on the dustjacket of the first volume, Knut Hagberg's *Gotland sommaren 1933* (Gotland in Summer 1933):

> In a series of independent, illustrated volumes, each focusing on a specific province, this province will be dealt with by a major Swedish author who has links with the area in the form of family connections or other interests and who, in a handful of essays, will deal with aspects of the province that have especially caught his [sic] eye or touched his [sic] heart. (Hagberg 1933)

As I have pointed out in an earlier study of *Tusen år i Småland*, the series became less extensive than planned, and the volume commissioned from Wägner was the last of only four to be published (Forsås-Scott 2001, 72). As I have also emphasised, the series should be viewed in the context of the economic and social changes that had been transforming Sweden since the second half of the nineteenth century. Orvar Löfgren has pointed to the emergence, from the second half of the nineteenth century onwards, of a 'landscape of recreation, [...] a landscape of consumption' side by side with the 'landscape of industrial production' (Löfgren 1996, 51), and one of many enthusiastic reviewers of *Tusen år i Småland*, Gustaf Näsström, explicitly recommended the volume for tourists not just in Småland but anywhere in Sweden (Näsström 1940, 186). Näsström was reading the book in the context of a sense of national urgency caused by the Second World War, but as Löfgren has underlined, the interest in history and the home district was bound up with the economic and social changes originating in the nineteenth century: '[a]s peasant culture was threatened by industrial development, the interest in the natural, indigenous people increased' (Löfgren 1996, 59). The majority of the reviewers did indeed read *Tusen år i Småland* as a book about Elin Wägner's home district (see Forsås-Scott 2001, 72-73), and this reading has been reinforced by Wägner's biographers (Isaksson and Linder 2003, 551-53). A bolder reading was offered by the art historian Andreas Lindblom, who highlighted the implications of what he perceived as the central thesis of Wägner's text, that 'the health of the earth [...] is fundamental to the life of the human being' (Lindblom 1940b) – but Lindblom was the exception.

I have explored the complex issue of the genre of *Tusen år i Småland* in my earlier study. Wägner's volume clearly cannot be categorised as 'a handful of essays', and I have concluded that *Tusen år i Småland* is a combination of history writing and a travelogue (Forsås-Scott 2001, 75-78). But I am now less keen on introducing genre categorisations prior to any textual analysis; and as in the case of *Väckarklocka*, I am going to explore the text and then return to the issue of genre.

Investigating the narrator and the narratees in my earlier study, I came to conclusions which also related to or implied gender, and which bear marked similarities to my findings about *Väckarklocka*. The visible narrator in *Tusen år i Småland* is certainly feminine, and given her early announcement that 'kvinnornas insatser och historia' (the contributions and history of women) will play a prominent role in the narrative due to the fact that 'de är så gott som undantagslöst överhoppade i historien om Småland eller välmenande men ytligt och enfaldigt behandlade' (Wägner 1939, 28) (almost without exception they have been ignored in the history of Småland or treated with good intentions but superficially and foolishly), I think we are also justified in reading her as feminist. As in *Väckarklocka*, the narrative emphasises the narratees, and the significance of pronouns such as *man* (one/you/they/people) and *vi* (we) is broadly parallel to that in the pamphlet (Forsås-Scott 2001, 85-86). In my earlier study, I have highlighted the community of narrator and narratees that develops in *Tusen år i Småland* (op. cit., 86), and although my focus on that occasion on the multiple narratees of the text did not involve a sustained attempt at gender categorisation, it seems to me that as in *Väckarklocka*, we are justified in reading these narratees as feminine, masculine, either-or, or gender neutral, depending on the context.

In *Tusen år i Småland* the sequential narrative, the fabula transformed into a story, is more coherent and prominent than the equivalent narrative in *Väckarklocka*, and the analysis that follows is an exploration of the constructions of gender and community, in their relations to each other, in this narrative. As I have shown in my earlier study, the narrative is underpinned by a chronological progression from the Stone Age to 1939, but with the story characterised by deviations and repetitions to the extent that an anecdote can hold up the progress of the fabula – 'Nu är historien slut och vi kan fortsätta ner till Helgasjön' (Wägner 1939, 165) (Now the anecdote is finished and we can continue down to Helgasjön) – *Tusen år i Småland* is markedly metatextual. It is a book that repeatedly challenges its readers to consider what the text is actually doing (Forsås-Scott 2001, 87).

The feminine and feminist narrator, the multiple narratees, and the prominent metatextuality are then the starting-points for our investigation into the constructions of gender and community. I have chosen to focus on a few specific sections of the text.

In the chapter entitled 'Frejs hustru för denna orten' (Freyr's Wife for this Neighbourhood), the narrator puts forward her most emphatic justification for the study of 'kvinnornas andel i vår kulturhistoria' (the women's share of our cultural history), arguing that while much of the research has in fact been done, the connections are still missing:

> När vetenskapen en gång får den idén att ta fram skärvorna och sätta ihop dem efter en ny metodik, så kommer den att få fram en ny bild av den småländska kulturhistorien med de särdrag som uppstått genom att kvinnorna så länge hållit sin ställning i arbete och kult. (Wägner 1939, 60-61)

> (When it will eventually occur to science to bring out the fragments and combine them in accordance with a new methodology, a new picture of cultural history in Småland will emerge, complete with the distinctive features that have resulted from the fact that the women for so very long have maintained their positions with regard to work and religion.)

The lack of any such cultural history is the narrator's excuse – the term is certainly the correct one in the context – for the text that follows with its combination of vividness, caveats, suggestiveness, and reservations: since nobody knows when a cultural history doing justice to the contribution of the women of Småland will be written, '*må* det *kanske* tillåtas mig att göra en historia i tre kapitel av det material jag plockat ihop under strövtåg i Blendabygden och Blendalitteraturen' (op. cit., 61; my italics) (*I may perhaps be permitted to put together a history in three chapters from the material I have gathered during excursions in the Blenda district and the Blenda literature*).

The narrative about Blenda and other mythical female figures is characterised by the kind of tentativeness that surfaces here: there is no single, coherent story being served up to the reader, but instead a series of interlocking stories to engage the narratees. According to the version in a seventeenth-century source, critiqued here for in turn having been stitched together from separate elements (Wägner 1939, 62), Blenda once gathered all the women of the area of Småland known as Värend to put a stop to incursions by Danish troops: having treated the Danes to a good meal with generous quantities of drink the women, on a signal from Blenda, cut the throats of the Danish soldiers. The narrative in *Tusen år i Småland* highlights its intertexts, quoting extensively from a wide range of sources including an epic poem by the Romantic poet Erik Johan Stagnelius (1793-1823), and the narrator also adds a summary of an interview about the Blenda tradition that she has conducted with a named informant, Blenda Andersson at Skörda (op. cit., 64). The seventeenth-century source, Petter Rudebeck, turns out to contain information that crucially reinforces the significance of the community of women that overcame the Danes, for after their deed the women, having travelled to Blotberget (The Sacrificial Mountain) by Lake Åsnen, erected two mounds of stones, '*den ena, Moderhögen, gudinnorna och särdeles Frigga till ära, den andra till gudarnas. Omkring dessa dansade sedan kvinnorna, sprang och förrättade offer*' (op. cit., 63-64; italics original) (*the one, the Mother Mound, in honour of the goddesses and of Frigg in particular, and the other in honour of the gods. Around these the women then danced, leapt, and conducted sacrifices*). In *Tusen år i Småland*, the climax of the narrative about Blenda is the section about the visit to Blotberget paid by the narrator and her companion, their guide a school-girl who lives by the mountain and whose grandmother they glimpse in a cottage complete with a wireless set and a modern coffee pot:

Var är vi egentligen? Rudebeck och flickan vet inte vart de har fört oss. De ville visa oss viken där Blenda och hennes kvinnor tvättade danskens blod av sina kläder, och de har fört oss till en av de platser i Värend där modergudinnan dyrkats med offer, tvagningar och danser. Denna vackra vårdag har löst sig ur sitt sammanhang och sjunkit tillbaka djupt i årtusendenas dunkel. (op. cit., 68)

(But where are we? Rudebeck and the girl do not know where they have brought us. They wanted to show us the inlet where Blenda and her women washed the blood of the Danes off their clothes, and they have brought us to one of the places in Värend at which the Mother Goddess used to be worshipped with sacrifices, ritual washings and dancing. This beautiful spring day has detached itself from its context and retreated deep into the obscurity of the millenia.)

The traditions about Blenda that Blenda Andersson and the school-girl are keeping alive underpin the combined material from the written sources and the narrator's observations to link Blenda to an ancient fertility cult conducted by women, a cult of which there are traces elsewhere in this part of Småland as is illustrated by the quotation, again from a named source, fleetingly linking Blenda to a lake that similarly appears to have been the site of ritual washings and to which '*Frejs hustru för denna orten*' (Wägner 1939, 70; italics original) (*Freyr's wife for this neighbourhood*) used to be brought. The foregrounding of the living tradition highlights the interdependence of memory with gender and community, for Blenda Andersson's story about Blenda is the one she has heard from her mother, 'som ännu hade allmogens stora traditions- och sägenskatt bevarad i sitt minne' (op. cit., 65) (who still preserved in her memory the great treasure of traditions and legends of the country people). Much later in *Tusen år i Småland*, memory is problematised as the narrator, listening to her fellow passengers on a bus, reflects that 'här lyssnade jag på den sista generationen smålänningar som ägde den gamla förmågan att minnas' (op. cit., 257) (here I was listening to the last generation of Smålanders who had retained the old ability to remember). As Ebba Witt-Brattström has emphasised, memory here is associated with a sense of 'loyalty to deep roots and interdependence between human beings' (Witt-Brattström 2003, 106). Again, memory is fundamental to the construction of community, and although there are references in this context to the impact of long-lasting conflicts, the narrator also highlights 'trevnaden i att tusen människor i en socken levde i evig nyfikenhet och fullkomlig kunskap om varandra' (Wägner 1939, 258) (the positive impact of the fact that a thousand people in a parish were living in never-ending curiosity and perfect knowledge about each other). Contrasting the survival of the remnants of this sense of community with 'stadens tråkighet' (ibid.) (the boredom of the town) arising from the fact that people do not know each other, the narrator develops the sense of community that can still be found in rural areas to include animals, both wild and domestic. The range of traditions represented here involving speaking animals and birds is traced back to a time when 'människorna visste mer om djuren [...] och följaktligen förstod dem bättre' (human beings knew more about animals [...] and so understood them better), in other words when 'människan levde mera på jämlik fot med dem' (op. cit., 259) (when humankind was on a more equal footing with them). The narrative of *Tusen år i Småland* is less markedly ecofeminist than that of *Väckarklocka*, and in the context of the quotations about humankind and animals above I again want to foreground Braidotti's concept of *zoe*, 'the affirmative power of life' that 'actualizes a set of both social and symbolic interactions that inscribe the human – animal bond' (Braidotti 2006, 109). Braidotti is concerned with philosophy and ethics, but although the 'philosophy of affirmative becoming' that she labels '[b]io-centred egalitarianism' may appear distant from the narrative of *Tusen år i Småland*, I want to highlight, as we move on to another section focusing on the representation of gender and community in Wägner's text, Braidotti's emphasis on the principle of non-profit and on the role of 'self-expression and communally held property rights over both biological and cultural artefacts' (op. cit., 110).

The old village consists of eight homesteads, the buildings grouped closely together surrounded by fields and grazing land which form a bright green patch in the darker forests. As late as 1939, the village is in the process of redistributing the land of the homesteads in accordance with a system which had been introduced in Sweden in the late eighteenth and early nineteenth centuries, and which aimed to relocate the land of each homestead to form a single unit. Up to the early nineteenth century, the land of this village had been divided according to the age-old principle that every homestead should have a share of every type of land, and the subsequent reform had still left several farmers with shares in each homestead: 'Man levde i en form av ättsamhälle, modifierad från den tid då ättens jord ej var till salu så länge ättemän levde som kunde bruka den' (Wägner 1939, 209) (People were living in a form of family community, modified from the time when the land of the family was not for sale as long as there were members of the family able to cultivate it). The farmer who is interviewed by the narrator and her companion, and whose occasional lines in direct discourse come complete with dialect syntax and vocabulary, has had half a share in a homestead co-owned with two other farmers and can outline the practicalities of a system rooted in negotiation and joint contributions. Having recently become independent, he still believes the old system worked well; and with the narrative about the old village also preceded by a passage about the *byalag* (village community), the body of villagers that used to manage the affairs of each village and that was still in existence in a modernised form in 1939, the narrative about the community of the old village signals a link with the old stone bridges that become prominent symbols of community early in the following chapter. One of these, by which the narrator and her companion have their picnic, is represented in some detail, and there is also a photo of this bridge, or a similar one, on the last page of illustrations in the volume:

> Bron smög sig in som en utsökt detalj i landskapet och gav det dess prägel av kultur. [...] Stenarna låg vackert och självklart sammanfogade utan murbruk som om de frivilligt bildade valv för att bära människorna över och deras med varje år ökade bördor. Innan vi helt övergick till smörgåsarna, gömde vi i vårt minne denna bild av den skönaste gemenskap att föra med oss under vår studieresa in i det moderna föreningsväsendet. (op. cit., 225)

> (The bridge fitted into the landscape like an exquisite detail and gave it its stamp of culture. [...] The stones were beautifully and naturally joined together, as if they were voluntarily forming arches to carry across the human beings and their ever-increasing burdens. Before we turned to our sandwiches, we stored in our memories this image of the most beautiful community to take with us during our study trip into the associations that predominate nowadays.)

But just as the old bridges are threatened as the roads are widened and straightened, the old village communities are changing and disappearing – and here issues of gender come to the forefront. The farmer who has been interviewed has represented the work on the homestead in almost exclusively masculine terms, but throughout the interview his wife, who has stopped to listen with a pail of milk in her hand, has been a silent reminder of the missing dimension. While her husband is pleased to be independent she, it turns out, is feeling constrained by her duties and glad that their three daughters have left the rural village to settle in urbanised areas. The contrast with the narrative in the earlier chapter about Blenda and the women who followed her could hardly be greater. There is an explanation, largely implicit, as the narrator turns to a summary of the regulations for villages in the county of Kronoberg printed in 1745, only to conclude that all these details about the organisation of work on the land and in the forests, about sowing and harvesting and about the grazing of animals, ignore the work and roles of the women. Given that the women effectively participated in 'så gott som alla de arbeten vilka reglerades av byordningen' (op. cit., 216) (virtually all the tasks defined by the village regulations), a range of sources are used to set out the contributions made by the women ranging from their work on the land, including heavy digging and the clearing of rocks, to their responsibilities for cattle and sheep, their work to prepare and preserve food, and the spinning, weaving, sewing, and knitting required to make clothing and household textiles. The women were also responsible for the care of the sick and the elderly, and for the early education of both boys and girls and then for the education of their daughters. It would have been impossible, the narrator underlines, 'att samarbetet inom byalaget kunnat gå jämnt om inte kvinnorna fullgjort sin del däri likaväl som männen' (op. cit., 219) (for the cooperation within the village community to run smoothly unless the women did their share like the men), yet the women had no say in the running of the village. The narrative implicitly connects this imbalance with the situation of the farmer's wife who is pleased that her daughters have moved to built-up areas.

But the growing lack of balance traced in the narrative of *Tusen år i Småland* is not just an imbalance between women and the land but an imbalance between humankind and nature. Concluding that the traditional farmer's calendars were put together by people with 'en enorm känslighet för de stora rytmiska böljeslagen och de små skiftningarna i naturen' (Wägner 1939, 143) (an immense sensitivity to the big rhythmic beats of the waves and the small changes in nature), the narrator summarises:

> Människan är ett finstämt instrument på vilket hela naturen spelar, safterna i hennes kropp, liksom i djurens och växternas, stiger och sjunker efter årstider och planeternas inbördes ställning. Det gäller att följa och hålla den rätta takten för arbete, vila, kärlek, måltider och fromma övningar. (ibid.)
>
> (The human being is a finely-tuned instrument on which the whole of nature is playing, the fluids in her or his body, as in those of the animals and the plants, rise and fall in accordance with the seasons and the relative positions of the planets. It is important to follow and observe the right pace for work, rest, love, meals, and spiritual exercises.)

While the old fertility cult can be glimpsed in the narrative of the big chapter on 'Småländsk magi' (Magic in Småland) from which the quotation above has been taken, I want to bring back into focus Braidotti's concept of *zoe*. The narratives spelling out the affinities between trees and human beings, including trees that speak, trees that function as foster-mothers, and *vårdträd*, those unique trees next to houses or farms that are so closely bound up with the generations living there that they inspire members of the family to take their names from them, as Linnaeus did, these narratives have a connection with magic that is wholly absent from Braidotti's concept, and the same is true of the narratives in this chapter about the relationships between human beings and rats, mice, ants, and snakes, including the grass snakes that used to be regarded as the guardians of dwellings and the plots of land surrounding them. But the instances of the affinity connecting plants and animals with human beings combine into a conspicuous thread in the narrative of *Tusen år i Småland*, starting, in one of the early chapters, with the dependence of the poor people of Svänans on wood and wooden objects – 'Dessa människor levde och dog utan att äga en järnspik' (Wägner 1939, 52) (These people lived and died without possessing a nail made of iron) – and culminating in the twentieth-century clash with the sustained exploitation of nature, defined in terms of the difference between a river and a discharge ditch:

> Ett utfallsdike är inte något mysterium. En flod däremot är ett mysterium. Den samlar sitt vatten ur tusen tillflöden, inom sitt uppsamlingsområde har den de finaste vattensträngar utgrenade. Även dimman över myren som avkyles till vatten hör till dess leverantörer. (op. cit., 249)

> (A discharge ditch is not a mystery. A river, on the other hand, is a mystery. It collects its waters from a thousand tributaries; within its catchment area it has the finest filaments of water spread far and wide. Even the mist over the bog, which is cooled down into water, is one of its suppliers. [Wägner 1997a, 46])

While the image of water, gathering naturally from a myriad sources and gaining strength as it joins into burns and rivers, recalls the water imagery of an opinion piece such as 'Två landskap' (see above, p.249-51), the contrast here with the drainage ditch, dug to reduce the level of a lake or drain it altogether, helps to bring into focus the significance of *zoe* as the economic history of Småland is likened to 'en kedja av tappningar och länsningar av rikedomskällor' (Wägner 1939, 249) (a series of tappings and emptyings of sources of wealth [Wägner 1997a, 47]): 'Liksom de tappat ut sjö efter sjö, så har de också tömt ut den ena efter den andra av naturens näringsdepåer. För varje gång de upptäckt en sådan, har de trott att den var outtömlig' (Wägner 1939, 249) (Just as they have drained the water from lake after lake, so they have emptied, one after another, nature's stores of sustenance. Each time they discovered one of these, they thought it was inexhaustible [Wägner 1997a, 47]).

Calling into question boundaries of register and genre, the text of *Tusen år i Småland* constructs humankind as part of the community of living beings; and as a perspective is opened up towards the future, any dividing lines are consequently no longer drawn by human beings but by nature: 'Vem vet var gränsen går för vad naturen tillåter och förbjuder?' (Wägner 1939, 252). (Who knows where the dividing line is between what nature allows and forbids? [Wägner 1997a, 48]).

Texts 1937-47

The ecofeminist and ecocritical perspectives clearly connect *Väckarklocka* and *Tusen år i Småland*. But how and in what ways does our next text, the biography of Selma Lagerlöf, relate to the two texts just analysed in terms of constructions of gender and community?

3. *Selma Lagerlöf*, 1-2

Shortly after the death of Selma Lagerlöf in March 1940, the publisher Tor Bonnier invited Elin Wägner to write a biography of the world-renowned author (Larsson 2003, 62). The work appeared in two volumes in 1942-43, was very well received, and helped pave the way for Wägner's election to the Swedish Academy in 1944.

Inger Larsson included the Lagerlöf biography in her doctoral dissertation about three Swedish literary biographies, published in 2003. Focusing on the biography as a literary text, Larsson highlights the similarities between the biographies she has selected, Elisabeth Tykesson on P.D.A. Atterbom and Fredrik Böök on Verner von Heidenstam along with Wägner on Lagerlöf, and the realistic novel with which, in the terminology of Stephen J. Walton, the 'realistic' or 'positivist' biography has both the narrative techniques and the conceptual world in common (Walton 2008, 79). By analysing 'the subjectivity of the biographers and the literariness of the texts' Larsson aims to pinpoint the extent to which her chosen biographies 'in their genesis and as texts, show a dependence on fictionalising working methods and stylistic features' (Larsson 2003, 54). Her theoretical starting-points consist of a combination – which is never problematised – of positivist approaches to the genre such as those of Leon Edel and Ira Bruce Nadel, and a postmodern one such as that of William Epstein; but with her preference for Nadel, Larsson foregrounds her reading of the narrator in the Lagerlöf biography as 'dramatic/expressive' (op. cit., 118-19). In Nadel's categorisation of narrators, the dramatic/expressive narrator 'emphasizes participation' and is present in the narrative 'either in terms of symbolic or actual presence through his [sic] role as a character [...] or commentator' (Nadel 1984, 170-71). Moreover, a 'specialized acquaintance with the subject also characterizes the dramatic narrative reflected in a unique relationship of the hero [sic] to the biographer which he [sic] frequently develops for dramatic effect' (op. cit., 171). Larsson does not believe that Nadel's argument about the development of the narrator constituting a second plot in biographies with dramatic/expressive narrators is relevant to the Lagerlöf biography, but it is possible to discern, she argues, 'how Wägner's previous innocence has changed into the awareness of the moment of writing' (Larsson 2003, 119). However, Larsson's analysis of the text about Lagerlöf is preceded by a section that in part reads like a fragment of a Wägner biography, and that surveys the interpretations of Lagerlöf in articles by Wägner over several decades in conjunction with the development of Wägner's feminism. Larsson's approach to the Lagerlöf biography thus rests on what she has defined as Wägner's understanding of Lagerlöf as someone with knowledge of the 'hidden connections that unite everything, dead and alive', in combination with 'Wägner's difference feminism with its core message about the affinity between woman and nature' (op. cit., 78, 147). Larsson has made no attempt to explore or critique 'Wägner's difference feminism', and rewarding though her analysis of the Lagerlöf biography is, it is also a major example of the types of restricted and skewed readings in which this notion can result.

In Marianne Egeland's reading, Nadel's typology does not do justice to the narratological distinction between narrators who participate in the plot and narrators who remain outside (Egeland 2000, 97) – but much more problematic, in my view, is the absence in Nadel of a distinction between the biographer and the narrator: Nadel's main example of the dramatic/expressive narrator is Boswell (Nadel 1984, 170). It is in this type of theoretical context that Larsson approaches Wägner in the Lagerlöf biography. Egeland has suggested that 'the more dramatised and present the narrator of a biography appears, the more s/he can be perceived as a rhetorical *persona* created by the author' (Egeland 2000, 98-99; italics original); but given my focus throughout this study on texts as narrative spaces, I prefer to continue to use Bal's terminology and categorise this as a 'specific version of the narrator', as another instance of a 'visible' narrator (Bal 1999, 18).

Texts 1937-47

As in my analyses of the essays on Schwimmer and Key in Chapter 4.2 above, I use inverted commas to denote the 'Selma Lagerlöf' constructed in Wägner's text.

There can be no mistaking the focal point of the construction of gender in the narrative of the biography: the central character is a woman who achieved international fame to the extent that, as the biography reminds us, by the time she turned 80 in 1938 she was the most widely translated Swedish author ever (Wägner 1943, 303). The text also makes some attempt to represent the ever-widening communities of readers underpinning this success. In addition, the narrator refers to sources throughout, although the details are not always given and there are no references. However, as a means of steering clear of that which is either too obvious or too vague, I have chosen here to focus on the constructions of gender and community in three specific sections of the biography. As Inger Larsson has pointed out, the representation of 'Lagerlöf' in the biography is based less on the fusion of life and work presented as an ideal approach in the introduction to volume 1, than on 'a focused reading of the works' (Larsson 2003, 64). I have chosen to analyse the sections about a handful of key texts by Lagerlöf, *Gösta Berlings saga* (1891; *Gösta Berling's Saga*), *Jerusalem* (1901-02), and *Nils Holgerssons underbara resa genom Sverige* (1906-07; *Nils Holgerssons's Wonderful Journey through Sweden*), because in my view these sections of the biography not only highlight constructions of gender and community but also represent the interrelations between gender and community in ways at once distinctive and varied.

Gösta Berlings saga was a long time in the making as Lagerlöf was struggling to combine writing with her day-to-day duties as a teacher and contending with trends in Swedish culture seemingly incompatible with her material. But Lagerlöf's first novel gradually became a huge success; and in retrospect it has become clear that it also marked a decisive shift in Swedish culture, away from the early phase of the Modern Breakthrough characterised by topical issues and social criticism along with realism and naturalism, to a later phase characterised by individualism and National Romanticism in combination with new freedoms with regard to genre and style. In

Wägner's text, two substantial chapters focus on *Gösta Berlings saga*, the first setting out the background and conditions for the production of the text, and the second analysing the novel. The narrative about 'Lagerlöf's' struggle to produce *Gösta Berlings saga* is a familiar one, as the narrator indicates in a phrase involving the narratee: 'Även *den som* vet hur det gick, blir nervös av att följa med i alla de misslyckanden som föregick den slutliga segern' (Wägner 1942, 99; my italics) (Even *s/he who* knows the outcome gets nervous from engaging in all the failures that preceded the eventual victory). Lagerlöf's well-known text about the writing of *Gösta Berlings saga*, 'En saga om en saga' (1902; A Saga about a Saga), is also an intertext in this section of the biography.

The narrative of the first of the chapters about *Gösta Berlings saga* constructs gender in terms of an outline of 'Lagerlöf's' professional life. At a time when few professions were open to women in Sweden, Lagerlöf was a teacher at a school where the staff was all-female; and by definition her former colleagues at the Women Teachers' College of Higher Education in Stockholm were also women. Emphasising the fact that it was three colleagues from the Teachers' College who posted, in 1886, some of Lagerlöf's sonnets to the editor of *Dagny*, the journal of the Fredrika Bremer Association, the narrative integrates 'Lagerlöf's' literary début into the struggle for women's emancipation. Indeed, 'Lagerlöf's' entire project is represented as emancipatory: 'Den ärelystnad Selma hyste för egen del hade tidigt smält ihop med en önskan att visa världen vad kvinnor dugde till' (Wägner 1942, 103) (Selma's personal ambitions had long before merged with a desire to demonstrate to the world what women could achieve). And the editor of *Dagny* was none other than Sophie Adlersparre (1823-95), the founder of the Fredrika Bremer Association, who played a prominent role in the early phase of the Swedish women's movement. The arrival of Adlersparre's letter inviting 'Selma Lagerlöf' to Stockholm marks a change in the rhythm of the story as 'Lagerlöf' moves to one side the student essays she is marking, and the significance of the moment is enhanced by an instance of free indirect thought, which also highlights the affinity with the realistic novel: 'Så hade då ödet äntligen förstått att det måste göra något för Selma Lagerlöf!' (op. cit., 104) (At long last fate had realised that something would have to be done for Selma Lagerlöf!). 'Lagerlöf' is also integrated into a feminine line of tradition, becoming a friend of Adlersparre's just like Ellen Key and Victoria Benedictsson; and the significance to 'Lagerlöf' of this encouragement is signalled by a single-sentence paragraph: 'Vid återkomsten till Landskrona skrev hon om balen på Borg' (op. cit., 105) (On her return to Landskrona, she wrote about the ball at Borg).

The narrative of the biography constructs its readers as familiar with 'Lagerlöf's' texts, and significantly nothing more is said about the prominent chapter in *Gösta Berlings saga* in which the male protagonist attempts to run away with the beautiful Anna Stjärnhök but is dramatically pursued and stopped by a flock of wolves. More importantly, however, the one-sentence paragraph recalls the place that is the key element of the fabula of this biography. In Lagerlöf's 'En saga om en saga', the saga 'som ville bli berättad och förd ut i världen' (that wanted to be told and brought into the world) takes centre stage:

> Den var ännu bara ett helt vimmel av historier, en hel formlös sky av äventyr, som drevo fram och åter likt en svärm vilsekomna bin en sommardag och inte visste var de skulle finna någon, som kunde samla dem i en kupa. (Lagerlöf 1911, 7)
>
> (It was still just a jumble of stories, a big shapeless cloud of adventures that was drifting to and fro like a swarm of bees that had got lost on a summer's day and did not know where to find someone who could gather them into a hive.)

In the biography, by contrast, centre stage is taken by Mårbacka, the small manor in Värmland where 'Lagerlöf' had been born, and which had been in the family since the land was first cultivated in the early seventeenth century. The narrative makes Mårbacka the key to 'Lagerlöf's' entire project, but the interweaving of the financial difficulties that culminated in the loss of Mårbacka in 1888 and 'Lagerlöf's' struggle with the narrative form of *Gösta Berlings saga* foregrounds a unique bond between the place and the text. In 'En saga om en saga' the protagonist, on a farewell visit to the farm where she has grown up, decides on the evening before her departure 'i all ödmjukhet att skriva boken på sitt eget sätt och efter egen fattig förmåga' (Lagerlöf 1911, 18) (in all humility to write the book in her own way and to the best of her poor ability). In the biography this pivotal moment also has the Värmland landscape as a key motif plus, most significantly, Mårbacka's feminine tradition as epitomised by 'Selma Lagerlöf's' paternal grandmother:

> en sista ensam rundtur fick hon väl tid till ändå, medan solen sjönk bakom kullarna i väster och alla höjderna omkring dalen blånade mot kväll.
> Aldrig hade gammelfrua haft ett sådant välde över sondottern som i det ögonblick hon sade farväl till hennes värld. Hon hade ett enda arv att ta med sig från Mårbacka och det var de gamla värmlandshistorierna. I åratal hade hon försökt skriva dem som man skriver då man vill vinna guld och ära. Men då Mårbackas öde ändå var avgjort, betydde guld och ära inte längre så mycket. Nu tog hon farväl till alla försök i klassisk och modern stil, till det ofullbordade versdramat, romanerna och den nyktra realistiska prosan. Hon insåg nu att hon skulle berätta på mårbackavis, vad så folk än sade därom. Detta kom över henne som en plötslig visshet. Men inom henne hade skett ett långt frigörelsearbete som nu var avslutat. Äntligen. (Wägner 1942, 102-103)

(surely she managed a final walk on her own around the land of the manor while the sun was setting behind the hills in the west and all the ridges surrounding the valley were turning blue with the approach of evening. The old woman had never had such power over her granddaughter as at the moment when she was saying goodbye to her world. She had a single inheritance to take with her from Mårbacka, the old stories from Värmland. For many years she had been trying to write them down the way one writes when one wants to win gold and glory. But when the fate of Mårbacka had already been decided, gold and glory no longer meant very much. Now she said goodbye to all attempts in classical and modern styles, to the incomplete drama in verse, to the romances and the sober realistic prose. She now realised that she should tell the stories the Mårbacka way, no matter what people would say about this. This struck her as a sudden certainty. But a long inner process of liberation had now been concluded. At last.)

Connections emerge in the narrative between Mårbacka in its Värmland landscape and the landscape that becomes a metaphor of the situation of 'Miss Lagerlöf', the teacher with the great ambitions who 'vandrade från svindlande höjder av trotsigt självförtroende ner i djupa dalar av ångest och förödmjukelse' (Wägner 1942, 99) (walked from the dizzying heights of defiant self-confidence down into deep valleys of anxiety and humiliation). It is a feature of the chapter about the writing of *Gösta Berlings saga* – ignored by Inger Larsson – that the construction of the subject of the biography gradually approaches that of a character in a work of prose fiction, and here this metaphor is reinforced to confirm the significance of 'Lagerlöf's' awareness that at long last, she has 'funnit författarförmågan' (discovered her ability to write): 'Hennes vandring mellan avgrunder och höjder ledde henne nu på branta och steniga vägar mot en bergstopp' (op. cit., 109) (Her trek between precipices and heights was now bringing her along steep and rocky paths towards the top of a mountain). The affinity between 'Selma Lagerlöf' and a character in a novel culminates in the identification of her with the text she is producing, an identification that also opens up perspectives towards a community of readers:

> hon känner att den [romanen] gör henne till människa och en god människa. En dag skall hon bli till nytta och glädje för en hel del människor, ty hon skall tillfredsställa eller väcka anlaget för poetisk njutning. Hon ser i de färdigskrivna sidorna ett bevis på sin förmåga att leta fram det poetiska var det finns. Andra poeters verk går ej upp mot deras drömmar, men hennes verk är större än drömmarna därom. (op. cit., 109-10)

> (she feels that it [the novel] is making her into a human being, and a good human being. One day her work will be useful and pleasurable to quite a few people, for she will satisfy or arouse the predisposition for poetic enjoyment. She regards the pages she has completed as proof of her ability to find that which is poetic wherever it is. The works of other poets do not match their dreams, but her work surpasses the dreams about it.)

With the bold claim of the final sentence taking the form of a maxim (Lanser 1992, 17), the object's uniqueness as well as the authority of the narrator are reinforced.

Given the heightening of the readers' expectations in the chapter about the production of *Gösta Berlings saga*, the opening of the chapter analysing the text comes as an anticlimax. The first six pages explore the extensive speculation about the real-life models for some of the characters in the novel and give an indication of the efforts that have gone into the attempts to pinpoint the drunken priest who became Gösta Berling, the enterprising woman who became the Major's Wife at Ekeby, and some of the talented and eccentric men who became the cavaliers. The list of these efforts highlights both the engagement and fascination of many readers and the awkwardness of approaching prose fiction in these terms, with the section representing 'Selma Lagerlöf's' reactions and responses to enquiries about the models for her characters, including replies in the form of direct speech, underlining the futility of this line of investigation and so effectively emphasising the significance of the narrative:

> hennes [Selma Lagerlöfs] allmänomdöme om boken var att den innehöll en sådan blandning av sanning och lögn, att ingen mer än hon själv visste var det ena började och det andra slutade.
> Man frågar sig om hon till slut visste det själv. (Wägner 1942, 119)
>
> (her [Selma Lagerlöf's] general verdict on the book was that it contained such a mixture of truth and lies that no one but she herself knew where one began and the other ended.
> One wonders if, in the last instance, she actually knew herself.)

It is in this context of textuality that the narrator offers the story of 'the model' of the Major's Wife, complete with the reproduction of a portrait and a photo of the manor at which she lived. As the narrative combines her with the Major's Wife in Lagerlöf's novel, the latter, with a metaphor that significantly links women to the earth, emerges as an exemplum: 'Jordmånen för sådana ståtliga kvinnoexemplar höll på att tunnas ut genom det ekonomiska livets förvandling' (Wägner 1942, 128-29) (The soil in which such magnificent specimens of women could grow was getting thinner as the economy was being transformed). The conclusion is that the Major's Wife

> är och förblir [...] den gestalt som i dikten bäst representerar en både stolt och svag svensk kvinnotyp i dess motsägelsefyllda ställning under en tid då traditionen låter dem utveckla regeringsduglighet och maktlystnad, medan moralen är obönhörlig mot deras seder, och lagen kan störta dem då den behagar träda i kraft. (op. cit., 129)

(is and remains [...] the literary character who best represents a typical Swedish woman, at once proud and weak, in the contradictory position she has at a time when tradition permits her to develop the ability to rule and the desire for power, while the moral standards are merciless in the face of her conduct, and the law can bring about her fall when it sees fit to come into force.)

In the analysis of *Gösta Berlings saga* developed here, gender is constructed in terms of powerful femininity and weak masculinity. For not even the abrupt transition that can be read as a protest by the narratee, 'Men boken är ju Gösta Berlings saga och inte majorskans' (Wägner 1942, 129) (But surely the book is the saga of Gösta Berling and not that of the Major's Wife), or the emphasis on the eponymous hero as a handsome young poet and genius, can hide the fact that Gösta and his fellow cavaliers in this narrative are mere instances of role-play, with the hero himself no more than a 'genomskinlig och vikande gestalt' (op. cit., 131) (diaphanous and receding character). The focal points in this analysis are the Major's Wife and the place of the fabula of the novel, the district of Lövsjö. For this district effectively represents 'ett enda förgrenat sammanhang' (a single continuity with many branches): 'Isolering finns inte i en sådan värld, ty allting angår alla' (op. cit., 135) (Isolation does not exist in this kind of world, because everything concerns everyone). This sense of community with its strong roots in the place and its history is shared and fostered by all the characters and also inspires their capacity for decisive action:

> Det är denna gemenskap, vilken är fullt förenlig med den största olikhet i levnadsvillkor, som ger livet innehåll och fyllighet. Gemenskapen ger varje situation djup och bredd. Djup emedan dess orsaker ligger öppna för dem som känner traktens historia, bredd genom att så många berörs av den. De stora ögonblicken, de hastiga livsavgörande besluten och offerhandlingarna inspireras av gemenskapen. (op. cit., 136)

> (It is this sense of community, quite compatible with the greatest differences with regard to living conditions, that gives life its substance and fullness. The sense of community endows every situation with depth and breadth. Depth because the causes of it are obvious to anyone who knows the history of the district, breadth because so many are affected by it. The great moments, the quick, all-important decisions and acts of sacrifice are inspired by the sense of community.)

The community in *Gösta Berlings saga* also embraces all animals, whether wild or domesticated, and even extends to the weather and the seasons. The narrator points up the belief in 'sambandet mellan människans handlingar och företeelserna i naturen' (the connection between the actions of humankind and the occurrences in nature) as at once age-old and universal; and just as age-old and universal, she asserts, again with a characteristic metaphor, 'är tron på kärleken som den äldsta av alla gudomligheter, som den makt vilken verkar i det slumrande frökornet likaväl som i människors hjärtan' (op. cit., 137) (is the belief in love as the oldest of all the deities, as the power at work in the dormant seed as well as in the hearts of human beings). As the narrative of the biography fuses 'Selma Lagerlöf' with the text of *Gösta Berlings saga*, a more elaborate and poetic version of the metaphor of the landscape that originally reinforced the connection between 'Lagerlöf' and the project of the novel sets out the effects of the text in terms of the affinities of all living beings across the ages:

> Hon [Selma Lagerlöf] förvandlas själv allteftersom hon för oss in i de olika tidsåldrar som finns upplagrade i samma landskap. Detta landskap förvandlas själv därvid. I gryningen då dimman fyller dalarna ända upp till bergens fot, återskapas det Urtidsvärmland där alla djup var fyllda till brädden med vatten. När solen står rätt över landskapet, när de farande molnen fördelar ljus och skugga i snabb växling, då står de skogklädda kullarnas djärvt svängda linjer än svarta mot gyllene bakgrund, än gudutritade mot metallblått mörker, alldeles så som mörker och ljus växlar över människoödena i boken. Men då den sjunkande solen bryter sig mot kvällsmolnen i väster, kastar den samma milda rosenskimmer över när och fjärran, över högt och lågt, över vida vatten, ljusa slätter, mörka skogar och vita kyrktorn. (op. cit., 138)

> (She [Selma Lagerlöf] is herself transformed as she brings us into the different chronological periods stored in a single landscape. As a result of this process, the landscape is also transformed. At dawn when the mist fills the valleys up to the foot of the hills, the prehistoric Värmland in which all depressions were filled to the brim with water is recreated. When the sun is high in the sky above the landscape, when the scudding clouds are making light and shadows spread and change, then the boldly curving lines of the forested hills are either black against a golden background, or outlined in gold against a metallic-blue darkness, just as

Texts 1937-47

darkness and light change over the fates of the characters in the book. But when the setting sun refracts against the evening clouds in the west, it is throwing the same mild, rosy glow over far and near, over high and low, over wide waters, pale fields, dark forests and white church towers.)

It is in this context of the novel as a kind of essence of the landscape that the power of the Major's Wife and the interdependence of the living beings and other elements of the landscape achieve their significance in this analysis. In the last instance, this is an analysis that foregrounds the role of the text.

In the analysis of the two-volume novel *Jerusalem* (1901-02), the narrative of the biography highlights community rather than gender, and in terms that bear only limited similarities to the construction in *Gösta Berlings saga*. In 1896, around forty people from the parish of Nås in Dalarna had emigrated to Jerusalem to join a commune which had been established in 1881 and which 'efter de första kristnas exempel levde i syskonliv och egendomsgemenskap under utövande av goda gärningar' (Wägner 1942, 205) (following the example of the first Christians were living as brothers and sisters, sharing their belongings while doing good deeds). Selma Lagerlöf had learnt about the emigrants from Nås in the press, and while the emphasis in this section of the narrative is on 'Lagerlöf's' admiration of great deeds, the subtext is about communities:

> hon beundrade dem som hade mod att följa sin ingivelse. Det var detta mod som gjort kavaljererna beundransvärda, trots allt som man kunnat invända mot dem. Historien om dalabönderna vittnade om att sådant mod inte bara tillhörde det förgångna. I hennes egen tid levde alltså människor som visat sig mäktiga att utföra ett vågstycke mot vilket kavaljerernas förbleknade. (ibid.)

> (she admired those who had the courage to act in accordance with that which inspired them. It was this courage that had made the cavaliers worth admiring, despite all the objections one might have to them. The story of the peasants from Dalarna was evidence of the fact that this kind of courage did not just belong to the past. There were actually people, in the present, who had shown themselves capable of realising a venture which made that of the cavaliers pale by comparison.)

The biography details Lagerlöf's preparations, including her journey in spring 1900 with her companion Sophie Elkan to Jerusalem, where they became the first Swedes to visit the emigrants from Nås since their arrival four years previously, and their visit to Nås in the autumn. But throughout, the narrative highlights 'Lagerlöf's' uncertainty about how to tackle the material.

Leaving the narratee in suspense while simultaneously exploiting the resonances of 'Lagerlöf's' major texts, the narrator switches to the opening sentence of *Jerusalem: 'Det var en ung karl som gick och plöjde sitt träde en sommarmorgon'* (Wägner 1942, 221; italics original) (A young man was ploughing his field one summer's morning) (Lagerlöf 1903, 3). In the narrative of the biography, the combination of the earlier short story called 'Gudsfreden' (God's Peace) with the narrative about 'Ingmarssönerna' (The Sons of Ingmar) becomes fundamental to the writing of *Jerusalem*, and in the pages about the two texts the emphasis is wholly on the communities they construct. In 'Ingmarssönerna' this is the community of the family reaching far back in time and epitomised by Young Ingmar's conversation, while continuing to plough his field, with his father who is in heaven surrounded by the previous generations of the family. But in the narrative of the biography this representation of community is interwoven with that of 'Gudsfreden', in which the community embraces the animals as well as humankind, and in which the failure to respect this interrelationship has profound consequences. The words of the widow of the Ingmar Ingmarsson killed by the bear are quoted in the biography: *'om julen har Gud satt fred mellan djur och människor, och det arma djuret höll Guds bud, men vi bröto det, och därför äro vi nu under Guds straff'* (Wägner 1942, 223; italics original) (*God has prescribed peace between animals and human beings at Christmas and the poor animal observed God's commandment, but we offended against this and this is why we are now being punished by God*). And the widow, as the narrator points out, 'använder uttrycket vi, ty hela ätten är ansvarig när *en* felar' (ibid.; italics original) (uses the word we, for the entire family is responsible when *one* [member] errs). In the narrative of the biography, then, it is the conflict between this construction of community, related to that in

Gösta Berlings saga yet different, and that of the commune in Jerusalem with its focus on the Christian faith that is pivotal to the fabula of *Jerusalem*: 'Kärleken till det himmelska Jerusalem kämpar mot den mäktiga kärleken till fädernejorden' (op. cit., 228) (The love of the heavenly Jerusalem is in conflict with the powerful love of the soil of the ancestors). The result is a consistent and persuasive reading of the novel which, however, marginalises constructions of gender.

This trend is more conspicuous in the chapter on *Nils Holgerssons underbara resa genom Sverige*, commissioned to be used as a reader in the schools in Sweden and completed in 1906-07. The narrative of the biography emphasises the difficulties caused by the requirements that the book convey information about the scenery, plants, and animals of the various provinces of Sweden along with cultural history as well as an outline of conditions in the country at the time of writing. Again, the biography traces a long period of uncertainty, and again the solution is bound up with a notion of community. In the case of *Nils Holgerssons underbara resa*, the community is one of animals, with the narrative combining Kipling's *The Jungle Book* and Lagerlöf's own short story about a tame goose joining the wild geese migrating north as sources of inspiration. As the naughty boy Nils travels north across Sweden on the back of a goose in a flock headed by Akka, his relations with the animals also make him a better human being as he 'blir alltmera mån om att öka och bevara sitt goda namn bland djuren' (becomes more and more keen to increase and preserve his good reputation among the animals): 'Han gör till slut vad som helst för att inte Akka skall behöva skämmas för honom' (Wägner 1943, 39) (In the end he will do anything to ensure that Akka will not feel ashamed of him). Here, then, the narrative constructs a community of animals with the capacity to educate the human being. The construction of gender, on the other hand, is marginalised, and the main references to gender in the chapter about *Nils Holgerssons underbara resa* are in fact to be found in a section about 'Lagerlöf's' growing involvement in the Swedish campaign for women's suffrage while she was working on the book. The construction of community, however, emerges in a new version with the narrative about the publication of the first volume, which attracts 'barn av olika åldrar och nationaliteter' (op.

cit., 47) (children of different ages and nationalities), and it is these growing communities of readers who go on to learn, generation after generation, not just about Sweden but also 'de gamla sagornas läxa om vikten av att göra sig vän med djuren och om alla de möjligheter som de små och svaga har att klara sig' (op. cit., 58) (the lesson of the ancient fairytales about the importance of becoming friends with the animals and about all the possibilities of those who are small and weak to survive). At once confirming and expanding the significance of the construction of community, this very chapter also includes the narrative of 'Lagerlöf's' purchase of Mårbacka, which coincided with the writing of the second volume about Nils Holgersson.

*

For all the obvious differences, then, between the pamphlet *Väckarklocka*, the travelogue-cum-local-history *Tusen år i Småland*, and the biography *Selma Lagerlöf*, there are clear similarities between the constructions of gender and community. In comparison with texts from the earlier periods of Wägner's career, up to around the mid-1930s, the community of all living beings emerges as a central construction in all three late texts and to some extent marginalises the constructions of gender, at least in comparison with texts from the earlier periods. How, then, do the three texts analysed above compare with the last three novels?

4. Prose Fiction

Genomskådad (Unmasked) and Hemlighetsfull (Secretive)

The two novels Wägner published in 1937 and 1938, *Genomskådad* (Unmasked) and *Hemlighetsfull* (Secretive), had a mixed reception. The novels were not included in the series of selected works published in 1950-54 and have not been reprinted, but with the publication of Isaksson and Linder's biography in 1977-80 they achieved a new visibility in the form of generous quotations. This use of the novels with their character-bound narration would not appear to be an attempt to enhance the fictionality of the genre of biography; on the contrary, the biographers declared in the opening pages that 'read in the right way, these two novels constitute, as far as they go, an account of Elin Wägner's own actual life as a woman in the twentieth century' (Isaksson and Linder 2003, 32).

I have distanced myself from this type of reading in the past (Forsås-Scott 1985, 5), and I am doing so again here. Prose fiction with character-bound narration of the kind that could be perceived as 'autobiographical fiction' had a high profile in Sweden in the 1930s, and especially in the output of the 'proletarian' writers, e.g. Jan Fridegård (1897-1968), Eyvind Johnson (1900-1976), Ivar Lo-Johansson (1901-1991), Harry Martinson (1904-1978), Moa Martinson (1890-1964), and Vilhelm Moberg (1898-1973). The prominence of these and other writers from working-class backgrounds – quite different from those that had previously predominated among Swedish writers – was bound up with some of the economic, political, social, and cultural developments outlined in Chapters 2 and 6 above. Another important element was the interest in the work of Freud that had begun to develop in Sweden in the 1920s.

The work of Freud is indeed prominent in the narrative of *Genomskådad* and *Hemlighetsfull*, and more so than in any other prose fiction by Wägner. Kristian Hoheneck, a member of the aristocracy with whom Agnes, the character-bound narrator, falls in love, repeatedly finds himself unable to develop and complete projects, to the extent that he cannot even carry out the basic tasks required to manage the accounts of the family estate: 'tror du att jag kommer mig för att räkna ner en kolumn och transportera till nästa sida?' (Wägner 1938, 88) (do you think I can bring myself to add up a column and carry forward to the next page?). Wanting to 'komma så långt att han kan ta ansvaret både i sitt personliga liv och sitt arbete' (op. cit., 115) (get far enough to take responsibility both in his private life and in his work), Kristian seeks treatment from a Freudian psychoanalyst in Switzerland who duly unveils his Oedipus complex and his relationships with his parents, only to find the remainder of his analysis jeopardised by the patient's failure to dream. The aim of the treatment is full integration into the existing social structures, 'ett normalt liv' (a normal life) defined as '[h]ustru och barn och arbete' (op. cit., 116) (a wife and children and a job).

However, the narrative context of this ironic deconstruction and re-subjectivation of the patient in accordance with Freudian psychoanalysis is a more far-reaching problematisation of subjectivity. Agnes, the character-bound narrator, represents herself as growing up believing she might have been the victim of a mix-up at the maternity hospital so that another girl 'kanske, kanske ännu går omkring och är jag' (Wägner 1937, 5) (perhaps, perhaps is still going round being me); and the difference between Agnes, born out of wedlock, and her half-brothers and half-sister born to her mother as Mrs Andersén leads up to young Agnes's declaration in class: '*Min mamma var inte med då jag föddes*' (op. cit., 21; italics original) (*My mother wasn't present when I was born*). Agnes's array of possible and actual surnames continue to flag up the confusion about who she is. As a patient in the maternity hospital her mother is 'Mrs Holm', but her father, one of the wealthiest men in the country, is Count Johan Sporre; and while Andersén is the name of the owner of the bookshop selling religious literature whom her mother subsequently marries, Stenås is the name of the Mayor of Åköping whose wife Agnes becomes. Once divorced from Julius Stenås, Agnes finds herself without a surname of her own: she is unable to use Stenås or Andersén or Sporre, 'och att kalla mig Trulson som jag trodde mamma hetat efter kyrkboken, det hade jag inte mod till' (Wägner 1938, 81) (and I did not have the courage to call myself Trulson, which I believed had been my mother's name according to the parish register).

The narrative of *Genomskådad* and *Hemlighetsfull* consistently problematises subjectivity, and feminine subjectivity in particular. And unlike the 'autobiographical' prose fiction that achieved such prominence in Sweden in the 1930s, the narrative of Wägner's two novels does not trace the construction of the identity of the protagonist as part of a process of integration into a society in its *status quo*, on the model of the integration of Kristian Hoheneck. In *Genomskådad* and *Hemlighetsfull*, by contrast, the narrative opens up the possibilities of radical alternatives and change, making these two novels a prime example of the transformative potential of narrative space.

Texts 1937-47

Two stories are intertwined in Agnes's character-bound narrative. The more prominent one traces her life from her birth in the early 1880s to a point in the 1920s, with her half-sister Karna as the addressee. The other one only emerges intermittently and indicates her situation at the time of writing, long after the events that make up the first story. And these reminders of the second story, phrases such as 'Inför uppgiften att skildra mitt äktenskap med Julius Stenås har jag hejdat mig' (Wägner 1937, 126) (Faced with the task of giving an account of my marriage to Julius Stenås I've checked my self), or 'Nu sitter jag här tjugu år efteråt' (op. cit., 335) (Now I'm sitting here twenty years later), do not merely have a metatextual function: they contribute to highlighting the role of the narrative as a transformative space. Narrative, as Middleton and Woods have pointed out, 'provides a means of presenting a coherent identity to others', but it also 'allows the subject the possibility of self-transformation through renarrativisation' (Middleton and Woods 2000, 69). Early on in *Genomskådad* the basis of this process is highlighted by the narrator:

> Ett minne är ett barn av händelsen själv i dess förbindelse med ens egen värdering därav i nästa ögonblick. Ett senare nu har en annan värdering och föder i förbindelsen med det första minnet ett nytt av andra generationen. Vad som sker då jag skriver är att jag fixerar vad sista generationen av minnen fått i arv av synbilder, hörselminnen, förnimmelser av lycka, skuld, smärta eller ånger. (Wägner 1937, 21-22)

(A memory is the child of the actual event in its relationship with one's evaluation of it at the next moment. A subsequent present has a different evaluation, and in its relationship with the first memory this gives birth to a new memory of the second generation. What happens as I write is that I define that which the latest generation of memories has inherited in terms of visual images, aural memories, sensations of happiness, guilt, pain or regret.)

Throughout, the unspoken factor underlying Agnes's argument is that of narrative.

Most prominently, the construction of gender in *Genomskådad* and *Hemlighetsfull* is synonymous with the construction of the character-bound narrator, Agnes. But the stories of this *Entwicklungsroman* (the planned third volume of which was never completed), relate the character of Agnes to a range of places, and in her narrative these become the focal points of differing constructions of both gender and community.

In Åköping, the provincial Swedish town in which Agnes grows up, gender as well as sexuality are constructed in terms of the dominant discourse on the family outlined in Chapter 3 above. In the strict class society of Åköping, Count Sporre's relationship with a servant from his estate has to remain a secret and his daughter illegitimate, the consequences of the etymology of 'not [being] lawfully begotten' underlined in this case by the fact that the Count's entailed estate can only be passed on to a male heir. Once Agnes has completed her schooling and starts work in the office of the Mayor of Åköping who is also her guardian, she gradually inscribes herself into the role of 'drömborgmästarinna' (Wägner 1937, 98) (dream mayoress). The constructions of gender are reinforced not just by the definition of the spouse as an appendage to the male official but by the Mayor's comments on Agnes's lack of erotic experience after he has kissed her for the first time: 'du ska mogna, Agnes, få sötma. [...] Agnes, en dag får jag kanske göra dig till kvinna ...' (ibid.) (you're going to ripen, Agnes, develop your sweetness. [...] Agnes, perhaps one day I will be the one to make you into a woman ...). Agnes's marriage to Julius, 23 years her senior, catapults her to the top of Åköping society, but her initial assumption that women's erotic power automatically translates into political and social power is gradually fragmented, and the death of her son before he is born marks the end not just of this section of Agnes's narrative but also of the predominance of the deeply traditional constructions of gender and community epitomised by the town of Åköping.

Agnes's separation and divorce from Julius Stenås, her move to Stockholm where she shares a flat with Ethel Westerdyk, the journalist and old class-mate whom she has once given permission to write a novel about her, and her growing involvement in the international efforts to help the victims of the First World War are elements of a story precipitating new constructions of gender and community. Here Miss Eglantyne Jebb, the founder of Save the Children, becomes a character in Agnes's narrative just as Ellen Key has been shortly before; and Miss Jebb's call for a Magna Carta for the children of the world, a document that 'ska fastslå mänsklighetens ansvar mot dem i klara satser' (Wägner 1938, 102) (will define humankind's responsibility for them in plain clauses), is indicative of the constructions of new communities across the boundaries of class and nationality: 'Härkomst och nationalitet får inte spela någon roll' (ibid.) (Origin and nationality must be of no consequence), Miss Jebb is reported as saying with reference to the children who will help build a new world. The innovative qualities of the constructions of gender and community are reinforced following Agnes's stay at the Swiss clinic at which Kristian Hoheneck is undergoing psychoanalysis, for '[k]atastrofen på Angelsdorf' (op. cit., 128) (the disaster at Angelsdorf), the haemorrage that Agnes suffers following Kristian's suggestion that they have sex, is represented by the narrator as proof not just of the splitting of Agnes's sense of identity but of the presence of an inner strength that inspires a new sense of dignity:

> Att den [kraften] fanns även hos en människa som varit så oviss och slarvig med sitt liv fyllde mig med respekt för människan och den som skapat henne. Ty någonstans måste ju kraften komma ifrån och någonstans måste den djupa jämviktens centrum finnas som förhindrade att ännu inte allt sprängts sönder fast vi gjorde vårt bästa därmed. (op. cit., 131)

> (The fact that it [the strength] was present even in a human being who had been so uncertain and careless about her life filled me with respect for humankind and its creator. For the strength would have to come from somewhere, and somewhere there would have to be that centre of perfect equilibrium that had so far prevented everything from being blown to pieces, despite the fact that we were doing our very best to do so.)

Agnes's narrative makes her visit in the early 1920s to a French-occupied part of the Ruhr take on exceptional proportions. In the midst of what is a highly-charged political stand-off, national identity is deconstructed as deserters from the French army who disagree with the occupation are smuggled through underground tunnels to re-emerge as workers in the German coal-mines. The narrative also provides close-ups of instances of masquerade across gender boundaries, as when von

Holst, a German who has been helping French deserters, is offered the opportunity to escape from the occupied area disguised in Agnes's leather coat and hood, garments that 'så ofta överskridit gränsen att fransmännen inte fäste sig mycket vid vad som var inne i dem' (op. cit., 189-90) (had crossed the border so often that the French did not care much about what was inside), or when Agnes saves her absent lover von Holst by sleeping in his bed and pretending to be him. It is this part of Agnes's narrative with its prominent instances of drag and performativity that represents her epiphanic experience as she realises that she is able to identify with and love the French soldiers who are queuing outside a German brothel, an insight that paves the way for a construction of community that knows no boundaries:

> Aldrig tror jag att de sotiga och astmatiska träden i denna park ska glömma denna stund med stjärnorna och med oss. Jag ska inte glömma den. En gång har jag varit mig själv som en del av universum och att vara sig själv är att ha fred. Splittringen, uppdelningen, sprickan som tränger in i jaget, når inte allra längst in ändå! (op. cit., 193)

> (I don't think the sooty and asthmatic trees in this park will ever forget this moment with the stars and with us. I won't forget it. I have once been myself as part of the universe, and to be oneself is to experience peace. In the last instance the fragmentation, the division, the crack that penetrates the self does not reach to the very core!)

Rosi Braidotti's concept of the nomadic subject is emphatically postmodern, but I would argue that it is still useful in helping us to assess where the process of self-transformation through renarrativisation in *Genomskådad* and *Hemlighetsfull* culminates. As Braidotti has emphasised, the nomadic subject is a performative image, with nomadic becoming, glossed by phrases such as 'emphatic proximity' and 'intensive interconnectedness' (Braidotti 1994, 5), also helping to point up the significance of boundary-crossings in establishing new communities. The definition of nomadic politics in terms of 'a matter of bonding, of coalitions, of interconnections' (op. cit., 35) also strikes me as contributing to shedding light on the new patterns of affinity which Agnes's narrative represents and which, although set in the 1920s, would clearly also have had distinctive resonances for readers

Texts 1937-47

in the late 1930s and arguably continues to have strong resonances. If, finally, we apply Braidotti's definition of writing for the nomad – by definition a polyglot – as 'a process of undoing the illusory stability of fixed identities' (op. cit., 15), it seems to me that we can also do justice to the openness, the absence of a conclusion with the multitude of possibilities that this absence entails, which the self-transformation through renarrativisation that the text of the first two volumes of this incomplete trilogy constitutes.

Vinden vände bladen (The Wind Turned the Leaves Over)

Wägner's last novel, *Vinden vände bladen* (1947; The Wind Turned the Leaves Over), is an historical novel in which the chronological sequence extends over well over 1,000 years, from the period just before the introduction of Christianity in Sweden to the spring of 1939. The place of much of the narrative is Småland, and the series of events grouped together here range from the confrontation between Ana who can make the land bear fruit and Assar who worships Odin, the god of battle, to Johan Stiernborg's return from Siberia after many years as a prisoner of war following the defeat of the Swedish army at Poltava in 1709, and on to the transformations through the subsequent centuries of the landscape on either side of Lake Smalen. In addition the place of one section of the narrative is Russia and more specifically Tobolsk, the town some distance east of the Ural Mountains where Johan Stiernborg and his servant Jöns Värdig live as prisoners of war. Their story engages Roda Pendrich, the feminist who becomes a central character in the twentieth-century section of this text.

While the reception of the novel was largely positive, some reviewers were troubled by what they perceived as a lack of coherence between the various sections of the fabula (see e.g. Österling 1947). Most of the reviewers read the novel in terms of the stories of the two families, Stiernborg and Värdig, and so too does Conny Svensson in *Den svenska litteraturen* (Svensson 1999, 458-59). Strangely, there is no mention of *Vinden vände bladen* in Linder's *Fem decennier av nittonhundratalet*, but in the biography Isaksson and Linder, having highlighted the disparate character of Wägner's source material, suggest that the novel can be read as 'Elin Wägner's will', centring on the demand for 'peace with the earth' (Isaksson and Linder 2003, 632).

The chronological sequence that makes *Vinden vände bladen* unique in Wägner's output problematises memory and history writing. Although there are some similarities here with the two strands or two stories that we have traced in *Genomskådad* and *Hemlighetsfull*, the new World War has arguably made issues of memory and history writing more urgent. In addition, they were highlighted by the ongoing construction of the Swedish welfare state which, to translate Orvar Löfgren, 'should be inhabited by individuals who had broken away from old collectives and connections' to form 'a united nation resolutely marching into a joint future':

> On this journey old baggage, out-of-date customs, traditions and loyalties had to be thrown into the ditch or handed in to the left-luggage offices provided by the museums. A good Swede had to be a modern Swede who had the future firmly in his sights and was not dragging his feet. For this reason accusations of traditionalism and conservatism could be directed both towards the old élite trying to cling on to outdated class privileges and towards the peasantry refusing to understand the blessings of the new era. (Löfgren 1999b, 54-55)

Vinden vände bladen strikingly illustrates the point made by Middleton and Woods that literary texts may be 'significant forms of contemporary historicism, in which shifting senses of the pastness of the past – its location and the mechanisms whereby it is maintained and transmitted – are explored in ways that are not available in other discursive modes' (Middleton and Woods 2000, 36). Published at a time when the pastness of the past appeared more marginal than ever in a Sweden that was also enjoying a post-war economic boom, *Vinden vände bladen* with its composite and kaleidoscopic text is a particularly interesting example of the potential of the narrative space. As I shall show, *Vinden vände bladen* explores the significance of the pastness of the past while simultaneously highlighting epistemic breaks, defined by Middleton and Woods as the 'discontinuities between different eras and their discourses' (op. cit., 29). The result is a foregrounding of gender and community in terms of narrative and textuality that differs from the constructions in Wägner's previous works of prose fiction.

The complex narrative of *Vinden vände bladen* effectively takes the form of two intertwined stories. One represents the Stiernborg family over many generations and includes characters such as Johan Stiernborg who fights in the army of Karl XII, becomes a prisoner of war, and is murdered by the woman he has married on his return to Sweden; his son Christoph who becomes a royal physician; Alexander, the chamberlain, whose purchase of the estate of Aneholm in the mid-nineteenth century ensures that it is returned to the family and becomes the focal point of a project of rapid modernisation; his twentieth-century descendant, also named Alexander, who runs the estate with its big dairy herd, arable land, and productive forest on an industrial basis; and Alexander's son Karl-Gustaf who is preparing to take over Aneholm. Epitomising the masculine line of descent, the Stiernborgs are not just linked with the mechanisation of agriculture but also with the other projects of modernisation on the east side of Lake Smalen, and more especially with the siting of the railway station just five kilometres from the manor-house, an arrangement that the first Alexander, as a member of the House of Nobility, has been able to secure before buying the estate (Wägner 1947, 100, 103-104).

Most of the story about the Stiernborgs is externally narrated, and in line with Susan Lanser's observation about this type of narrative (Lanser 2004, 129), the gender of the narrator is not defined. On the other hand, this is a narrative of many voices: it includes three letters, from Roda Pendrich, from Oscar Sjömalm né Värdig, and from Livia Värdig, as well as a speech by Alexander Stiernborg, and an essay by Livia extending to nearly six pages of the novel. But one section of the narrative about the Stiernborgs differs from the rest, and this is where the second of the intertwined stories becomes apparent. The narrator of the novel's opening section about Ana and Assar clearly is not identical with the narrator who begins the section about Johan Stiernborg, the officer in the army of Karl XII, in the following way:

En sentida ättling av Johan som fått Christophs Minnen i händerna står till en början helt oförstående inför överskriften: 'I fångenskapen fri', och förskräckes över den mänskliga föränderligheten. Först efter mycken begrundan och möda tror man sig ha genomträngt den livssyn som ligger bakom och vet ändå inte om man förstått Christoph rätt. (Wägner 1947, 19)

(A late descendant of Johan who has come across Christoph's Memories will initially be utterly baffled by the rubric 'Free in Captivity' and will be alarmed by humankind's propensity for change. It is only after much thought and effort that you believe you have penetrated the underlying perspective on life, but you still do not know if you have interpreted Christoph correctly.)

Unlike the omniscient narrator in the opening section of the novel, this visible narrator positions herself/himself in relation to specific source material, expresses his/her uncertainty as regards the reading of it, and is prominently present thanks to the use of the pronoun *man* (one/you/they/ people). But it is only much later in the novel, in the section of the narrative set in the twentieth century, that Roda Pendrich appears, a feminist and activist who is distantly related to the Stiernborgs, but whose interviews with members of the Värdigs, the family that has played a key role in serving and assisting the noble family, have made her feel transported 'till en värld som var så mycket äldre än Johan Stiernborgs, att hon tyckte att hon lyssnade till en historia som skulle ske, fast den hade skett' (op. cit., 261) (to a world that was so much older than that of Johan Stiernborg that she felt she was listening to a story that was about to happen although it had happened). As I have pointed out in an earlier study, the section about Johan Stiernborg clearly has Roda Pendrich as its narrator and, indeed, fictitious author, although this only becomes apparent in retrospect (Forsås-Scott 2002, 275). Roda's narration illustrates the tactic that Bal has described as '[g]oing back – in retroversion – to the time in which the place was a different kind of space', and has characterised as 'a way of countering the effects of colonizing acts of focalization that can be called mapping' (Bal 1999, 147). In other words, the most bellicose section of the novel, the narrative about the officer Johan Stiernborg, is deconstructed by being narrated by a feminist and pacifist. It is no accident that Roda, as part of the novel's second story, is editing the manuscript she has put together on Good Friday 1939, the day she learns of Italy's attack against Albania (Wägner 1947, 360): linking violence and warfare across the centuries, the narrative simultaneously deconstructs violence and warfare thanks to Roda's roles as the narrator of the section on Johan Stiernborg and as a central character in much of the section set in the twentieth century.

Throughout the section on Johan Stiernborg there are reminders of the fact that the narrator is dependent on an existing source: phrases such as 'som Christoph uttryckte det' (Wägner 1947, 26) (as Christoph put it) or 'han [nämner] ingenting därom i sina memoarer' (op. cit., 36-37) (he does not [mention] anything about it in his memoirs) help highlight both metatextuality and the significance of interpretation. But there is another category of narratorial comment too, one that points up the additional contributions of the narrator, as in the following lines:

> Det lär väl från början ha varit luckor i Värdigs berättelse och blivit fler under tidens lopp, men den behöll en prägel av ärlighet och sanning. Den som skriver ner detta måste säga som sin mening att när den ställdes bredvid det som fanns känt och bevittnat från andra håll, visade den sig hålla provet. (op. cit., 55)

> (There were probably gaps in Värdig's narrative from the start and more of these as time went by, but it retained its stamp of honesty and truth. I who am writing this want to state my opinion that when his narrative was placed side by side with what was known and attested from other sources, it turned out to pass the test.)

This narrator has clearly not just edited Christoph's manuscript: she has also worked to corroborate the information. There are traces of this process too in her narrative about Johan Stiernborg: 'Emedan familjen Värdig var begåvad med den förmögenhet som kallas minne, vandrade historien från generation till generation. Aldrig ett ord blev nedskrivet, men en bleknad tradition fanns kvar ännu efter tvåhundra år' (op. cit., 56) (Since the Värdig family was gifted with the asset known as memory, this story migrated from one generation to the next. Not a single word was written down, but a faded tradition was still in existence two hundred years later). Roda Pendrich, the twentieth-century feminist and pacifist, has complemented Christoph's story about his father by talking to the descendants of Jöns Värdig, Johan Stiernborg's servant. And thanks to the Värdigs she has got to know not just the narratives about Jöns who served in the army of Karl XII, but the way of life based on traditional farming that has continued on the west side of Lake Smalen. Braidotti's concept of *zoe* is relevant to *Vinden vände bladen* also.

In other words, the feminist and pacifist narrator ensures that the perspective on the nobleman warrior is complemented by the prominent role of his servant, to the extent that Jöns Värdig frequently appears to play the more significant part in the story. When Johan Stiernborg is made responsible for the colonel's housekeeping he becomes totally dependent on Jöns for provisions, just as it is Jöns who attends to him when he has been wounded in a skirmish with the enemy. The emphasis on the duty of Jöns to provide food focuses the narrative not on military triumphalism but on the suffering of the civilian population as Värdig takes from them their cattle and their grain: 'Det var lett då barnen grät och kvinnorna ömsom bad och ömsom knöt näven, men krig är krig' (Wägner 1947, 22) (It was bad when the children cried and the women either prayed or clenched their fists, but war is war). In Jöns's perspective, food is 'det viktigsta utå allt i ett krig' (op. cit., 23) (the most important of all in a war); and the provision of food remains his responsibility at the school in Tobolsk where Johan Stiernborg becomes a teacher. Here a community across ethnic and religious boundaries emerges as Jöns Värdig trades with Orthodox Russians who farm the land, with the pagan Tatars who keep huge herds of cattle, with Samoyedans and Ostiacs who live from hunting and fishing, with Greek Catholics and with Muslims: 'Om jorden också var svart som fan själv, så kom ju ändå från den det bröd som bröts i skolan under tack och pris till Gud i himmelen' (op. cit., 41) (Even if the soil was black as the devil himself, it produced the bread that was broken at the school as God in heaven was being praised for it). The narrative of *Vinden vände bladen* consistently links the Värdigs to the soil and that which grows in it, and there are connections between the character of Jöns in the eighteenth century and Rina in the twentieth with her herb garden and knowledge of the medicinal properties of plants and on to

Livia, who is gathering spruce roots for basketry when she is spotted by Karl-Gustaf on the Stiernborg estate,

> i ett regn av mull, som hon rev upp under sitt arbete. Han stod en stund och betraktade hur hon högg av granrötterna som låg tätt under ytan och slet upp dem från stam till spets. Plötsligt rätade hon på ryggen, vände sig om, brun i ansiktet, på armar och ben som om hon kommit direkt upp ur jorden, ruskade på sig så att det yrde om henne och sa: har du nu sett på länge nog, så du kan hjälpa te? (op. cit., 230-31)

> (in a cloud of soil that she was dislodging as she worked. He stood for a while looking at how she was cutting off the spruce roots that grew just below the surface and tearing them out from the trunk to their points. Suddenly she straightened up, turned round, brown in her face, on her arms and legs as if she had come straight from the earth, shook herself so that the soil flew around her and said, have you been looking long enough so that you can help me?)

Narrated by a feminist and pacifist, the section about Johan Stiernborg amounts to a deconstruction of militarism, but despite the representations in subsequent sections of the novel of characters such as Rina and Livia, there is no simple grid in *Vinden vände bladen* linking male characters to warfare and female characters to the soil and to peace. Ulrika, Johan Stiernborg's second wife, has her husband murdered; Johan's conversion to pietism in Tobolsk turns the warrior into a man of peace; and the example of his servant Jöns also defies the stereotypes. So too, in my reading, does the character of Roda. Discerning parallels with the biography of the author, Holger Ahlenius has read Roda in binary terms: 'Like Elin Wägner, Roda turns her back on the rootless, public work of lectures, committees and meetings, moves back home to Småland, engages in regenerating, life-giving relations with the life of the district and its living traditions' (Ahlenius 1954, 27). I prefer to look beyond identifications to connections, reading Roda, like Agnes in *Genomskådad* and *Hemlighetsfull*, in terms of the Braidottian nomadic subject who

> functions as a relay team: s/he connects, circulates, moves on; s/he does not form identifications but keeps on coming back at regular intervals. The nomad is a transgressive identity, whose transitory nature is precisely

the reason why s/he can make connections at all. Nomadic politics is a matter of bonding, of coalitions, of interconnections. (Braidotti 1994, 35)

Roda's role as a narrator in part of the novel reinforces her significance as a nomadic subject in much of the twentieth-century section of the text. And it is not just the mutual relationship, the interdependence of the Värdigs and the Stiernborgs that her narrative highlights, but also the interconnections that link all living beings and that are epitomised by the question she poses in spring 1939, once she has learnt about the attack against Albania and the local plans for evacuations and bomb-proof shelters: 'Jag undrade bara [...] om livet skall börja knyta sin långa kedja på nytt, ifall människan försvinner från jorden?' (Wägner 1947, 382) (I was just wondering [...] if life will begin to weave its long chain again if humankind disappears from the earth?).

In *Vinden vände bladen*, the significance of *zoe* emerges in an intricate narrative space that foregrounds textuality and dialogism. Pointing out that there is 'no primacy of text or originating memory' (Middleton and Woods 2000, 86), Middleton and Woods have quoted Mary Carruthers: 'reading a book extends the process whereby one memory engages another in a continuing dialogue' (quoted ibid.). As one reviewer pointed out, parallel motifs help link the different sections of the text (Österling 1947), and these parallels, which include the killing on the railway of Oscar Värdig, the lineman and trades union activist who is Livia's father, and the accident on the same spot several decades later, contribute to highlighting the dialogism of the text.

*

As my analyses have emphasised, the novels *Genomskådad* and *Hemlighetsfull* on the one hand and *Vinden vände bladen* on the other are similar in the sense that they each have stories covering (very) considerable chronological spans which are complemented and problematised by stories covering the period of the writing of the whole or part of the narratives. The prominent metatextuality of all three novels helps foreground constructions of gender and community in relation to memory and history writing, but there is a difference between the focus on the problematisation of feminine subjectivity within the framework of the *Entwicklungsroman* in *Genomskådad* and *Hemlighetsfull*, and the focus on *zoe*, 'the affirmative power of life' (Braidotti 2006, 109) in *Vinden vände bladen*. In terms of the outcome of the narrative in Wägner's last novel, the affirmative power of life would appear to be the loser as Livia's son with Karl-Gustaf, Adel Värdig, moves to his father's family and a new future at Aneholm, while Livia returns with her cat and her cows to her relatives on the west side of Lake Smalen. It is the narrative space of this novel, dominated as it is by stories that extend over many centuries and that centre on mutuality and interdependence, across all boundaries, that opens up the possibilities of a different outcome.

Chapter 10:
Gender and Community 1922-47: Pacifism into Ecocentrism

Although Swedish women had been granted full citizenship in 1919 and had participated in national elections for the first time in 1921, the surveys above of the political as well as the economic and social contexts have shown numerous instances of deepening gender segregation during the interwar period. While there were some cracks in this process, for example with regard to married women in the labour market (Frangeur 1998), there can be no doubt that the introduction of the welfare state, 'the home of the people', had the effect of reinforcing binary constructions of gender as illustrated, in Yvonne Hirdman's periodisation, by the notion of 'the housewife contract'. The state intervention in the wake of the demographic crisis from 1934 onwards added to this binarism, with the significance of the new community of the state highlighted by the ethnologist who has referred to the individual being 'förstatligad' (nationalised) as a citizen (Frykman and Löfgren 1985, 137). While the dominant discourse on citizenship was based on binary and traditionalist constructions of gender along with the construction of community epitomised by 'the home of the people', some of the most significant alternative discourses, exemplified by the National Association of Liberal Women and the National Association of Women on the Left, by the weekly *Tidevarvet* and the Women Citizens' College at Fogelstad, highlighted innovative constructions of gender as the basis of new types of inclusive communities; as I have emphasised, concepts such as Plumwood's 'self-in-relationship' (Plumwood 1993, 154) and Frazer and Lacey's 'dialogic communitarianism' (Frazer and Lacey 1993, 203) are relevant in this context.

Along with texts such as *Tusen år i Småland* (1939) and *Väckarklocka* (1941), Wägner's prose fiction from the years 1922-47 has traditionally been read in terms of a trajectory from religious preoccupations in the 1920s to a new focus from the late 1930s onwards on 'her' district of rural Sweden, on the significance of the soil and of a matriarchal past, all of which has been perceived as not just regressive but, in the context of the modern welfare state, deeply conservative. As my study has demonstrated, the combination of opinion pieces, texts such as *Från Seine, Rhen och Ruhr* (1923), and novels from the 1920s points up not religious preoccupations but the political tensions in Europe in the wake of the First World War and the underpinning of these by the new technology of warfare. In novels such as *Den namnlösa* (1922) and *De fem pärlorna* (1927), constructions of gender in accordance with the dominant discourse are deconstructed and power in terms of agency is separated out from domination as love in equal, heterosexual relationships emerges as a basis of new communities. Variations on these communities are pointed up and, indeed, constructed in the transgressive, metatextual texts of *Från Seine, Rhen och Ruhr*, in which gender remains binary but is to some extent sidelined by the project of transcending boundaries and borders by means of new communities, a project in which, as I have tried to show, the textual space of the volume plays a prominent role. Wägner's limited output, in the first half of the 1930s, of drama for radio also distanced itself from the dominant discourse on femininity in this new medium, but it was novels such as *Dialogen fortsätter* (1932) and the comparatively neglected *Mannen vid min sida* (1933) that reinforced the construction of feminine citizenship in terms that reached far beyond the national boundaries of Sweden. It is no coincidence that both texts also problematise the cultural centrality of the west and invite postcolonial approaches.

In my reading the pamphlet *Väckarklocka* (1941) is anything but conservative: its narrator, feminine, feminist, feminist-pacifist, ecofeminist, engages a narratee so wide ranging that it is perhaps best thought of as multiple in a textual space that is exceptionally dynamic and many-faceted, peppered as it is with quotations and with sections involving the narratees by means of the personal pronoun *vi* (we), and by questions and italicisation. The immediate Swedish context was the building of 'the home of the people', albeit temporarily in abeyance as a result of the Second World War, but the significance of the home constructed in *Väckarklocka* bears no relation to the home of the nuclear family that was one of the corner-stones of the Swedish welfare state. The home in Wägner's text is the focal point of a critique of 'the system' and has a revolutionary potential as the basis of alternative communities. The plurality of these communities, peaceful and inclusive to the extent that I have argued for the relevance here of Braidotti's concept of *zoe*, 'the affirmative power of life, [...] a vector of transformation, a conveyor or a carrier that enacts in-depth transformations' (Braidotti 2006, 109), needs to be read in light of the fact that the notion of 'the matriarchal past' is in no way held up as a model for the future but destabilised by the many versions of this narrative that instead contribute to a rather more complex instance of textual memory '[looking] forward' (Middleton and Woods 2000, 5). Relating gender and community to memory, the narrative of *Tusen år i Småland* (1939) traces a growing imbalance between humankind and nature as it contrasts twentieth-century communities based on the exploitation of all 'natural resources' with communities integrating all living beings. The construction of alternative communities is again prominent in the biography *Selma Lagerlöf* (1942-43), with the all-embracing community of *Gösta Berlings saga* making the novel emerge as the essence of the Värmland landscape, while in *Jerusalem* (1901-02) communities consisting of many generations of the same family as well as of animals co-existing with human beings are contrasted with the different construction of the Jerusalem commune with its basis in the Christian faith. In *Nils Holgerssons underbara resa* (1906-07) the focus is wholly on the community of animals. In the first two novels from this concluding period of Wägner's career, *Genomskådad* and *Hemlighetsfull* (1937-38), constructions of gender again become more prominent in relation to constructions of community. With *Genomskådad* and *Hemlighetsfull* arguably a riposte to the 'autobiographical fiction' popular in Sweden in the 1930s, feminine subjectivity is problematised in terms of character-bound narration and related first to the deeply traditional community of Åköping around the turn of the century 1900 and then to Europe just after the First World War, with innovative and inclusive communities across the boundaries of gender and nationhood preparing the ground for a more peaceful future. In *Vinden vände bladen* the masculinisation of a community that is technologically based, selective, and competitive is contrasted with a community that is inclusive of all living beings and that foregrounds femininity.

In view of my focus in Chapter 7 on constructions of gender and community in terms of discourses on citizenship, a current concept such as environmental citizenship might seem to be relevant here. But in their book entitled *Environmental Citizenship* (2006), Andrew Dobson and Derek Bell have tentatively defined the concept in terms which, in the context of the present study, appear at once vague and timid, as no more than '[having] something to do with the relationship between individuals and the common good' (Dobson and Bell 2006, 4). The key difference, with regard to the texts studied here, is the prominence of gender; and as I have shown, the work of theorists such as Plumwood and Braidotti helps highlight the environmental significance of new constructions of gender and community in these texts by Wägner.

Chapter 11:
Connecting, Circulating, Moving On

In *The Companion Species Manifesto* (2003), Donna Haraway has written about 'the practice of feminist theory as I have experienced it' in terms that can help point up some of the approaches to the study I have undertaken here and also some of the implications of it:

> This feminist theory, in its refusal of typological thinking, binary dualisms, and both relativisms and universalisms of many flavors, contributes a rich array of approaches to emergence, process, historicity, difference, specificity, co-habitation, co-constitution, and contingency. Dozens of feminist writers have refused both relativism and universalism. Subjects, objects, kinds, races, species, genres, and genders are the products of their relating. None of this work is about finding sweet and nice – 'feminine' – worlds and knowledges free of the ravages and productivities of power. Rather, feminist inquiry is about understanding how things work, who is in the action, what might be possible, and how worldly actors might somehow be accountable to and love each other less violently. (Haraway 2003, 6-7)

Haraway highlights an emphasis on openness and processes. In the context of historical specificity and with a focus, in the present study, on discursivity and the potential of textual spaces, the exploration of constructions of gender and community has shown up both the workings of power and the possibilities of change.

The present study has taken its starting-point in the full range of Elin Wägner's published texts. While the texts have been related to the contexts in which they were produced and initially consumed, and where the landmarks in the first half of the twentieth century were the introduction of democracy and the building of the Swedish welfare state, I have taken care to detach my analyses from the notions of the biographically determined phases that have hitherto guided the reading of Wägner's texts. My focus on constructions of gender and community has instead been related to dominant and alternative discourses on gender and community, as defined in terms of discourses on the family during the period leading up to 1921 (when female suffrage was introduced in Sweden), and as defined during the subsequent period in terms of discourses on citizenship.

As we have seen, the Swedish literary histories quickly established a reading of Wägner's texts, i.e. of her prose fiction plus a pamphlet such as *Väckarklocka*, that has predominated to this day: the young journalist who also wrote fiction introduced in her early novels the new professional woman in Swedish literature, but a subsequent shift to a preoccupation with ethical and religious issues dominated her literary output in the 1920s, and her move to rural Småland then prepared the ground for what has been perceived – with just the occasional exception – as the conservative turn of her late work with its focus on a matriarchal past, the environment, and pacifism. So what are the conclusions of the present text-centred study?

The foregrounding in the analyses above of the potential of the textual space has been underpinned by material drawn from a combination of gender theory and feminist poststructuralism, with texts by Chris Weedon, Judith Butler, Susan S. Lanser, and Rosi Braidotti providing the corner-stones. Concepts such as performativity and role-play are prominent in my analyses; the problematisation of gendered subjectivation is highlighted by the relatively numerous examples of character-bound narration, including the two series of light-hearted columns and the novels drawing on the diary format; and my reading in terms of constructions of gender and community has pinpointed the centrality in many of these texts of notions of power, developed in terms of agency as well as domination. Throughout I have underlined the prominence of narratees and readers: contrary to the locking of Wägner's prose fiction into categories such as 'tendentious texts', e.g. the early novels about the New Woman, and works of art (see e.g. Landquist 1949), I have emphasised the openness and continuing potential of the textual spaces.

The structure of this study is in effect an argument for texts such as journalism, prose fiction, pamphlets, biographies, and travelogues to be read side by side, illuminating and speaking to each other in a dialogic relationship. In what follows, I am going to select a handful of clusters of texts and look more closely at the interrelationships between different texts dating from more or less the same periods in time.

The series of light-hearted columns entitled *Klubben*, the novel *Norrtullsligan*, and the series of reportages on 'Kvinnan som arbetar' were all published in 1907-08, with the exception of the final reportage which appeared in March 1909. These texts have not previously been placed side by side, but as they are compared and contrasted with regard to constructions of gender and community, the many facets and the dynamic potential of these texts become apparent. While the reportages on 'Kvinnan som arbetar' map some of the new economic roles of women in Sweden along with the social implications of these roles, the problematisations of constructions of gender and community in *Klubben* and *Norrtullsligan* provide instances of radicalising counterpoint. In both the series of light-hearted columns and the novel the dominant discourse on the family is deconstructed, with the role of mimicry in constructing femininity highlighted in the former, and subjectivation enhanced by the diary format in the latter. In both texts gender emerges as a social construct underpinned by erotic as well as economic power, and in *Norrtullsligan* in particular, this analysis reinforces the agency of the four professional female characters who constitute the gang of the title. The dialogic relationship between all these early texts is at once destabilising and radicalising, unsettling the apparent straightforwardness of the reportages and drawing the previously neglected series of light-hearted columns into a kaleidoscope of texts that takes the explorations of the constructions of both gender and community further than has been observed so far. The remarkable queering that I have traced in *Pennskaftet* (1910) can be read as an extension of the explorations and experimentation in these early texts.

Another illuminating cluster consists of texts published in 1919, i.e. the essay on Ellen Key and the two novels *Den befriade kärleken* and *Kvarteret Oron*. Written in the wake of the First World War, these texts all investigate constructions of gender in terms of power. Despite the prominence of the war and its aftermath, the texts of the novels do not equate masculinity with war and femininity with peace along the lines of for example one of the reportages from the Congress at The Hague in 1915: instead the trope of the-world-upside-down facilitates explorations of masculinity and femininity in terms of shifting patterns of domination and agency. In the narratives of these novels, the war and the revolutions sparked off by it provide laboratory conditions for investigations into gender and power, with any alternative communities merely sketched in. But these investigations are arguably deepened in the essay on Key, with all three texts enhanced by being read in relation to each other. The construction familiar from the texts of Key of masculinity in terms of the brain and femininity in terms of the heart is countered in the essay by the prominence of the professional woman who combines the heart and the brain, but the focus here on the role of reason also invites readings of the construction of gender in terms of phallogocentrism. The focus on language and philosophy in the essay complements the sometimes breathtaking twists of the stories of the novels. It also helps point up the implications and potential of the character-bound narration in *Kvarteret Oron*, probably also the text in which feminine agency becomes most prominent.

My next cluster consists of texts dating from 1922-23: the novel *Den namnlösa*, the two opinion pieces 'Liv eller död' and 'En negerstat i staten', and the volume entitled *Från Seine, Rhen och Ruhr*. Published at a time when Swedish women had recently been granted full citizenship and were being integrated into the women's associations of the political parties where the focus was on national and predominantly social issues, these texts, as I have demonstrated, need to be read in the context of alternative discourses on citizenship. The feminine citizens who emerge here belong in Europe – and beyond – with the threat of rearmament and a new war necessitating both more radical explorations of gender and power, as in *Den namnlösa* and 'En negerstat i staten' and, most importantly, the construction of alternative communities. In *Den namnlösa* the exploration of gender and phallogocentrism is more emphatic and far-reaching than in any previous text analysed in this study; however, this is not just paralleled but expanded by the perspective on race glimpsed in *Den namnlösa* and developed along with colonialism in 'En negerstat i staten'. In these two texts the gender hierarchy is topped by the white western man. This adds to both the difficulty and urgency of constructing alternative communities. The character-bound narrator who bridges the chasms between the characters in *Den namnlösa* and so begins to point up a new community or communities is paralleled by the linkages that underpin the collage of texts constituting *Från Seine, Rhen och Ruhr* and that help construct communities across national borders.

I am not proposing to continue this exercise; the present study offers ample material for similar comparisons. I would like to highlight, however, the argument that is implicit both in my selection of texts and the structuring of this study, namely that there is a need not just for literary histories but for histories of texts representing a far wider range of genres, including for example travelogues, journalism, and pamphlets. By relating texts to their contexts and analysing them side by side and in relation to each other, such more inclusive textual histories could help clarify aspects of culture at specific points in time, contributing also to destabilising generalisations of the kind which, to take but one example, the standard histories of Swedish literature have done so much to reinforce. Given recent projects in Scandinavia which have resulted in volumes such as *Den svenska pressens historia* (2000-2002; The History of the Swedish Press), *Dansk mediehistorie* (1996-97; History of Danish Media), and *Norsk litteraturhistorie. Sakprosa fra 1750 til 1995* (1998; Norwegian Literary History: Ordinary Prose from 1750 to 1995), along with the Swedish project on *sakprosa* (ordinary prose) that was launched in 1996 and has resulted in several books (Englund and Ledin 2003, 13-31), the ground is certainly being prepared for more wide-ranging histories of texts. In the meantime, some feminist approaches in particular have pointed the way by ranging across genre boundaries.

Elin Wägner's texts, then, still belong chiefly in the literary histories; and literary histories, as David Perkins has reminded us, 'are made out of literary histories' (Perkins 1992, 73). Histories of Swedish literature have long had a preference for periodisation in terms of decades. In Lönnroth and Delblanc's *Den svenska litteraturen*, Conny Svensson has written about Wägner in a chapter headed 'Tiotalets borgerliga realister' (The Bourgeois Realists of the 1910s), with the other authors categorised under this heading being Ludvig Nordström (1882-1942), Gustaf Hellström (1882-1953), Sigfrid Siwertz (1882-1970), and Sven Lidman (1882-1960). Preferring to place greater emphasis on 'borgerliga' (bourgeois) and 'realister' (realists) than on 'tiotalets' (belonging to the 1910s), Svensson has characterised the literature produced by these writers, including Wägner, as coloured by their bourgeois background (in Svensson's overview the reference is to class only, while gender is not mentioned); as being solidly realistic in the tradition of the nineteenth century; and as being markedly moderate with regard to social criticism (Svensson 1999, 453).

As I have shown, issues of gender are key to any readings of Wägner's texts. The constructedness of gender is prominent in a number of the texts investigated in the present study, and the emphatic relationship between gender and power shows up power in terms of agency as well as domination. Among the most striking texts in this context are the reportages and works of prose fiction from the years immediately after the First World War which explore constructions of gender and gender relations in terms of the trope of the-world-upside-down. Feminist pacifism inevitably also foregrounds gender, but here my readings have differed from previous ones in that they have found the constructions of gender in the relevant texts to be less essentialist, tempered instead by the prominence of constructedness and relations of power. And while the environmentalism of a text such as *Väckarklocka* has been read in terms of ecofeminism, notably by Leppänen, my readings of this and other texts from the last phase of Wägner's output have again distanced themselves from essentialism, highlighting instead the significance of the construction of communities that embrace all living beings along with humankind. Braidotti's concept of *zoe*, the 'primacy of life as production', allows us to bypass gendered essentialism and focus instead on '[b]io-centred egalitarianism', defined as 'a philosophy of affirmative becoming, which activates a nomadic subject into sustainable processes of transformation' (Braidotti 2006, 110). The concluding chapter of *Väckarklocka* is a good example, but as I have shown others can be found in for instance the Lagerlöf biography and the last novels.

The 'bourgeois realists', Conny Svensson has assured us, produced nothing but realist texts. As I have shown, a work of prose fiction such as *Den förödda vingården* has several modernist features. Many of Wägner's texts, moreover, experiment with narrative form and highlight metatextuality in ways which are much more akin to modernism than to realism. Here I am not just thinking of the great variations between the novels analysed here, between, say, the representations of contemporary urban society in *Pennskaftet* and of a rural community in the second half of the nineteenth century in *Åsa-Hanna*; between character-bound narration in *Den namnlösa* on the one hand and in *Genomskådad* and *Hemlighetsfull* on the other and the differing problematisations of gendered subjectivity that emerge as a result; and between the explorations of issues of war and peace in a realistic narrative with symbolic elements such as *De fem pärlorna* and a seemingly lightweight novel in the form of a travelogue such as *Mannen vid min sida*. I am of course also thinking of all the other texts that problematise issues of genre, of the light-hearted columns that sometimes have so much in common with prose fiction; of some of the opinion pieces that have so many similarities with essays; of a text such as *Väckarklocka* which so many scholars have categorised in so many different ways; and of volumes such as *Från Seine, Rhen och Ruhr* and *Tusen år i Småland* which do not fit easily into any existing categories. There are some similarities here with Catrine Brödje's findings about Anna Lenah Elgström's (1884-1968) prose fiction from the 1910s, which Brödje to some extent relates to texts by Elgström that represent other genres, and the analysis of which amounts to a new understanding of 'early Swedish modernism from a feminist perspective' (Brödje 1998, 11).

Feminist research over the past several decades has resulted in major contributions to our understanding of Swedish literary modernism. Another example is Gunilla Domellöf's readings of Karin Boye's reviews and essays in relation to three of her novels from the 1930s, the study highlighting the significance of the conjunction of gender and modernism (Domellöf 1986). With much Swedish literary modernism in the 1920s and 1930s being characterised by primitivism and vitalism, Ebba Witt-Brattström has demonstrated the extent to which Moa Martinson's first published novel, *Kvinnor och äppelträd* (1933; *Women and Apple Trees*, 1985) was a 'highly sophisticated response and a challenge to the masculine doctrine of love (with its related image of woman) of this period' (Witt-Brattström 1988, 91). Wägner's texts also distance themselves from any simplistic identification of the female body with the earth. In Wägner's texts, by contrast, the earth emerges as the basis of a radically new society characterised by interdependence, mutual respect, and peace. In the case of Wägner, as we have seen, Svensson's claim about the moderate social criticism of the 'bourgeois realists' does not stand up either: what emerges in many of Wägner's texts is an increasingly comprehensive and radical critique of western civilisation in the first half of the twentieth century.

In other words, the categorisation of Wägner as a 'bourgeois realist of the 1910s' does not take us very far. Not only has the wide range of texts by Wägner studied here shown up far-reaching problematisations of the construction of gender, but the constructions of new communities and, by extension, new societies have also been prominent. In the context of the interwar period in Sweden these texts, then, outline alternatives to the welfare state. With regard to such alternatives, however, more research is clearly needed, and while Irene Andersson's work on *Föreningen Frisinnade Kvinnor* and *Frisinnade Kvinnors Riksförbund* will fill a major gap, both *Tidevarvet* and the Women Citizens' College at Fogelstad are crying out for comprehensive research projects. In the context of the twenty-first century, the constructions of new communities and societies inevitably merge with the environmentalism of a number of Wägner's texts from the 1930s and 1940s in particular. While a recent study such as Lennart J. Lundqvist's *Sweden and Ecological Governance: Straddling the Fence* (2004) highlights Sweden's advanced policies and strategies with regard to 'ecologically rational governance' (Lundqvist 2004, vii), it does so without referring to issues of gender. On the other hand, ecofeminism and ecocriticism have become increasingly prominent over the past few decades. Wägner's contribution was highlighted in a chapter co-written with Abby Peterson in Carolyn Merchant's *Earthcare: Women and the Environment* (1995), and the publication in English of Katarina Leppänen's study of *Väckarklocka* (2005) has obviously helped make some of Wägner's work more visible in an international context. The ecocriticism that has been flourishing for several decades in the United States and Canada has only recently begun to make an impact in Scandinavia, with the first Swedish volume published only in 2007 (Schulz 2007), but here, too, change is clearly on the way.

In the last instance, we are back where we began, with the text and its readers. Inspired by Deleuze, Rosi Braidotti has written about the 'truth' of a text as residing 'in the kind of outward-bound interconnections or relations that it enables, provokes, engenders and sustains' (Braidotti 2006, 171). With the nomadic subject functioning as a 'relay team: s/he connects, circulates, moves on' (Braidotti 1994, 35), a conclusion, inevitably, is a contradiction in terms. The relay continues.

Chronology

1882	16 May: birth of Elin Mathilda Elisabeth Wägner, first child to Anna Wägner, née Ekedahl, daughter of a minister from the parish of Tolg in Småland, and Dr Sven Wägner, son of a farmer from Vä in Skåne and headmaster in Lund, in the south of Sweden.
1884	Birth of Ester, Anna and Sven Wägner's second child.
1885	Birth of Harald, Anna and Sven Wägner's third child. Anna Wägner dies from puerperal fever.
1887	Sven Wägner appointed Headmaster at the State Secondary Grammar School in Nyköping, some distance south of Stockholm.
1888	Sven Wägner re-marries; his new wife is Augusta Ulfsparre.
1890	Birth of Ruth, Augusta and Sven Wägner's first child.
1896	Birth of Robert, Augusta and Sven Wägner's second child.
1897	Sven Wägner appointed Headmaster at the State Secondary Grammar School for Boys in Helsingborg, in the south of Sweden.
1898	Elin Wägner leaves the Appelgren School for Girls at her own request, the year before she is due to take her final exams.
1899	Awarded a prize for a short story in the magazine *Linnéa*.
1900	Spends January-March in Tolg and Berg in Småland, being prepared for her confirmation by the minister, Alfred Ekedahl, who is her uncle. Then works as a clerk in the Headmaster's office at the State Secondary Grammar School for Boys in Helsingborg.
1901	Autumn: reviews published in a local conservative paper, *Helsingborgs-Posten*.
1902	Contributes reviews, short stories, and light-hearted columns to *Helsingborgs-Posten*. Sweden's first Association for Women's Political Suffrage is formed, in Stockholm.
1903	Employed as a journalist at *Helsingborgs-Posten*. The National Association for Women's Political Suffrage is formed.
1904	Leaves her post at *Helsingborgs-Posten*. In spring travels to London. Becomes engaged to a colleague from *Helsingborgs-Posten*, Hjalmar Jönsson. In December in Stockholm, as a contributor to the conservative journal *Vårt land*. Awarded third prize in a competition arranged by the women's weekly *Idun* for 'Fröknarna von Uhrn: skiss' (The Misses von Uhrn: A Sketch).

Chronology

1905　Spends the spring at her uncle's in Berg in an attempt to recuperate from illness. Her engagement broken off in August. Ruth, her halfsister, drowns in a lake in Berg. Elin Wägner starts a notebook, 'Interiörer ur mitt privathelvete' (Interiors from My Private Hell).

1906　In Växjö, a town just south of Berg; deeply depressed. Attended by Linnéa Johansson, who is the same age as Elin Wägner, and gradually recovers. Sixteen short texts, 'snapshots', published in *Idun*.

1907　Publication of Wägner's first book, *Från det jordiska museet* (From the Human Museum), a collection of short stories and sketches. Develops her career in Stockholm: appointed Assistant Editor-in-Chief at *Idun*, and takes on freelance work at the liberal daily *Dagens Nyheter* and the magazine *Puck*. Instalments of *Norrtullsligan* (The Norrtull Gang) begin to appear in *Dagens Nyheter* in November.

1908　Publication in book form of the novel *Norrtullsligan*.
Becomes involved in work for suffrage for women. Linnéa Johansson arrives in Stockholm to keep house for Elin Wägner.

1909　Attends the Fifth Congress of the International Woman Suffrage Alliance in London.
The General Strike in Sweden. Sweden introduces universal suffrage for men.

1910　The novel *Pennskaftet* (*Penwoman*).
Norrtullsligan published in German.
October: Elin Wägner engaged to Dr John Landquist. They marry on 6 November.

1911　'Fru Hillevis dagbok' (Mrs Hillevi's Diary), a series of light-hearted columns, is published in *Idun*. Wägner writes the script of the film *Hon fick platsen* (She Got the Job), which has its première the same year with Wägner playing a woman journalist looking for a job.
Norrtullsligan published in Norwegian.
Pennskaftet published in Danish.
The Sixth Congress of the International Woman Suffrage Alliance takes place in Stockholm in June. Wägner produces a newspaper, Rösträtt för kvinnor (Votes for Women), which is sold at the Congress.

1912　Writes the script of the film *Systrarna* (The Sisters), which receives its première the same year. *Pennskaftet* and *Norrtullsligan* published in Russian.

1913　The novel *Helga Wisbeck*.

1914　*Mannen med körsbären* (The Man with the Cherries), a collection of short stories.

371

Pennskaftet published in German.

Wägner involved in the formation of *Föreningen Frisinnade Kvinnor* (the Swedish Women's Liberal Association). Signatures collected as part of the campaign for women's suffrage, with a famous photo showing Wägner next to a pile of ringbinders considerably taller than herself: these contain 351,454 signatures.

The First World War begins.

1915 *Camillas äktenskap* (Camilla's Marriage), a novel.

Takes part in the Women's International Congress at The Hague, 27 April – 1 May, the immediate aim of which is to bring about a ceasefire. At the Congress, the International Committee of Women for Permanent Peace is formed; this subsequently becomes the Women's International League for Peace and Freedom.

1916 *Släkten Jerneploogs framgång* (The Rise of the House of Jerneploog), a novel.

Camillas äktenskap published in Dutch.

Leaves *Idun*. Sven Wägner dies in June. Wägner's sister-in-law, Ellen Landquist, dies in November.

1917 *Vansklighetens land* (The Perilous Land), a novel.

With Anna Lenah Elgström and Frida Stéenhoff Elin Wägner edits a volume in honour of the Hungarian pacifist campaigner Rosika Schwimmer, *Den kinesiska muren. Rosika Schwimmers kamp för rätten och hennes krig mot kriget* (The Great Wall of China: Rosika Schwimmer's Struggle for Justice and her War against the War). Wägner contributes four essays.

1918 The novel *Åsa-Hanna*, i.e. *Vansklighetens land* with minor changes and a new title.

End of the First World War.

1919 Two novels published, *Den befriade kärleken* (Love Liberated), and *Kvarteret Oron* (District of Unrest).

Camillas äktenskap published in Finnish.

With Anna Lenah Elgström, Naima Sahlbom and Frida Stéenhoff, Wägner edits *En bok om Ellen Key* (A Book about Ellen Key) on the occasion of Key's seventieth birthday. Wägner contributes an essay on Key and the women's cause.

A Swedish section of The Women's International League for Peace and Freedom is formed.

The Swedish *Rädda Barnen* (Save the Children) is formed in December, with Wägner as one of five founder members.

Chronology

In May the bill introducing suffrage for women is passed by the *riksdag*.

1920   The novel *Den förödda vingården* (The Ravaged Vineyard).
Wägner in Vienna, assisting with the first relief action organised by the Swedish Save the Children.

1921   *Nyckelknippan* (The Bunch of Keys), a collection of short stories. Commissioned with Gunnar Vall, minister in Vingåker in Södermanland, by *Förbundet för kristet samhällsliv* (The Society for Christianising Social Life) to visit the French-occupied Rhineland and report on their findings. Vall and Wägner spend 20 Feb. – 3 March in the Rhineland. Wägner subsequently spends several months in London.
Harald Wägner gets divorced. Just over a year old his son, Harald Giovanni (Vanni), comes to live with Elin Wägner and John Landquist.
The Swedish Women's Liberal Association becomes the National Association of Swedish Liberal Women in the autumn.
For the first time, women in Sweden are entitled to vote in an election to the *riksdag*. The first women, five in all, take their seats in the *riksdag*.

1922   The novel *Den namnlösa* (The Anonymous Woman).
January: Wägner and Landquist divorce.
Summer: the first course at what will become the Women Citizens' College at Fogelstad.
November: second trip to the Rhineland, this time with the English Quaker Marion Fox.

1923   Publication of *Från Seine, Rhen och Ruhr. Små historier från Europa* (From the Seine, the Rhine and the Ruhr: Anecdotes from Europe).
Norrtullsligan is turned into a film, the script having been written by the author Hjalmar Bergman. The film is premièred in December.
France occupies the Ruhr District in January, and Wägner visits the occupied area in February.
Awarded Grand Prize by *Samfundet De Nio* (The Society of Nine) in May. Discovers Gandhi during the summer. Augusta Wägner, Wägner's step-mother, dies in September. Wägner moves to Lund in October. On 24 November publication of the first issue of *Tidevarvet* (The Epoch), with Wägner on the editorial board. In autumn buys plot of land in Berg, Småland.

1924   The novel *Silverforsen* (The Silver Rapids).

In spring with Quakers in Pfalz; also visits the occupied section of the Rhineland. July: becomes Editor of *Tidevarvet*.

1925 Lilla Björka built on the plot of land in Berg; the architect is Carl Bergsten.

The Women Citizens' College at Fogelstad arranges its first regular course.

Death of Harald Wägner.

Elin Wägner has an affair with the author Sigfrid Siwertz.

1926 The novel *Natten till söndag* (Saturday Night). A slightly different version serialised in *Tidevarvet*, March – September.

1927 The novel *De fem pärlorna* (The Five Pearls). In a version entitled *Credo* it has been serialised in *Tidevarvet* between March and September and subsequently published in *Tidevarvets romanbibliotek* (The Epoch Novel Library).

The film *Ungdom* (Youth), the script written by Elin Wägner and Ragnar Hyltén-Cavallius, is premièred in August.

Elin Wägner moves to Lilla Björka on a near-permanent basis. At the end of the year she resigns as Editor of *Tidevarvet* but remains on the editorial board.

1928 *Den odödliga gärningen* (The Immortal Act), a collection of short stories.

1929 The novel *Svalorna flyga högt* (The Swallows are Flying High).

1930 *Korpungen och jag* (The Young Raven and Me), a collection of articles from *Tidevarvet*.

Svalorna flyga högt published in Danish.

Three radio dramas are broadcast, *Barnjungfrun* (The Nurse Maid) in February, *Tre åldrar* (Three Ages) in June, and *En helgonlegend* (A Legend) in December.

1931 *Gammalrödja. Skildring från en bygd som ömsar skinn* (Gammalrödja: Stories from a District Changing its Skin), a collection of short stories.

Two radio dramas: *Han som blödde* (He who Bled) in May, and *Sjömansbruden* (The Sailor's Bride) in September.

The National Association of Liberal Women becomes *Svenska Kvinnors Vänsterförbund* (The Association of Swedish Women on the Left).

1932 The novel *Dialogen fortsätter* (The Dialogue is Continuing).

As she turns 50 on 16 May, Wägner is honoured with a copy of the specially made journal *Bergsluft* (Berg/Mountain Air). The

contributors include the journalist Barbro Alving, the author Karin Boye, Linnéa Johansson, the journalist and author Ester Blenda Nordström, the theologian Emilia Fogelklou Norlind, and the journalist Ria Wägner.
With the end of the year, Wägner resigns from the editorial board of *Tidevarvet*.

1933 The novel *Mannen vid min sida* (The Man at my Side).
In early spring travels to Spain and North Africa. Later in the year visits Orrefors in Småland and meets Flory Gate and her husband Simon, a famous glass designer.
Adolf Hitler becomes Chancellor of Germany.

1934 *Credo*, a drama for radio.
In May travels to Leningrad and Moscow on a trip organised by *Morgonbris*, the journal of the Social Democratic Women's Association.

1935 The novel *Vändkorset* (The Turnstile) is serialised in *Konsumentbladet*, the magazine of the Swedish Cooperative movement. The novel is published in book form later in the year.
During the summer, Wägner is involved in organising the Women's Unarmed Revolt against War and is part of the delegation sent to the League of Nations in Geneva in September. On this occasion, Wägner also takes part in the founding of Women's Organisation for World Order (WOWO).
October: Italy attacks Abyssinia.

1936 Wägner and Flory Gate participate in the WOWO Congress in Salzburg.
With the end of the year, *Tidevarvet* ceases publication.
The Spanish Civil War begins.

1937 The novel *Genomskådad* (Unmasked).
Wägner and Flory Gate participate in the WOWO Congress in Bratislava. One of the speakers is Mina Hofstetter, an ecological farmer from Switzerland.
Wägner visits Greece.

1938 The novel *Hemlighetsfull* (Secretive).
Wägner is elected a member of *Samfundet De Nio* (The Society of Nine). Wägner and Gate visit Mina Hofstetter in Switzerland.
The annexation of Austria by Germany takes place in March. In September Hitler makes claims to the Sudetenland. The Munich agreement between Hitler and Neville Chamberlain: 'Peace in our

time'.
1939 *Tusen år i Småland* (A Thousand Years in Småland), a travelogue-cum-local-history with an ecofeminist slant.
End of the Spanish Civil War. Hitler occupies the remainder of Czechoslovakia. The Second World War begins on 1 September.
1940 *Fred med jorden* (Peace with the Earth), a pacifist/ecofeminist pamphlet by Elisabeth Tamm and Elin Wägner.
Flory Gate buys a farm in Rösås in Berg, Småland, and embarks on farming in accordance with ecological principles.
1941 The pamphlet *Väckarklocka* (Alarm Clock).
Spinnerskan (The Spinster), a radio drama.
1942 Publication of *Selma Lagerlöf, 1: Från Mårbacka till Jerusalem* (Selma Lagerlöf, 1: From Mårbacka to Jerusalem), the first part of a biography of the Swedish Nobel laureate.
Åsa-Hanna and *Väckarklocka* are published in Danish.
1943 *Selma Lagerlöf, 2: Från Jerusalem till Mårbacka* (Selma Lagerlöf, 2: From Jerusalem to Mårbacka).
The first part of the biography is published in Danish.
1944 Wägner is elected a member of the Swedish Academy, succeeding the philosopher Hans Larsson. Publication of *Hans Larsson*, the speech with which she takes her entry.
The two volumes of the Lagerlöf biography are published in Finnish.
Film version of *Vändkorset*, after a script written by Ragnar Hyltén-Cavallius and Bengt Janzon.
1945 *Svalorna flyga högt* and *Vändkorset* are published in Finnish.
The second volume of the Lagerlöf biography is published in Danish.
The first atomic bomb is dropped over Hiroshima on 6 August, and the second over Nagasaki on 9 August. End of the Second World War.
1946 Film version of *Åsa-Hanna*, after a script by Barbro Alving.
Åsa-Hanna and *Väckarklocka* are published in Norwegian.
1947 The novel *Vinden vände bladen* (The Wind Turned the Leaves Over).
1948 *Spinnerskan* (The Spinster), a collection of short stories.
November: Wägner has surgery for cancer.
1949 Wägner dies in Flory Gate's house at Rösås on 7 January. Funeral in the church in Berg, 13 January. Burial in Anna Wägner's grave at *Norra kyrkogården* in Lund, with Wägner's friend Emilia Fogelklou conducting the service.
Fredrika Bremer. Minnesteckning (Fredrika Bremer: A Memorial Sketch) is published posthumously.

Select Bibliography

The alphabetical order used here is the Swedish one, i.e. [...] z, å, ä, ö.

I. Unpublished material

(a) *Manuscript material*
(i) Göteborg University Library: The Women's History Collections
Andrea Andreen-Svedberg's Collection, A 49.
Ada Nilsson's Collection, A 22.

(ii) Sveriges Radios arkiv, Stockholm
Elin Wägner, *Barnjungfrun*, broadcast 25 Feb. 1930, 'Kvinnans kvart'; RTEA MI:226
Elin Wägner, *Tre åldrar*, broadcast 3 June 1930, 'Kvinnans kvart'; RTEA MI:289
Elin Wägner, *En helgonlegend*, broadcast 29 Dec. 1930, 'Kvinnans kvart'; RTEA MI:344
Elin Wägner, *Han som blödde. Sketch*, broadcast 8 May 1931; RTEA MI:402
Elin Wägner, *Sjömansbruden. Pjäs*, broadcast 26 Sept. 1931; RTEA MI:437
Elin Wägner and Ragnar Hyltén-Cavallius, *Credo. Pjäs i fem akter*, broadcast 24 Oct. 1934; RTEA MI: 762
Elin Wägner, *Spinnerskan. Radiospel*, broadcast 8 May 1941; RTEA MI:1752

(b) *Other unpublished material*
Andersson, Irene. 1993. 'Wiener Call-Club' och 'Womens [sic] Organisation for World Order – WOWO'. En internationell organisations kamp för en ny värld. Lund: University of Lund, Dept. of History.
Death, Sarah. 1985. The Female Perspective in the Novels of Fredrika Bremer and Elin Wägner: A Comparative Study of Some Central Themes. London: University of London.
Halvardson, Margret and Susanne Töringe. 1979. *Elin Wägner. Bidrag till en bibliografi*. Borås: Bibliotekshögskolan. (Specialarbete 1979:39).

II. Published material

(a) Material by Elin Wägner (and co-authors/co-editors)

(Any signatures used have been given here. In the case of the serial 'Fru Hillevis dagbok', there is some variation between the use of signature/neither signature nor full name/full name, as shown here.)

Wägner, Elin. (sign. [drawing of wasp about to sting]). 1907a. Klubben. Upprinnelsen. Första sammanträdet. *Puck* 8 May.
- (sign. [drawing of wasp about to sting]). 1907b. Klubben. Andra sammanträdet. *Puck* 16 May.
- (sign. [drawing of wasp about to sting]). 1907c. Klubben. Tredje sammanträdet. *Puck* 23 May.
- (sign. [drawing of wasp about to sting]). 1907d. Klubben. Fjärde sammanträdet. *Puck* 30 May.
- (sign. [drawing of wasp about to sting]). 1907e. Klubben. Femte sammanträdet. *Puck* 6 June.
- (sign. [drawing of wasp about to sting]). 1907f. Klubben. Sjätte sammanträdet. *Puck* 13 June.
- (sign. [drawing of wasp about to sting]). 1907g. Klubben. Sjunde sammanträdet. *Puck* 27 June.
- (sign. [drawing of wasp about to sting]). 1907h. Klubben. Den hotas med upplösning. *Puck* 4 July.
- (sign. [drawing of wasp about to sting]). 1907i. Klubben. Ingenuen och Kvinnan med ett Förflutet. *Puck* 13 July.
- (sign. [drawing of wasp about to sting]). 1907j. Klubben. *Puck* 20 July.
- (sign. [drawing of wasp about to sting]). 1907k. Klubben sammanträder i en syrénberså. *Puck* 27 July.
- (sign. [drawing of wasp about to sting]). 1907l. Klubben. Journalistens historia. *Puck* 3 Aug.
- (sign. [drawing of wasp about to sting]). 1907m. Klubben. Fröken Julies födelsedag. *Puck* 24 Aug.
- (sign. [drawing of wasp about to sting]) 1907n. Klubben. Storstadsfröken på landet. *Puck* 31 Aug.
- (sign. [drawing of wasp about to sting]). 1907o. Klubben. Ingenuens afsättning. *Puck* 5 Oct.
- 1907p. *Från det jordiska museet. Skisser.* Stockholm: Albert Bonniers förlag.
- (sign. Elisabeth). 1907q. Norrtullsligans krönika. Lösryckta blad ur en

Select Bibliography

dagbok, I. *Dagens Nyheter* 3 Nov.
- (sign. Elisabeth). 1907r. Norrtullsligans krönika. Lösryckta blad ur en dagbok, II. *Dagens Nyheter* 10 Nov.
- 1907s. Norrtullsligans krönika, III. *Dagens Nyheter* 14 Nov.
- 1907t. Norrtullsligans krönika, IV. *Dagens Nyheter* 17 Nov.
- (sign. Elisabeth). 1907u. Norrtullsligans krönika. Lösryckta blad ur en dagbok, V. *Dagens Nyheter* 23 Nov.
- (sign. Elisabeth). 1907v. Norrtullsligans krönika. Lösryckta blad ur en dagbok, VI. *Dagens Nyheter* 24 Nov.
- (sign. Elisabeth). 1907x. Norrtullsligans krönika. Lösryckta blad ur en dagbok, VII. *Dagens Nyheter* 1 Dec.
- (sign. Elisabeth). 1907y. Norrtullsligans krönika. Lösryckta blad ur en dagbok, VIII [erroneously numbered IX]. *Dagens Nyheter* 8 Dec.
- (sign. Elisabeth). 1907z. Norrtullsligans krönika. Lösryckta blad ur en dagbok, IX. *Dagens Nyheter* 13 Dec.
- (sign. Elisabeth). 1907aa. Norrtullsligans krönika. Lösryckta blad ur en dagbok, X. *Dagens Nyheter* 15 Dec.
- (sign. Elisabeth). 1907ab. Norrtullsligans krönika. Lösryckta blad ur en dagbok, XI. *Dagens Nyheter* 22 Dec.
- (sign. Elisabeth). 1907ac. Norrtullsligans krönika. Lösryckta blad ur en dagbok, XII [erroneously numbered XIII]. *Dagens Nyheter* 28 Dec.
- (sign. Elisabeth). 1907ad. Norrtullsligans krönika. Lösryckta blad ur en dagbok, XIII [erroneously numbered XIV]. *Dagens Nyheter* 29 Dec.
- (sign. Elisabeth). 1908a. Norrtullsligans krönika. Lösryckta blad ur en dagbok, XIV [erroneously numbered XV]. *Dagens Nyheter* 5 Jan.
- (sign. Elisabeth). 1908b. Norrtullsligans krönika. Lösryckta blad ur en dagbok, XV [erroneously numbered XVI]. *Dagens Nyheter* 12 Jan.
- (sign. Elisabeth). 1908c. Norrtullsligans krönika. Lösryckta blad ur en dagbok, XVI [erroneously numbered XVII]. *Dagens Nyheter* 19 Jan.
- (sign. Elisabeth). 1908d. Norrtullsligans krönika. Lösryckta blad ur en dagbok, XVII [erroneously numbered XVIII]. *Dagens Nyheter* 26 Jan.
- (sign. Elisabeth). 1908e. Norrtullsligans krönika. Ligan skingrad. – Ett bref till Baby från Elisabeth. *Dagens Nyheter* 2 Feb.
- (sign. E-ER.). 1908f. En timme hos Ellen Key. *Idun* 6 Feb.: 73-74.
- 1908g. Kvinnan som arbetar. I. Tjänarinnan. *Idun* 30 Jan.: 56-57.
- 1908h. Kvinnan som arbetar. II. De kvinnliga poststationsföreståndarna. *Idun* 5 March: 118-19.
- 1908i. Kvinnan som arbetar. III. Fabriksarbeterskan. *Idun* 23 April: 202-203.

- 1908j. Kvinnan som arbetar. IV. Fabriksarbeterskan. *Idun* 23 July: 362-63.
- 1908k. Kvinnan som arbetar. V. Kvinnliga hönsodlare. *Idun* 24 Sept.: 473.
- 1908l. Kvinnan som arbetar. VI. Kvinnorna och restaurantrörelsen. *Idun* 26 Nov.: 584-85.
- 1908m. Kvinnan som arbetar. VII. Hvita Bandets restaurantrörelse. *Idun* 3 Dec.: 601.
- 1908n. *Norrtullsligan. Elisabeths krönika.* Stockholm: Aktiebolaget Ljus.
- 1909. Kvinnan som arbetar. Kontorister och stenografer. *Idun* 28 March: 155.
- 1910. *Pennskaftet.* Stockholm: Aktiebolaget Ljus.
- (sign. Hillevi). 1911a. Fru Hillevis dagbok, I. *Idun* 8 Jan.: 5.
- 1911b. Fru Hillevis dagbok, II. *Idun* 22 Jan.: 39.
- 1911c. Fru Hillevis dagbok, III. *Idun* 5 Feb.: 73.
- 1911d. Fru Hillevis dagbok, IV. *Idun* 19 Feb.: 102-103.
- 1911e. Fru Hillevis dagbok, V. *Idun* 5 March: 139.
- 1911f. Fru Hillevis dagbok, VI. *Idun* 19 March: 171.
- 1911g. Fru Hillevis dagbok, VII. *Idun* 2 April: 200.
- 1911h. Fru Hillevis dagbok, VIII. *Idun* 16 April: 235.
- 1911i. Fru Hillevis dagbok, IX. *Idun* 30 April: 267.
- 1911j. Fru Hillevis dagbok, X. *Idun* 28 May: 331.
- 1911k. Fru Hillevis dagbok, XI. *Idun* 17 Sept.: 602-03.
- 1911l. Fru Hillevis dagbok, XII. *Idun* 26 Nov.: 763.
- 1911m. Fru Hillevis dagbok, XIII. *Idun* 17 Dec.: 806.
- 1911n. Fru Hillevis dagbok, XIV. *Idun* 24 Dec.: 826.
- 1912a. Fru Hillevis dagbok. Tredje könet håller möte. *Idun* 3 March: 137.
- 1912b. *Norrtullsligan. Elisabeths krönika.* Stockholm: Albert Bonniers förlag. (Albert Bonniers 25-öresböcker, 18).
- 1915a. Ett vackert föredöme i enighet och fredsvilja: Kongressen öppnas. *Idun* 16 May: 309-12.
- 1915b. Ett vackert föredöme i enighet och fredsvilja: Förhandlingar och beslut. *Idun* 16 May: 312-13.
- 1915c. Ett vackert föredöme i enighet och fredsvilja: Trots allt. *Idun* 16 May: 313-14.
- (sign. E.W.). 1915d. Färden genom Tyskland. *Idun* 23 May: 327-28.
- (sign. E.W.). 1915e. Croquiser från Haag. *Idun* 23 May: 328.

Select Bibliography

- 1915f. Kvinnornas fredsombud. *Idun* 13 June: 373-74.
- 1915g. Ett vägrödjningsarbete. *Idun* 22 Aug.: 534-35.
- 1917a. Katastrofen. In *Den kinesiska muren. Rosika Schwimmers kamp för rätten och hennes krig mot kriget*, ed. Anna Lenah Elgström, Frida Stéenhoff, Elin Wägner, 58-71. Stockholm: AB Dahlberg & Co:s förlag.
- 1917b. Erövringen av Amerika. In *Den kinesiska muren. Rosika Schwimmers kamp för rätten och hennes krig mot kriget*, ed. Anna Lenah Elgström, Frida Stéenhoff, Elin Wägner, 74-79. Stockholm: AB Dahlberg & Co:s förlag.
- 1917c. Underverket. In *Den kinesiska muren. Rosika Schwimmers kamp för rätten och hennes krig mot kriget*, ed. Anna Lenah Elgström, Frida Stéenhoff, Elin Wägner, 138-60. Stockholm: AB Dahlberg & Co:s förlag.
- 1917d. Se drömmaren. In *Den kinesiska muren. Rosika Schwimmers kamp för rätten och hennes krig mot kriget*, ed. Anna Lenah Elgström, Frida Stéenhoff, Elin Wägner, 269-72. Stockholm: AB Dahlberg & Co:s förlag.
- 1917e. *Vanslighetens land. Roman.* Stockholm: Iduns redaktion. (Iduns romanbibliotek, No. LXIX).
- 1918. *Åsa-Hanna. Roman.* Stockholm: Albert Bonniers förlag.
- 1919a. De tre kraven. Ett kapitel om Ellen Key och kvinnosaken. In *En bok om Ellen Key*, 131-56. Stockholm: Albert Bonniers förlag.
- 1919b. *Den befriade kärleken. Roman.* Stockholm: Albert Bonniers förlag.
- 1919c. *Kvarteret Oron. En Stockholmshistoria.* Stockholm: Albert Bonniers förlag.
- 1920a. I förödmjukelsens dal. 'Vi ha', försäkra tyskarna, 'fått högsta priset i nöd'. *Dagens Nyheter* 11 Jan.
- 1920b. Inför barnens martyrium. *Dagens Nyheter* 19 Jan.
- 1920c. Människor med eldsjäl i kamp för barnens väl: intryck från Genève. *Dagens Nyheter* 20 Jan.
- 1920d. Med 'ententetåget' Zürich – Wien. *Dagens Nyheter* 25 Jan.
- 1920e. 'Alla onda drömmars land'[.] Wiens tragedi – en paralell [sic] till Jerusalems undergång. *Dagens Nyheter* 3 Feb.
- 1920f. Hur Sverge ger i Wien. Den nyaste hjälpformen bespisning av ungdomar. *Dagens Nyheter* 7 Feb.
- 1920g. Bland ödelagda hjärtan, hungrande och hatande, i ungerska huvudstaden. *Dagens Nyheter* 27 Feb.

- 1920h. Mellan tiggaren och miljonpälsen. *Dagens Nyheter* 13 March.
- 1920i. Effektiv hjälp till studenterna i Wien härifrån. *Dagens Nyheter* 17 March.
- 1920j. Brottsligheten i det hemsökta Wien förfärande. *Dagens Nyheter* 18 March.
- 1920k. Tre hus. *Dagens Nyheter* 22 March.
- 1920l. Det dödströtta Europa. *Dagens Nyheter* 7 April.
- 1920m. Terrorism i Ungern. *Dagens Nyheter* 4 May.
- 1920n. Svenskt sjukhus uppföres i Wien. *Dagens Nyheter* 20 May.
- 1920o. *Den förödda vingården*. Stockholm: Albert Bonniers förlag.
- 1922. *Den namnlösa*. Stockholm: Albert Bonniers förlag.
- 1923a. Liv eller död. *Tidevarvet* 1 Dec.: 1-2. Reprinted in Elin Wägner. 1999. *Vad tänker du, mänsklighet?*, ed. Helena Forsås-Scott, 90-93. Stockholm: Norstedts förlag.
- 1923b. En negerstat i staten. *Tidevarvet* 8 Dec.: 1, 5, 6. Reprinted in Elin Wägner. 1999. *Vad tänker du, mänsklighet?*, ed. Helena Forsås-Scott, 94-100. Stockholm: Norstedts förlag.
- 1923c. *Från Seine, Rhen och Ruhr. Små historier från Europa*. Stockholm: Albert Bonniers förlag.
- 1927. *De fem pärlorna*. Stockholm: Albert Bonniers förlag.
- 1930. Hemmet i den nya världen. Stockholmsutställningen 1930. *Tidevarvet* 29 March: 1, 6.
- 1932. *Dialogen fortsätter. Roman*. Stockholm: Albert Bonniers förlag.
- 1933. *Mannen vid min sida*. Stockholm: Albert Bonniers förlag.
- 1935a. Lysistrates och fredens timma. *Dagens Nyheter* 11 Jan. Reprinted in Elin Wägner. 1999. *Vad tänker du, mänsklighet?*, ed. Helena Forsås-Scott, 172-79. Stockholm: Norstedts förlag.
- 1935b. Vad tänker du, mänsklighet? *Tidevarvet* 7 Sept.: 3-5. Reprinted in Elin Wägner. 1999. *Vad tänker du, mänsklighet?*, ed. Helena Forsås-Scott, 184-90. Stockholm: Norstedts förlag.
- 1935c. *Vändkorset. Roman*. Stockholm: Albert Bonniers förlag.
- 1936. Två landskap. Ett resebrev. *Tidevarvet* 8 Aug.: 1, 4. Reprinted in Elin Wägner. 1999. *Vad tänker du, mänsklighet?*, ed. Helena Forsås-Scott, 204-08. Stockholm: Norstedts förlag.
- 1937. *Genomskådad. Roman*. Stockholm: Albert Bonniers förlag.
- 1938. *Hemlighetsfull. Roman*. Stockholm: Albert Bonniers förlag.
- 1939. *Tusen år i Småland*. Stockholm: Wahlström & Widstrand.
- 1941. *Väckarklocka*. Stockholm: Albert Bonniers förlag.
- 1942. *Selma Lagerlöf*, Vol. 1, *Från Mårbacka till Jerusalem*.

Stockholm: Albert Bonniers förlag.
- 1943. *Selma Lagerlöf*, Vol. 2, *Från Jerusalem till Mårbacka*. Stockholm: Albert Bonniers förlag.
- 1944. *Läs den!*. Katrineholm.
- 1946. *Åsa-Hanna. Roman*. Stockholm: Albert Bonniers förlag.
- 1947. *Vinden vände bladen*. Stockholm: Albert Bonniers förlag.
- 1948. *Spinnerskan. Noveller*. Stockholm: Albert Bonniers förlag.
- 1978. *Väckarklocka. Med inledning av Erik Hjalmar Linder*. Wägner's text orig. publ. 1941. Stockholm: Bonnier. (Delfinserien).
- 1997a. The River and the Discharge Ditch. Extract from *Tusen år i Småland*. Tr. Sarah Death. *Swedish Book Review*, Supplement, 45-48.
- 1997b. Alarm Clock. Extract from *Väckarklocka*. Tr. Sarah Death. *Swedish Book Review*, Supplement, 49-52.
- 1999. *Vad tänker du, mänsklighet? Texter om feminism, fred och miljö*, ed. Helena Forsås-Scott. Stockholm: Norstedts förlag.
- 2002. *Stockholm Stories* [*Norrtullsligan* and *Kvarteret Oron*]. Tr. Betty Cain and Ulla Sweedler. XLibris Corporation.
- 2003. *Pennskaftet*. Orig. publ. 1910. Ed. Helena Forsås-Scott. Stockholm: Atlantis (Svenska Klassiker utgivna av Svenska Akademien).
- 2007. *Väckarklocka*. Orig. publ. 1941. Stockholm: Albert Bonniers förlag. (Bonniers klassiker).
- 2009. *Penwoman*. Sw. orig. publ. 1910. Tr. Sarah Death. London: Norvik Press.

Elgström, Anna Lenah, Naima Sahlbom, Frida Stéenhoff, and Elin Wägner. 1917. Förord. In *Den kinesiska muren. Rosika Schwimmers kamp för rätten och hennes krig mot kriget*, 5. Stockholm: AB Dahlberg & Co:s förlag.

Gustafson, Ruth, Rut Grubb and Elin Wägner. 1938. Kvinnornas kris. Bilaga till SOU 1938:19, Yttrande med socialetiska synpunkter på befolkningsfrågan avlämnat av Befolkningskommissionen. Stockholm. Reprinted in Elin Wägner. 1999. *Vad tänker du, mänsklighet?*, ed. Helena Forsås-Scott, 236-50. Stockholm: Norstedts förlag.

Kellin, Sam and Elin Wägner. 1907. *Sommarflirt*. *Dagens Nyheter* 30 June – 8 Aug.

Tamm, Elisabeth and Elin Wägner. 1985. *Fred med jorden*. Orig. publ. 1940. Knivsta: Arkturus.

(b) Other material
(Note: Pamphlets etc. published by *Frisinnade Kvinnors Riksförbund* and other political associations and having no named author/s have been listed here as anonymous. Ada Nilsson in *Barrikaden valde oss* (1940) gives Wägner as the author of several of them, but since this programmatic material was published on behalf of political associations and not as the work of specific individuals, I have preferred to stick to the anonymity of the published texts. Some of these pamphlets are scarce, and below I have given details of the manuscript collections in which I have found them.)

Anon. 1905. Junidagarna 1905. *Dagny*: 237-38.
Anon. 1910. Till Rosa Mayreders porträtt. *Dagny*: 169-70.
Anon. 1911. Rösträttskvinnan i hemmet. *Iduns kongressnummer*: 378.
Anon. 1920. Spalten om böckerna [review of *Den förödda vingården*, by Elin Wägner]. *Idun* 5 Dec.: 826-27, 833.
Anon. 1923a. Program och stadgar för Frisinnade Kvinnors Riksförbund. Stockholm (Föreningen Frisinnade Kvinnors Småskrifter, 4) [Göteborg University Library, The Women's History Collections, Ada Nilsson's Collection, A 22].
Anon. 1923b. Tidevarvet. *Tidevarvet* 24 Nov.: 1.
Anon. 1925a. Kvinnliga medborgarskolan i Fogelstad. *Tidevarvet* 21 Feb.: 1.
Anon. 1925b. Kvinnlig medborgarbildning. *Tidevarvet* 21 Feb.: 1, 4.
Anon. 1928. Uttalande inför Andrakammarvalen 1928. Frisinnade Kvinnors Riksförbund, Katrineholm [Göteborg University Library, The Women's History Collections, Andrea Andreen-Svedberg's Collection, A 49].
Anon. 1932. Uttalande inför Andrakammarvalen 1932. Radikala gruppen av Svenska Kvinnors Vänsterförbund, Stockholm [Göteborg University Library, The Women's History Collections, Andrea Andreen-Svedberg's Collection, A 49].
Anon. 1935. Representantmötets resolution. *Tidevarvet* 7 Sept.: 1.
Anon. 1940. 'Omistliga värden'. Uttalanden och synpunkter. Radikala Föreningen [Göteborg University Library, The Women's History Collections, Andrea Andreen-Svedberg's Collection, A 49].
Anon. 1944. Förslag till representationsreform på grundval av 50/50, framlagt av Sveriges Radikala Kvinnoförbund [Göteborg University Library, The Women's History Collections, Andrea Andreen-Svedberg's Collection, A 49; pp. 3-4 missing from this copy].
Addams, Jane, Emily G. Balch, and Alice Hamilton. 2003. *Women at The*

Select Bibliography

Hague: The International Congress of Women and its Results. Orig. publ. 1915. Introduction by Harriet Hyman Alonso. Urbana and Chicago: University of Illinois Press.
Adorno, Theodor W. 1984. The Essay as Form. Orig. publ. 1958. Tr. Bob Hullot-Kentor and Frederic Will. *New German Critique*: 151-71.
Ahlenius, Holger. 1932. Review of *Dialogen fortsätter*, by Elin Wägner. *Morgontidningen* 3 Dec.
– 1950. Inledning. In *Åsa-Hanna*, by Elin Wägner, ed. Holger Ahlenius, 7-22. Stockholm: Albert Bonniers förlag. (Valda skrifter, 2).
– 1954. Inledning. In *Vinden vände bladen*, by Elin Wägner, ed. Holger Ahlenius, 7-30. Stockholm: Albert Bonniers förlag. (Valda skrifter, 13-14).
Allan, Tuzyline Jita. 1993. A Voice of One's Own: Implications of Impersonality in the Essays of Virginia Woolf and Alice Walker. In *The Politics of the Essay: Feminist Perspectives*, ed. Ruth-Ellen Boetcher Joeres and Elizabeth Mittman, 131-47. Bloomington and Indianapolis: Indiana University Press.
Alonso, Harriet Hyman. 2003. Introduction to the Illinois Edition. In *Women at The Hague: The International Congress of Women and its Results*, ed. Jane Addams, Emily G. Balch and Alice Hamilton, vii-xl. Urbana and Chicago: University of Illinois Press.
Alving, Barbro. 1968. Från Pennskaft till Väckarklocka. Rösträttskamp och mödraauktoritet hos Elin Wägner. In *Könsroller i litteraturen från antiken till 1960-talet*, ed. Karin Westman Berg, 123-39. Stockholm: Prisma.
Anderson, Benedict. 2003. *Imagined Communities: Reflections on the Origin and Spread of Nationalism*. Revised and extended ed. orig. publ. 1991. London and New York: Verso.
Anderson, Harriet. 1992. *Utopian Feminism: Women's Movements in fin-de-siècle Vienna.* New Haven and London: Yale University Press.
Andersson, Irene. 2001. *Kvinnor mot krig. Aktioner och nätverk för fred 1914-1940.* Lund: University of Lund, Dept. of History.
Andreen, Andrea. 1947. Fred genom samarbete. *Vi kvinnor.* Jan.: 1.
– 1964. *Svenska Kvinnors Vänsterförbund. En femtioårsberättelse.* Stockholm: Esselte.
Ardis, Ann L. 1990. *New Women, New Novels: Feminism and Early Modernism.* New Brunswick and London: Rutgers University Press.
Asplund, Johan. 1991. *Essä om Gemeinschaft och Gesellschaft.* Göteborg: Bokförlaget Korpen.

Aston, Elaine and George Savona. 1991. *Theatre as Sign-System: A Semiotics of Text and Performance*. London and New York: Routledge.

Auerbach, Nina. 1978. *Communities of Women: An Idea in Fiction*. Cambridge, MA and London: Harvard University Press.

Backberger, Barbro. 1979. Elin Wägner i dag politiskt omöjlig. *Dagens Nyheter* 28 June.

Bakhtin, M. M. 1994. *The Dialogic Imagination: Four Essays*. Tr. Caryl Emerson and Michael Holquist. Orig. publ. 1981. Austin: University of Texas Press.

Bal, Mieke. 1997. *Narratology: Introduction to the Theory of Narrative*. 1st edition orig. publ. 1985. Tr. Christine van Boheem. Toronto, Buffalo, London: University of Toronto Press.

– 1999. *Narratology: Introduction to the Theory of Narrative*. 2nd edition orig. publ. 1997. Toronto, Buffalo, London: University of Toronto Press.

Berger, Margareta. 1977. *Pennskaft. Kvinnliga journalister i svensk dagspress 1690-1975*. Stockholm: P.A. Norstedt & Söners förlag.

Bergman, Bo (sign. B. B-n.). 1920. Review of *Den förödda vingården*, by Elin Wägner. *Dagens Nyheter* 22 Nov.

Bergstrand, Allan (sign. A. B-nd.). 1918. Review of *Åsa-Hanna*, by Elin Wägner. *Social-Demokraten* 23 Dec.

– 1933. Review of *Mannen vid min sida*, by Elin Wägner. *Arbetet* 20 Dec.

Berkman, Joyce Avrech. 1989. *The Healing Imagination of Olive Schreiner: Beyond South African Colonialism*. Amherst: The University of Massachusetts Press.

Bibeln. 1917 translation.

The Bible. Authorised King James version.

Björck, Staffan. 1968. *Romanens formvärld. Studier i prosaberättarens teknik*. Orig. publ. 1953. Stockholm: Natur & Kultur.

Björk, Gunnela. 1999. *Att förhandla sitt medborgarskap. Kvinnor som kollektiva politiska aktörer i Örebro 1900-1950*. Lund: Arkiv förlag.

Björkenlid, Bertil. 1982. *Kvinnokrav i manssamhälle. Rösträttskvinnorna och deras metoder som opinionsbildare och påtryckargrupp i Sverige 1902-21*. Uppsala: University of Uppsala, Dept. of Literature.

Björkman-Goldschmidt, Elsa, ed. 1956a. *Fogelstad. Berättelsen om en skola*. Stockholm: P.A. Norstedt & Söners förlag.

– 1956b. Ebba Holgersson. In *Fogelstad. Berättelsen om en skola*, ed. Elsa Björkman-Goldschmidt, 69-77. Stockholm: P.A. Norstedt & Söners förlag.

Blom, Ida, 1996. Nation – Class – Gender: Scandinavia at the Turn of the Century. *Scandinavian Journal of History* 21: 1-16.
Bolander, Carl-August. 1927. Review of *De fem pärlorna*, by Elin Wägner. *Dagens Nyheter* 18 Nov.
Bolander, Carl-August (sign. C.-A.B.). 1933. Review of *Mannen vid min sida*, by Elin Wägner. *Dagens Nyheter* 29 Nov.
Boye, Karin. 1936. Elin Wägner. En översikt. *Ord & Bild*: 415-26.
– 1948. *Kallocain*. Orig. publ. 1940. Stockholm: Albert Bonniers förlag. (Samlade skrifter, 5).
Braidotti, Rosi. 1994. *Nomadic Subjects: Embodiment and Sexual Difference in Contemporary Feminist Theory*. New York: Columbia University Press.
– 2006. *Transpositions: On Nomadic Ethics*. Cambridge and Malden, MA: Polity Press.
Brandell, Elin (sign. Regan). 1908. Norrtullsligan i bok. Dess författarinna berättar om medlemmarna i ligan. *Dagens Nyheter* 16 April.
Brandell, Gunnar. 1967. *Svensk litteratur 1900-1950*. 2nd ed. First ed. publ. 1958. Stockholm: Aldus/Bonnier.
Brödje, Catrine. 1998. *Ett annat tiotal. En studie i Anna Lenah Elgströms tiotalsprosa*. Stehag: Förlags AB Gondolin.
Burwell, Jennifer. 1997. *Notes on Nowhere: Feminism, Utopian Logic, and Social Transformation*. Minneapolis and London: University of Minnesota Press.
Bussey, Gertrude and Margaret Tims. 1965. *Women's International League for Peace and Freedom 1915-1965: A Record of Fifty Years' Work*. London: George Allen & Unwin.
Butler, Judith. 1993. *Bodies that Matter: On the Discursive Limits of 'Sex'*. New York and London: Routledge.
– 2006. *Gender Trouble: Feminism and the Subversion of Identity*. Orig. publ. 1990. New York and London: Routledge.
Böök, Fredrik (sign. F. B.). 1927. Review of *De fem pärlorna*, by Elin Wägner. *Svenska Dagbladet* 24 Nov.
Carey, John. 1989. Introduction. In *The Faber Book of Reportage*, ed. John Carey, ixxx-xxxviii. Orig. publ. 1987. London: Faber & Faber.
Carlsson, Christina. 1986. *Kvinnosyn och kvinnopolitik. En studie av svensk socialdemokrati 1880-1910*. Lund: Arkiv förlag.
Carlsson, Sten. 1968a. Befolkningsutvecklingen 1860-1965. In *Den svenska historien*, vol. 9, ed. Jan Cornell, 30-34. Stockholm: Albert Bonniers förlag.

- 1968b. Den stora folkvandringen västerut. In *Den svenska historien*, vol. 9, ed. Jan Cornell, 35-42. Stockholm: Albert Bonniers förlag.
- 1968c. Sverige under första världskriget. In *Den svenska historien*, vol. 9, ed. Jan Cornell, 298-315. Stockholm: Albert Bonniers förlag.
- 1968d. Borgare och arbetare. In *Den svenska historien*, vol. 10, ed. Jan Cornell, 16-29. Stockholm: Albert Bonniers förlag.

Carlsson Wetterberg, Christina. 1994. Penningen, kärleken och makten. Frida Stéenhoffs feministiska alternativ. In *Det evigt kvinnliga. En historia om förändring*, ed. Ulla Wikander, 80-102. Stockholm: Tidens förlag.
- 2002. Med den fria kärleken på programmet. Frida Stéenhoff utmanar kyrkofäder och gammalfeminism. In *Rummet vidgas. Kvinnor på väg ut i offentligheten 1880-1940*, ed. Eva Österberg and Christina Carlsson Wetterberg, 166-208. Stockholm: Atlantis.

Childs, Marquis. 1936. *Sweden: The Middle Way*. London: Faber & Faber.

Cixous, Hélène and Catherine Clément. 1987. *The Newly Born Woman*. French orig. publ. 1975. Tr. Betsy Wing. Manchester: Manchester University Press.

Claréus, Ingrid. 1981. *Ellen Key och Elin Wägner*. Ellen Key-Sällskapet.

Clayhills, Harriet. 1983. 'Likhet' eller 'egenart'. Ett tema i feministisk debatt i Sverige under 1900-talet. In *Kvinnornas litteraturhistoria*, vol. 2, *Nittonhundratalet*, ed. Ingrid Holmquist and Ebba Witt-Brattström, 11-33. Stockholm: Författarförlaget.
- 1991. *Kvinnohistorisk uppslagsbok*. Stockholm: Rabén & Sjögren.

Cominos, Peter T. 1973. Innocent Femina Sensualis in Unconscious Conflict. In *Suffer and Be Still: Women in the Victorian Age*, ed. Martha Vicinus, 155-72. Bloomington and London: Indiana University Press.

Connell, R.W. 2005. *Gender*. Orig. publ. 2002. Cambridge and Malden, MA: Polity Press.

Crawford, Elizabeth. 2001. *The Women's Suffrage Movement: A Reference Guide 1866-1928*. Orig. publ. 1999. London and New York: Routledge.

Crook, Tim. 1999. *Radio Drama: Theory and Practice*. London and New York: Routledge.

Currie, Mark. 1998. *Postmodern Narrative Theory*. Basingstoke and London: Macmillan.

Dahlerup, Drude. 1973. *Socialisme og kvindefrigørelse i det 19. århundrede. En analyse af Charles Fourier, Karl Marx, Fr. Engels, August Bebel og Clara Zetkin m.fl*. Århus: GMT.

Death, Sarah. 1983. Sexual Politics and the Defeat of Sisterhood in Elin

Select Bibliography

Wägner's *Släkten Jerneploogs framgång* (The Rise of the House of Jerneploog). In *Mothers – Saviours – Peacemakers: Swedish Women Writers in the Twentieth Century*, ed. Karin Westman Berg and Gabriella Åhmansson, 125-44. Uppsala: University of Uppsala, Dept. of Literature.

– 1985. The Sleeping Fury: Symbol and Metaphor in Elin Wägner's *Silverforsen*. *Scandinavica*: 183-95.

Degler, Carl N. 1966. Introduction to the Torchbook Edition. In *Women and Economics: A Study of the Economic Relation between Men and Women as a Factor in Social Evolution*, by Charlotte Perkins Gilman. Orig. publ. 1898. vi-xxxv. New York, Hagerstown, San Francisco, London: Harper & Row.

Delanty, Gerard. 2008. *Community*. Orig. publ. 2003. London and New York: Routledge.

Dobson, Andrew and Derek Bell. 2006. Introduction. In *Environmental Citizenship*, ed. Andrew Dobson and Derek Bell, 1-17. Cambridge, MA and London: The MIT Press.

Domellöf, Gunilla. 1986. *I oss är en mångfald levande. Karin Boye som kritiker och prosamodernist*. Umeå: University of Umeå, Dept. of Literature.

– 2001. Elin Wägner. In *Mätt med främmande mått. Idéanalys av kvinnliga författares samtidsmottagande och romaner 1930-1935*, by Gunilla Domellöf, 217-57. Hedemora: Gidlunds förlag.

– 2003. Opinionsbildningen i *Tidevarvet* 1923-1936. Upptakten och anknytningen till det liberalfeministiska arvet. In *Kvinnorna skall göra det! Den kvinnliga medborgarskolan vid Fogelstad – som idé, text och historia*, ed. Ebba Witt-Brattström and Lena Lennerhed, 122-42. Huddinge: Södertörns Högskola, Samtidshistoriska institutet.

DuPlessis, Rachel Blau. 1985. *Writing Beyond the Ending: Narrative Strategies of Twentieth-Century Women Writers*. Bloomington: Indiana University Press.

Edling, Nils. 1996. *Det fosterländska hemmet. Egnahemspolitik, småbruk och hemideologi kring sekelskiftet 1900*. Stockholm: Carlssons bokförlag.

Egeland, Marianne. 2000. *Hvem bestemmer over livet? Biografien som historisk og litterær genre*. Oslo: Universitetsforlaget.

Ellis, Havelock. 1919. Ellen Key och hennes inflytande i England. In *En bok om Ellen Key*, 121-30. Stockholm: Albert Bonniers förlag.

Elshtain, Jean Bethke. 1981. *Public Man, Private Woman: Women in Social and Political Thought.* Oxford: Martin Robertson.

Engdahl, Horace. 2003. En roman om entusiasm och förälskelse. In *Pennskaftet*, by Elin Wägner, ed. Helena Forsås-Scott, vii-xvi. Stockholm: Atlantis. (Svenska Klassiker utgivna av Svenska Akademien).

Englund, Boel and Per Ledin. 2003. Inledning. In *Teoretiska perspektiv på sakprosa*, ed. Boel Englund and Per Ledin, 13-31. Lund: Studentlitteratur.

– er–. 1908. Review of *Norrtullsligan*, by Elin Wägner. *Vårt land* 9 May.

Erdmann, Nils. 1933. Review of *Mannen vid min sida*, by Elin Wägner. *Nya Dagligt Allehanda* 22 Nov.

Ericsson, Christina. 1994. Att vara eller inte vara. 1800-talets aktriser och kvinnligheten. In *Det evigt kvinnliga. En historia om förändring*, ed. Ulla Wikander, 162-87. Stockholm: Tidens förlag.

Eskilsson, Lena. 1991. *Drömmen om kamratsamhället. Kvinnliga medborgarskolan på Fogelstad 1925-35.* Stockholm: Carlssons bokförlag.

Esslin, Martin. 1970. *The Theatre of the Absurd.* Revised and enlarged ed., orig. publ. 1968. Harmondsworth: Penguin Books.

Fahlgren, Margaretha, Yvonne Hirdman and Ebba Witt-Brattström. 1996. Erotik, etik och emancipation. Om 1920-talets nya kvinna, Marika Stiernstedt och emancipationsromanen. In *Nordisk kvinnolitteraturhistoria*, vol. 3, ed. Elisabeth Møller Jensen, 373-78. Höganäs: Bra Böcker.

Fairclough, Norman. 2006. *Discourse and Social Change.* Orig. publ. 1992. Cambridge and Malden, MA: Polity Press.

Fernberg, Magnus. 2004. *Kåseristil.* Göteborg: University of Göteborg, Dept. of Swedish Language.

First, Ruth and Ann Scott. 1980. *Olive Schreiner.* London: André Deutsch.

Fjelkestam, Kristina. 2002. *Ungkarlsflickor, kamrathustrur och manhaftiga lesbianer. Modernitetens litterära gestalter i mellankrigstidens Sverige.* Stockholm/Stehag: Brutus Östlings Bokförlag Symposion.

Forsås-Scott, Helena. 1983. Kvinnoroll och kvinnosak. En studie i Elin Wägners romankonst. *Samlaren* 104: 7-20.

– 1985. 'En kvinnas självbiografi'. Om Elin Wägners romankonst. *Kvinnovetenskaplig tidskrift* 3: 3-16.

– 1986. Bibeln, kvinnan och romanen. En studie av Elin Wägners *Åsa-Hanna. Samlaren* 107: 35-57.

– 1991. Swedish 'Literature of Preparedness' and Feminist Pacifism: The

Select Bibliography

Example of Elin Wägner. In *Proceedings of the Ninth Biennial Conference of the British Association of Scandinavian Studies, 8-11 April 1991*, 97-111. Norwich: University of East Anglia, School of Modern Languages and European History.
- 1996. Gasmaskmadonnan. Om Elin Wägner. In *Nordisk kvinnolitteraturhistoria*, vol. 3, ed. Elisabeth Møller Jensen, 174-78. Höganäs: Bra Böcker.
- 1999. Inledning. In *Vad tänker du, mänsklighet? Texter om feminism, fred och miljö*, by Elin Wägner, ed. Helena Forsås-Scott, 13-60. Stockholm: Norstedts förlag.
- 2001. Narratologi i kontext. Elin Wägners *Tusen år i Småland*, berättandet och civilisationskritiken. *Tidskrift för litteraturvetenskap*: 70-94.
- 2002. Elin Wägner. In *Dictionary of Literary Biography*, Vol. 259, *Twentieth Century Swedish Writers before World War II*, ed. Ann-Charlotte Gavel Adams, 268-77. Detroit, San Francisco, London, Woodbridge, CT: Gale Group.
- 2003a. 'Tänk själv, säger denna bok.' Om Elin Wägners *Väckarklocka*. In *Kvinnorna skall göra det! Den kvinnliga medborgarskolan vid Fogelstad – som idé, text och historia*, ed. Ebba Witt-Brattström and Lena Lennerhed, 23-48. Huddinge: Södertörns högskola, Samtidshistoriska institutet.
- 2003b. Kommentarer och ordförklaringar. In *Pennskaftet*, by Elin Wägner, ed. Helena Forsås-Scott, 207-30. Stockholm: Atlantis. (Svenska Klassiker utgivna av Svenska Akademien).
- 2004. Verbal Power, Visual Power, and the Construction of Feminine Subjectivity: Elin Wägner's *Norrtullsligan* as Prose Fiction and Film. In *The New Woman and the Aesthetic Opening: Unlocking Gender in Twentieth-Century Texts*, ed. Ebba Witt-Brattström, 83-100 Huddinge: Södertörns högskola.
- 2007. Förord. In *Väckarklocka*, by Elin Wägner, 5-26. Stockholm: Albert Bonniers förlag. (Bonniers klassiker).
- 2009. Vems är rösten? Berättare, genus och auktoritet i tre romaner. *In Det första fotstegets moder. Antologi*, ed. Marianne Enge Swartz. Växjö: Artéa förlag.

Foucault, Michel. 1990. *The History of Sexuality: An Introduction*, vol.1. Orig. publ. 1976. Tr. Robert Hurley. Harmondsworth: Penguin Books.

Fowler, Alastair. 1997. *Kinds of Literature: An Introduction to the Theory of Genres and Modes*. Orig. publ. 1982. Oxford: Clarendon Press.

Frangeur, Renée. 1998. *Yrkeskvinna eller makens tjänarinna? Striden om yrkesrätten för gifta kvinnor i mellankrigstidens Sverige.* Lund: Arkiv förlag.

Franklin, John Hope and Alfred Moss, Jr. 1994. *From Slavery to Freedom: A History of African Americans.* New York: Alfred A. Knopf.

Frazer, Elisabeth and Nicola Lacey. 1993. *The Politics of Community: A Feminist Critique of the Liberal-Communitarian Debate.* Toronto, Buffalo: University of Toronto Press.

Frostegren, Margareta. 1979. Damernas egen. Idun 1906. In *Veckopressen i Sverige. Analyser och perspektiv*, ed. Anita Alveus et al., 11-46. Löderup: Förlagshuset Mälargården.

Frye, Northrop. 1983. *The Great Code: The Bible and Literature.* Orig. publ. 1981, 1982. London, Melbourne, Henley: Ark Paperbacks.

Frykman, Jonas and Orvar Löfgren, ed. 1985. *Modärna tider. Vision och vardag i folkhemmet.* Malmö: Liber förlag.

Fröding, Gustaf. 1902. *Samlade dikter*, vol. 2. Stockholm: Albert Bonniers förlag.

Furhammar, Leif. 2003. *Filmen i Sverige. En historia i tio kapitel och en fortsättning.* 3rd ed. First ed. publ. 1991. Stockholm: Dialogos in collaboration with the Swedish Film Institute.

Gadamer, Hans-Georg. 2003. *Truth and Method.* 2nd rev. ed. German orig. publ. 1960. Tr. rev. by Joel Weinsheimer and Donald G. Marshall. New York: Continuum.

Genette, Gérard. 1994. *Narrative Discourse Revisited.* Orig. publ. 1983. Tr. Jane E. Lewin. Ithaca, New York: Cornell University Press.

– 1995. *Narrative Discourse: An Essay in Method.* Orig. publ. 1972. Tr. Jane E. Lewin. Ithaca, New York: Cornell University Press.

– 2001. *Paratexts: Thresholds of Interpretation.* Orig. publ. 1987. Tr. Jane E. Lewin. Cambridge, New York and Melbourne: Cambridge University Press.

Gilbert, Sandra M. and Susan Gubar. 1989. *No Man's Land: The Place of the Woman Writer in the Twentieth Century*, vol. 2, *Sexchanges*. New Haven and London: Yale University Press.

Gilman, Charlotte Perkins. 1911. *The Man-Made World or, Our Androcentric Culture.* New York: Charlton Company. Sw. tr. Alma Faustman. 1912. *Den av mannen skapade världen eller Vår maskulina kultur.* Stockholm: Norstedts förlag.

– 1966. *Women and Economics: A Study of the Economic Relation between Women and Men as a Factor in Social Evolution.* Orig. publ.

1898. New York, Hagerstown, San Francisco, London: Harper & Row.
- 1979. *Herland*. Orig. publ. in instalments in *The Forerunner* 1915. London: The Women's Press.
- 2002. *The Home: Its Work and Influence*. Orig. publ. 1903. Walnut Creek, Lanham, New York, Oxford: Altamira Press. Sw. tr. Frigga Carlberg. 1907. *Hemmet: dess verksamhet och inflytande*. Stockholm: Wahlström & Widstrand.

Grepstad, Ottar. 1997. *Det litterære skattkammer. Sakprosaens teori og retorikk*. Oslo: Det Norske Samlaget.

Grosz, Elizabeth. 1995. *Space, Time, and Perversion: Essays on the Politics of Bodies*. New York and London: Routledge.

Gualtieri, Elena. 1998. The Essay as Form: Virginia Woolf and the Literary Tradition. *Textual Practice*: 49-67.

Göransson, Anita. 1996. Kön som analyskategori i den ekonomiska historien. Några linjer och resultat. In *Kvinnovetenskapens vadan och varthän. Rapport från en konferens*, ed. Eva Borgström and Anna Nordenstam, 49-67. Göteborg: University of Göteborg, Dept. of Women's Studies.

Hackman, Boel. 2005. *Elin Wägner*. Stockholm: Albert Bonniers förlag.

Hadenius, Stig, Björn Molin and Hans Wieslander. 1971. *Sverige efter 1900. En modern politisk historia*. Orig. publ. 1967. Stockholm: Bokförlaget Aldus/Bonniers.

Hadenius, Stig and Lennart Weibull. 2003. *Massmedier. En bok om press, radio & TV*. 8th ed. First ed. publ. 1970. Stockholm: Albert Bonniers förlag.

Hagberg, Knut. 1933. *Gotland sommaren 1933*. Stockholm: Wahlström & Widstrand.

Hagemann, Gro and Klas Åmark. 2004. Fra 'husmorkontrakt' til 'likestillingskontrakt'. Yvonne Hirdmans genusteori. In *Om makt. Teori og kritikk*, ed. Fredrik Engelstad, 174-206. Orig. publ. 1999. Oslo: Gyldendal Akademisk.

Hallberg, Mikael and Tomas Jonsson. 1993. *'Allmänanda och självtukt'. Per Albin Hanssons ideologiska förändring och folkhemretorikens framväxt*. Uppsala: University of Uppsala, Centre for Rhetoric. (Arbetarrörelsen och språket, 1993:5).

Hallingberg, Gunnar. 1965. *Radioteater i 40 år. Den svenska repertoaren*. Stockholm: Sveriges Radio.
- 1967. *Radiodramat. Svensk hörspelsdiktning – bakgrund, utveckling och formvärld*. Stockholm: Sveriges Radios förlag.

Hansson, Per Albin. 1982. *Från Fram till folkhemmet. Per Albin Hansson som tidningsman och talare*, ed. Anna Lisa Berkling. Solna: Metodica Press.

Haraway, Donna J. 1991. *Simians, Cyborgs, and Women: The Reinvention of Nature*. London: Free Association Books.

– 2003. *The Companion Species Manifesto: Dogs, People, and Significant Otherness*. Chicago: Prickly Paradigm Press.

Harvey, David. 2001. *The Condition of Postmodernity: An Enquiry into the Origins of Cultural Change*. Orig. publ. 1990. Cambridge, MA and Oxford: Blackwell.

Hatje, Ann-Katrin. 1974. *Befolkningsfrågan och välfärden. Debatten om familjepolitik och nativitetsökning under 1930- och 1940-talen*. Stockholm: Allmänna förlaget.

Heggestad, Eva. 2003. Elin Wägners *Norrtullsligan*. 'Män må icke under någon förevändning taga plats i damkupé'. In *En bättre och lyckligare värld. Kvinnliga författares utopiska visioner 1850-1950*, by Eva Heggestad, 83-97. Stockholm/Stehag: Brutus Östlings Bokförlag Symposion.

Hermelin, Carin (sign. C.H.). 1935. Representanterna för 20.000 kvinnor i arbete. *Tidevarvet* 7 Sept.: 3-4.

Hermelin, Carin. 1956. Varför kom du till Fogelstad?. In *Fogelstad. Berättelsen om en skola*, ed. Elsa Björkman-Goldschmidt, 112-22. Stockholm: P.A. Norstedt & Söners förlag.

Hermelin, Honorine. 1939. *Kvinnliga medborgarskolan vid Fogelstad*. Stockholm: Saxon & Lindströms förlags tryckeri.

– 1956. På avsiktsfri mark. Orig. publ. 1935. In *Fogelstad. Berättelsen om en skola*, ed. Elsa Björkman-Goldschmidt, 202-04. Stockholm: P.A. Norstedt & Söners förlag.

Hermodsson, Elisabet. 1979. *Ord i kvinnotid. Essäer, polemik och dagliga blad*. Stockholm: Rabén & Sjögren.

Herrmann, Anne. 1989. *The Dialogic and Difference: 'An/Other Woman' in Virginia Woolf and Christa Wolf*. New York: Columbia University Press.

Hirdman, Yvonne. 1983. Den socialistiska hemmafrun. Den socialdemokratiska kvinnorörelsen och hemarbetet 1890-1939. In *Vi kan, vi behövs – kvinnorna går samman i egna föreningar*, by Brita Åkerman *et al.*, 11-59. Stockholm: Förlaget Akademilitteratur.

– 1987. Makt och kön. In *Maktbegreppet*, ed. Olof Petersson, 188-206. Stockholm: Carlssons bokförlag.

Select Bibliography

- 1990. Genussystemet. In *Demokrati och makt i Sverige.* Stockholm: Statens offentliga utredningar 1990, 44: 73-116.
- 1993. *Att lägga livet till rätta – studier i svensk folkhemspolitik.* Orig. publ. 1989. Stockholm: Carlssons bokförlag.
- 1996. Kvinnorna i välfärdsstaten. Sverige 1930-1990. In *Kvinnohistoria. Om kvinnors villkor från antiken till våra dagar,* 203-18. Orig. publ. 1992. Stockholm: Utbildningsradion.
- 2001. *Genus – om det stabilas föränderliga former.* Malmö: Liber.
- 2006. Feminismens dilemma. Varationer på ett (oändligt) tema... In *Att se det osedda. Vänbok till Ann-Sofie Ohlander,* 117-30. Stockholm: Hjalmarsson & Högberg.

Hogan, Rebecca. 1991. Engendered Autobiographies: The Diary as a Feminine Form. In *Autobiography and Questions of Gender,* ed. Shirley Neuman, 95-107. London and Portland, OR: Frank Cass.

Holm, Birgitta. 2002. Kvinnans kärlek och kvinnans verk. In *Tusen år av ögonblick. Från den heliga Birgitta till den syndiga,* by Birgitta Holm, 149-60. Stockholm: Albert Bonniers förlag.

Holmberg, Claes-Göran. 1995. De sagolika nyheterna. In *Medietexter och medietolkningar. Läsningar av massmediala texter,* ed. Claes-Göran Holmberg and Jan Svensson, 101-12. Nora: Bokförlaget Nya Doxa.

Holquist, Michael. 1991. *Dialogism: Bakhtin and his World.* Orig. publ. 1990. London and New York: Routledge.

Hughes, Linda K. and Michael Lund. 1995. Textual/Sexual Pleasure and Serial Publication. In *Literature in the Marketplace: Nineteenth-Century British Publishing and Reading Practices,* ed. John O. Jordan and Robert L. Patten, 143-64. Cambridge: Cambridge University Press.

Hultman, Tor G. 2003. *Svenska Akademiens språklära.* Stockholm: Svenska Akademien.

Hägg, Göran. 1978. *Övertalning och underhållning. Den svenska essäistiken 1890-1930.* Stockholm: Wahlström & Widstrand.

Irigaray, Luce. 1993. *This Sex which Is not One.* Fr. orig. publ.1977. Eng. tr. Catherine Porter with Carolyn Burke. Eng. tr. orig. publ. 1985. Ithaca, New York: Cornell University Press.

Isaksson, Ulla and Erik Hjalmar Linder. 2003. *Elin Wägner: Amason med två bröst 1882-1922, Dotter av Moder Jord 1922-1949.* Orig. publ. 1977 and 1980 respectively. Stockholm: Albert Bonniers förlag.

Jackson, Margaret. 1994. *The Real Facts of Life: Feminism and the Politics of Sexuality c. 1850-1940.* London: Taylor & Francis.

Joeres, Ruth-Ellen Boetcher and Elizabeth Mittman. 1993. An Introductory

Essay. In *The Politics of the Essay: Feminist Perspectives*, ed. Ruth-Ellen Boetcher Joeres and Elizabeth Mittman, 12-20. Bloomington and Indianapolis: Indiana University Press.

Johannisson, Karin. 1994. *Den mörka kontinenten. Kvinnan, medicinen och fin-de-siècle*. Stockholm: Norstedts förlag.

Johanson, Klara (sign. K.J.). 1908. Review of *Norrtullsligan*, by Elin Wägner. *Stockholms Dagblad* 7 May.

– 1910. Review of *Pennskaftet*, by Elin Wägner. *Stockholms Dagblad* 30 Oct.

– 1915. Introduction to Rosa Mayreder om kön och kultur. *Hertha*: 212-13.

Johanson, Klara. 1953. *Brev*. Stockholm: Wahlström & Widstrand.

Jonsson, Bibi. 2001. *I den värld vi drömmer om. Utopin i Elin Wägners trettiotalsromaner*. Löderup: Werstam Media.

Jonsson, Tomas. 1998. *'Att anpassa sig efter det möjliga'. Utsugningsbegreppet och SAP:s ideologiska förändringar 1911-1944*. Göteborg: University of Göteborg, Dept. of Intellectual History.

Karlsson, Sten O. 2001. *Det intelligenta samhället. En omtolkning av socialdemokratins idéhistoria*. Stockholm: Carlssons bokförlag.

Kellgren, Ragna, ed. 1971a. *Kvinnor i politiken. Artiklar ur den politiska, radikala veckotidningen Tidevarvet (1923-1936)*. Stockholm: LTs förlag.

– 1971b. Inledning. In *Kvinnor i politiken. Artiklar ur den politiska, radikala veckotidningen Tidevarvet (1923-1936)*, ed. Ragna Kellgren, 9-16. Stockholm: LTs förlag.

– 1973. *Klasslöst. Tre veckor i nutid och forntid vid Fogelstad Kvinnliga Medborgarskola. Ur kursprotokoll och egen erfarenhet*. Julita: Kvinnliga medborgarskolan vid Fogelstad.

Key, Ellen. 1900. *Barnets århundrade*, vols. 1-2. Stockholm: Albert Bonniers förlag. Eng. tr. 1909. *The Century of the Child*. New York and London: Putnam's.

– 1911. *Kärleken och äktenskapet* (*Lifslinjer*, Part 1), vol. 2. Orig. publ. 1903. Stockholm: Albert Bonniers förlag.

– 1912. *The Woman Movement*. Eng. tr. Mamah Bouton Borthwick. New York and London: G.P. Putnam's Sons. Sw. orig. publ. 1909. *Kvinnorörelsen*. Stockholm: Albert Bonniers förlag.

– 1914a. Missbrukad kvinnokraft. In *Missbrukad kvinnokraft och Kvinnopsykologi*, by Ellen Key, 11-56. Orig. publ. 1896. Stockholm: Albert Bonniers förlag.

Select Bibliography

- 1914b. Naturenliga arbetsområden för kvinnan. In *Missbrukad kvinnokraft och Kvinnopsykologi*, by Ellen Key, 57-77. Orig. publ. 1896. Stockholm: Albert Bonniers förlag.
- 1976a. Fredsrörelsen och kulturen. Orig. publ. 1908. In *Hemmets århundrade*, by Ellen Key, ed. Ronny Ambjörnsson, 60-78. Stockholm: Aldus.
- 1976b. Skönhet i hemmen. Några utläggningar till Ehrensvärds text. Orig. publ. 1899. In *Hemmets århundrade*, by Ellen Key, ed. Ronny Ambjörnsson, 79-108. Stockholm: Aldus.
- 1976c. Samhällsmoderlighet. Orig. publ. 1903. In *Hemmets århundrade*, by Ellen Key, ed. Ronny Ambjörnsson, 156-85. Stockholm: Aldus.

Kleen, Ingeborg. 1897. Olive Schreiners diktning. *Ord & Bild*: 521-24.

Kleman, Ellen (sign. E. K-n.). 1910. Review of *Kvinnlighet, manlighet och mänsklighet*, by Rosa Mayreder. *Dagny*: 294-95.

Kock, Karin. 1942a. Den borttappade yrkeskvinnan. Några reflexioner kring Elin Wägners nya bok. I. *Social-Demokraten* 4 Jan.

- 1942b. Den borttappade yrkeskvinnan. Några reflexioner kring Elin Wägners nya bok. II. *Social-Demokraten* 7 Jan.

Koskinen, Maaret. 1983. Med ljudfilmen försvann kvinnorna. In *Kvinnor i svensk film*. Published in connection with the Film Festival, 12-20 Feb., 2-4. [Stockholm].

Kræmer, Vera von (sign. V.v.K.). 1908. Review of *Norrtullsligan*, by Elin Wägner. *Social-Demokraten* 8 May.

Kyle, Gunhild. 1980. Kvinnan under 1900-talet – konflikten mellan produktion och reproduktion. *Historisk Tidskrift* [Sweden]: 355-69.

Kyle, Gunhild and Gunnar Qvist. 1974. *Kvinnorna i männens samhälle. Ur den officiella debatten om kvinnans villkor i Sverige*. Stockholm: Esselte Studium.

Lagerkvist, Pär. 1955. Hellensk morgondröm. Orig. publ. 1934. In *Prosa*, by Pär Lagerkvist, 126-31. Stockholm: Albert Bonniers förlag.

Lagerlöf, Selma. 1903. *Jerusalem*. Sw. orig. publ. 1901-02. Eng. tr. Jessie Bröchner. London: William Heinemann.

- 1911. *En saga om en saga och andra sagor*. Orig. publ. 1902. Stockholm: Albert Bonniers förlag.
- 1915. Hem och stat. In *Troll och människor*, by Selma Lagerlöf, 245-61. Stockholm: Albert Bonniers förlag.

Lamberth, Pia. 1991. Som ensamma fyrar i natten? En främst kvantitativ undersökning av kvinnliga svenskspråkiga författares aktivitet 1900-

1949. *Tidskrift för litteraturvetenskap* 3: 31-42.
Landquist, John. 1949. Några drag av Elin Wägners berättarkonst. *Svensk litteraturtidskrift*: 73-102
Lane, Ann J. 1979. Introduction. In *Herland*, by Charlotte Perkins Gilman, v-xxiv. London: The Women's Press.
Lanser, Susan Sniader. 1992. *Fictions of Authority: Women Writers and Narrative Voice*. Ithaca and London: Cornell University Press.
– 2004. Sexing Narratology: Toward a Gendered Poetics of Narrative Voice. In *Narrative Theory: Critical Concepts in Literary and Cultural Studies*, vol. 3, ed. Mieke Bal, 123-39. London and New York: Routledge.
Larsson, Carl. 1969. *Ett hem. 24 målningar*. Orig. publ. 1899. Stockholm: Albert Bonniers förlag. Eng. tr. Olive Jones. 1976. *Our Home*. London: Methuen.
Larsson, Inger. 2003. *Text och tolkning i svenska författarbiografier. Elin Wägners Selma Lagerlöf, Elisabeth Tykessons Atterbom och Fredrik Bööks Verner von Heidenstam*. Hedemora: Gidlunds förlag.
Larsson, Lisbeth. 2001. *Sanning och konsekvens. Marika Stiernstedt, Ludvig Nordström och de biografiska berättelserna*. Stockholm: Norstedts förlag.
Law, Graham. 2001. New Woman Novels in Newspapers. *Media History*: 17-31.
Ledin, Per and Staffan Selander. 2003. Institution, text och genre. In *Teoretiska perspektiv på sakprosa*, ed. Boel Englund and Per Ledin, 91-122. Lund: Studentlitteratur.
Leffler, Anne-Charlotte. 1883. *Sanna kvinnor. Skådespel i tre akter*. Stockholm: Z. Hæggströms förlagsexpedition.
Lengefeld, Cecilia. 1997. Translation and Transformation: Carl Larsson's Books in Europe. In *Carl and Karin Larsson: Creators of the Swedish Style*, ed. Michael Snodin and Elisabet Stavenow-Hidemark, 196-211. London: V&A Publications.
Leppänen, Katarina. 2005. *Rethinking Civilisation in a European Feminist Context: History, Nature, Women in Elin Wägner's Väckarklocka*. Göteborg: University of Göteborg, Dept. of History of Ideas and Theory of Science. Republ. 2008. *Elin Wägner's Alarm Clock: Ecofeminist Theory in the Interwar Era*. Lanham, Boulder, New York, Toronto, Plymouth UK: Lexington Books.
Lindberger, Örjan. 1949. Hjärtat och nycklarna. Några synpunkter på Elin Wägners författarskap. *Bonniers litterära magasin*: 271-78.

Select Bibliography

Lindblad, Göran. 1918. Review of *Åsa-Hanna*, by Elin Wägner. *Svenska Dagbladet* 11 Nov.
Lindblom, Andreas. 1940a. Review of *Tusen år i Småland*, by Elin Wägner, I. *Social-Demokraten*, 6 Oct.
– 1940b. Review of *Tusen år i Småland*, by Elin Wägner, II. *Social-Demokraten* 7 Oct.
Lindén, Claudia. 2002. *Om kärlek: Litteratur, sexualitet och politik hos Ellen Key*. Stockholm/Stehag: Brutus Östlings Bokförlag Symposion.
Linder, Erik Hjalmar. 1949. Elin Wägner. In *Fyra decennier av nittonhundratalet*, by Erik Hjalmar Linder, 90-106. Stockholm: Natur & Kultur. (*Illustrerad svensk litteraturhistoria*, ed. Henrik Schück and Karl Warburg, vol. 8).
– 1965. Elin Wägner. In *Fem decennier av nittonhundratalet*, by Erik Hjalmar Linder, vol. 1, 118-30. Stockholm: Natur & Kultur.
– 1966. *Fem decennier av nittonhundratalet*, vol. 2. Stockholm: Natur & Kultur.
– 1978. Om Väckarklocka. In *Väckarklocka*, by Elin Wägner, 7-11. Stockholm: Bonniers förlag. (Delfinserien).
Lindholm, Margareta. 1990. *Talet om det kvinnliga. Studier i feministiskt tänkande i Sverige under 1930-talet*. Göteborg: University of Göteborg, Dept. of Sociology.
Lindqvist, Karl. 1980. *Individ grupp gemenskap. Studier i de unga tiotalisternas litteratur*. Uppsala: University of Uppsala, Dept. of Literature.
Lindqvist, Märta (sign. Quelqu'une). 1933. Review of *Mannen vid min sida*, by Elin Wägner. *Svenska Dagbladet* 14 Dec.
Lindqvist, Ola. 1968. Arbetarrörelsen växer fram. In *Den svenska historien*, vol. 9, ed. Jan Cornell, 158-64. Stockholm: Albert Bonniers förlag.
Ljungquist, Ivar. 1953. *Kampen om läsarna. Ur Dagens Nyheters historia 1889-1921*, vol. 2. Stockholm: Albert Bonniers förlag.
Lloyd, Genevieve. 1993. *The Man of Reason: 'Male' and 'Female' in Western Philosophy*, 2nd ed. First ed. publ. 1984. London: Routledge.
Loomba, Ania. 2007. *Colonialism/Postcolonialism*. 2nd ed., first publ. 2005. First ed. publ. 1998. London and New York: Routledge.
Lundberg, Anders P. 2005. *Om gemenskap. En sociologisk betraktelse*. Lund: University of Lund, Dept. of Sociology.
Lundgren, Kristina and Birgitta Ney, ed. 2000. *Tidningskvinnor 1690-1960*. Lund: Studentlitteratur.
Lundgren, Kristina, Birgitta Ney and Torsten Thurén. 1999. *Nyheter – att*

läsa tidningstext. Stockholm: Ordfront förlag.
Lundquist, Tommie. 1982. *Den disciplinerade dubbelmoralen. Studier i den reglementerade prostitutionens historia i Sverige 1859-1918*. Göteborg: University of Göteborg, Dept. of History.
Lundqvist, Lennart J. 2004. *Sweden and Ecological Governance: Straddling the Fence*. Manchester and New York: Manchester University Press.
Löfgren, Orvar. 1996. Rational and Sensitive: Changing Attitudes to Time, Nature, and the Home. In *Culture Builders: A Historical Anthropology of Middle-Class Life*, by Jonas Frykman and Orvar Löfgren, 11-153. Eng. tr. Alan Crozier. Orig. publ. 1987. New Brunswick, NJ: Rutgers University Press. Sw. orig. 1979.
– 1999a. Känslans förvandling.Tiden, naturen och hemmet i den borgerliga kulturen. In *Den kultiverade människan*, by Jonas Frykman and Orvar Löfgren, 21-130. Orig. publ. 1979. Lund: Gleerup.
– 1999b. Nationella arenor. In *Försvenskningen av Sverige. Det nationellas förvandlingar*, by Billy Ehn, Jonas Frykman and Orvar Löfgren, 21-117. Orig. publ. 1993. Stockholm: Natur & Kultur.
Lövgren, Britta. 1993. *Hemarbete som politik. Diskussioner om hemarbete, Sverige 1930-40-talen, och tillkomsten av Hemmens forskningsinstitut*. Stockholm: University of Stockholm, Dept. of History.
–m. 1919. Review of *Kvarteret Oron*, by Elin Wägner. *Ny Tid* 14 June.
Marshall, T.H. and Tom Bottomore. 1992. *Citizenship and Social Class*. London and Concord, MA: Pluto Press.
Mayreder, Rosa. 1910. Slutsatser. Ur Rosa Mayreders *Kvinnlighet, manlighet och mänsklighet*. *Dagny*: 175-76.
– 1913. *A Survey of the Woman Problem*. Eng. tr. Herman Scheffauer. London: William Heinemann. Orig. publ. 1905. *Zur Kritik der Weiblichkeit*. Jena: E. Diederichs. Sw. tr. 1910. *Kvinnlighet, manlighet och mänsklighet*. Stockholm: Wahlström & Widstrand.
– 1915a. Rosa Mayreder om kön och kultur, I. Ed. and tr. 'K.J.' [Klara Johanson]. *Hertha*: 212-17.
– 1915b. Rosa Mayreder om kön och kultur, II. *Hertha*: 230-35.
– 1923a. *Geschlecht und Kultur. Essays*. Jena: E. Diederichs.
– 1923b. *Sexualitet och kultur*. Tr. Klara Johanson. Stockholm: Wahlström & Widstrand.
Merchant, Carolyn, with Abby Peterson. 1995. Peace with the Earth: Women and the Swedish Environment. In *Earthcare: Women and the Environment*, by Carolyn Merchant, 167-84. New York: Routledge.

Select Bibliography

Mezei, Kathy. 1996. Who is Speaking here? Free Indirect Discourse, Gender, and Authority in *Emma, Howards End*, and *Mrs Dalloway*. In *Ambiguous Discourse: Feminist Narratology and British Women Writers*, ed. Kathy Metzei, 66-92. Chapel Hill and London: University of North Carolina Press.

Middleton, Peter and Tim Woods. 2000. *Literatures of Memory: History, Time and Space in Postwar Writing*. Manchester and New York: Manchester University Press.

Moi, Toril. 1985. *Sexual/Textual Politics: Feminist Literary Theory*. London and New York: Methuen.

Molin, Karl. 1974. *Försvaret, folkhemmet och demokratin. Socialdemokratisk riksdagspolitik 1939-1945*. Stockholm: Allmänna förlaget.

Myrdal, Alva. 1945. *Nation and Family: The Swedish Experiment in Democratic Family and Population Policy*. Orig. publ. 1941. London: Kegan Paul, Trench, Trubner & Co.

Myrdal, Alva and Viola Klein. 1956. *Women's Two Roles: Home and Work*. London: Routledge and Kegan Paul.

Myrdal, Alva and Gunnar Myrdal. 1934. *Kris i befolkningsfrågan*. Stockholm: Albert Bonniers förlag.

Määttä, Sylvia. 1997. *Kön och evolution. Charlotte Perkins Gilmans feministiska utopier 1911-1916*. Nora: Nya Doxa.

Nadel, Ira Bruce. 1984. *Biography: Fiction, Fact and Form*. Basingstoke: Macmillan.

Ney, Birgitta. 1999. *Reporter i rörelse. Lotten Ekman i dagspressen vid förra sekelskiftet*. Nora: Nya Doxa.

Nicklasson, Stina. 1992. *Högerns kvinnor. Problem och resurs för Allmänna valmansförbundet perioden 1900-1936/1937*. Uppsala: University of Uppsala, Dept. of History.

Nilsson, Ada. 1940. *Barrikaden valde oss. 25 år ur en kämpande förenings historia*. Stockholm: Axel Holmströms förlag.

Nilsson, Anders and Lars Pettersson. 1996. Utbildning, ekonomisk omvandling och tillväxt. In *Äventyret Sverige. En ekonomisk och social historia*, ed. Birgitta Furuhagen, 168-88. Stockholm: Utbildningsradion and Bokförlaget Bra Böcker.

Nilsson, Sven. 1975. *Det offentliga samtalet. Storstadspressen som medium för kulturinformation och kulturdebatt*. Lund: Liber Läromedel.

Nissen, Ingjald. 1934. *Seksualitet og disiplin*. Oslo: H. Aschehoug & Co.

Nordberg, Karin. 1998. *Folkhemmets röst. Radion som folkbildare 1925-*

1950. Stockholm/Stehag: Brutus Östlings Bokförlag Symposion.

Nordisk Familjebok. Ny, reviderad och rikt illustrerad upplaga. 1904-26. 38 vols. Stockholm: Nordisk Familjeboks Förlags Aktiebolag.

Norström, Vitalis. 1912. Verkliga skäl för kvinnans rösträtt och skenbara. *Idun* 18 Feb.: 102-103.

Näsström, Gustaf. 1940. Review of *Tusen år i Småland*, by Elin Wägner. *Svenska Turistföreningens Tidning*: 184-86.

Ohrlander, Kajsa. 1996. Moderniserad kvinnlighet – gammal manlighet. Socialpolitiska betydelser av genus i formeringen av den tidiga svenska välfärdsstaten 1900-1914. *Arkiv för studier i arbetarrörelsens historia*: 33-67.

Olsson, Jan Olof. 1968. Sverige och världen. In *Den svenska historien*, vol. 10, ed. Jan Cornell, 142-53. Stockholm: Albert Bonniers förlag.

Palme, Sven Ulric. 1969. Vid valurnan och i riksdagen under femtio år. In *Kvinnors röst och rätt*, ed. Ruth Hamrin-Thorell, Ulla Lindström and Gunborg Stenberg, 41-110. Stockholm: Allmänna förlaget.

Pateman, Carole. 1997. *The Sexual Contract.* Orig. publ. 1988. Cambridge: Polity Press.

Pearce, Lynne. 1994. *Reading Dialogics.* London, New York, Melbourne, Auckland: Edward Arnold.

Perkins, David. 1992. *Is Literary History Possible?* Baltimore and London: The Johns Hopkins University Press.

Petersson, Birgit. 2001. Tidningar som industri och parti (1880-1897). In *Den svenska pressens historia*, vol. 2, ed. Karl Erik Gustafsson and Per Rydén, 236-342. Stockholm: Ekerlids förlag.

Plumwood, Val. 1993. *Feminism and the Mastery of Nature.* London and New York: Routledge.

– 2002. *Environmental Culture: The Ecological Crisis of Reason.* London and New York: Routledge.

Prince, Gerald. 1996. Introduction to the Study of the Narratee. Orig. publ. 1973. In *Essentials of the Theory of Fiction*, ed. Michael J. Hoffman and Patrick D. Murphy, 213-33. 2nd ed. Durham, NC: Duke University Press.

Randall, David. 2000. *The Universal Journalist*, 2nd ed.. First ed. 1996. London and Ann Arbor, MI: Pluto Press.

Ricoeur, Paul. 1988. *Time and Narrative*, vol. 3. Orig. publ. 1985. Tr. Kathleen Blamey and David Pellauer. Chicago and London: University of Chicago Press.

Rimmon-Kenan, Shlomith. 1988. *Narrative Fiction: Contemporary*

Select Bibliography

Poetics. Orig. publ. 1983. London and New York: Methuen.
Rinman, Sven. 1967. Strindberg. In *Ny illustrerad svensk litteraturhistoria*, 2nd ed., vol. 4, 30-143. Stockholm: Natur & Kultur.
Riviere, Joan. 1989. Womanliness as a Masquerade. Orig. publ. 1929. In *Formations of Fantasy*, ed. Victor Burgin, James Donald and Cora Kaplan, 35-61. Orig. publ. 1986. London and New York: Routledge.
Rochefort, Christiane. 1981. Are Women Writers Still Monsters? In *New French Feminisms: An Anthology*, ed. Elaine Marks and Isabelle de Courtivron, 183-86. New York, London, Toronto, Sydney, Tokyo: Harvester Wheatsheaf.
Romberg, Bertil. 1962. *Studies in the Narrative Technique of the First-Person Novel*. Stockholm, Göteborg, Uppsala: Almqvist & Wiksell.
Runeberg, Johan Ludvig. 1974. *Fänrik Ståls sägner*. Orig. publ. 1848-60. In *Samlade skrifter*, vol. 5, ed. Gunnar Tideström and Carl-Eric Thors. Helsingfors. (Svenska författare utgivna av Svenska vitterhetssamfundet, 16.).
Rydberg, Viktor. 1945. Förord till de två första upplagorna. In *Viktor Rydberg, Den siste atenaren*, orig. publ. 1859, ed. Ingemar Wizelius, 11-15. Stockholm: Albert Bonniers förlag. (Skrifter av Viktor Rydberg, 5).
Rydin, Lena. 1997. Karin Larsson. In *Carl and Karin Larsson: Creators of the Swedish Style*, ed. Michael Snodin and Elisabet Stavenow-Hidemark, 160-83. London: V&A Publications.
Rönnbäck, Josefin. 2004. *Politikens genusgränser. Den kvinnliga rösträttsrörelsen och kampen för kvinnors politiska medborgarskap 1902-1921*. Stockholm: Atlas Akademi.
Sandel, Maria. 1908. *Vid svältgränsen*. Stockholm: Geber.
Schreiner, Olive. 1900. Kvinnorörelsens mål. *Dagny*: 233-41.
– 1978. *Woman and Labour*. Orig. publ. 1911. London: Virago. Sw. tr. H. Flygare. 1911. *Kvinnan och arbetet*. Stockholm: Hugo Gebers förlag.
– 1979. *The Story of an African Farm*. Orig. pub. 1883. Harmondsworth: Penguin Books. Sw. tr. K. B-n. 1890. *Under Afrikas himmel: historien om en farm i Kaplandet*. Stockholm: H. Geber.
Schulz, S.L. 2007. *Ekokritik: Naturen i litteraturen*. Uppsala: CEMUS.
Schön, Lennart. 2000. *En modern svensk ekonomisk historia. Tillväxt och omvandling under två sekel*. Stockholm: SNS Förlag.
Scott, Joan Wallach. 1988a. Introduction. In *Gender and the Politics of History*, by Joan Wallach Scott, 1-11. New York: Columbia University Press.

- 1988b. Gender: A Useful Category of Historical Analysis. Orig. publ. 1986. In *Gender and the Politics of History*, by Joan Wallach Scott, 28-50. New York: Columbia University Press.
- 1994. Deconstructing Equality-versus-Difference: or, The Uses of Poststructuralist Theory for Feminism. Orig. publ. 1988. In *Defining Women: Social Institutions and Gender Divisions*, ed. Linda McDowell and Rosemary Pringle, 253-64. Cambridge: Polity Press in association with The Open University.
- 1998. *Only Paradoxes to Offer: French Feminists and the Rights of Man.* Orig. publ. 1996. Cambridge MA and London, England: Harvard University Press.

Selander, Sten (sign. S. S-r.). 1927. Review of *De fem pärlorna*, by Elin Wägner. *Stockholms Dagblad* 15 Dec.

Showalter, Elaine. 1978. *A Literature of Their Own: British Women Novelists from Brontë to Lessing*. Orig. publ. 1977. London: Virago.
- 1992. *Sexual Anarchy: Gender and Culture at the Fin de Siècle*. Orig. publ. 1991. London: Virago.

Siim, Birte. 2000. *Gender and Citizenship: Politics and Agency in France, Britain and Denmark*. Cambridge, New York, Oakleigh, Madrid, Cape Town: Cambridge University Press.

Silenstam, Per. 1970. *Arbetskraftsutbudets utveckling i Sverige 1870-1965*. Stockholm: Almqvist & Wiksell.

Sjöholm, Carina. 2003. *Gå på bio. Rum för drömmar i folkhemmets Sverige*. Stockholm/Stehag: Brutus Östlings Bokförlag Symposion.

Sjöstrand, Wilhelm. 1968. Skola, universitet och vetenskaper. In *Den svenska historien*, vol. 9, ed. Jan Cornell, 234-43. Stockholm: Albert Bonniers förlag.

Sköld, Lars. 1968. Socialsverige växer fram. In *Den svenska historien*, vol. 10, ed. Jan Cornell, 118-23. Stockholm: Albert Bonniers förlag.

Spacks, Patricia Meyer. 1985. *Gossip*. New York: Alfred A. Knopf.

Spivak, Gayatri Chakravorty. 1988. Can the Subaltern Speak? In *Marxism and the Interpretation of Culture*, ed. Cary Nelson and Lawrence Grossberg, 271-313. Urbana and Chicago: University of Illinois Press.

S.R.O. 1920. Review of *Den förödda vingården*, by Elin Wägner. *Göteborgs Handels- och Sjöfartstidning* 3 Dec.

Stanley, Liz. 1983. Olive Schreiner: New Women, Free Women, All Women. In *Feminist Theorists: Three Centuries of Women's Intellectual Traditions*, ed. Dale Spender, 229-43. London: The Women's Press.

Steene, Birgitta. 1999. Radio- och tv-teatern. In *Den svenska litteraturen*, vol. 3, *Från modernism till massmedial marknad 1920-1995*, ed. Lars Lönnroth, Sven Delblanc and Sverker Göransson, 516-17. Stockholm: Albert Bonniers förlag.

Stéenhoff, Frida (Harold Gote). 1896. *Lejonets unge. Nutidsskildring i fyra akter.* Stockholm: Wahlström & Widstrand.

— 1903. *Feminismens moral. Föredrag hållet i Sundsvall den 30 juni 1903.* Stockholm: Wahlström & Widstrand.

— 1908. *Penningen och kärleken.* Stockholm: Björck & Börjesson.

Stéenhoff, Frida. 1912. *Kärleken som kulturproblem.* Stockholm: Frams Förlag.

Still, Judith and Michael Worton. 1990. Introduction. In *Intertextuality*, ed. Michael Worton and Judith Still, 1-44. Manchester and New York: Manchester University Press.

Strindberg. August. 1984. *Fadren. Fröken Julie. Fordringsägare*, ed. Gunnar Ollén. Orig. publ. 1887, 1888, 1889. Stockholm: Almqvist & Wiksell. (August Strindbergs Samlade Verk, 27).

Stål, Margareta. 2002. *Signaturen Bansai. Ester Blenda Nordström. Pennskaft och reporter i det tidiga 1900-talet.* Göteborg: University of Göteborg, Dept. of Journalism and Mass Communication.

Svanberg, Birgitta. 1989. *Sanningen om kvinnorna. En läsning av Agnes von Krusenstjernas romanserie Fröknarna von Pahlen.* Stockholm: Gidlunds förlag.

Svedjedal, Johan. 1993. *Bokens samhälle. Svenska Bokförläggareföreningen och svensk bokmarknad 1887-1943*, vols. 1-2. Stockholm: Svenska Bokförläggareföreningen.

— 1994. Kvinnorna i den svenska bokbranschen. Om feminisering, integrering och segregering. In *Författare och förläggare och andra litteratursociologiska studier*, by Johan Svedjedal, 70-113. Hedemora: Gidlunds förlag.

Svensson, Conny. 1999. Tiotalets borgerliga realister. In *Den svenska litteraturen*, vol. 2, *Genombrottstiden 1830-1920*, ed. Lars Lönnroth and Sven Delblanc, 453-76. First ed. publ. 1988, 1989. Stockholm: Albert Bonniers förlag.

Sveriges socialdemokratiska ungdomsförbund. 1948. *Vår levnadsstandard.* Stockholm: Frihets Förlag.

Söderhjelm, Henning (sign. H. S-m.). 1927. Review of *De fem pärlorna*, by Elin Wägner. *Göteborgs Handels- och Sjöfartstidning* 19 Nov.

Sörlin, Sverker. 1988. *Framtidslandet. Debatten om Norrland och naturresurserna under det industriella genombrottet.* Stockholm:

Carlssons bokförlag.
Tamm, Elisabeth. 1923. *Vår politiska väg*. Ansvaret. *Tidevarvet* 24 Nov.
Therborn, Göran. 1988. Hur det hela började. När och varför det moderna Sverige blev vad det blev. In *Sverige – vardag och struktur. Sociologer beskriver det svenska samhället*, ed. Ulf Himmelstrand and Göran Svensson, 23-53. Stockholm: Norstedts förlag.
Thorell, Olof. 1973. *Svensk grammatik*. Stockholm, Göteborg, Lund: Scandinavian University Books, Esselte Studium.
Thorsell, Lennart. 1957. Den svenska parnassens 'demokratisering' och de folkliga bildningsvägarna. *Samlaren* 88: 53-135.
Tomson, Bengt. 1948. *Släkten Jerneploogs framgång* och *De fem pärlorna*. Något om Elin Wägners pacifism. *Edda*: 172-219.
Tornbjer, Charlotte. 2002. *Den nationella modern. Moderskap i konstruktioner av svensk nationell gemenskap under 1900-talets första hälft*. Lund: University of Lund, Dept. of History.
Turner, Victor W. 1969. *The Ritual Process: Structure and Anti-Structure*. London: Routledge & Kegan Paul.
Vaerting, M. 1921. *Neubegründung der Psychologie von Mann und Weib*, vol. 1, *Die weibliche Eigenart im Männerstaat und die männliche Eigenart im Frauenstaat*. Karlsruhe: G. Braun.
– 1923. *Neubegründung der Psychologie von Mann und Weib*, vol. 2, *Wahrheit und Irrtum in der Geschlechterpsychologie*. Karlsruhe: G. Braun.
Vaerting, Mathilde and Mathias. 1923. *The Dominant Sex: A Study in the Sociology of Sex Differentiation*. Tr. Eden and Cedar Paul. New York: George H. Doran Company.
Wahlström, Lydia. 1933. *Den svenska kvinnorörelsen. Historisk översikt*. Stockholm: P.A. Norstedt & Söners förlag.
Wallberg, Klas. 1968. Utbildningsexplosionen. In *Den svenska historien*, vol. 10, ed. Jan Cornell, 253-59. Stockholm: Albert Bonniers förlag.
Walton, Stephen J. 2008. *Skaff deg eit liv! Om biografi*. Oslo: Det Norske Samlaget.
Warren, Karen J. 1994. Introduction. In *Ecological Feminism*, ed. Karen J. Warren, 1-7. London and New York: Routledge.
Waugh, Patricia. 1989. *Feminine Fictions: Revisiting the Postmodern*. London and New York: Routledge.
Weedon, Chris. 1997. *Feminist Practice and Poststructuralist Theory*, 2nd ed. First ed. 1987. Oxford and Cambridge, MA: Blackwell.
Werner, Gösta. 1970. *Den svenska filmens historia. En översikt*. Stockholm:

PAN/Norstedt.
Westerståhl Stenport, Anna. 2004. *Making Space: Stockholm, Paris and the Urban Prose of Strindberg and His Contemporaries*. Berkeley: University of California.
Widerberg, Karin. 1980. *Kvinnor, klasser och lagar 1750-1980*. Stockholm: Liber förlag.
Wieselgren, Greta. 1969. *Den höga tröskeln. Kampen för kvinnas rätt till ämbete*. Lund: Gleerup. (Kvinnohistoriskt arkiv, 7).
Wikander, Ulla. 1988. *Kvinnors och mäns arbeten: Gustavsberg 1880-1980*. Lund: Arkiv förlag.
– 1993. Periodisering av kapitalismen – med kvinnor. In *Genus i historisk forskning*, ed. Christina Ericsson, 84-95. Lund: Studentlitteratur.
– 1999. *Kvinnoarbete i Europa 1789-1950. Genus, makt och arbetsdelning*. Stockholm: Atlas Akademi.
Williams, Anna. 1997. *Stjärnor utan stjärnbilder. Kvinnor och kanon i litteraturhistoriska översiktsverk under 1900-talet*. Hedemora: Gidlunds förlag.
Williams, Raymond. 1988. *Keywords: A Vocabulary of Culture and Society*. Rev. and expanded ed. first publ. 1983. London: Fontana Press.
Wiltsher, Anne. 1985. *Most Dangerous Women: Feminist Peace Campaigners of the Great War*. London, Boston and Henley: Pandora.
Wirmark, Margareta. 1987. Från *Barnjungfrun* till *Spinnerskan*. Elin Wägners radiodramatik. In *Läskonst, skrivkonst, diktkonst. Aderton betraktelser över dikt och diktande jämte en bibliografi över Thure Stenströms skrifter*, ed. Pär Hellström and Tore Wretö, 335-49. Stockholm: Askelin & Hägglund. Reprinted 2002 in Elin Wägner-Sällskapets skriftserie, 13. Växjö: Elin Wägner-sällskapet.
Wistrand, Birgitta. 2006. *Elin Wägner i 1920-talet. Rörelseintellektuell och internationalist*. Uppsala: Uppsala University, Dept. of Literature.
Witt-Brattström, Ebba. 1977. Maria Sandel – trikåstickerska, kvinnokämpe, tidningsskribent och författare. In Maria Sandel, *Virveln*, orig. publ. 1913, 267-75. Stockholm: Ordfront.
– 1988. *Moa Martinson. Skrift och drift i trettiotalet*. Stockholm: Norstedts förlag.
– 1996a. Jag är lag i mig själv. Om Edith Södergran. In *Nordisk kvinnolitteraturhistoria*, vol. 3, ed. Elisabeth Møller Jensen, 14-33. Höganäs: Bra Böcker.
– 1996b. Begäret på landsbygden. In *Nordisk kvinnolitteraturhistoria*, vol. 3, ed. Elisabeth Møller Jensen, 390-97. Höganäs: Bra Böcker.

- 2003. Elin Wägner. Feminismen, internationalismen och svenskheten. In Ebba Witt-Brattström, *Ur könets mörker Etc. Litteraturanalyser 1993-2003*, 97-109. Stockholm: Norstedts förlag.
- 2004. Introduction: The New Woman Specter in Modernist Aesthetics. In *The New Woman and the Aesthetic Opening: Unlocking Gender in Twentieth-Century Texts*, ed. Ebba Witt-Brattström, 1-14. Huddinge: Södertörns högskola.

Woolf, Virginia. 1977. *A Room of One's Own*. Orig. publ. 1929. St Albans: Triad/Panther Books.

Worton, Michael and Judith Still, ed. 1990. *Intertextuality: Theories and Practices*. Manchester and New York: Manchester University Press.

Zade, Beatrice. 1935. *Frida Stéenhoff. Människan. Kämpen. Verket.* Stockholm: Albert Bonniers förlag.

Zauderer, Naomi B. 1999. Consumption, Production, and Reproduction in the Work of Charlotte Perkins Gilman. In *Charlotte Perkins Gilman: Optimist Reformer*, ed. Jill Rudd and Val Gough, 151-72. Iowa City: University of Iowa Press.

Zweigbergk, Eva von (sign. Colomba). 1942. Låt hemmen ta ledningen på väg till en ny värld! *Dagens Nyheter* 30 Jan.

Åberg, Åke. 1983. Folket läste. In *Den svenska boken 500 år*, ed. Harry Järv, 365-401. Stockholm: Liber förlag.

Åhlander, Lars, ed. 1986. *Svensk filmografi*, vol. 1, *1897-1919*. Stockholm: Svenska filminstitutet.

Östberg, Kjell. 2000. *Efter rösträtten. Kvinnors utrymme efter det demokratiska genombrottet*. Stockholm/Stehag: Brutus Östlings Bokförlag Symposion.

Österberg, Carin, Inga Lewenhaupt and Anna Greta Wahlberg. 1990. *Svenska kvinnor. Föregångare Nyskapare*. Lund: Bokförlaget Signum.

Österling, Anders. 1918. Review of *Åsa-Hanna*, by Elin Wägner. *Göteborgs Handels- och Sjöfartstidning* 27 Nov.

Österling, Anders. 1947. Review of *Vinden vände bladen*, by Elin Wägner. *Stockholms Dagblad* 12 Oct.

Select Bibliography: Second Edition, updates

Bohlin, Anna. 2008. *Röstens anatomi. Läsningar av politik i Elin Wägners Silverforsen, Selma Lagerlöfs Löwensköldtrilogi och Klara Johansons Tidevarvskåserier*. Umeå: Bokförlaget h:ström.
Enge Swartz, Marianne, ed. 2009. *Elin Wägner. Det första fotstegets moder. Antologi*. Växjö: Artéa Förlag.
Forsgren, Peter. 2009. *I vansklighetens land. Genus, genre och modernitet i Elin Wägners smålandsromaner*. Stockholm/Göteborg: Makadam.
Forsås-Scott, Helena. 2011. 'Nuet och framtiden'. In *Elin Wägner i litteraturhistorien*, ed. Marianne Enge Swartz. Elin Wägner-sällskapets skriftserie, No. 22, 58-66.
Forsås-Scott, Helena. Forthcoming 2014. Texts for Change: Constructions of Feminine Citizenship. *In Love and Modernity: Scandinavian Literature, Drama and Letters. Essays in Honour of Professor Janet Garton*, eds. Claire Thomson and Elettra Carbone. London: Norvik Press.
Jonsson, Bibi. 2008. *Blod och jord i trettiotalet. Kvinnorna och den antimoderna strömningen*. Stockholm: Carlsson Bokförlag.
Qvarnström, Sofi. 2009. *Motståndets berättelser. Elin Wägner, Anna Lenah Elgström, Marika Stiernstedt och första världskriget*. Hedemora/Möklinta: Gidlunds förlag.

In addition, the 2003 edition of Wägner's novel *Pennskaftet*, complete with Horace Engdahl's introduction and my commentary, is now available, free of charge, on the Swedish Academy website, www.svenskaakademien.se/publikationer/svenska_klassiker

Nordisk kvinnolitteraturhistoria is available, free of charge, in the original Danish and Swedish as well as in English translation, on www.nordicwomensliterature.net

An updated bibliography of material about Wägner and her work is available on http://lillabjorka.se/litteraturen/

The 2003 edition of Ulla Isaksson's and Erik Hjalmar Linder's biography of Wägner is available as an e-book.

Kvinnohistoriska samlingarna at Göteborg University Library is now simply KvinnSam (www.ub.gu.se/kvinn)

Index

The alphabetical order used here is the Swedish one, i.e. [...] z, å, ä, ö.

Index of Texts written by Elin Wägner or to which Wägner contributed.

Barnjungfrun (The Nurse Maid) 262, 264
Credo [radio drama] 261, 262, 267-71, 272
De fem pärlorna (The Five Pearls) 39, 65, 261, 267-68, 272, 278-83, 295-96, 358, 367
'De tre kraven' (The Three Requirements) 128-32, 194, 329, 363-64
Den befriade kärleken (Love Liberated) 60, 144, 178-82, 187, 189, 190-91, 194-95, 291, 363-64
Den förödda vingården (The Ravaged Vineyard) 102, 113, 144, 185-91, 195, 252, 253, 258, 367
Den kinesiska muren (The Great Wall of China) 123-28, 129, 132, 194, 329
Den namnlösa (The Anonymous Woman) 21, 272-78, 279, 280, 285, 292, 295-96, 358, 364-65, 367
Dialogen fortsätter (The Dialogue is Continuing) 21, 272, 283-88, 295-96, 358

En helgonlegend (A Legend) 262, 265-66, 268, 271
'En negerstat i staten' (A Negro State within the State) 240-42, 249, 251-52, 364-65
Fru Hillevis dagbok (Mrs Hillevi's Diary) 133, 134, 137-43, 145, 193-94
Från det jordiska museet (From the Human Museum) 100
Från Seine, Rhen och Ruhr (From the Seine, the Rhine and the Ruhr) 14, 15, 21, 43, 237, 252-60, 271-72, 278, 296, 358, 364-65, 367
Genomskådad (Unmasked) 340-47, 348, 353-55, 359-60, 367
Han som blödde (He who Bled) 262, 266-67, 271
Hemlighetsfull (Secretive) 340-47, 348, 353-55, 359-60, 367
Hon fick platsen (She Got the Job) 64
'I Helsingborg' (In Helsingborg) 100
Klubben (The Club) 40, 133, 134-37, 138, 143, 145, 150, 193-94, 363

411

Kvarteret Oron (District of Unrest) 144, 178, 179, 182-85, 187, 189, 190-91, 194-95, 291, 363-64
'Kvinnan som arbetar' (The Working Woman) 101, 102-05, 110, 120-21, 143, 145, 193, 363
'Kvinnornas kris' (The Women's Crisis) 205
'Liv eller död' (Life or Death) 239-40, 246, 251-52, 364-65
'Lysistrates och fredens timma' (The Hour of Lysistrata and of Peace) 242-45
Mannen vid min sida (The Man at My Side) 21, 272, 289-96, 358, 367
Norrtullsligan (The Norrtull Gang) 37, 40, 59, 100, 141, 144, 145-53, 154, 155, 162-63, 182, 183, 190, 191, 194, 195, 210, 363
Pennskaftet (*Penwoman*) 49-50, 63, 91, 144, 153-64, 181, 189, 190, 191, 194, 195, 363, 367
Radio drama 14, 21, 43, 209, 237, 260-71, 272, 296, 358
Reportages from The Hague 1915-16 101, 105-13, 114, 120-21, 124, 125, 194, 240, 244-45, 246, 260, 269, 302, 307, 309, 364
Reportages from Vienna 1920 101-02, 113-21, 185-86, 189-91, 195, 252-53, 258
Selma Lagerlöf, vols. 1-2 14, 15, 20, 41, 43, 297, 327-40, 359, 367
Silverforsen (The Silver Rapids) 40
Sjömansbruden (The Sailor's Bride) 262, 267
Släkten Jerneploogs framgång (The Rise of the House of Jerneploog) 39, 40
Spinnerskan (The Spinster) [radio drama] 261
Spinnerskan (The Spinster) [short story] 261
Systrarna (The Sisters) 64
Tre åldrar (Three Ages) 262, 264-65, 266, 271
Tusen år i Småland (A Thousand Years in Småland) 14, 15, 20, 43, 297, 316-27, 340, 358, 359, 367
'Två landskap' (Two Landscapes) 249-52, 326
'Vad tänker du, mänsklighet?' (Humankind, What are You Thinking?) 245-48, 252
Vansklighetens land (The Perilous Land) 60, 165
Vinden vände bladen (The Wind Turned the Leaves Over) 347-55, 360
Väckarklocka (Alarm Clock) 14, 15, 20, 21, 26, 30-31, 41, 43, 247, 297-316, 318-19, 322, 340, 358-59, 362, 366-67, 369
Vändkorset (The Turnstile) 62, 210
Åsa-Hanna 60, 144, 165-77, 178, 181, 190, 191, 194, 210, 272, 274, 285, 367

Index of Names

Adamov, Arthur 186-87
Addams, Jane 106-07, 111
Adler, Alfred 252
Adlersparre, Sophie 330, 331
Adorno, Theodor W. 121-22
Ahlenius, Holger 39-40, 168-69, 284, 353
Alonso, Harriet Hyman 111
Alva, Jorge de 288
Alving, Barbro 40, 154, 210
Anderson, Benedict 68-69
Anderson, Harriet 80, 82-83
Andersson, Blenda 320, 321
Andersson, Irene 41, 224, 245-46, 368
Andersson, Kaj 218-19
Andrée, Elfrida 286
Andreen, Andrea 225-26
Andreen-Svedberg, Andrea 229-30
Ardis, Ann 151, 159
Aristophanes 242, 243
Asplund, Johan 32
Atterbom, P.D.A. 327
Auerbach, Nina 37, 146
Bachofen, Johann Jacob 83, 299
Backberger, Barbro 306-07
Bacon, Francis 122-23
Bakhtin, Mikhail 21, 38, 256, 290-91
Bal, Mieke 18, 19-20, 21-23, 37, 38-39, 103, 105, 124, 133, 135, 170, 179, 187, 252, 253-54, 273, 289, 328, 350
Balch, Emily G. 106-07
Baldwin, Stanley 247
Barthes, Roland 38
Beauvoir, Simone de 25
Bebel, August 76, 221

Beckett, Samuel 186-87
Bell, Derek 360
Bellamy, Edward 88
Benedictsson, Victoria 331
Berger, Margareta 49-50, 62
Bergman, Hjalmar 210
Bergman, Ingmar 209
Björck, Staffan 170, 172, 272-73
Björk, Gunnela 211, 214, 215, 218
Björkenlid, Bertil 40, 138, 162
Björkman-Goldschmidt, Elsa 232
Bjørnson, Bjørnstjerne 70
Blom, Ida 69
Bonnier, Tor 327
Boswell, James 328
Boye, Karin 39, 295, 367-68
Braidotti, Rosi 18-19, 23, 27, 29, 30, 35-36, 39, 142, 195, 312-13, 315, 322, 325, 346-47, 352, 353-54, 359, 360, 362, 366-67, 369
Brandell, Elin 147
Brandes, Georg 128
Branting, Anna 149
Branting, Hjalmar 51, 204
Bremer, Fredrika 40, 142
Briand, Aristide 229
Brittain, Vera 85
Brödje, Catrine 367
Bunkers, Suzanne 141, 147
Bunyan, John 268
Burwell, Jennifer 31
Butler, Josephine 70
Butler, Judith 16, 27-29, 39, 139, 148, 150, 158, 162, 164, 362
Böök, Fredrik 204, 279, 280, 327
Carey, John 101
Carlberg, Frigga 88

413

Carlsson, Christina 76
Carlsson Wetterberg, Christina 92, 94
Carruthers, Mary 354
Carson, Rachel 298
Chamberlain, Austen 229
Childs, Marquis 199, 216
Cixous, Hélène 157
Clayhills, Harriet 25, 26
Cleghorn, Sarah 240, 242
Collett, Camilla 244
Connell, R.W. 83
Crook, Tim 263
Curie, Marie 137, 141
Currie, Mark 19
Dawes, Charles G. 229
Death, Sarah 40
Delanty, Gerard 33
Delblanc, Sven 144, 165, 283, 366
Deleuze, Gilles 369
Descartes, René 122
Dobson, Andrew 360
Domellöf, Gunilla 42, 283, 367-68
DuPlessis, Rachel Blau 139
Durkheim, Émile 33
Ebert, Friedrich 114
Edel, Leon 327
Edling, Nils 47, 54-55, 56
Egeland, Marianne 328
Einstein, Albert 290-91
Ekman, Lotten 101, 132-33
Elgström, Anna Lenah 96, 123, 367
Eliot, George 23
Elkan, Sophie 338
Ellis, Havelock 70, 85, 128
Elshtain, Jean Bethke 234, 235
Engdahl, Horace 153, 159, 164
Engels, Friedrich 76, 83, 86, 93-94, 221
Epstein, William 327

Eriksson, Arne 216
Eskilsson, Lena 31-32, 41, 227, 233
Esslin, Martin 186-87
Fahlgren, Margaretha 208
Fairclough, Norman 20, 115, 238, 242
Faustman, Alma 88
Fernberg, Magnus 132, 133
First, Ruth 84, 85, 86, 87
Fjelkestam, Krsitina 208
Ford, Henry 96, 125-27, 132
Foucault, Michel 17-18
Fourier, Charles 88
Fowler, Alastair 15, 260, 298
Fox, Marion 253
Frangeur, Renée 201
Frazer, Elizabeth 16, 34-35, 227, 235, 357
Freud, Sigmund 114, 341-42
Fridegård, Jan 341
Frostegren, Margareta 62
Frye, Northrop 118
Frykman, Jonas 204
Fröding, Gustaf 127, 137, 138, 140-41, 186
Gadamer, Hans-Georg 309
Gandhi, Mahatma 240, 288, 304
Garbo, Greta 65
Gate, Flory 251
Genet, Jean 186-87
Genette, Gérard 19, 22-23, 186
Gilbert, Sandra M. 178-79, 181, 187
Gilman, Charlotte Perkins 79, 88-91, 95, 97, 102, 114, 120-21, 125, 131, 149, 178, 181, 221
Greimas, Algirdas Julien 22
Grepstad, Ottar 298
Griffin, Susan 300
Grosz, Elizabeth 23

Grubb, Rut 205
Grønbech, Vilhelm 304
Gubar, Susan 178-79, 181, 187
Gustafson, Ruth 205
Guy-Blaché, Alice 64
Göransson, Anita 47-48, 49
Haar, Michel 148
Hackman, Boel 42
Hadenius, Stig 209
Hagberg, Knut 317
Hagemann, Gro 218
Hallberg, Mikael 213-14
Hallingberg, Gunnar 261, 262, 268
Halvardson, Margret 100
Hamilton, Alice 106-07
Hansson, Per Albin 73, 201, 213, 214, 216, 234
Haraway, Donna 29-30, 361
Harvey, David 125-26
Haydn, Joseph 186
Heard, Gerald 304
Heggestad, Eva 37, 146, 152
Heidenstam, Verner von 327
Hellström, Gustaf 366
Hermelin, Honorine 230-31, 232-33
Hermodsson, Elisabet 43
Herrmann, Anne 310
Hildegard of Bingen 306
Hirdman, Yvonne 25, 26, 73, 75, 76, 77, 78, 156, 201, 208, 216-18, 221-222, 223, 238, 275-76, 307, 357
Hitler, Adolf 225, 249, 258, 270-71, 294, 298
Hofman-Uddgren, Anna 64
Holm, Birgitta 145, 149
Holmberg, Claes-Göran 107-08
Holquist, Michael 256-57
Horthy, Miklós 114

Hrosvita 306
Hufton, Olwen 49
Hughes, Linda K. 139
Huxley, Aldous 304
Hyltén-Cavallius, Ragnar 14, 261, 268, 271
Hägg, Göran 123
Ibsen, Henrik 70
Ionesco, Eugène 186-87
Irigaray, Luce 136, 150
Isaksson, Ulla 13, 39, 40, 42, 134, 138, 145, 162-63, 165, 185, 193, 253, 258, 261, 277, 278, 289, 299, 300, 340-41, 347-48
Jacobs, Aletta 111
Jaenzon, Julius 64-65
Jeanne d'Arc 306
Jebb, Eglantyne 344-45
Joeres, Ruth-Ellen Boetcher 121, 122, 123
Johanson, Klara 82, 155, 273
Johnson, Eyvind 295, 341
Jonsson, Bibi 14, 41, 283, 289
Jonsson, Tomas 213-14
Karl XII 349, 352
Kellgren, Ragna 228, 232
Key, Ellen 25-26, 70-72, 73, 76, 77-79, 93, 95, 96-97, 103, 114, 124, 128-32, 152, 158, 194, 217, 306, 329, 331, 344-45, 363-64
Kipling, Rudyard 339
Klein, Viola 222
Kleman, Ellen 80
Kock, Karin 54, 202, 299
Kreuger, Ivar 201
Krusenstjerna, Agnes von 37
Kyle, Gunhild 222
Lacey, Nicola 16, 34-35, 227, 235, 357

Lagerkvist, Pär 295
Lagerlöf, Selma 64-65, 73, 84, 128, 327-40
Lamberth, Pia 60, 207
Landquist, Ellen 62-63
Landquist, John 39, 62-63, 134
Lanser, Susan S. 22-23, 37-38, 39, 107, 147, 153, 157, 272, 273, 278, 279, 280, 349, 362
Larsson, Carl 56, 67-68, 69, 72, 74, 75
Larsson, Inger 41, 327-28, 329, 333
Larsson, Karin 68
Larsson, Lisbeth 13
Law, Graham 145
Lawrence, D. H. 304
Leffler, Anne-Charlotte 140
Leppänen, Katarina 14, 41, 298, 299-300, 311, 366, 369
Levertin, Oscar 150
Lidman, Sven 366
Lindberg, Per 209, 262, 263-64
Lindberger, Örjan 39
Lindblom, Andreas 317-18
Lindén, Claudia 71
Linder, Erik Hjalmar 13, 14-15, 39, 40, 42, 134, 138, 145, 162-63, 165, 185, 193, 253, 258, 260, 261, 268, 277, 278, 289, 298, 299, 300, 340-41, 347-48
Lindholm, Margareta 40-41, 218, 219, 220, 221, 222
Lindqvist, Karl 40, 133, 134, 135, 136
Linnaeus, Carolus 325
Ljungquist, Ivar 100
Lloyd, Genevieve 122, 128
Lo-Johansson, Ivar 341
Loomba, Ania 288

Lukács, Georg 122
Lund, Michael 139
Lundberg, Anders P. 32, 211
Lundgren, Kristina 42, 100
Lundqvist, Lennart J. 368
Luther, Martin 166
Löfgren, Orvar 69-70, 75, 204, 317, 348
Lönnroth, Lars 144, 165, 283, 366
Macdonald, Nina 179, 181
Marshall, T. H. 212, 214-15, 224-25, 235
Martinson, Harry 341
Martinson, Moa 208, 341, 368
Marx, Eleanor 85
Marx, Karl 76, 88
Mayreder, Rosa 79, 80-83, 86, 87-88, 93, 97, 131, 299
Merchant, Carolyn 369
Mezei, Kathy 173
Middleton, Peter 23, 38, 118, 165, 172, 177, 185-86, 292, 311-12, 343, 348-49, 354
Mittman, Elizabeth 121, 122, 123
Moberg, Vilhelm 295, 341
Molander, Olof 209
Montaigne, Michel de 122-23, 309
Morgan, Lewis Henry 83
Mumford, Lewis 304
Mussolini, Benito 249
Myrdal, Alva 25, 40-41, 205, 217, 218, 220-21, 222, 234, 238, 242-43, 245
Myrdal, Gunnar 205, 217, 221, 234, 238, 242-43, 245
Nadel, Ira Bruce 327-28
Napoleon Bonaparte 254
Ney, Birgitta 42, 100, 101, 132-33
Nietzsche, Friedrich 71

Index

Nilsson, Ada 224
Nissen, Ingjald 243
Nordberg, Karin 261
Nordström, Ester Blenda 62
Nordström, Ludvig 40, 366
Norström, Vitalis 141-43
Näsström, Gustaf 317
Ohrlander, Kajsa 56-57
Owen, Robert 88
Pateman, Carole 234
Pearce, Lynne 21, 310
Pearson, Karl 85
Perkins, David 365
Peterson, Abby 369
Petersson, Birgit 62
Pethick-Lawrence, Emmeline 109, 110
Pfeiffer, Ehrenfried 304
Plumwood, Val 212, 226-27, 235, 357, 360
Prince, Gerald 38, 116
Randall, David 237-38
Ricoeur, Paul 254
Rimmon-Kenan, Shlomith 20, 37, 173
Riviere, Joan 150
Rochefort, Christiane 24
Rolland, Romain 128
Romberg, Bertil 146-47
Rosaldo, Michelle Zimbalist 70
Rudebeck, Petter 320
Runeberg, Johan Ludvig 142
Rydberg, Viktor 110, 286
Rönnbäck, Josefin 53-54
Sandel, Maria 75
Saussure, Ferdinand de 17
Schreiner, Olive 79, 84-90, 94, 97, 120-21, 125, 131, 178, 221
Schwimmer, Rosika 96, 109, 110, 123-28, 129, 132, 194, 329
Schön, Lennart 47, 48, 54-55, 199, 200
Scott, Ann 84, 85, 86, 87
Scott, Joan Wallach 26-27, 155-56, 218
Selander, Sten 279, 280
Shiva, Vandana 300
Showalter, Elaine 84, 85
Siim, Birte 212, 214, 234, 235
Siwertz, Sigfrid 366
Sjöberg, Alf 209
Sjöström, Victor 64
Spacks, Patricia Meyer 169, 170, 171, 172, 173, 177
Spielberg, Steven 21
Spivak, Gayatri Chakravorty 241
St. Athanasius 266
St. Bridget of Sweden 306
Stagnelius, Erik Johan 320
Stanley, Liz 84
Steene, Birgitta 260-61
Stéenhoff, Frida 63, 79, 91-96, 97, 102, 114, 123, 125, 178
Steinbeck, John 306
Steiner, Rudolf 304
Stiernstedt, Marika 208
Still, Judith 176-77, 309
Stiller, Mauritz 64, 65
Stresemann, Gustav 229
Strindberg, August 64, 136, 137, 140-41, 187
Stål, Margareta 42, 62, 63
Suttner, Bertha von 120
Svanberg, Birgitta 37
Svedjedal, Johan 57-58, 59, 60-61, 207-08
Svensson, Conny 30-31, 144, 165, 283, 347, 366, 367, 368

417

Svensson, D. 105
Svensson, I. 105
Söderberg, Hjalmar 128, 147
Södergran, Edith 208
Tacitus 306
Tamm, Elisabeth 224, 229, 232
Theresa of Avila 292, 293, 306
Tomson, Bengt 39
Tornbjer, Charlotte 77
Turner, Victor 33, 293-94
Tykesson, Elisabeth 327
Tönnies, Ferdinand 32-33, 82-83
Töringe, Susanne 100
Vaerting, Mathias 83
Vaerting, Mathilde 83, 93, 244, 245, 252, 299
Vall, Gunnar 253
Veblen, Thorstein 88
Wahlström, Lydia 200-01
Walker, Alice 21
Walton, Stephen J. 327
Ward, Lester F. 88
Warren, Karen 300, 313
Waugh, Patricia 164, 227
Weedon, Chris 17, 18, 20, 23, 39, 106, 362
Weibull, Lennart 209
Westerståhl Stenport, Anna 149
Wieselgren, Greta 200
Wikander, Ulla 49, 50, 199, 200, 201
Williams, Anna 15
Williams, Raymond 22, 32-33
Wilson, Woodrow 126
Wiltsher, Anne 125-26
Wirmark, Margareta 261, 262, 263, 264, 268, 270
Wistrand, Birgitta 14, 15, 41-42, 238, 253

Witt-Brattström, Ebba 18, 164, 208, 321, 368
Wohlin, Margit 222
Wolf, Christa 310
Wolzogen, Ernst von 142
Woods, Tim 23, 38, 118, 165, 172, 177, 185-86, 292, 311-12, 343, 348-49, 354
Woolf, Virginia 16, 178-79, 250, 310
Worton, Michael 176-77, 309
Zetkin, Clara 76, 77-78, 96-97
Åberg, Åke 58
Åhrén, Uno 223
Åmark, Klas 218
Östberg, Kjell 51, 52, 202-03

www.ingramcontent.com/pod-product-compliance
Lightning Source LLC
Chambersburg PA
CBHW050417170426
43201CB00008B/444